The Best Bed & Breakfast
in England, Scotland & Wales
2002–2003

Sigourney Welles

Jill Darbey

Joanna Mortimer

The finest Bed & Breakfast accommodations in the

British Isles

from the Scottish Hebrides to

London's Belgravia

Country Houses, Town Houses, City Apartments, Manor
Houses, Village Cottages, Farmhouses, Castles

U.K.H.M. Publishing, London, U.K.

The Globe Pequot Press, Guilford, Connecticut, U.S.A.

Library of Congress Catalog Card Number: 91-074158

U.S. ISBN 0-7627-1189-2

Typeset by U.K.H.M. Publishing Ltd., London.
Printed and bound in China.
Produced by Phoenix Offset Ltd.

U.K.H.M. Publishing Ltd. P.O. Box 2070, London W12 8QW, England. U.K.

Contents

Foreword 4
How to use this Guide 5
Making a Reservation 6
The Discount Offer 7
Regions 8
County Map........................... 9
General Information 10
Motorway Map 12
Rail Map 13
Tube/Subway Map 14
London Map 15
London Homes 16
Avon/Bath *see Somerset*............
Beds/Berks/Bucks/Herts ... 27
Bristol *see Somerset*.................
Cambridge & Northants 38
Cheshire & Lancashire 46
Cornwall 56
Cumbria............................... 75
Derbyshire / Staffordshire.. 99
Devon 108
Dorset 135
Durham *see Northumbria* ....
Essex 149
Gloucestershire 153

Hampshire/Isle of Wight .. 175
Hereford. & Worcester 189
Isle of Wight *see Hampshire* ....
Kent 198
Lancashire *see Cheshire* ....
Leicester/ Notts./Rutland . 214
Lincolnshire 222
Nottinghamshire *see Leicester.*
Norfolk............................... 229
Northumbria....................... 238
Oxfordshire 245
Rutland *see Leicester/Notts*........
Shropshire 257
Somerset 267
Staffordshire *see Derbyshire* ...
Suffolk 294
Surrey 301
Sussex............................... 307
Warwickshire 326
Wiltshire 345
Yorkshire........................... 357
Scotland 378
Wales 422
Towns: Counties Index 454
Recommendations 457

Foreword

Bed & Breakfast has suddenly become the fashionable way to travel. The secret has escaped & thousands of people are discovering for themselves that it is possible to combine high quality accommodation with friendly, personal attention at very reasonable prices. The New York Times said about us that "...after an unannounced inspection of rooms booked through The Worldwide Bed & Breakfast Association it is clear that the standards of comfort & cleanliness are exemplary ...at least as good as in a five star hotel & in most cases, better, reflecting the difference between sensitive hosts taking pride in their homes & itinerant hotel staff doing as little as they can get away with..."

Discerning travellers are turning away from the impersonal hotels with the expensive little refridgerators & microwave breakfasts in each room. How much nicer to have a real English breakfast to begin the day, enough to keep you going until evening. Many of our houses will provide dinner too - often the hostess will be a Cordon Bleu cook & the price will be within your range. We try to provide the best accommodation possible within a wide range of prices, some as little as £15.00 per person per night, whilst others will be up to £60.00 per person per night. The choice is yours, but you can be certain that each will be the best available in that particular area of the country at that price.

Our inspectors are out & about visiting our homes to ensure that standards are maintained. We encourage everyone to use the recommendations & complaints page at the back of the book. Let us know your opinion of the accommodation or inform us of any delightful homes you may have come across & would like to recommend for future inclusion.

In order to avoid the classification trap, which we feel is invidious, we encourage you to read about each home, what they offer & their respective price range, so that you find the one that best suits your expectations. Our hosts in turn offer hospitality in their own unique style, so each home naturally retains its individuality & interest. We have found this to be a very successful recipe which often leads to lasting friendships.

Bed & Breakfast really is a marvellous way to travel, meeting a delightful cross section of fellow travellers with whom to exchange information & maybe the address of ...that lovely little place which was discovered by chance and which serves the most delicious dinner or... the best route to take to a particular farmhouse but make sure you get there by 5 o'clock so that you're in time to watch the evening milking...

This is the fun & real pleasure that is part of Bed & Breakfasting. Once you've tried it you will be a dedicated Best Bed & Breakfaster.

How to use this Guide

To get the full benefits of staying at our Bed & Breakfast homes it is important to appreciate how they differ from hotels, so both hosts & guests know what to expect.

Arrival & Departure

These times are more important to a family than to hotel desk clerks, so your time of arrival (E.T.A.) is vital information when making a reservation either with the home directly or with one of our agencies. This becomes even more important to your reception if you intend travelling overnight & will be arriving in the early morning. So please have this information & your flight number ready when you book your rooms. **At most B & Bs the usual check-in time is 6 P.M. & you will be expected to check out by 10 A.M. on the morning of departure.** These arrangements do vary from home to home. The secret to an enjoyable visit is to let your hosts know as much about your plans as possible & they will do their best to meet your requirements.

Other personal requests

There are a few other details that you should let your hosts know when planning your Bed & Breakfast trip that will make everyone much happier during your visit. Do you smoke? Would you prefer to be in a non-smoking home? Do you suffer from any allergies? Some families have cats, dogs, birds & other pets in the house....Can you make it up a flight of stairs? Would you prefer the ground floor? Do you have any special dietary requirements? Will you be staying for dinner?

Do you prefer a private bathroom or are you prepared to share facilities? Do you prefer a shower instead of a bath? The ages of any children travelling.

In all these cases let your host know what you need & the details can be arranged before you arrive rather than presenting a problem when you are shown to your rooms.

Prices

The prices quoted throughout the guide are the *minimum* per person per night for two sharing. Single occupancy usually attracts a supplement. Prices will increase during busy seasons. You should always confirm the prevailing rate when you make a reservation.

Facilities

The bathroom & toilet facilities affect the prices. Sharing is the cheapest, private is a little more costly & en-suite carries a premium.

Descriptions

Rooms are described as follows: Single:1 bed (often quite small). Double:1 large bed (sometimes King or Queensize).
Twin: 2 separate single beds.
Four-poster: a King or Queen size bed with a canopy above supported by four corner posts.
Bathrooms and toilets are described as follows;
Shared: these facilities are shared with some other guests or perhaps the hosts.
Private: for your use only, however they may occasionally be in an adjacent room.
En-suite: private facilities within your bedroom suite.

Making a Reservation

Once you have chosen where you want to stay, have all the following information ready & your reservation will go smoothly without having to run & find more travel documents or ask someone else what they think you should do. Here is a brief check list of what you will probably be asked & examples to illustrate answers:

Dates & number of nights...August 14-19(6 nights).

Estimated time of arrival at the home ...7 P.M.(evening) & flight number.

Type & number of rooms...1 Double & 2 Single.

Toilet & Bathroom facilities...1 Double en-suite) & 2 singles (shared)

Smoking or Non-smoking?

Any allergies?

Special dietary requests?

Children in the party & their ages?

Any other preferences... Is a shower preferred to a bath?

Maximum budget per person per night based on all the above details.

The London Reservation Agency

There is a minimum two night consecutive stay at our London homes.

Reservations for London homes can only be made through one of our World-wide Bed & Breakfast Agencies. They can be contacted by 'phone, fax, e-mail or on-line from our website at http://www.bestbandb.co.uk.

All reservations must be confirmed with advance payments which are non-re-fundable in the event of cancellation. You simply pay the balance due after you arrive at the home. The advance payment can be made with major credit & charge cards or by cheque. Cash is the preferred method of paying the balance & always in pounds sterling.

The advance payments confirm each night of your visit, **not just the first one**.

When arriving at a later date or departing at an earlier date than those confirmed, the guest will be liable to pay only the appropriate proportion of the stated balance that is due. For example, staying three nights out of four booked means paying 3/4 of the stated balance due. The advance payment is non-refundable. A minimum of 2 nights will always apply.

Outside London

We encourage you to make use of the information in this guide & contact the homes directly. The hosts may require varying amounts of advance payments & may or may not accept credit & charge cards. Remember, many B&Bs are small, family-run establishments and are unable to accept payment by credit card. The confirmed prices shall be those prevailing on the dates required... as previously mentioned, *the prices shown in this guide are the* **minimum** *& will increase during the busy seasons.*

Alterations

If you wish to alter or change a previously confirmed booking through one of the agencies there will be a further fee of £15 per alteration.

Cancellations

All advance payments for London are non-refundable.

All booking fees outside London are non-refundable.

Notice of cancellation must be given as soon as possible & the following suggested rates shall apply outside London only;

30 - 49 days notice - 80% refund.

10-29 days notice -50% refund.

0 - 9 days notice - No refund.

The Worldwide Bed & Breakfast Agencies reserve the right to alter your accommodation should it be necessary & will inform you of any alteration as soon as possible

London Reservation Agency

Website:http://www.bestbandb.co.uk

We offer an outstanding selection of accommodation in London. As with all our accommodation each one has been personally inspected so you can be sure of the highest standards. We offer an immensely wide range of accommodation. We have a type, style and location to suit everyone. From city apartments close to shops, museums and galleries to spacious homes in leafy residential suburbs near the river, parks and restaurants. No matter what your reason for visiting London we can accommodate you. Whether on business or vacation the Best Bed & Breakfast provides great accommodation together with a fast, efficient reservation service. Our helpful staff are always happy to advise you on all your accommodation requirements. We are located in London, we know the city and all our hosts. We know how to provide an enjoyable, affordable, hassle free trip. There are plenty of ways to contact us. To make a reservation simply do one of the following;

Worldwide call Tel: +44 (0)20 8742 9123 (24Hrs.)

North America call Toll Free: 011 800 852 26320

Australia call Toll Free: 0011 800 852 26320

E-mail: bestbandb@atlas.co.uk

Fax: +44 (0)20 8749 7084

The Discount Offer

This offer is made to people who have bought this book & wish to make reservations for Bed & Breakfast in London through our London Reservation Agency. The offer only applies to a minimum stay of three consecutive nights at one of our London homes between the following dates; January 7. 2002 & April 1. 2002 then from September 15. 2002 to December 1. 2002. Only one discount per booking is allowed. Call the reservation office to make your booking in the normal way & tell the clerk that you have bought the book & wish to have the discount. After a couple of questions the discount will be deducted from the advance payment required to confirm the reservation.

Regions

To assist tourists with information during their travels, counties have been grouped together under Regional Tourist Boards that co-ordinate the various efforts of each county.

The British Tourist Authority has designated these areas in consultation with the English, Scottish & Wales Tourist Boards & we have largely adopted these areas for use in this guide

Counties are listed alphabetically throughout our guide & then have a sub-heading indicating which Tourist Region they belong to.

ENGLAND
Cumbria
County of Cumbria
Northumbria.
Counties of Cleveland, Durham, Northumberland, Tyne & Wear.
North West
Counties of Cheshire, Greater Manchester, Lancashire, Merseyside, High Peaks of Derbyshire.
Yorkshire & Humberside
Counties of North Yorkshire, South Yorkshire, West Yorkshire, Humberside.
Heart of England
Counties of Gloucestershire, Herefordshire & Worcestershire, Shropshire, Staffordshire, Warwickshire, West Midlands.
East Midlands
Counties of Derbyshire, Leicestershire, Nottinghamshire, Rutland, Lincolnshire & Northamptonshire,
East Anglia
Counties of Cambridgeshire, Essex, Norfolk, Suffolk.
West Country
Counties of Cornwall, Devon, Dorset (parts of), Somerset, Wiltshire, Isles of Scilly.
Southern
Counties of Hampshire, Dorset (East & North), Isle of Wight.
South East
Counties of East Sussex, Kent, Surrey, West Sussex.

SCOTLAND
The subdivisions of Scottish Regions in this guide differ slightly from the current Marketing Regions of the Scottish Tourist Board.

The Borders, Dumfries & Galloway
Districts & counties of Scottish Borders, Dumfries & Galloway.
Lothian & Strathclyde
City of Edinburgh, Forth Valley, East Lothian, Kirkaldy, St. Andrews & North-East Fife, Greater Glasgow, Clyde Valley, Ayrshire & Clyde Coast, Burns Country.
Argyll & The Isles
Districts & counties of Oban & Mull, Mid Argyll, Kintyre & Islay, Dunoon, Cowal, Rothesay & Isle of Bute, Isle of Arran.
Perthshire, Loch Lommond & The Trossachs.
Districts & counties of Perthshire, Loch Lomond, Stirling & Trossachs.
The Grampians
Districts & counties of Banff & Buchan, Moray, Gordon, Angus, City of Aberdeen, Kincardine & Deeside, City of Dundee.
The Highlands & Islands
Districts & counties of Shetland, Orkney, Caithness, Sutherland, Ross & Cromarty, Western Isles, South West Ross & Isle of Skye, Inverness, Loch Ness & Nairn, Aviemore & Spey Valley, Fort William & Lochaber.

WALES
The regions are defined as follows:
North Wales
Counties of Anglesey, Conwy, Denbighshire, Flintshire & Gwynedd.
Mid Wales
Counties of Ceredigion & Powys.
South Wales
Counties of Carmarthenshire, Glamorgan, Monmouthshire, Newport, Pembrokeshire & Swansea.
The photographs appearing in the Introductions & Gazeteers are by courtesy of the appropriate Tourist Board for each county or W.W.B.B.A.

Counties map

Each county has been assigned a page number where a more detailed map can be found. These maps include principal towns, major roads & the location of each Bed & Breakfast establishment.

OUTER HEBRIDES
WESTERN ISLES
INNER HEBRIDES

HIGHLANDS

MORAY

ABERDEENSHIRE

ABERDEEN

SCOTLAND
468

PERTHSHIRE & KINROSS

ANGUS

DUNDEE

FIFE

ARGYLL & BUTE

STIRLING

EAST LOTHIAN

1 INVERCLYDE
2 DUNBARTON & CLYDEBANK
3 RENFREWSHIRE
4 EAST RENFREWSHIRE
5 GLASGOW
6 EAST DUNBARTONSHIRE
7 NORTH LANARKSHIRE
8 FALKIRK
9 CLACKMANNAN
10 WEST LOTHIAN
11 EDINBURGH
12 MID LOTHAIN

NORTH AYRSHIRE

SOUTH LANARK-SHIRE

EAST AYRSHIRE

BORDERS

North Sea

SOUTH AYRSHIRE

DUMFRIES & GALLOWAY

NORTHUMBERLAND

TYNE AND WEAR
289

CUMBRIA
88

DURHAM

CLEVELAND

YORKSHIRE

435 HUMBERSIDE

LANCASHIRE
52

Irish Sea

MANCHESTER
MERSEYSIDE

ENGLAND

FLINTSHIRE
DENBIGHSHIRE

ANGLESEY

CONWY

CHESHIRE
52

122

LINCOLNSHIRE

WREXHAM

DERBYSHIRE & STAFFORD-SHIRE

260

NOTTINGHAM-SHIRE,

268

GWYNEDD

SHROP-SHIRE

LEICESTERSHIRE & RUTLAND

NORFOLK
276

WALES
524

311

WARWICK-SHIRE
397

CAMBRIDGE-SHIRE & NORTHAMPTON-SHIRE
43

SUFFOLK
359

CEREDIGION

POWYS

HEREFORD & WORCESTER
225

BEDFORDSHIRE, BERKSHIRE, BUCKINGHAMSHIRE, & HERTFORDSHIRE
31

ESSEX
178

CARMARTHENSHIRE

MONMOUTH-SHIRE

183

296

OXFORD-SHIRE

PEMBROKESHIRE

GLOUCESTER-SHIRE

LONDON
15

SWANSEA

NEWPORT
CARDIFF

1 BRIDGEND
2 RHONDA CYNON TAFF
3 MERTHYR TYDFIL
4 CAERPHILLY
5 BLAENAU GWENT
6 TORFAEN

NEATH & PORT TALBOT

VALE OF GLAMORGAN

WILTSHIRE
422

365
SURREY

KENT
238

SOMERSET
323

HAMPSHIRE
209

SUSSEX
374

165

DEVON
135

DORSET

64
CORNWALL

English Channel

General Information

To help overseas visitors with planning their trip to Britain, we have compiled the next few pages explaining the basic requirements & customs you will find here.

Before you arrive

Documents you will have to obtain before you arrive;
Valid passports & visas. Citizens of Commonwealth countries or the U.S.A. don't need visas to enter the U.K. Bring your local Driving Licence.

Medical Insurance.

This is strongly recommended although visitors will be able to receive free emergency treatment. If you have to stay in hospital in the U.K. you will be asked to pay unless you are a citizen of European Community Countries.

Restrictions on arrival

Immigration procedures can be lengthy & bothersome, be prepared for questions like:
a) where are you staying in the U.K.?
b) do you have a round trip ticket?
c) how long do you intend to stay?
d) how much money are you bringing in?
e) do you have a credit card?
Do not bring any animals with you as they are subject to 6 months quarantine & there are severe penalties for bringing in pets without appropriate licences. Do not bring any firearms, prohibited drugs or carry these things for anyone else. If you are in doubt about items in your possession, declare them by entering the Red Channel at Customs & seek the advice of an officer.

After you have arrived

You can bring in as much currency as you like. You can change your own currency or travellers cheques at many places at varying rates.

Airports tend to be the most expensive places to change money & the 'Bureau de Change" are often closed at nights. So bring enough Sterling to last you at least 2 or 3 days. Banks often charge commission for changing money. Some Cashcard machines (or A.T.M.'s) will dispense local currency using your charge card, if they are affiliated systems, & don't charge commissions to your account. Major credit cards/charge cards are widely accepted & you may only need to carry small amounts of cash for "pocket money".

Driving

Don't forget to drive on the Left... especially the first time you get into a car... at the airport car hire parking lot... or from the front of a railway station... or straight after breakfast... old habits are hard to shake off. If you need to know the rules, get a copy of the Highway Code. You must wear a seat belt & so must any other front seat passenger. The speed limits are clearly shown in most areas - generally 30 mph. in residential areas (48 kph) & 70 mph on motorways (113 kph.). Traffic lights are at the side of the road & not hanging overhead. Car hire is relatively expensive in the U.K. & it is often a good idea to arrange this before you arrive. Mileage charges, V.A.T. (Sales Tax) & insurance are usually charged extra & you will need to be over 21 to hire a car in the U.K. Petrol (gas) is also relatively expensive & you may find petrol stations hard to find or closed at night in rural areas... so fill up often. Driving in London is not a recommended experience for newcomers & parking is also a very complex arrangement which can become a nightmare if the car gets "clamped" (immobilised) or towed away.

General Information

Buses & Coaches

If you are not driving & only want to travel 5-10 miles there are good bus services within most towns & cities, however, rural routes have seriously declined over the last few years. There are regular & fast coach services between the major towns which are very popular - so book ahead to be sure of a seat.

Trains

There is an extensive railway system throughout the U.K. which serves the major towns on a fast & frequent basis. These services are relatively expensive & like most railway systems are subject to delays.

Tubes (Subways)

London is the only city with an extensive subway system although some other towns do have "Metro" trains of linked under & overground systems.

The "tube" is a very popular means of getting around London, but it can get very crowded & unpleasant at "rush hours". It is often the preferred way to get into London from Heathrow Airport in the early morning, when there are long delays on the roads that hold up both buses & taxis with increasingly expensive rides into the city centre, £40 is not unusual for this cab fare, compared with a few pounds on the "tube".

The "tube" in London is operated by London Transport which also operates the London bus service ... the famous red buses. They sell tickets which allow you to travel all over London on tubes, buses & trains at very good rates, called Travelcards... a transfer system. Ask your local travel agent about these & other travel passes throughout the U.K.

Telephones

When calling the U.K. from abroad always drop the 0 from the area code.

In the U.K. the only free calls are the operator - 100, enquiries - 192 (international 153) & emergencies - 999.

You may use your calling card to call home which is billed to your account or call collect, ask the operator to "reverse charge" the call. The famous red telephone kiosks are slowly being replaced with new glass booths & they differ in that the old boxes only take 10 & 50 pence pieces & don't give any change, whereas the new ones take many combinations of coins & do give change. Phonecards are becoming more popular as the number of boxes that only accept these cards increases. Cards can be bought at Post Offices & many newsagents & shops.

Doctors/Chemists

All local police stations have lists of chemists & doctors should you need one, at night, for instance.

Voltage

The standard voltage throughout the country is 240v AC.50Hz. If you bring small electrical appliances with you, a converter will be required.

Tipping

Is not obligatory anywhere but a general guide if you wish to leave a tip for service is between 10%-15%.

Pubs

Most open between 11 a.m. & 11 p.m. every day.

You must be over 18 years old to buy & drink alcohol in pubs .

Motorway map

Approximate
driving time

8 hrs
7 hrs
6 hrs
5 hrs
4 hrs
3 hrs
2 hrs

North Sea

Irish Sea

English Channel

Inverness
Aberdeen
M90
M9
M8 Edinburgh
Glasgow
M74
Newcastle
Carlisle   A1(M)
M6
Windermere
York
M55
M62
M58   M180
Holyhead
M53   Manchester
Chester   M56
M6   M1
Shrewsbury   M54
M69
Birmingham   M42
M45
M5   M40   M1   A1(M)   Cambridge
M11
Fishguard   Oxford   M25
M4   LONDON
Cardiff   M4
M25   M20   Dover
M3   M23
M5   M27
Southampton
Plymouth

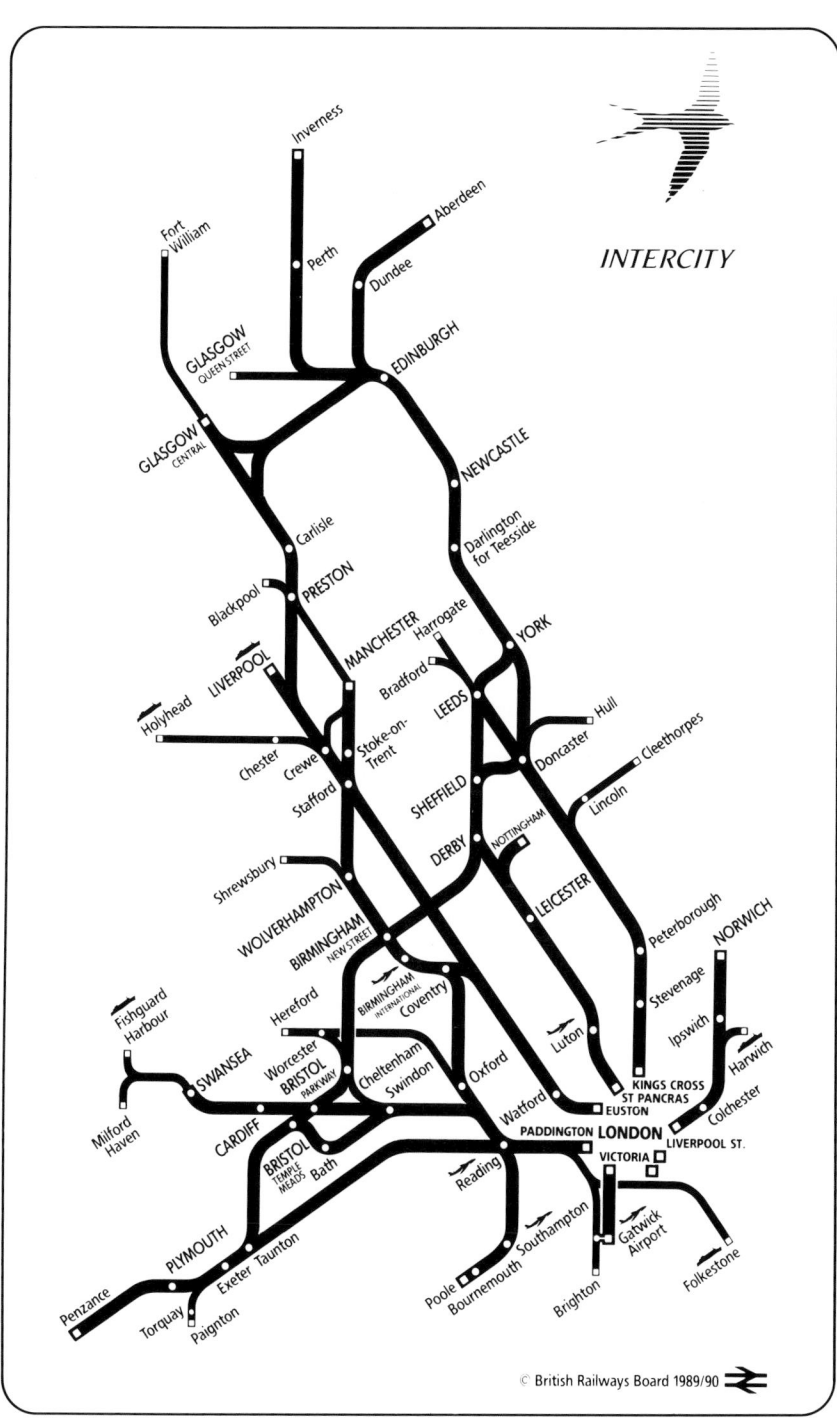

INTERCITY

© British Railways Board 1989/90

UNDERGROUND

©Copyright London Regional Transport

91/1258

LONDON MAP

London

Visit our website: www.bestbandb.co.uk

	rate £ from - to per person	evening meals children taken	animals taken

		rate £ from - to per person	evening meals	children taken	animals taken
Home No. 01. London. Tel: +44 (0)20-8742-9123 Fax: +44 (0)20-8749-7084 U.S., Canada call: Toll Free 011-800-852-26320 Australia call: Toll Free 0011-800-852-26320 E-mail: bestbandb@atlas.co.uk	Nearest Tube: Putney Bridge An attractive Victorian terraced house, situated in a quiet residential street, yet only 3 mins' walk from the station. 1 spacious double-bedded room with an en-suite bathroom & a twin-bedded room with a private bathroom. Each room is tastefully furnished & has a T.V. & hairdryer. Breakfast is served in the very pleasant dining room. Many good pubs, restaurants & shops locally. An excellent location from which to explore London. Parking by arrangement. Children over 12.	£31.00 to £50.00	Y	N	N
Home No. 06. London. Tel: +44 (0)20-8742-9123 Fax: +44 (0)20-8749-7084 U.S., Canada call: Toll Free 011-800-852-26320 Australia call: Toll Free 0011-800-852-26320 E-mail: bestbandb@atlas.co.uk	Nearest Tube: East Putney A Victorian terraced house with a traditional family atmosphere & set in a quiet residential street. The friendly hosts offer 1 comfortable twin-bedded room with T.V., overlooking the rear garden, & with an adjacent private bathroom. A large Continental or Full English breakfast is served. Putney is a delightful area with many good shops & restaurants. Excellent transport facilities provide easy access to central London & the sights.	£26.00 to £40.00	Y	N	N
Home No. 07. London. Tel: +44 (0)20-8742-9123 Fax +44 (0)20-8749-7084 U.S., Canada call: Toll Free 011-800-852-26320 Australia call: Toll Free 0011-800-852-26320 E-mail: bestbandb@atlas.co.uk	Nearest Tube: Fulham Broadway Set in the heart of Fulham, this is an attractive Victorian maisonette which is elegantly furnished throughout with antiques. The charming host, who has an in-depth knowledge of London, offers 2 beautifully furnished double-bedded rooms. Each is attractively decorated & has tea/coffee-making facilities & an en-suite or private bathroom. In summer, breakfast can be taken in the delightful garden. Only 8 mins' walk from the tube this is an ideal base for exploring London. Many good restaurants & antique shops close by.	£37.00 to £50.00	N	N	N
Home No. 08. London. Tel: +44 (0)20-8742-9123 Fax: +44 (0)20-8749-7084 U.S., Canada call: Toll Free 011-800-852-26320 Australia call: Toll Free 0011-800-852-26320 E-mail: bestbandb@atlas.co.uk	Nearest Tube: Maida Vale An attractive Victorian maisonette very well situated only 3 mins' walk from the tube. Offering 1 spacious & comfortably furnished twin-bedded room with T.V., tea/coffee-making facilities & an en-suite shower room. Breakfast is served in the dining area looking out onto the pretty garden. Good local pubs & restaurants. An excellent central location providing easy access to many attractions; with a direct tube link to Piccadilly Circus & the Embankment. Also, Paddington Station for the Heathrow Express.	£32.00 to £50.00	N	N	N
Home No. 12. London. Tel: +44 (0)20-8742-9123 Fax: +44 (0)20-8749-7084 U.S., Canada call: Toll Free 011-800-852-26320 Australia call: Toll Free 0011-800-852-26320 E-mail: bestbandb@atlas.co.uk	Nearest Tube: Parsons Green Set in a quiet residential street, yet only 5 mins' walk from the station, this is a delightful Victorian terraced house. It has been beautifully decorated & is furnished throughout with antiques. The charming hosts offer 1 attractive King-size double/twin-bedded room with T.V., tea/coffee-making facilities & an en-suite shower room. Breakfast is taken in the elegant dining room which overlooks the garden. A number of interesting antique shops & good restaurants just a short walk away.	£40.00 to £78.00	N	N	N

Home No. 17. London.

London
Visit our website: www.bestbandb.co.uk

	per person rate £ from - to	children taken	evening meals	animals taken

Home No. 17. London.
Tel: +44 (0)20-8742-9123
Fax: +44 (0)20-8749-7084
U.S., Canada call:
Toll Free 011-800-852-26320
Australia call:
Toll Free 0011-800-852-26320
E-mail: bestbandb@atlas.co.uk

Nearest Tube: Richmond
Situated in an excellent 17th-century terrace, this is an outstanding home, elegantly furnished throughout with antiques. 3 guest rooms: 1 double 4-poster, 1 twin-bedded room & a triple with a 4-poster & a single bed. Each has a super private bathroom. 2 bedrooms have French doors leading onto an Italiante garden, the triple room commands views of the Thames. Historic Richmond with its wealth of shops & riverside restaurants are a few mins walk. Waterloo 12 mins by train.

£45.00 to £88.00 — N N N

see PHOTO over p. 17

Home No. 18. London.
Tel: +44 (0)20-8742-9123
Fax: +44 (0)20-8749-7084
U.S., Canada call:
Toll Free 011-800-852-26320
Australia
Toll Free 0011-800-852-26320
E-mail: bestbandb@atlas.co.uk

Nearest Tube: High St. Ken.
A beautiful house, furnished with many interesting paintings & situated in the heart of Kensington. The charming host offers 1 light & airy, twin-bedded room with a private bathroom. Also another, equally attractive twin-bedded room, which is ideal for a third or fourth member of the party. Each bedroom is well-furnished & a T.V. is available. Only a short walk from the High Street with its many shops & restaurants & within easy reach of Kensington Palace & gardens, Knightsbridge & the museums. Children over 12.

£32.00 to £50.00 — Y N N

Home No. 19. London.
Tel: +44 (0)20-8742-9123
Fax: +44 (0)20-8749-7084
U.S., Canada call:
Toll Free 011-800-852-26320
Australia call:
Toll Free 0011-800-852-26320
E-mail: bestbandb@atlas.co.uk

Nearest Tube: Parsons Green
Located in the quiet Parsons Green area of Fulham. This superb house offers accommodation in 1 king-size double-bedded room with private facilities & 2 doubles which share a bathroom. Each room is beautifully decorated & very comfortably furnished. This is a delightful home & the ideal base for visitors to London. Many of the attractions including Buckingham Palace & Knightsbridge are only 15 mins away by tube.

£31.00 to £60.00 — N N N

Home No. 21. London.
Tel: +44 (0)20-8742-9123
Fax: +44 (0)20-8749-7084
U.S., Canada call: Toll Free
011-800-852-26320
Australia call:
Toll Free 0011-800-852-26320
E-mail: bestbandb@atlas.co.uk

Nearest Tube: Hammersmith
This is a charming Victorian terraced house, where the welcoming hosts offer 1 spacious, attractive & comfortably furnished twin-bedded room with sitting area & a private bathroom & 1 equally attractive king-size double/twin room with private shower room. Each with T.V. & tea/coffee & hairdryer. Breakfast is served in the dining room. A delightful home set in a quiet street, yet only 8 mins walk from Hammersmith with its many restaurants etc. Excellent transport facilities provide easy access to Heathrow & central London.

£32.00 to £50.00 — Y N N

Home No. 24. London.
Tel: +44 (0)20-8742-9123
Fax: +44 (0)20-8749-7084
U.S., Canada call:
Toll Free 011-800-852-26320
Australia call:
Toll Free 0011-800-852-26320
E-mailbestbandb@atlas.co.uk

Nearest Tube: Parsons Green
An elegantly furnished Victorian terraced house, situated in a quiet street yet only 5 mins walk from all transport facilities. The most charming hosts offer 1 delightful double-bedded room which overlooks the rear garden & an equally attractive king-size double/twin-bedded room. Each has a private bathroom & is beautifully decorated. There are 2 small dogs. Parsons Green is an ideal base from which to explore the delights of London & has many excellent restaurants & antique shops.

£35.00 to £60.00 — N N N

London

Visit our website: www.bestbandb.co.uk

	rate £ from - to per person	children taken	evening meals	animals taken

Home No. 31. London. **Tel:** +44 (0)20-8742-9123 **Fax:** +44 (0)20-8749-7084 **U.S., Canada call:** Toll Free **011-800-852-26320** **Australia call:** Toll Free **0011-800-852-26320** E-mail: bestbandb@atlas.co.uk	Nearest Tube: Parsons Green A charming Victorian terraced house, situated only minutes from many excellent shops & restaurants in Fulham. The welcoming host has elegantly furnished this property throughout. Accommodation is in 1 attractive double-bedded room. It is very comfortable & has a good private bathroom. There is also a cosy single room for a third member of the party. A large Continental breakfast is served. Situated only a short walk from the station, this is an excellent base from which to explore London. Children over 12.	£30.00 to £50.00	Y	N	N
Home No. 35. London. **Tel:** +44 (0)20-8742-9123 **Fax:** +44 (0)20-8749-7084 **U.S., Canada call:** Toll Free **011-800-852-26320** **Australia call:** Toll Free **0011-800-852-26320** E-mail: bestbandb@atlas.co.uk	Nearest Tube: Fulham Broadway Located in the cosmopolitan area of Fulham, this modern townhouse is set in a quiet street & yet is only 5 mins walk from all transport facilities, providing easy access to central London & the sights. The friendly & very helpful host offers 1 twin-bedded room with an adjacent private bathroom. Also, 1 double room is available for another member of the party. Each room is tastefully furnished & well-appointed with T.V. & tea/coffee-making facilities. Local restaurants offer a wide choice of international cuisine. Children over 12.	£29.00 to £50.00	Y	N	N
Home No. 38. London. **Tel:** +44 (0)20-8742-9123 **Fax:** +44 (0)20-8749-7084 **U.S., Canada call:** Toll Free **011-800-852-26320** **Australia call:** Toll Free **0011-800-852-26320** E-mail: bestbandb@atlas.co.uk	Nearest Tube: Earls Court A lovely apartment situated on the top floor of a Victorian mansion block (with lift access) & only 3 mins walk from Earls Court station. The charming host offers 1 spacious & attractively furnished double bedded room with an en-suite bathroom & T.V. Breakfast is served in the attractive dining area. Easy access to Knightsbridge, South Kensington & the museums & Heathrow. Many good local restaurants.	£30.00 to £50.00	Y	N	N
Home No. 39. London. **Tel:** +44 (0)20-8742-9123 **Fax:** +44 (0)20-8749-7084 **U.S., Canada call:** Toll Free **011-800-852-26320** **Australia call:** Toll Free **0011-800-852-26320** E-mail: bestbandb@atlas.co.uk	Nearest Tube: Earls Court A superb home, designer decorated & furnished to the highest standard with antiques throughout. 2 double & 1 twin bedded rooms. Each beautiful bedroom is large & airy with a lovely bathroom en-suite, T.V. & tea/coffee facilities. A large dining room. A delightful garden where breakfast can be served if the weather is good. Guests have their own private entrance. Only 10 mins. to Harrods. Children over 12 years. Parking.	£49.00 to £80.00 *see PHOTO over p. 20*	Y	N	N
Home No. 40. London. **Tel:** +44 (0)20-8742-9123 **Fax:** +44 (0)20-8749-7084 **U.S., Canada call:** Toll Free **011-800-852-26320** **Australia call:** Toll Free **0011-800-852-26320** E-mail: bestbandb@atlas.co.uk	Nearest Tube: Gunnersbury A large Victorian residence, with garden, only minutes from the tube station, with easy access to Heathrow, central London, Richmond & beautiful Kew Gardens. The charming host offers 2 spacious guest rooms suitable for doubles or twins & ideal for families. Each room has an en-suite bathroom, T.V., tea/coffee-making facilities & is decorated in natural tones with stripped pine. Children are especially welcome.	£29.00 to £54.00	Y	N	N

Home No. 39. London.

London

Visit our website: www.bestbandb.co.uk

	rate £ from - to per person	children taken	evening meals	animals taken
Home No. 42. London. Tel: +44 (0)20-8742-9123 Fax: +44 (0)20-8749-7084 U.S., Canada call: Toll Free 011-800-852-26320 Australia call: Toll Free 0011-800-852-26320 E-mail: bestbandb@atlas.co.uk Nearest Tube: Hammersmith An imposing 4-storey Victorian terraced house situated in a quiet residential street approx. 8-10 mins' walk from the tube. The charming & artistic hosts have furnished their home with flair & imagination & offer 2 attractive (Gothic inspired) double bedrooms each with an en-suite or private bathroom. There is easy access to central London & the sights by both bus & tube. Many good local restaurants offer a fine selection of international cuisine. An elegant home.	£32.00 to £52.00	Y	N	N
Home No. 43. London. Tel: +44 (0)20-8742-9123 Fax: +44 (0)20-8749-7084 U.S., Canada call: Toll Free 011-800-852-26320 Australia call: Toll Free 0011-800-852-26320 E-mail: bestbandb@atlas.co.uk Nearest Tube: Earls Court This is a traditional London mews house set in a quiet location, yet only 5 mins walk from the tube. The charming host offers 1 attractive & comfortably furnished double-bedded room with T.V., tea/coffee-making facilities & fridge. The private bathroom is adjacent. A Continental breakfast is served. There are a good selection of restaurants & pubs within walking distance. A great location within easy reach of many attractions. Also, easy access to Heathrow & Gatwick Airports.	£45.00 to £70.00	N	N	N
Home No. 44. London. Tel: +44 (0)20-8742-9123 Fax: +44 (0)20-8749-7084 U.S., Canada call: Toll Free 011-800-852-26320 Australia call: Toll Free 0011-800-852-26320 E-mail: bestbandb@atlas.co.uk Nearest Tube: Richmond Situated in the heart of delightful Richmond this really is the perfect location for a relaxing break in London. The charming host, who is an interior designer has refurbished this Victorian home & offers 1 double-bedded room with a private bathroom. Delicious Continental breakfasts are served in the lovely kitchen/diner which overlooks a pretty plantsmans garden. Richmond abounds with fashionable shops & restaurants. Within easy reach of several stately homes. Central London is only 25 mins. Easy access to Heathrow Airport.	£37.00 to £50.00	N	N	N
Home No. 48. London. Tel: +44 (0)20-8742-9123 Fax: +44 (0)20-8749-7084 U.S., Canada call: Toll Free 011-800-852-26320 Australia call: Toll Free 0011-800-852-26320 E-mail: bestbandb@atlas.co.uk Nearest Tube: Parsons Green A beautifully decorated, very stylish late Victorian house, situated in Parsons Green & only 20 mins. from Harrods by tube. Offering 2 attractive double/twin-bedded rooms & 1 very pleasant single room, all are en-suite & have T.V. & tea/coffee-making facilities. Each room is furnished to the highest standards of comfort. A delicious country house breakfast is served. This is a no smoking house.	£41.00 to £60.00	N	N	N
Home No. 50. London. Tel: +44 (0)20-8742-9123 Fax: +44 (0)20-8749-7084 U.S., Canada call: Toll Free 011-800-852-26320 Australia call: Toll Free 0011-800-852-26320 E-mail: bestbandb@atlas.co.uk Nearest Tube: Parsons Green This is a delightful Victorian terraced house which has been beautifully decorated & furnished throughout. The lovely hosts offer 1 very comfortable king-size double-bedded room & 1 attractive single-bedded room. Each room has a T.V. & bottled water etc. & an excellent private bathroom. There are a variety of good bars, bistros & restaurants nearby. Located only 5 mins' walk from the tube station, this is a perfect spot from which to explore London. A charming home.	£35.00 to £50.00	N	N	N

London

Visit our website: www.bestbandb.co.uk

	Description	rate £ from - to per person	children taken	evening meals	animals taken
Home No. 51. London. Tel: +44 (0)20-8742-9123 Fax: +44 (0)20-8749-7084 U.S., Canada call: Toll Free 011-800-852-26320 Australia call: Toll Free 0011-800-852-26320 E-mail: bestbandb@atlas.co.uk	Nearest Tube: Holland Park Set in a quiet, secluded street, this is a modern mews house with an original brick kiln which has been converted into an elegant dining room. Only a few minutes walk from fashionable restaurants, antique shops, Portobello Market & beautiful Holland Park. It has been attractively furnished throughout by the host who is an interior designer. 1 delightful & spacious en-suite double-bedded room which is well-appointed with T.V. etc. & a dressing room. A Continental breakfast is served. Easy access to many of London's attractions.	£37.00 to £60.00	N	N	N
Home No. 52. London. Tel: +44 (0)20-8742-9123 Fax: +44 (0)20-8749-7084 U.S., Canada call: Toll Free 011-800-852-26320 Australia call: Toll Free 0011-800-852-26320 E-mail: bestbandb@atlas.co.uk	Nearest Tube: South Kensington Located in Chelsea, in a quiet residential street yet, only a short walk from many fashionable shops & restaurants. A charming Victorian town house which has been attractively decorated throughout with many interesting prints & artifacts. The friendly hosts offer 1 spacious double-bedded room & a comfortable twin-bedded room. Each has an excellent en-suite shower room, T.V. & tea/coffee-making facilities. A delightful home with easy access to the museums at South Kensington, Knightsbridge & Harrods.	£34.00 to £50.00	Y	N	N
Home No. 56. London. Tel: +44 (0)20-8742-9123 Fax: +44 (0)20-8749-7084 U.S., Canada call: Toll Free 011-800-852-26320 Australia call: Toll Free 0011-800-852-26320 E-mail: bestbandb@atlas.co.uk	Nearest Tube: Hammersmith A lovely house, pleasantly situated in leafy Brook Green mid-way between Hammersmith & Kensington. Offering a spacious & comfortably furnished double bedded room with private bathroom & tea/coffee making facilities which overlooks the rear garden. A pretty lounge with T.V. is often available & in which guests may choose to relax. An ideal base, with good access to Heathrow & central London.	£32.00 to £50.00	Y	N	N
Home No. 59. London. Tel: +44 (0)20-8742-9123 Fax: +44 (0)20-8749-7084 U.S., Canada call: Toll Free 011-800-852-26320 Australia call: Toll Free 0011-800-852-26320 E-mail: bestbandb@atlas.co.uk	Nearest Tube: Fulham Broadway Situated in Fulham, with many good restaurants, pubs & antique shops nearby. This is a charming Victorian house, standing in a quiet street. The delightful hosts offer 1 spacious King-size double/twin-bedded room with an exquisite marble en-suite bathroom & another lovely, light & airy twin-bedded room with a beautiful private bathroom adjacent. Each bedroom is well-furnished & has colour T.V., hairdryer & tea/coffee-making facilities. Very good access to central London & the sights by bus or tube.	£31.00 to £62.00	Y	N	N
Home No. 60. London. Tel: +44 (0)20-8742-9123 Fax: +44 (0)20-8749-7084 U.S., Canada call: Toll Free 011-800-852-26320 Australia call: Toll Free 0011-800-852-26320 E-mail: bestbandb@atlas.co.uk	Nearest Tube: High St. Ken. A beautifully appointed home located in a quiet cul-de-sac, close to Kensington Palace. A lift will take you to the 2nd floor accommodation. A delightful, spacious double room with brass bed, T.V., tea/coffee-making facilities & biscuits are also provided. A delicious varied breakfast is also served. Knightsbridge, Kensington & Hyde Park are all just a short walk from here.	£37.00 to £60.00	N	N	N

London
Visit our website: www.bestbandb.co.uk

	rate £ from - to per person	children taken	evening meals	animals taken

Home No. 61. London.
Tel: +44 (0)20-8742-9123
Fax: +44 (0)20-8749-7084
U.S., Canada call:
Toll Free 011-800-852-26320
Australia call:
Toll Free 0011-800-852-26320
E-mail: bestbandb@atlas.co.uk

Nearest Tube: Holland Park
A lovely apartment situated on the 7th floor of an Edwardian mansion block with lift access. Offering 1 spacious & attractive double bedded room with a private bathroom, T.V. & a small balcony with rooftop views. A large Continental breakfast is served. The charming host has an extensive knowledge of London & is happy to give advice on what to see do. Easy access to central London & the sights, beautiful Holland Park, Kensington High Street & many good shops & restaurants. Heathrow Airbus stops nearby.

£33.00 to £50.00 — N N N

Home No. 63. London.
Tel: +44 (0)20-8742-9123
Fax: +44 (0)20-8749-7084
U.S., Canada call:
Toll Free 011-800-852-26320
Australia call:
Toll Free 0011-800-852-26320
E-mail: bestbandb@atlas.co.uk

Nearest Tube: Sloane Square
An attractive 2-storey penthouse apartment with prize-winning roof garden, situated in the heart of fashionable Chelsea & only minutes from the River Thames & the trendy shops & restaurants of the King's Road. The delightful host, who is an artist, is always happy to advise guests on what to see & do. 1 comfortable en-suite double-bedded room. A Continental breakfast is served in the attractive dining room which is adorned with many of the hosts interesting pictures.

£33.00 to £50.00 — N N N

Home No. 64. London.
Tel: +44 (0)20-8742-9123
Fax: +44 (0)20-8749-7084
U.S., Canada call:
Toll Free 011-800-852-26320
Australia call:
Toll Free 0011-800-852-26320
E-mail: bestbandb@atlas.co.uk

Nearest Tube: Camden Town
A unique timber & glass house (designed by the host who is an architect), only a short walk from the station, the market & many excellent shops & restaurants. 1 attractive double-bedded room with T.V. & tea/coffee facilities & a single room for a third member of the party. Each room is light & airy, comfortable & modern in design. A private bathroom. Breakfast is served in the lovely open-plan kitchen/dining area which overlooks the garden. Easy access to the West End & theatreland.

£40.00 to £58.00 — Y N N

Home No. 65. London.
Tel: +44 (0)20-8742-9123
Fax: +44 (0)20-8749-7084
U.S., Canada call:
Toll Free 011-800-852-26320
Australia call:
Toll Free 0011-800-852-26320
E-mail: bestbandb@atlas.co.uk

Nearest Tube: Baker Street
An elegant Georgian townhouse situated only moments from Baker Street, Regent's Park & Mayfair. It is pleasantly furnished throughout. A selection of charming guest rooms including double, single & triple rooms. Each bedroom is spacious, attractively decorated & has an en-suite/private bathroom, T.V. & 'phone. An elegant guest lounge where tea/coffee is available. A Continental breakfast is served. A marvellous location only minutes from the West End.

£54.00 to £85.00 — N N N

Home No. 66. London.
Tel: +44 (0)20-8742-9123
Fax: +44 (0)20-8749-7084
U.S., Canada call:
Toll Free 011-800-852-26320
Australia call:
Toll Free 0011-800-852-26320
E-mail: bestbandb@atlas.co.uk

Nearest Tube: Earls Court
A spacious apartment located at garden level offering contemporary accommodation in 1 double bedded room with en-suite facilities, T.V., fridge & 'phone. The friendly host has tastefully furnished & pleasantly decorated this apartment with many interesting paintings. Guests may relax in the garden which is accessible from their room. Situated only a few minutes walk from the underground station, this home is within easy reach of museums, galleries, shops & theatres.

£32.00 to £50.00 — N N N

London

		rate £ from - to per person	children taken	evening meals	animals taken
Home No. 69. London. Tel: +44 (0)20-8742-9123 Fax: +44 (0)20-8749-7084 U.S., Canada call: Toll Free **011-800-852-26320** Australia call: Toll Free **0011-800-852-26320** E-mail: bestbandb@atlas.co.uk	Nearest Tube: South Kensington A super home from which to explore London, situated only a very short walk from the Natural History & Science Museums & the station. An attractively furnished apartment, located on the 1st floor of an Edwardian conversion, where the friendly host offers 1 King-size double/twin-bedded room with full en-suite bathroom & T.V. A large Continental breakfast is served. An excellent location with many good restaurants etc.	£32.00 to £50.00 🚭	N	N	N
Home No. 72. London. Tel: +44 (0)20-8742-9123 Fax: +44 (0)20-8749-7084 U.S., Canada call: Toll Free **011-800-852-26320** Australia call: Toll Free **0011-800-852-26320** E-mail: bestbandb@atlas.co.uk	Nearest Tube: Baker Street A traditional 4-storey Georgian townhouse in a marvellous location, only moments from Madame Tussauds, the Sherlock Holmes museum, Lord's Cricket Ground & Regents Park. The charming hosts, who are artists, offer 1 king-size double/twin-bedded room & an attractive double room with 1 with low-beamed ceilings. Each has an en-suite bathroom, T.V., tea/coffee facilities & views towards Regents Park. An ideal base from which to explore London on foot; the West End, theatreland & Piccadilly are only 10 mins away.	£37.00 to £60.00	Y	N	N
Home No. 73. London. Tel: +44 (0)20-8742-9123 Fax: +44 (0)20-8749-7084 U.S., Canada call: Toll Free **011-800-852-26320** Australia call: Toll Free **0011-800-852-26320** E-mail: bestbandb@atlas.co.uk	Nearest Tube: Sloane Square A delightful Victorian townhouse in fashionable Chelsea, & very close to Harrods, stylishly decorated throughout & offering 2 lovely guest rooms. 1 a king-size double/twin-bedded room with en-suite shower room & the other a double with a spacious en-suite bathroom & access to a pretty garden. Each has T.V. & tea/coffee-making facilities. A wonderful location, only a short walk from Sloane Square, Knightsbridge, the museums at South Kensington & superb restaurants.	£37.00 to £60.00	Y	N	N
Home No. 76. London. Tel: +44 (0)20-8742-9123 Fax: +44 (0)20-8749-7084 U.S., Canada call: Toll Free **011-800-852-26320** Australia call: Toll Free **0011-800-852-26320** E-mail: bestbandb@atlas.co.uk	Nearest Tube: Earls Court One king-size double or twin-bedded room with very large en-suite bath & separate shower & 1 king-size double with adjacent private bath & shower. Each room has a colour T.V. & clock/radio & has been beautifully decorated & furnished by this most helpful host. This charming Victorian house is very close to all the best places for shopping, museums, sight-seeing & within walking distance of many excellent restaurants. Easy access to Gatwick & Heathrow Airports.	£30.00 to £62.00 🚭	N	N	N
Home No. 77. London. Tel: +44 (0)20-8742-9123 Fax: +44 (0)20-8749-7084 U.S., Canada call: Toll Free **011-800-852-26320** Australia call: Toll Free **0011-800-852-26320** E-mail: bestbandb@atlas.co.uk	Nearest Tube:Clapham Jt.(B.R.) A large Edwardian house built for Earl Spencer backing onto a private park. Breakfast may be served in the dining room or large conservatory. There is 1 double en-suite room, 1 family room en-suite, 1 twin bedded room with private facilities, also, 1 double room with shared bathroom. Plenty of car parking space. There are two cats & a friendly dog. A charming & most friendly host. Smoking permitted on the ground floor.	£32.00 to £50.00 *see PHOTO over p. 25*	N	N	N

Home No. 77 . London.

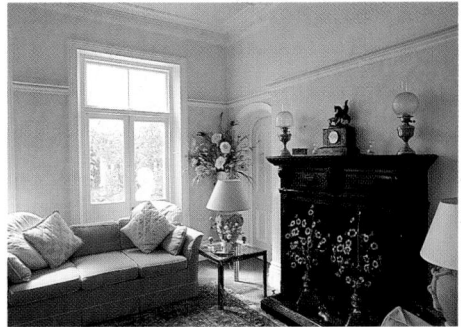

London

Visit our website: www.bestbandb.co.uk

	rate £ from – to per person	children taken	evening meals	animals taken

Home No. 78. London.	Nearest Tube: Parsons Green	£33.00 to £50.00	N	N	N
Tel: +44 (0)20-8742-9123 Fax: +44 (0)20-8749-7084 U.S., Canada call: Toll Free 011-800-852-26320 Australia call: Toll Free 0011-800-852-26320 E-mail: bestbandb@atlas.co.uk	An impressive Victorian house with pretty garden in a fashionable area facing a park with a public tennis court. Easy access to central London & excellent shops & restaurants nearby. The charming host is a well-travelled author, with 1 cat. There are 2 bedrooms, each with a double bed, completely private facilities, T.V. & hairdryer. A full English breakfast is served. Charming guest sitting-room (rare in a private home).				

Home No. 79. London.	Nearest Tube: East Putney	£32.00 to £50.00	Y	N	N
Tel: +44 (0)20-8742-9123 Fax: +44 (0)20-8749-7084 U.S., Canada call: Toll Free 011-800-852-26320 Australia call: Toll Free 0011-800-852-26320 E-mail: bestbandb@atlas.co.uk	An elegant Victorian house with a pretty garden located in the residential area of Putney. The charming hosts offer 2 stylishly decorated guest rooms, located on the 3rd floor. An attractive & spacious twin room with a lovely private bathroom & one large, sunny double bedroom with an excellent shower room en-suite. Each room has a colour T.V. & tea/coffee-making facilities. Only 25 minutes to central London & the main attractions by tube, or 35 mins' to Windsor by train. There are many excellent local restaurants.				

Home No. 83. London.	Nearest Tube: Stamford Brook	£31.00 to £50.00	Y	N	N
Tel: +44 (0)20-8742-9123 Fax: +44 (0)20-8749-7084 U.S., Canada call: Toll Free 011-800-852-26320 Australia call: Toll Free 0011-800-852-26320 E-mail: bestbandb@atlas.co.uk	A spacious Edwardian house set in a quiet street only 4 mins' walk from the station. The charming hosts offer 1 spacious & beautifully decorated Queen-size double-bedded room with Victorian-style brass bedstead, fridge, T.V./video, trouser press, tea/coffee-making facilities & an excellent bathroom en-suite. Breakfast is served in the conservatory overlooking the garden. Only 7 mins' walk from the River Thames with its variety of riverside pubs. Easy access to central London & Heathrow Airport. Children over 8.				

Home No. 85. London.	Nearest Tube: Fulham Broadway	£32.00 to £50.00	N	N	N
Tel: +44 (0)20-8742-9123 Fax: +44 (0)20-8749-7084 U.S., Canada call: Toll Free 011-800-852-26320 Australia call: Toll Free 0011-800-852-26320 E-mail: bestbandb@atlas.co.uk	Situated in the heart of Fulham, this is a delightful 3 storey Victorian house conveniently located only 3 mins' walk from the tube. The very friendly hosts offer 1 double-bedded room with an en-suite bathroom & another double-bedded room with a shower room en-suite. Each bedroom is beautifully decorated & very comfortable. T.V. & tea/coffeee facilities are available. There are many famous bars, bistros & restaurants in Fulham Broadway. Heathrow Airport & Londons' many attractions are easily accessible by tube.				

Home No. 88. London.	Nearest Tube: Sloane Square	£36.00 to £60.00	N	N	N
Tel: +44 (0)20-8742-9123 Fax: +44 (0)20-8749-7084 U.S., Canada call: Toll Free 011-800-852-26320 Australia call: Toll Free 0011-800-852-26320 E-mail: bestbandb@atlas.co.uk	This is an elegantly furnished apartment situated less than 10 mins' walk from the tube. The friendly hosts offer 1 attractive twin-bedded room with a private bathroom. Breakfast is served in the elegant dining room. Situated in the heart of Chelsea within easy reach of the fashionable shops in the King's Road & good restaurants. Many of London's attractions are only a short distance away by bus or tube.				

Beds:Berks:Bucks:Herts.

Bedfordshire
(Thames & Chilterns)

The county of Bedfordshire is an area of great natural beauty from the Dunstable Downs in the south to the great River Ouse in the north, along with many country parks & historic houses & gardens.

Two famous wildlife parks are to be found, at Woburn &Whipsnade. The Woburn Wild Animal Kingdom is Britain's largest drive-through safari park, with entrance to an exciting leisure park all included in one admission ticket.

Whipsnade Zoo came into existence in the 1930's as a country retreat for the animals of London Zoo, but is now very much a zoo in its own right & renowned for conservation work.

Woburn Abbey, home of the Dukes of Bedford for three centuries, is often described as one of England's finest showplaces. Rebuilt in the 8th century the Abbey houses an important art collection & is surrounded by a magnificent 3,000 acre deer park.

John Bunyan drew on local Bedfordshire features when writing the Pilgrims Progress, & the ruins of Houghton House, his "House Beautiful" still remain.

Buckinghamshire
(Thames & Chilterns)

Buckinghamshire can be divided into two distinct geographical regions: The high Chilterns with their majestic beechwoods & the Vale of Aylesbury chosen by many over the centuries as a beautiful & accessible place to build their historical homes.

The beechwoods of the Chilterns to the south of the county are crisscrossed with quiet lanes & footpaths., Ancient towns & villages like Amersham & Chesham lie tucked away in the

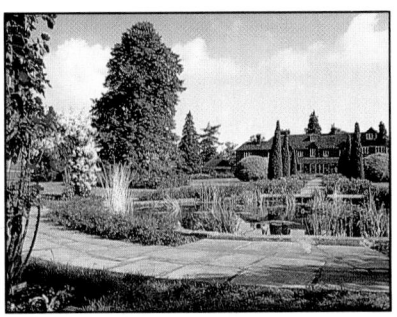

Rose gardens. St.Albans. Herts.

folds of the hills & a prehistoric track; the Ichnield Way winds on its 85 mile journey through the countryside.

The Rothschild family chose the Vale of Aylesbury to create several impressive homes, & Waddesdon House & Ascott House are both open to the public. Benjamin Disraeli lived at Hughenden Manor, & Florence Nightingale, "the Lady with the Lamp", at Claydon House. Sir Francis Dashwood, the 18th century eccentric founded the bizarre Hellfire Club, which met in the man-made caves near West Wycombe House.

Berkshire
(Thames & Chilterns)

Berkshire is a compact county but one of great variety & beauty.

In the East is Windsor where the largest inhabited castle in the world stands in its majestic hilltop setting. Nine centuries of English monarchy have lived here, & it is home to the present Queen. The surrounding parkland, enormous yards, vast interior & splendour of the State Apartments make a trip to Windsor Castle an unforgettable experience.

To the West are the gently rolling Berkshire Downs where many a champion racehorse has been trained.

Beds:Berks:Bucks:Herts.

To the north of the county, the River Thames dominates the landscape - an opportunity for a river-bank stroll & a drink at a country pub.

In the south is the Kennet & Avon Canal, a peaceful waterway with horse-drawn barges.

Historically, Berkshire has occupied an important place due to its strategic position commanding roads to & from Oxford & the north, & Bath & the west. Roundheads & Cavaliers clashed twice near Newbury during the 17th century English Civil Wars. Their battles are colourfully recreated by historic societies like the Sealed Knot.

The Tudor period brought great wealth from wool-weaving. Merchants built wonderful houses & some built churches but curiously, there is no cathedral in Berkshire.

Hertfordshire
(Thames & Chilterns)

Old & new exist side by side in Hertfordshire. This attractive county includes historic sites, like the unique Roman theatre in St. Albans, as well as new additions to the landscape such as England's first Garden City at Letchworth.

The countryside varies from the chalk hills & rolling downlands of the Chilterns to rivers, lakes, canals & pretty villages. The county remains largely rural despite many large towns & cities. The Grand Union Canal, built at the end of the 18th century to link the Midlands to London, passes through some glorious scenery, particularly at Cassiobury Park in Watford.

Verulamium was a newly-built town of the Roman Empire. It was the first name of Alban, himself a Roman, who became the first Christian to be martyred for his faith in England. The great Abbey church was built by the Normans around his original church, & it was re-established under the Rule of St. Benedict & named St. Albans some 600 years after his death.

Windsor Castle.

Beds:Berks:Bucks:Herts.

Bedfordshire

Gazeteer

Area of outstanding natural beauty.
Dunstable Downs, Ivinghoe Beacon.

Historic Houses

Woburn Abbey - house & gardens, extensive art collection, deer park, antiques centre.
Luton Hoo - the Wernher collection of Old Masters, tapestries, furniture, ivories & porcelain, unique collection of Russian Faberge jewellry. Parkland landscaped by Capability Brown.

Other Things to see & do

Woburn Wildlife Park
Whipsnade Zoo-Whipsnade
Old Warden - the village houses a collection of working vintage aeroplanes with flying displays each month from April to October.

Berkshire

Gazeteer

Areas of outstanding natural beauty.
North West Downs.

Historic Houses & Castles

Windsor Castle - Royal Residence at Windsor
State apartments, house, historic treasures. The Cloisters, Windsor Chapel. Mediaeval house.
Basildon Park - Nr. Pangbourne
Overlooking the Thames. 18th century Bath stone building, massive portico & linked pavilions. Painted ceiling in Octagon Room, gilded pier glasses. Garden & wooded walks.
Cliveden - Nr. Taplow
Once the home of Nancy Astor.

Churches

Lambourn (St. Michael & All Saints)
Norman with 15th century chapel. 16th century brasses, glass & tombs.
Padworth (St. John the Baptist)
12th century Norman with plastered exterior, remains of wall paintings, 18th century monuments.
Warfield (St. Michael & All Angels)
14th century decorated style. 15th century wood screen & loft.

Museums

Newbury Museum - Newbury
Natural History & Archaeology - Paleolithic to Saxon & Mediaeval times.
Household Cavalry Museum - Windsor

Other Things to see & do

Racing - at Newbury, Ascot & Windsor
Highlight of the racing year is the Royal Meeting at Ascot each June, attended by the Queen & other members of the Royal Family.
Antiques - Hungerford is a famous centre for antiques.

Buckinghamshire

Gazeteer

Area of outstanding natural beauty.
Burnham Beeches - 70 acres of unspoilt woodlands, inspiration to poet Thomas Gray.

Historic Houses

Waddesdon Manor & Ascott House - homes of the Rothschilds.
Chalfont St. Giles - cottage home of great English poet John Milton.
Old Jordans & the Meeting House - 17th century buildings associated with William Penn, the founder of Pennsylvania & with the Society of Friends, often called the Quakers.

Things to see & do

Buckinghamshire Railway Centre - at Quainton
Vintage steam train rides & largest private railway collection in Britain.
Chalfont Shire Horse Centre - home of the gentle giants of the horse world.

Beds:Berks:Bucks:Herts.

Hertfordshire

Gazeteer
Areas of outstanding natural beauty.
Parts of the Chilterns.

Historic Houses & Castles
Hatfield House - Hatfield
Home of the Marquess of Salisbury.
Jacobean House & Tudor Palace -
childhood home of Queen Elizabeth I.
Knebworth House - Knebworth
Family home of the Lyttons. 16th century
house transformed into Victorian High
Gothic. Furniture, portraits. Formal
gardens & unique Gertrude Jekyll herb
garden.
Shaw's Corner - Ayot St. Lawrence
Home of George Bernard Shaw.

Cathedrals & Churches
St. Albans Cathedral - St. Albans
9th century foundation, murals, painted
roof over choir, 15th century reredos,
stone rood screen.

Stanstead St. Abbots (St. James)12th
century nave, 13th century chancel, 15th
century tower & porch, 16th century
North chapel, 18th century box pews
& 3-decker pulpit.
Watford (St. Mary)
13 - 15th century. Essex chapel.
Tuscan arcade. Morryson tombs.

Museums
**Rhodes Memorial Museum &
Commonwealth Centre** - at Bishop
Stortford
Zoological Museum - Tring
Gardens
Gardens of the Rose - Chiswell Green
Nr. St Albans
Showgrounds of the Royal National Rose
Society
Capel Manor
Extensive grounds of horticultural
college.
Many fine trees, including the largest
copper beech in the country.

Bledlow Village; Bucks.

BEDS/BUCKS
BERKSHIRE
HERTS

Map reference

01	Must	09	Sanders-Rose
02	Kirchner	10	Thornely
03	Codd	11	Carke
04	Cook	12	Pibworth
05	Rashleigh	13	Knowles
06	Goldstein	14	Pollock-Hill
07	Digby	15	Dunn
09	Steeds		

31

Bedfordshire & Berkshire

Church Farm

Nearest Road: A.1, A.421

Church Farm is a Grade II listed, 17th-century part-timber framed house. It is a perfect base for those wanting somewhere a little special & a comfortable place to stay. 3 delightful en-suite bedrooms, each with a T.V. & a welcome tray. (In the twin room, there is the 'Coat of Arms' of the Stuart Kings.) A lounge with open fire is available for relaxation. Breakfast is served in the attractive beamed 17th-century dining room. There are walks around the village & countryside, & inns for evening meals.

E-mail: churchfarm@amserve.net

| | £25.00 to £30.00 | N | N | Y |

Janet Must   Church Farm   High Street   Roxton   Bedford   MK44 3EB   Bedfordshire
Tel: (01234) 870234   Fax 01234 870234   Open: ALL YEAR   Map Ref No. 01

The Old Vicarage

Nearest Road: A.418

Only 45 mins from central London, this imposing Gothic house is set in mature gardens in a pictur-esque Rothschild estate village. Mentmore boasts a good pub in addition to architectural interest & a fine setting. It is very much a family home with plenty of activity. The guest rooms are spacious with en-suite bathrooms, enjoying uninterrupted views over rolling countryside. Meals are served in the 'William Morris' dining room using garden produce when available.

E-mail: susie.kirchner@tesco.net

| | £27.50 to £32.50 | Y | N | N |

Charles & Susie Kirchner   The Old Vicarage   Mentmore   Leighton Buzzard   LU7 0QG   Bedfordshire
Tel: (01296) 661243   Fax 01296 661243   Open: ALL YEAR   Map Ref No. 02

Highfield Farm

Nearest Road: A.1

A tranquil & very welcoming house with comfort, warmth & a friendly atmosphere in a lovely setting on an arable farm. There are 6 attractive bedrooms, 4 en-suite, including 3 ground-floor rooms in taste-fully converted stables. Highfield Farm is set back off the A.1, giving peaceful seclusion & yet easy access to London, Cambridge, Bedford, the Shuttleworth Collection, the R.S.P.B. & the east-coast ports. Ample parking. (Dogs by arrange-ment.) Most guests return to this lovely home.

E-mail: margaret@highfield-farm.co.uk

| | £25.00 to £30.00 | Y | N | Y |

VISA: M'CARD:

Margaret Codd   Highfield Farm   Great North Road   Sandy   SG19 2AQ   Bedfordshire
Tel: (01767) 682332   Fax 01767 692503   Open: ALL YEAR   Map Ref No. 03

Lodge Down

Nearest Road: B.4000

A warm welcome is assured at Lodge Down, a country house with superb accommodation & en-suite bathrooms, set in lovely grounds. Excellent & varied dining in surrounding villages. Easy access to the M.4 motorway at Jts 14 & 15. 1 hr or less for Heathrow (60 miles), Bath (43 miles) & Oxford (26 miles). This location provides a central base for excursions to Stonehenge, Salisbury & the Cotswolds, etc., or an easy drive to Heathrow & London. A charming home.

E-mail: lodgedown@hotmail.com

| | £22.50 to £25.00 | Y | N | N |

see PHOTO over p. 33

Mrs S. Cook   Lodge Down   Lambourn   Hungerford   RG17 7BJ   Berkshire
Tel: (01672) 540304   Fax 01672 540304   Open: ALL YEAR   Map Ref No. 04

![Lodge Down. Lambourn.]

Lodge Down. Lambourn.

Dumbledore

Nearest Road: A.4

A charming (part-16th-century) Tudor country house, located in the pretty village of Warren Row, close to the picturesque town of Henley-on-Thames. 2 elegantly furnished bedrooms, 1 en-suite & each with T.V. & tea/coffee-making facilities. Breakfast is served in the attractive dining room. A residents' lounge is available throughout the day in which guests may choose to relax. Easy access to Windsor, Marlow & Heathrow & Gatwick Airports. Children over 12. Animals by arrangement.
E-mail: laviniarashleigh@faxvia.net

£28.00 to £35.00 | Y | N | Y

Lavinia Rashleigh Dumbledore Warren Row Maidenhead RG10 8QS Berkshire
Tel: (01628) 822723 Fax 01628 822723 Open: ALL YEAR Map Ref No. 05

Beehive Manor

Nearest Road: A.404 (M.)

Beehive Manor offers all the charm & country house atmosphere of a Tudor home set in a traditional English garden. Yet, amongst the massive oak beams, latticed windows & linenfold panelling are also all the comforts of the 20th century. Within its wisteria-clad walls, 3 superb bedrooms are available to guests, as well as a sunny drawing & a delightful dining room. London is just 35 mins away by train. Children over 12.
E-mail: beehivemanor@cs.com

£35.00 to £55.00 | Y | N | N

VISA: M'CARD:

Lesley Goldstein Beehive Manor Cox Green Lane Maidenhead SL6 3ET Berkshire
Tel: (01628) 620980 Fax 01628 621840 Open: ALL YEAR (Excl. Xmas & New Year) Map Ref No. 06

Rookwood Farmhouse

Nearest Road: A.4

This charming & comfortable former farmhouse combines ease of access with rural views & a large garden. The lovely guest bedrooms are in a newly converted coach house which is traditionally furnished & yet affords all modern facilities. In winter, there is a welcoming log fire in the guests' sitting room, while in summer, breakfast is served in the conservatory overlooking the swimming pool. Rookwood Farmhouse is an ideal base for touring & is a perfect spot for a relaxing break.

£35.00 to £45.00 | Y | N | N

VISA: M'CARD:

Charlotte Digby Rookwood Farmhouse Stockcross Newbury RG20 8JX Berkshire
Tel: (01488) 608676 Fax 01488 657961 Open: ALL YEAR Map Ref No. 07

Highwoods

Nearest Road: A.4, M.4

A friendly & relaxing atmosphere at this fine Victorian country house set in 4 acres of attractive grounds, with unspoilt, far-reaching views. Accommodation is in 3 spacious, comfortable & attractively furnished rooms (1 en-suite), all with colour T.V. etc. Guests are welcome to use the garden & hard tennis court. Also, a gallery specialising in English watercolours & prints. Easy access to London, Heathrow Airport, Windsor, Oxford & Bath. Non-smokers preferred.
E-mail: janesteeds@aol.com

£25.00 to £30.00 | Y | N | N

Mrs Jane Steeds Highwoods Hermits Hill Burghfield Common Reading RG7 3BG Berkshire
Tel: (0118) 9832320 Fax 0118 9831070 Open: ALL YEAR (Excl. Xmas & New Year) Map Ref No. 09

Column headers (rotated): rate £ from - to per person | children taken | evening meals | animals taken

---

£35.00 to £35.00 — N Y N (No smoking)

The Old Manor

Nearest Road: A.4

A beautiful country house in 10 acres of secluded grounds yet a mere 2 miles from Junction 12 on the M.4. Very large, elegant, beamed, en-suite bedrooms. The west suite has a 4-poster bed & jacuzzi bath. The east suite has a bath, separate shower & dressing room. Evening meals are of a very high standard & include wine. A beautiful drawing room is available & the dining room & morning room are furnished with elegance. Relaxation, hospitality & quality are the keynotes at The Old Manor.
E-mail: rags-r@theoldmanor.fsbusiness.co.uk

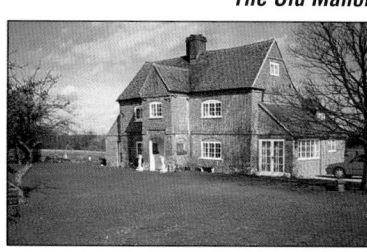

Mrs R. Sanders-Rose   The Old Manor   Whitehouse Green   Sulhamstead   Reading RG7 4EA Berks.
Tel: (0118) 9832423   Fax 0118 9836262   Open: ALL YEAR (Excl. Xmas & New Year) Map Ref No. 09

£28.00 to £32.00 — Y N N

Bridge Cottage

Nearest Road: A.4

A warm welcome awaits the visitor to this delightful 300-year-old riverside cottage, offering 5 attractive bedrooms with beamed ceilings including 2 twin-bedded en-suite rooms. Breakfast can be served on the patio, when weather permits, overlooking the River Kennet, where old narrow boats pass by. It is surrounded by lovely countryside. The local pub serves excellent home-cooked suppers. London 1 hr away. Ideal for Heathrow & rail/air connections to Reading & London, etc.
E-mail: jthornely@talk21.com

Jill Thornely   Bridge Cottage   Station Road   Woolhampton   Reading   RG7 5SF   Berkshire
Tel: (01189) 713138   Fax 01189 714331   Open: ALL YEAR (Excl. Xmas)   Map Ref No. 10

£27.50 to £27.50 — Y N Y

Field Cottage

Nearest Road: A.413

Field Cottage is a 17th-century thatched & stone farmhouse which is set in 4 acres in a small hamlet with stunning views. The house retains many original features including beams & old fireplaces, yet offers guests every modern-day comfort. Guest rooms include includes 1 double bedroom with an en-suite bathroom & a twin-bedded room & a single room which share a bathroom. Waddesdon Manor, Claydon House, Stowe Gardens, Silverstone, Oxford & the Cotswolds are within easy reach.
E-mail: martin.tessa@virgin.net

Martin & Tessa Clarke   Field Cottage   Hillesden Hamlet   MK18 4BX   Buckinghamshire
Tel: (01280) 815360   Fax 01280 815360   Open: ALL YEAR   Map Ref No. 11

£28.50 to £28.50 — Y N N (No smoking)   VISA: M'CARD:

Home Farm

Nearest Road: A.509, A.428

The Pibworths' offer a warm welcome to their stone farmhouse. 3 individually decorated en-suite rooms offer colour T.V., mini-fridge & tea/coffee facilities. Guest lounge. A traditional breakfast is served in the dining room. A kitchen is also available. Summer use of outdoor heated pool & gardens. Home Farm is an arable farm 1 1/2 miles north of Olney. 10 miles from Bedford, Northampton & Milton Keynes. Central for Cotswolds, Oxford, Cambridge, Stratford-upon-Avon & London.
E-mail: ruth@oldstonebarn.co.uk

Mrs Ruth Pibworth   Home Farm   Warrington   Olney MK46 4HN   Buckinghamshire
Tel: (01234) 711655   Fax 01234 711855   Open: ALL YEAR   Map Ref No. 12

	rate £ from - to per person	children taken	evening meals	animals taken

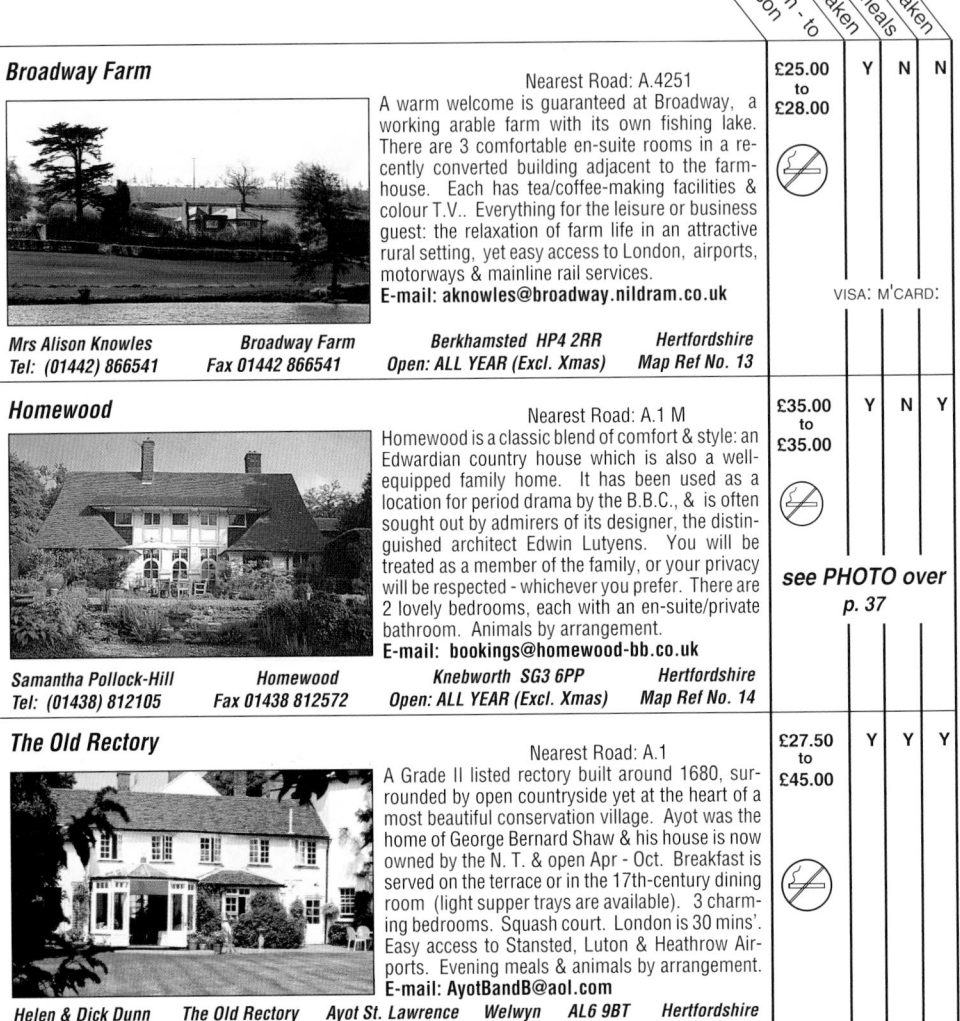

Broadway Farm

Nearest Road: A.4251

A warm welcome is guaranteed at Broadway, a working arable farm with its own fishing lake. There are 3 comfortable en-suite rooms in a recently converted building adjacent to the farmhouse. Each has tea/coffee-making facilities & colour T.V.. Everything for the leisure or business guest: the relaxation of farm life in an attractive rural setting, yet easy access to London, airports, motorways & mainline rail services.

E-mail: aknowles@broadway.nildram.co.uk

£25.00 to £28.00 — Y N N

VISA: M'CARD:

Mrs Alison Knowles	Broadway Farm	Berkhamsted HP4 2RR	Hertfordshire
Tel: (01442) 866541	Fax 01442 866541	Open: ALL YEAR (Excl. Xmas)	Map Ref No. 13

Homewood

Nearest Road: A.1 M

Homewood is a classic blend of comfort & style: an Edwardian country house which is also a well-equipped family home. It has been used as a location for period drama by the B.B.C., & is often sought out by admirers of its designer, the distinguished architect Edwin Lutyens. You will be treated as a member of the family, or your privacy will be respected - whichever you prefer. There are 2 lovely bedrooms, each with an en-suite/private bathroom. Animals by arrangement.

E-mail: bookings@homewood-bb.co.uk

£35.00 to £35.00 — Y N Y

see PHOTO over p. 37

Samantha Pollock-Hill	Homewood	Knebworth SG3 6PP	Hertfordshire
Tel: (01438) 812105	Fax 01438 812572	Open: ALL YEAR (Excl. Xmas)	Map Ref No. 14

The Old Rectory

Nearest Road: A.1

A Grade II listed rectory built around 1680, surrounded by open countryside yet at the heart of a most beautiful conservation village. Ayot was the home of George Bernard Shaw & his house is now owned by the N. T. & open Apr - Oct. Breakfast is served on the terrace or in the 17th-century dining room (light supper trays are available). 3 charming bedrooms. Squash court. London is 30 mins'. Easy access to Stansted, Luton & Heathrow Airports. Evening meals & animals by arrangement.

E-mail: AyotBandB@aol.com

£27.50 to £45.00 — Y Y Y

Helen & Dick Dunn	The Old Rectory	Ayot St. Lawrence	Welwyn	AL6 9BT	Hertfordshire
Tel: (01438) 820429/820603	Fax 01438 821844	Open: ALL YEAR			Map Ref No. 15

Visit our website at:
http://www.bestbandb.co.uk

Homewood. Knebworth.

Cambridge & Northants

Cambridgeshire
(East Anglia)

A county very different from any other, this is flat, mysterious, low-lying Fenland crisscrossed by a network of waterways both natural & man-made.

The Fens were once waterlogged, misty marshes but today the rich black peat is drained & grows carrots, sugar beet, celery & the best asparagus in the world.

Drive north across the Fens & slowly you become aware of a great presence dominating the horizon. Ely cathedral, the "ship of the Fens", sails closer. The cathedral is a masterpiece with its graceful form & delicate tracery towers. Begun before the Domesday Book was written, it took the work of a full century before it was ready to have the timbered roof raised up. Norman stonemasons worked with great skill & the majestic nave is glorious in its simplicity. Their work was crowned by the addition of the Octagon in the 14th century. Despite the ravages of the Reformation, the lovely Lady Chapel survives as one of the finest examples of decorated architecture in Britain with its exquisitely fine stone carving.

To the south, the Fens give way to rolling chalk hills & fields of barley, wheat & rye, & Cambridge. Punts gliding through the broad river, between smooth, lawned banks, under willow trees, past college buildings as extravagant as wedding cakes. The names of the colleges resound through the ages - Peterhouse, Corpus Christi, Kings, Queens, Trinity, Emmanuel. A city of learning & progress, & a city of great tradition where cows graze in open spaces, just 500 yards from the market square.

Northamptonshire
(East Midlands)

Northamptonshire has many features to attract & interest the visitor, from the town of Brackley in the south with its charming buildings of mellow stone, to ancient Rockingham Forest in the north. There are lovely churches, splendid historic houses & peaceful waterways.

The Waterways Museum at Stoke Bruerne makes a popular outing, with boat trips available on the Grand Union Canal beside the museum. Horse-racing at Towcester & motor-racing at Silverstone draws the crowds, but there are quieter pleasures in visits to Canons Ashby, or to Sulgrave Manor, home of George Washington's ancestors.

In the pleasantly wooded Rockingham Forest area are delightful villages, one of which is Ashton with its thatched cottages, the scene of the World Conker Championships each October. Mary Queen of Scots was executed at Fotheringay, in the castle of which only the mound remains.

Rockingham Castle has a solid Norman gateway & an Elizabethan hall; Deene Park has family connections with the Earl of Cardigan who led the Charge of the Light Brigade & Kirby Hall is a dramatic Elizabethan ruin.

The county is noted for its parish churches, with fine Saxon examples at Brixworth & at Earl's Barton, as well as the round Church of the Holy Sepulchre in the county town itself.

Northampton has a fine tradition of shoemaking, so it is hardly surprising that boots & shoes & other leather-goods take pride of place in the town';s museums. The town has one of the country's biggest market squares, an historic Royal Theatre & a mighty Wurlitzer Organ to dance to at Turner's Musical Merry-go-round ! !

Cambridge & Northants

Cambridgeshire Gazeteer

Areas of outstanding natural beauty
The Nene Valley

Historic Houses & Castles

Anglesy Abbey - Nr. Cambridge
Origins in the reign of Henry I. Was redesigned into Elizabethan Manor by Fokes family. Houses the Fairhaven collection of Art treasures - stands in 100 acres of Ground.

Hinchingbrooke House - Huntingdon
13th century nunnery converted mid-16th century into Tudor house. Later additions in 17th & 19th centuries.

King's School - Ely
12th & 14th centuries - original stonework & vaulting in the undercroft, original timbering 14th century gateway & monastic barn.

Kimbolton Castle - Kimbolton
Tudor Manor house - has associations with Katherine of Aragon. Remodelled by Vanbrugh 1700's - gatehouse by Robert Adam.

Longthorpe Tower - Nr. Peterborough
13th & 14th century fortification - rare wall paintings.

Peckover House - Wisbech
18th century domestic architecture - charming Victorian garden.

University of Cambridge Colleges

Peterhouse	1284
Clare	1326
Pembroke	1347
Gonville & Caius	1348
Trinity Hall	1350
Corpus Christi	1352
King's	1441
Queen's	1448
St. Catherine's	1473
Jesus	1496
Christ's	1505
St. John's	1511
Magadalene	1542
Trinity	1546
Emmanuel	1584
Sidney Sussex	1596
Downing	1800

Wimpole Hall - Nr. Cambridge
18th & 19th century - beautiful staterooms - aristocratic house.

Cathedrals & Churches

Alconbury (St. Peter & St. Paul)
13th century chancel & 15th century roof. Broach spire.

Babraham (St. Peter)
13th century tower - 17th century monument.

Ely Cathedral
Rich arcading - west front incomplete. Remarkable interior with Octagon - unique in Gothic architecture.

Great Paxton (Holy Trinity)
12th century.

Harlton (Blessed Virgin Mary)
Perpendicular - decorated transition. 17th century monuments

Hildersham (Holy Trinity)
13th century - effigies, brasses & glass.

Lanwade (St. Nicholas)
15th century - mediaeval fittings

Peterborough Cathedral
Great Norman church fine example - little altered. Painted wooden roof to   nave - remarkable west front - Galilee Porch & spires later additions.

Ramsey (St. Thomas of Canterbury)
12th century arcades - perpendicular nave. Late Norman chancel with Angevin vault.

St. Neots (St. Mary)
15th century

Sutton (St. Andrew)
14th century

Trumpington (St. Mary & St. Nicholas)
14th century. Framed brass of 1289 of Sir Roger de Trumpington.

Westley Waterless (St. Mary the Less)
Decorated. 14th century brass of Sir John & Lady Creke.

Wimpole (St. Andrew)
14th century rebuilt 1749 - splendid heraldic glass.

Yaxley (St. Peter)
15th century chancel screen, wall paintings, fine steeple.

Museums & Galleries

Cromwell Museum - Huntingdon
Exhibiting portraits, documents, etc. of the Cromwellian period.

Fitzwilliam Museum - Cambridge
Gallery of masters, old & modern, ceramics, applied arts, prints & drawing, mediaeval manuscripts, music & art library.

Cambridge & Northants

Scott Polar Research Institute - Cambridge
Relics of expeditions & the equipment used. Current scientific work in Arctic & Antarctic.
University Archives - Cambridge
13th century manuscripts, Charters, Statutes, Royal letters & mandates. Wide variety of records of the University.
University Museum of Archaeology & Anthropology - Cambridge
Collections illustrative of Stone Age in Europe, Africa & Asia.
Britain prehistoric to mediaeval times. Prehistoric America.

Ethnographic material from South-east Asia, Africa & America.
University Museum of Classical Archaeology - Cambridge
Casts of Greek & Roman Sculpture - representative collection.
Whipple Museum of the History of Science - Cambridge16th, 17th & 18th century scientific instruments - historic collection.

Other Things to see & do

Nene Valley Railway
Steam railway with locomotives & carriages from many countries.

Caius College; Cambridge.

Cambridge & Northants

Northamptonshire Gazeteer

Historic Houses & Castles

Althorp - Nr. Northampton
Family home of the Princess of Wales, with fine pictures & porcelain.

Boughton House - Nr. Kettering
Furniture, tapestries & pictures in late 17th century building modelled on Versailles, in beautiful parkland.

Canons Ashby House - Nr. Daventry
Small 16th century manor house with gardens & church.

Deene Park - Nr. Corby
Family home for over 4 centuries, surrounded by park, extensive gardens & lake.

Holdenby House - Nr. Northampton
Gardens include part of Elizabethan garden, with original entrance arches, terraces & ponds. Falconry centre. Rare breeds.

Kirby Hall - Nr. Corby
Large Elizabethan mansion with fine gardens.

Lamport Hall - Nr. Northampton
17th & 18th century house with paintings, furniture & china. One of the first garden rockeries in Britain. Programme of concerts & other special events.

Rockingham Castle - Rockingham, Nr. Market Harborough
Norman gateway & walls surrounding mainly Elizabethan house, with pictures & Rockingham china. Extensive gardens with 16th century yew hedge.

Rushton Triangular Lodge - Nr. Kettering
Symbolic of the Trinity, with 3 sides, 3 floors, trefoil windows.

Sulgrave Manor - Nr. Banbury
Early English Manor, home of George Washington's ancestors.

Museums

Abington Museum - Northampton
Domestic & social life collections in former manor house.

Museum of Leathercraft - Northampton
History of leather use, with Queen Victoria's saddle, & Samuel Pepys' wallet.

Waterways Museum - Stoke Bruerne Nr. Towcester
200 years of canal & waterway life, displayed beside the Grand Union Canal.

Cathedrals & Churches

Brixworth Church - Nr. Northampton
One of the finest Anglo-Saxon churches in the country, mostly 7th century.

Earls Barton Church - Nr. Northampton
Fine Anglo-Saxon tower & Norman arch & arcading.

Church of the Holy Sepulchre - Northampton
Largest & best preserved of four remaining round churches in England, dating from 1100.

Other Things to see & do

Billing Aquadrome - Nr. Northampton
Boating, fishing, swimming & amusements.

Wicksteed Park - Kettering
Large playground & variety of amusements for families.

Lilford Park - Nr. Oundle
Birds & farm animals in parkland setting where many special events are held.

Rushton Triangular Lodge.

CAMBRIDGESHIRE & NORTHAMPTONSHIRE

Map reference

01 Percival
02 Hindley
03 Scott
04 Nix
05 Roper
06 Elbourn
07 Barlow
08 Clarke

Cambridgeshire

Column headers (rotated): rate £ from - to per person | children taken | evening meals | animals taken

---

46 Panton Street

£35.00 to £35.00	Y	N	N

(no smoking symbol)

Nearest Road: M.11, A.14

A 19th-century cottage situated in the historic centre of Cambridge with the great advantage of private car parking. An excellent location near the Botanical Gardens & Fitzwilliam Museum, & only 10 mins' walk from the station, Kings College Chapel & the many beautiful colleges. 2 comfortable bedrooms are provided with a tea tray & T.V.. A full English breakfast is served. (A self-contained flat is also available for short stays.) A charming home & the perfect location from which to explore Cambridge. Children over 10. Single supplement.

VISA: M'CARD:

Mrs Alice Percival   46 Panton Street   Cambridge   CB2 1HS   Cambridgeshire
Tel: (01223) 365285   Fax 01223 461142   Open: ALL YEAR   Map Ref No. 01

Purlins

£24.50 to £29.00	Y	N	N

(no smoking symbol)

Nearest Road: A.10

Lovely, individually designed family home, with 2 acres of parkland, situated in a quiet, pretty village on the Cam, 4 miles south of Cambridge. An ideal centre for Colleges, Audley End House, the Imperial War Museum & bird watching. There are 3 well-appointed double bedrooms (2 ground-floor), all with en-suite bathrooms, colour T.V. & tea/coffee-making facilities. Varied breakfasts (special diets by arrangement). Restaurants nearby. Children over 8 welcome. Single supplement.
E-mail: dgallh@ndirect.co.uk

Olga & David Hindley   Purlins   12 High Street   Little Shelford   Cambridge   CB2 5ES   Cambridgeshire
Tel: (01223) 842643   Fax (01223) 842643   Open: FEB - Mid DEC   Map Ref No. 02

Church Farm

£36.00 to £37.50	Y	Y	N

(no smoking symbol)

Nearest Road: A.1198

This elegant & spacious listed farmhouse, which retains original 16th- & 17th-century features with 19th-century additions, is set in over 3 acres of rural peace. A wealth of oak beams, antiques, English watercolours, open log fires, comfortable beds & imaginative country-house cooking make for a relaxing stay. Ely Cathedral, Wimpole Hall, Kings College Chapel, Audley End & the Fitzwilliam Museum are all within easy reach. A delightful home. Children over 8.
E-mail: Churchfarm@aol.com

VISA: M'CARD: AMEX:

Peter & Maggie Scott   Church Farm   Gransden Road   Caxton   Cambridge   CB3 8PL   Cambridgeshire
Tel: (01954) 719543   Fax 01954 718999   Open: ALL YEAR   Map Ref No. 03

Hill House Farm

£22.00 to £24.00	Y	N	N

(no smoking symbol)

Nearest Road: A.142, A.10

A warm welcome awaits you at this spacious Victorian farmhouse, situated in the quiet village of Coveney, 3 miles from the cathedral city of Ely. Open views of the surrounding countryside & easy access to Cambridge, Newmarket & Huntingdon. Ideal for touring Cambridgeshire, Norfolk & Suffolk. Wicken Fen & Welney wildfowl refuge are nearby. 3 tastefully furnished bedrooms, 1 twin & 2 double en-suite rooms, 1 ground floor. All have their own entrance, T.V., clock/radio & tea/coffee facilities. Children over 12. Single supplement.

VISA: M'CARD:

Mrs Hilary Nix   Hill House Farm   9 Main Street   Coveney   Ely CB6 2DJ   Cambridgeshire
Tel: (01353) 778369   Fax 01353 778369   Open: ALL YEAR (Excl. Xmas)   Map Ref No. 04

Cambridgeshire & Northamptonshire

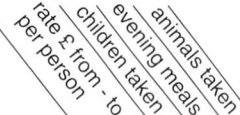

	rate £ from - to per person	children taken	evening meals	animals taken

Queensberry

Nearest Road: A.14, A.142, A.10

A delightful Georgian home, as featured on several T.V. travel programmes, set in large grounds with croquet lawn & parking. Ideally situated for touring East Anglia, Cambridge, Ely Cathedral, Newmarket, Bury St. Edmunds, & many National Trust properties. Equine tours can be arranged. 3 attractive bedrooms, 1 with en-suite facilities in the house & 3 bedrooms in a cottage in the grounds (self-catering). Fordham is the 1st village off the A.14 on the Newmarket to Ely A.142 road. Good local restaurants. Children & animals by arrangement.

£25.00 to £30.00 — Y | N | Y

Jan & Malcolm Roper   Queensberry   196 Carter Street   Fordham   CB7 5JU   Cambridgeshire
Tel: (01638) 720916   Fax 01638 720233   Open: ALL YEAR   Map Ref No. 05

Model Farm

Nearest Road: A.1198

A warm & friendly welcome awaits visitors to this traditional 1870s farmhouse situated on a working family farm. The house, providing comfortable accommodation & lovely views, is set in open countryside between the villages of Little Gransden & Longstowe. Guests are welcome to walk around the farm & garden. Cambridge can be reached in 20 mins via the B.1046 which takes the motorist on a picturesque drive through villages.
E-mail: bandb@modelfarm.org.uk

£22.50 to £22.50 — Y | N | Y

Mrs Sue Barlow   Model Farm   Longstowe Road   Little Gransden   SG19 3EA   Cambridgeshire
Tel: (01767) 677361   Fax 01767 677883   Open: ALL YEAR (Excl. Xmas Day)   Map Ref No. 07

Chiswick House

Nearest Road: A.10

A beautiful timber-framed farmhouse dating from the 16th century. The royal crest of King James I is to be found above the fireplace, suggesting this was his hunting lodge in the early 1600s. Jacobean panelling, oak beams & open fireplaces create a wonderful atmosphere. Accommodation is in 6 delightful en-suite rooms, with tea/coffee-making facilities. T.V. is available. There are many excellent inns nearby. An ideal base for touring Cambridge, Suffolk & Hertfordshire.

£24.00 to £24.00 — Y | N | Y

see PHOTO over p. 45

Bernice & John Elbourn   Chiswick House   Chiswick End   Meldreth   Royston   SG8 6LZ   Cambridgeshire
Tel: (01763) 260242   Open: FEB - NOV   Map Ref No. 06

Dairy Farm

Nearest Road: A.14

Situated in an idyllic Northamptonshire village, Dairy Farm is a charming 17th-century farmhouse, featuring oak beams & inglenook fireplaces. There are comfortable bedrooms, all with en-suite/private bathroom. Families are well catered for. There is a delightful garden, containing an ancient circular dovecote & a charming summer house, for guests to enjoy in a relaxed & friendly atmosphere. Delicious meals, using farmhouse produce (if ordered in advance.) Animals by arrangement.

£25.00 to £35.00 — Y | Y | Y

Mrs A. Clarke   Dairy Farm   12 St. Andrews Lane   Cranford St. Andrew   Kettering NN14 4AQ
Northamptonshire   Tel: (01536) 330273   Open: ALL YEAR   Map Ref No. 08

Chiswick House, Royston

Cheshire & Lancashire

Cheshire
(North West)

Cheshire is located between the Peak District & the mountains of North Wales & is easily accessible from three major motorways. It has much to attract long visits but is also an ideal stopping-off point for travellers to the Lake District & Scotland, or to North Wales or Ireland. There is good access eastwards to York & the east coast & to the south to Stratford-upon-Avon & to London.

Cheshire can boast seven magnificent stately homes, the most visited zoo outside London, four of Europe's largest garden centres & many popular venues which feature distinctive Cheshire themes such as silk, salt, cheese, antiques & country crafts.

The Cheshire plain with Chester, its fine county town, & its pretty villages, rises up to Alderley Edge in the east from where there are panoramic views, & then climbs dramatically to meet the heights of the Peaks.

To the west is the coastline of the Wirral Peninsula with miles of sandy beaches & dunes &, of course, Liverpool.

The countryside shelters very beautiful houses. Little Moreton Hall near Congleton, is one of the most perfect imaginable. It is a black & white "magpie" house & not one of its walls is perpendicular, yet it has withstood time & weather for nearly four centuries, standing on the waterside gazing at its own reflection.

Tatton Hall is large & imposing & is splendidly furnished with many fine objects on display. The park & gardens are a delight & especially renowned for the azaleas & rhododendrons. In complete contrast is the enormous radio telescope at Jodrell Bank where visitors can be introduced to planetary astronomy in the planetarium.

Chester is a joy; a walk through its streets is like walking through living history. The old city is encircled by city walls enclosing arcaded streets with handsome black & white galleried buildings that blend well with modern life. There are many excellent shops along these "Rows". Chester Cathedral is a fine building of monastic foundation, with a peaceful cloister & outstanding wood carving in the choir stalls. Boat rides can be taken along the River Dee which flows through the city.

Manchester has first rate shopping, restaurants, sporting facilities, theatres & many museums ranging from an excellent costume museum to the fascinating Museum of Science & Industry.

Little Moreton Hall.

Liverpool grew from a tiny fishing village on the northern shores of the Mersey River, receiving its charter from King John in 1207. Commercial & slave trading with the West Indies led to massive expansion in the 17th & 18th centuries. The Liverpool of today owes much to the introduction of the steam ship in the mid 1900s, which enabled thousands of Irish to emigrate when the potatoe famine was at its height in Ireland. This is a city with a reputation for patronage of art, music & sport.

Cheshire & Lancashire

Lancashire
(North West)

Lancashire can prove a surprisingly beautiful county. Despite its industrial history of cotton production, there is magnificent scenery & there are many fine towns & villages. Connections with the Crown & the clashes of the Houses of Lancaster & York have left a rich heritage of buildings with a variety of architecture. There are old stone cottages & farmhouses, as well as manor houses from many centuries.

For lovers of the countryside, Lancashire has the sweeping hills of Bowland, the lovely Ribble Valley, the moors of Rossendale & one mountain, mysterious Pendle Hill.

The Royal Forest of Bowland is a forest without trees, which has provided rich hunting grounds over the centuries. An old windswept pass runs over the heights of Salter Fell & High Cross Fell from Slaidburn, where the Inn, the "Hark to Bounty", was named after the noisiest hound in the squire's pack & used to be the courtroom where strict forest laws were enforced.

Further south, the Trough of Bowland provides an easier route through the hills, & here is the beautiful village of Abbeystead in Wynesdale where monks once farmed the land. The church has stained glass windows portraying shepherds & their flocks & there are pegs in the porch where shepherds hung their crooks.

Below the dramatic hills of Bowland, the green valley of the Ribble climbs from Preston to the Yorkshire Dales. Hangridge Fell, where the tales of witches are almost as numerous as those of Pendle Hill, lies at the beginning of the valley.

Pendle Hill can be reached from the pretty village of Downham which has Tudor, Jacobean & Georgian houses, village stocks & an old inn. Old Pendle rises abruptly to 1831 feet & is a strange land formation. It is shrouded in legend & stories of witchcraft.

Between Pendle Hill & the moors of Rossendale are the textile towns of Nelson, Colne, Burnley, Accrington & Blackburn. The textile industry was well established in Tudor times & the towns grew up as markets for the trading of the cloth woven in the Piece Halls.

The moors which descend to the very edges of the textile towns are wild & beautiful & have many prehistoric tumuli & earthworks. Through the towns & the countryside, winds the Liverpool & Leeds canal, providing an excellent towpath route to see the area.

Lancaster is an historic city boasting the largest castle in England, dating back to Norman times.

Lancashire's coastal resorts are legendary, & Blackpool is Queen of them all with her miles of illuminations & millions of visitors.

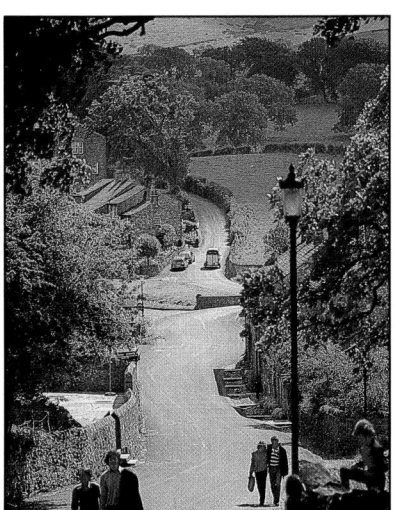

Downham Village.

Cheshire & Lancashire

Lancashire Gazeteer

Areas of outstanding natural beauty.
The Forest of Bowland, Parts of Arnside & Silverdale.

Historic Houses & Castles

Rufford Old Hall - Rufford
15th century screen in half-timbered hall of note. Collection of relics of Lancashire life.
Chingle Hall - Nr. Preston
13th century - small manor house with moat. Rose gardens. Haunted!
Astley Hall - Chorley
Elizabethan house reconstructed in 17th century. Houses pictures, tapestries, pottery & furniture.
Gawthorpe Hall - Padiham
17th century manor house with 19th century restoration. Moulded ceilings & some fine panelling. A collection of lace & embroidery.
Bramall Hall - Bramall
Fine example of half-timbered (black & white) manor house built in 14th century & added to in Elizabethan times. .
Lancaster Castle - Lancaster
Largest of English castles - dates back to Norman era.
Astley Hall - Chorley
16th century half-timbered grouped around central court. Rebuilt in the Jacobean manner with long gallery. Unique furniture.
Hoghton Tower - Nr. Preston
16th century - fortified hill-top mansion - magnificent banquet hall. Dramatic building - walled gardens & rose gardens.
Thurnham Hall - Lancaster
13th century origins. 16th century additions & 19th century facade. Beautiful plasterwork of Elizabethan period. Jacobean staircase.

Cathedrals & Churches

Lancaster (St. Mary)
15th century with 18th century tower. Restored chapel - fine stalls.
Whalley (St. Mary)
13th century with 15th century tower, clerestory & aisle windows. Fine wood carving of 15th century canopied stalls.
Halsall (St. Cuthbert)
14th century chancel, 15th century perpendicular spire. 14th century tomb. Original doors, brasses & effigies. 19th century restoration.
Tarleton (St. Mary)
18th century, part 19th century.
Great Mitton (All Hallows)
15th century rood screen, 16th century font cover, 17th century pulpit.

Museums & Galleries

Blackburn Museum - Blackburn
Extensive collections relating to local history archeology, ceramics, geology & natural history. One of the finest collection of coins & fine collection of mediaeval illuminated manuscripts & early printed books.
Bury Museum & Art Gallery - Bury
Houses fine Victorian oil & watercolours. Turner, Constable, Landseer, de Wint.
City Gallery - Manchester
Pre-Raphaelites, Old Masters, Impressionists, modern painters all represented in this fine gallery; also silver & pottery collections.
Higher Mill Museum - Helmshaw
One of the oldest wool textile finishing mills left in Lancashire. Spinning wheels, Hargreave's Spinning Jenny, several of Arkwrights machines, 20 foot water wheel.
Townley Hall Art Gallery & Museum, & Museum of Local Crafts & Industries - Burnley.

Cheshire Gazeteer

Area of outstanding natural beauty
Part of the Peaks National Park
Addington Hall - Macclesfield
15th century Elizabethan Black & White half timbered house.
Bishop Lloyd's House - Chester
17th century half timbered house (restored). Fine carvings. Has associations with Yale University & New Haven, USA.
Chorley Old Hall - Alderley Edge
14th century hall with 16th century Elizabethan wing.
Forfold Hall - Nantwich
17th century Jacobean country house, with fine panelling.

Cheshire & Lancashire

Gawsworth Hall - Macclesfield
Fine Tudor Half timbered Manor House.
Tilting ground. Pictures, furniture, sculptures, etc.
Lyme Park - Disley
Elizabethan with Palladian exterior by Leoni. Gibbons carvings. Beautiful park with herd of red deer.
Peover Hall - Over Peover, Knutsford
16th century- stables of Tudor period; has the famous magpie ceiling.
Tatton Park - Knutsford
Beautifully decorated & furnished Georgian House with a fine collection of glass, china & paintings including Van Dyke & Canaletto. Landscaping by Humphrey Repton.
Little Moreton Hall - Nr. Congleton
15th century timbered, moated house with 16th century wall-paintings.

Cathedrals & Churches

Acton (St. Mary)
13th century with stone seating around walls. 17th century effigies.
Bunbury (St. Boniface)
14th century collegiate church - alabaster effigy.
Congleton (St. Peter)
18th century - box pews, brass candelabrum, 18th century glass.
Chester Cathedral - Chester
Subjected to restoration by Victorians - 14th century choir stalls.
Malpas (St. Oswalds)
15th century - fine screens, some old stalls, two family chapels.
Mobberley (St. Wilfred)
Mediaeval - 15th century rood screen, wall paintings, very old glass.
Shotwick (St. Michael)
Twin nave - box pews, 14th century quatre - foil lights, 3 deck pulpit.
Winwick (St. Oswald)
14th century - splendid roof. Pugin chancel.
Wrenbury (St. Margaret)
16th century - west gallery, monuments & hatchments. Box pews.
Liverpool Cathedral - the Anglican Cathedral was completed in 1980 after 76 years of work. It is of massive proportions, the largest in the U.K. with much delicate detailed work.

Museums & Galleries

Grosvenor Museum - Chester
Art, folk history, natural history, Roman antiquities including a special display of information about the Roman army.
Chester Heritage Centre - Chester
Interesting exhibition of the architectural heritage of Chester.
Cheshire Military Museum - Chester
The three local Regiments are commemorated here.
King Charles Tower - Chester
Chester at the time of the Civil War illustrated by dioramas.
Museum & Art Gallery - Warrington
Anthropology, geology, ethnology, botany & natural history. Pottery, porcelain, glass, collection of early English watercolours.
West Park Museum & Art Gallery - Macclesfield
Egyptian collection, oil paintings, watercolours, sketches by Landseer & Tunnicliffe.
Norton Priory Museum - Runcorn
Remains of excavated mediaeval priory. Also wildlife display.
Quarry Bank Mill - Styal
The Mill is a fine example of industrial building & houses an exhibition of the cotton industry: the various offices retain their original furnishing, & the turbine room has the transmission systems & two turbines of 1903.
Nether Alderley Mill - Nether Alderley
15th century corn mill which was still used in 1929. Now restored.
The Albert Dock & Maritime Museum - Liverpool
Housing the Liverpool Tate Gallery, the Tate of the North.
Walker Art Gallery - Liverpool
Jodrell Bank - radio telescope & planetarium.

Historic Monuments

Chester Castle - Chester
Huge square tower remaining.
Roman Amphitheatre - Chester
12th legion site - half excavated.
Beeston Castle - Beeston
Remains of a 13th century fort.
Sandbach Crosses - Sandbach
Carved stone crosses date from the 9th C.

CHESHIRE & LANCASHIRE

Map reference

01 **D.Taylor**   05 **I. Taylor**   08 **M. Smith**
02 **Ikin**   06 **Butler**   09 **G. Smith**
03 **West**   07 **Rothwell**
04 **Sutcliffe**   08 **Townend**

Cheshire

rate £ from - to per person	children taken	evening meals	animals taken

---

£29.00 to £34.50

Y | N | N

🚭

VISA: M'CARD: AMEX:

Ash Farm Guest House

Nearest Road: A.56

Set in beautiful National Trust countryside. David & Janice have renovated this 18th-century farmhouse to a very high standard. Bedrooms are en-suite & have many features to delight the discerning traveller. The residents' lounge & dining area is furnished with an antique oak dining suite & open log fire. Excellent farmhouse food. 5 mins' walk to Dunham Deer Park; 2 miles M.56, M.6 less than 6 miles. Manchester Airport 10 mins. Easy access to Manchester & Chester. Children over 12.

E-mail: jan@ashfarm97.fsnet.co.uk

David Taylor   Ash Farm Guest House   Park Lane   Little Bollington   Altrincham   WA14 4TJ   Cheshire
Tel: (0161) 9299290   Fax 0161 9285002   Open: ALL YEAR (Excl. Xmas)   Map Ref No. 01

£30.00 to £35.00

Y | Y | N

🚭

Golborne Manor

Nearest Road: A.41

Golborne Manor is an elegant 19th-century country residence with glorious views, renovated to a high standard & set in 3 1/2 acres of gardens & grounds. Beautifully decorated with spacious en-suite bedrooms. Farmhouse breakfasts. Evening meals (available Mon-Fri) by arrangement. Piano & croquet set available for guests' use. Large car park. Easy access for motorways. 10 mins' drive south from Chester on the A.41, turning right a few yards after D.P. Motors (on the left).

E-mail: ann.ikin@golbornemanor.co.uk

Ann Ikin   Golborne Manor   Platts Lane   Hatton Heath   Chester   CH3 9AN   Cheshire
Tel: (01829) 770310   Fax 01829 770370   Open: ALL YEAR   Map Ref No. 02

£34.75 to £65.00

Y | Y | Y

VISA: M'CARD: AMEX:

Longview Hotel & Restaurant

Nearest Road: A.50

Set in this pleasant Cheshire market town overlooking the common is this lovely, friendly hotel, furnished with many antiques that reflect the elegance of this Victorian building. Care has been taken to retain its character, while also providing all required comforts for the discerning traveller. All of the 26 en-suite bedrooms are prettily decorated, giving them that cared-for feeling which is echoed throughout the hotel. You are assured of a warm welcome as you step into reception.

E-mail: enquiries@longviewhotel.com

Mr & Mrs S. West Longview Hotel & Restaurant 51-55 Manchester Rd Knutsford WA16 0LX Cheshire
Tel: (01565) 632119   Fax 01565 652402   Open: ALL YEAR (Excl. Xmas)   Map Ref No. 03

£25.00 to £40.00

Y | N | N

🚭

Roughlow Farm

Nearest Road: A.54

An 18th-century sandstone farmhouse set in a magnificent position with wonderful views to Shropshire & Wales. A friendly family home elegantly furnished & decorated to a very high standard. 3 comfortable, well-equipped bedrooms (double or twin), all en-suite. 1 has its own private entrance & spacious sitting room. A superb home in a very peaceful situation. Ideal location for exploring Roman Chester (good for shopping), historic Welsh castles & lovely gardens & walks close by.

E-mail: sutcliffe@roughlow.freeserve.co.uk

Mrs Sally Sutcliffe   Roughlow Farm   Willington   Tarporley   CW6 0PG   Cheshire
Tel: (01829) 751199   Fax 01829 751199   Open: ALL YEAR   Map Ref No. 04

The Bower. Yealand Conyers.

rate £ from - to per person	children taken	evening meals	animals taken

£28.00 to £40.00

🚭 (non-smoking)

The Manor

| | Y | Y | N |

Nearest Road: A.525, A.41

Surrounded by rolling Cheshire Plains, Welsh Marches & National Trust properties, Worthenbury Manor makes the ideal setting for a relaxing break. In this full restored Grade II listed building with oak panelling & 4-poster beds, you can indulge yourself with dinner, prepared by a qualified chef using fresh local produce. Guaranteed to be an experience you will want to repeat again & again. An elegant home, situated 2 miles from Bangor on Dee & 4 miles from Malpas. Children over 12.

Ian Taylor   The Manor   Worthenbury   Wrexham LL13 0AW   Cheshire
Tel: (01948) 770342   Fax 01948 770711   Open: FEB - OCT   Map Ref No. 05

£25.00 to £35.00

🚭 (non-smoking)

Eaves Barn Farm

| | Y | Y | N |

Nearest Road: A.679, M.65

Eaves Barn Farm is a working farm situated in a semi-rural location. Superb accommodation in the luxuriously furnished 18th-century farmhouse. The en-suite bedrooms are individually styled, tastefully furnished & very comfortable. Excellent dinner by arrangement, using fresh local produce. A traditional full English breakfast is served in the conservatory. Winner of major tourism award in Lancashire. Easy access to all Lancashire's tourist attractions & Manchester Airport by using the extensive motorway network. Children over 10.

Mrs Mavis Butler   Eaves Barn Farm   Hapton   Burnley BB12 7LP   Lancashire
Tel: (01282) 771591   Fax 01282 771591   Open: ALL YEAR   Map Ref No. 06

£28.50 to £33.50

🚭 (non-smoking)

see PHOTO over p. 52

VISA: M'CARD:

The Bower

| | Y | Y | N |

Nearest Road: A.6

A beautiful, small Georgian country house, set in an Area of Outstanding Natural Beauty. Superb walks right from the door, including to Leighton Moss RSPB reserve. 2 lovely bedrooms, 1 with a double & single bed & en-suite bathroom, & 1 with double bed & private bathroom. Both have T.V., etc. 4-course dinners, by arrangement. Perfect for exploring the Lake District & Yorkshire Dales. 10 mins' from M.6. Very peaceful, & ideal for stop-overs to or from Scotland. Children over 12.
E-mail: info@thebower.co.uk

Mrs S. A. Rothwell   The Bower   3 Yealand Road   Yealand Conyers Carnforth   LA5 9SF   Lancashire
Tel: (01524) 734585   Fax 01524 730710   Open: ALL YEAR   Map Ref No. 07

£33.00 to £39.00

🚭 (non-smoking)

see PHOTO over p. 54

VISA: M'CARD:

New Capernwray Farm

| | Y | Y | Y |

Nearest Road: A.6, M.6 Ex. 35

Ideal stop London-Scotland, 3 miles from Ex. 35, M.6. Ideal, also, for touring the Lake District & Yorkshire Dales. Wonderfully relaxed, friendly atmosphere. Superb accommodation in 17th-century former farmhouse, full of character, in beautiful countryside. Luxuriously equipped king, queen & twin bedrooms with en-suite/private facilities. Renowned for excellent, 4-course candle-lit dinners. Manchester Airport 1 1/4 hours. Winner Best Bed & Breakfast Award. Children over 10.
E-mail: info@newcapfarm.co.uk

Sally & Peter Townend   New Capernwray Farm   Capernwray   Carnforth   LA6 1AD   Lancashire
Tel: (01524) 734284   Fax 01524 734284   Open: Easter - OCT   Map Ref No. 08

New Capernwray Farm. Carnforth.

Lancashire

rate £ from - to per person	children taken	evening meals	animals taken		
£23.00 to £25.00	Y	Y	N	Nearest Road: A.6 **Capernwray House** Capernwray House is a tastefully furnished country home set in rolling countryside with panoramic views. Offering 3 en-suite bedrooms, all with tea/coffee, hairdryer, T.V., etc. A comfortable residents' lounge with T.V., books, magazines & games. Conveniently situated & within easy reach of the Lake District, Yorkshire Dales, the coast, Lancaster & RSPB Leighton Moss. Ideal stop-over en-route North/South. Dinner by arrangement. Also, many traditional pubs & inns close by. Children over 6. E-mail: thesmiths@capernwrayhouse.com	

VISA: M'CARD:

Mrs Melanie Smith   Capernwray House   Capernwray   Carnforth   LA6 1AE   Lancashire
Tel: (01524) 732363   Fax 01524 732363   Open: ALL YEAR (Excl. Xmas & New Year)   Map Ref No. 08

| £24.00 to £25.00 | Y | N | N |

Peter Barn Country House

Nearest Road: A.59
Nestling on the edge of the Forest of Bowland, & surrounded by a beautiful garden with stream & ponds, is the award-winning Peter Barn. Superb accommodation, oak beams & log fires in the sitting room with panoramic views of the Ribble Valley. All 3 bedrooms are attractive, & each has an en-suite or private bathroom & tea/coffee-making facilities. The home-made marmalade is delicious. Good walking & exploring - Browsholme Hall, Whalley Abbey ... or just relaxing. Children over 12.
E-mail: jean@peterbarn.fsnet.co.uk

Mr & Mrs G. Smith   Peter Barn Country House   Cross Lane   Waddington   Clitheroe BB7 3JH Lancs.
Tel: (01200) 428585   Open: ALL YEAR (Excl. Xmas & New Year)   Map Ref No. 09

All the establishments mentioned in this guide are members of
The Worldwide Bed & Breakfast Association

When booking your accommodation please mention
The Best Bed & Breakfast

Cornwall

Cornwall
(West Country)

Cornwall is an ancient Celtic land, a narrow granite peninsula with a magnificent coastline of over 300 miles & wild stretches of moorland.

The north coast, washed by Atlantic breakers, has firm golden sands & soaring cliffs. The magnificent beaches at Bude offer excellent surfing & a few miles to the south you can visit the picturesque harbour at Boscastle & the cliff-top castle at Tintagel with its legends of King Arthur. Newquay, with its beaches stretching for over seven miles, sheltered coves & modern hotels & shops, is the premier resort on Cornwall's Atlantic coast. St. Ives, another surfing resort, has great charm which has attracted artists for so long & is an ideal place from which to explore the Land's End peninsula.

The south coast is a complete contrast - wooded estuaries, sheltered coves, little fishing ports, & popular resorts. Penzance, with its warmth & vivid colours, is an all-the-year-round resort & has wonderful views across the bay to St. Michael's Mount. Here are excellent facilities for sailing & deep-sea fishing, as there are at Falmouth & Fowey with their superb harbours. Mevagissey, Polperro & Looe are fine examples of traditional Cornish fishing villages.

In the far west of Cornwall, you can hear about a fascinating legend: the lost land of Lyonesse - a whole country that was drowned by the sea. The legend goes that the waters cover a rich & fertile country, which had 140 parish churches. The Anglo-Saxon Chronicle records two great storms within a hundred years, which drowned many towns & innumerate people. Submerged forests are known to lie around these coasts - & in Mount's Bay beech trees have been found with the nuts still hanging on the branches, so suddenly were they swamped.

Today, St Michael's Mount & the Isles of Scilly are said to be all that remains of the vanished land. St. Michael's Mount, with its tiny fishing village & dramatic castle, can be visited on foot at low tide or by boat at high water. The Isles of Scilly, 28 miles beyond Land's End, have five inhabited islands, including Tresco with its sub-tropical gardens. Day trips to the numerous uninhabited islands are a special feature of a Scilly holiday.

Inland Cornwall also has its attractions. To the east of Bodmin, the county town, are the open uplands of Bodmin Moor, with the county's highest peaks at Rough Tor & Brown Willy. "Jamaica Inn", immortalised in the novel by Daphne du Maurier, stands on the lonely road across the moor, & "Frenchman's Creek" is on a hidden inlet of the Helford River.

There is a seemingly endless number & variety of Cornish villages in estuaries, wooded, pastoral or moorland settings, & here customs & traditions are maintained. In Helston the famous "Fleury Dance" is still performed, & at the ancient port of Padstow, May Day celebrating involves decorating the houses with green boughs & parading the Hobby Horse through the street to the tune of St. George's Song.

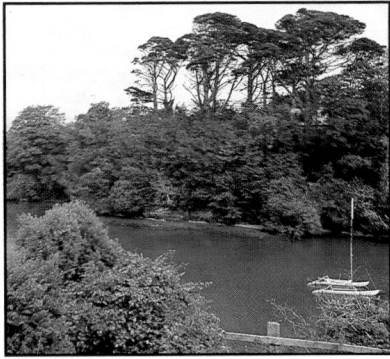

Helford Creek

Cornwall

Areas of outstanding natural beauty.
Almost the entire county.

Historic Houses & Castles

Anthony House - Torpoint
18th century - beautiful & quite unspoiled Queen Anne house, excellent panelling & fine period furnishings.

Cotehele House - Calstock
15th & 16th century house, still contains the original furniture, tapestry, armour, etc.

Ebbingford Manor - Bude
12th century Cornish manor house, with walled garden.

Godolphin House - Helston
Tudor - 17th century colonnaded front.

Lanhydrock - Bodmin
17th century - splendid plaster ceilings, picture gallery with family portraits 17th/20th centuries.

Mount Edgcumbe House - Plymouth
Tudor style mansion - restored after destruction in 1949. Hepplewhite furniture & portrait by Joshua Reynolds.

St. Michael's Mount - Penzance
Mediaeval castle & 17th century with 18th & 19th century additions.

Pencarrow House & Gardens - Bodmin
18th century Georgian Mansion - collection of paintings, china & furniture - mile long drive through fine woodlands & gardens.

Old Post Office - Tintagel
14th century manor house in miniature - large hall used as Post Office for a period, hence the name.

Trewithen - Probus Nr. Truro
Early Georgian house with lovely gardens.

Trerice - St. Newlyn East
16th century Elizabethan house, small with elaborate facade. Excellent fireplaces, plaster ceilings, miniature gallery & minstrels' gallery.

Cathedral & Churches

Altarnun (St. Nonna)
15th century, Norman font, 16th century bench ends, fine rood screen.

Bisland (St. Protus & St. Hyacinth)
15th century granite tower - carved wagon roofs, slate floor. Georgian wine - glass pulpit, fine screen.

Kilkhampton (St. James)
16th century with fine Norman doorway, arcades & wagon roofs.

Laneast (St. Michael or St. Sedwell)
13th century, 15th century enlargement, 16th century pulpit, some painted glass.

Lanteglos-by-Fowley (St. Willow)
14th century, refashioned 15th century, 13th century font, 15th century brasses & altar tomb, 16th century bench ends.

Launcells (St. Andrew)
Interior unrestored - old plaster & ancient roofs remaining, fine Norman font with 17th century cover, box pews, pulpit, reredos, 3 sided alter rails.

Probus (St. Probus & St. Gren)
16th century tower, splendid arcades, three great East windows.

St. Keverne (St. Keverne)
Fine tower & spire. Wall painting in 15th century interior.

St. Neot (St. Neot)
Decorated tower - 16th century exterior, buttressed & double-aisled. Many windows of mediaeval glass renewed in 19th century.

Museums & Galleries

Museum of Witchcraft - Boscastle
Relating to witches, implements & customs.

Military Museum - Bodmin
History of Duke of Cornwall's Light Infantry.

Public Library & Museum - Cambourne
Collections of mineralogy, archaeology, local antiquities & history.

Cornish Museum - East Looe
Collection of relics relating to witchcraft customs & superstitions. Folk life & culture of district.

Helston Borough Museum - Helston
Folk life & culture of area around Lizard.

Museum of Nautical Art - Penzance
Exhibition of salvaged gold & silver treasures from underwater wreck of 1700's.

Museum of Smuggling - Polperro
Activities of smugglers, past & present.

Cornwall

Penlee House Museum - Penlee, Penzance
Archaeology & local history & tin mining exhibits.
Barbara Hepworth Museum - St. Ives
Sculpture, letters, documents, photographs, etc., exhibited in house where Barbara Hepworth lived.
Old Mariners Church - St. Ives
St. Ives Society of Artists hold exhibitions here.
County Museum & Art Gallery - Truro
Ceramics, art local history & antiquities, Cornish mineralogy.

Historic Monuments

Cromwell's Castle - Tresco (Scilly Isles)
17th century castle.
King Charles' Fort - Tresco (Scilly Isles)
16th century fort.
Old Blockhouse - Tresco (Scilly Isles)
16th century coastal battery.
Harry's Wall - St. Mary's (Scilly Isles)
Tudor Coastal battery
Ballowall Barrow - St. Just
Prehistoric barrow.
Pendennis Castle - Falmouth
Fort from time of Henry VII.

Restormel Castle - Lostwithiel
13th century ruins.
St. Mawes Castle - St. Mawes
16th century fortified castle.
Tintagel Castle - Tintagel
Mediaeval ruin on wild coast, King Arthur's legendary castle.

Things to see & do

Camel trail - Padstow to Bodmin
12 miles of recreation path along scenic route, suitable for walkers, cyclists & horse-riders.
Tresco Abbey Gardens - Tresco
Collection of sub-tropical flora
Trethorne Leisure Farm - Launceston
Visitors are encouraged to feed & stroke the farm animals
Seal sanctuary - Gweek Nr. Helston
Seals, exhibition hall, nature walk, aquarium, seal hospital, donkey paddock.
Dobwalls Theme Park - Nr. Liskeard
2 miles of scenically dramatic miniature railway based on the American railroad.
Padstow tropical bird gardens - Padstow
Mynack Theatre - Porthcurno

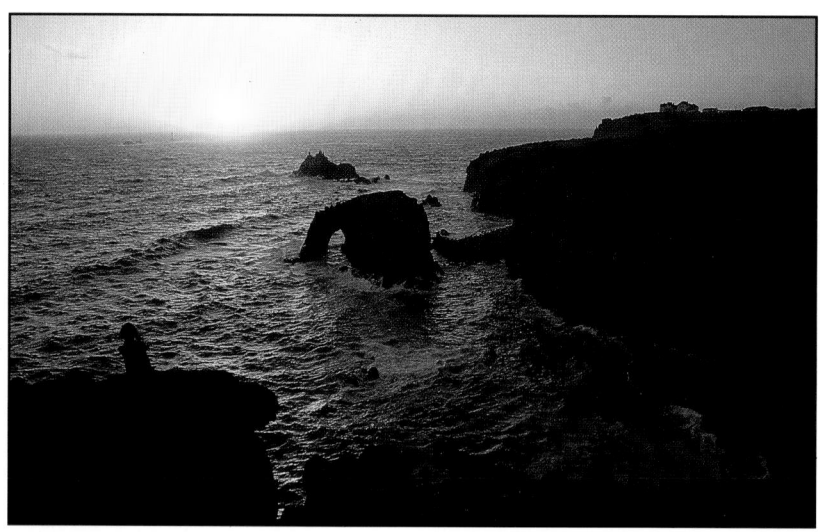

Lands End.

CORNWALL

Map reference

02	Purslow	34	Studley
04	Knight	36	Epperson
06	Tremayne	38	Dodds
10	Sleep	40	Nancarrow
12	Griffin	42	Martin
14	Rowe	44	Sykes
15	Leith	46	Semmens
16	Stanley	48	Fry
18	Eades	50	Devlin
20	Mackenzie	52	Poole
22	Woodley	54	Heasman
24	Walker	56	Vichniakov
28	Wilson	58	Barstow
30	Taylor	60	A. Tremayne
32	Tuckett	62	Dymond

Cornwall

Orchard Lodge

Nearest Road: A.39

Orchard Lodge, set in its own attractive gardens, is a large, delightful base for a relaxing holiday. It offers 5 very pleasant guest rooms, decorated & furnished to a high standard, with modern facilities. A delicious full English or Continental breakfast is served in the pretty dining room, with pine furnishings, which overlooks the garden. Ample parking. Orchard Lodge is an ideal base for touring Cornwall. A warm & friendly welcome awaits you at this charming home.

| £22.00 to £24.00 | N | N | N |

William & Eileen Purslow   Orchard Lodge   Gunpool Lane   Boscastle PL35 0AT   Cornwall
Tel: (01840) 250418   Open: APR - OCT   Map Ref No. 02

Manor Farm

Nearest Road: A.39

A really super 11th-century manor house, retaining all its former charm & elegance. Mentioned in the 1086 Domesday book, it belonged to the Earl of Mortain, half-brother to William the Conqueror. Delightfully located in a beautiful & secluded position, & surrounded by both attractive gardens & 40 acres of farmland. Guest rooms have private facilities. Dining at Manor Farm is considered the highlight of the day. Only 1 mile from the beach. Non-smokers only. West Country winner of the Best Bed & Breakfast award.

| £30.00 to £35.00 | N | Y | N |

Mrs Muriel Knight   Manor Farm   Crackington Haven EX23 0JW   Cornwall
Tel: (01840) 230304   Open: ALL YEAR (Excl. Xmas Day)   Map Ref No. 04

'The Home' Country House Hotel

Nearest Road: A.39

A quiet & charming country house, with views over Maenporth & Falmouth Bay. Accommodation is in 17 comfortable rooms, 16 with a private/en-suite bath/shower. All have tea/coffee-making facilities. A colour-T.V. lounge & bar are available, & guests may relax in the beautiful sheltered garden. A golf course & boating facilities nearby. A friendly host, who prepares delicious meals using local produce. Special diets provided by arrangement. Children over 6 years welcome. Animals by arrangement.

| £26.00 to £32.00 | Y | Y | Y |

VISA: M'CARD: AMEX:

T. P. Tremayne   'The Home' Country House Hotel   Penjerrick   Budock Water   Falmouth TR11 5EE
Tel: (01326) 250427   Fax 01326 250143   Open: APR - OCT   Map Ref No. 06

Trevadlock Farm

Nearest Road: A.30

Trevadlock Farm, is a character farmhouse situated 1 1/2 miles off the A.30 on the edge of Bodmin Moor, offering magnificent views & a relaxing atmosphere. Ideally placed for touring, north/south coasts of Cornwall/Devon, National Trust properties, Eden Project (20 miles) or just walking in peaceful surroundings. The pretty, spacious bedrooms, 1 en-suite & 1 with a private bathroom, each have tea/coffee facilities, T.V. & hairdryer. Enjoy a special break (just 4 hours from London.)
E-mail: trevadlockfarm@compuserve.com

| £20.00 to £24.00 | Y | N | N |

VISA: M'CARD:

Barbara Sleep   Trevadlock Farm   Trevadlock   Launceston PL15 7PW   Cornwall
Tel: (01566) 782239   Open: FEB - NOV   Map Ref No. 10

Cornwall

Wheatley Farm

| £19.00 to £24.00 | Y | Y | N |

Nearest Road: A.39

You will be made very welcome at Wheatley, a spacious farmhouse, built by the Duke of Bedford in 1871, which stands in landscaped gardens on a working family farm in the peaceful Cornish countryside. Excellent touring base for exploring Cornwall/Devon. Spectacular coastline nearby. Beautiful en-suite bedrooms, 1 with romantic 4-poster; each with T.V. & tea/coffee-making facilities. Splendid food using local produce. Log fires. Special breaks April, May, Sept. Children over 8.

VISA: M'CARD:
E-mail: wheatley@farming.co.uk

Mrs Valerie Griffin   Wheatley Farm   Maxworthy   Launceston PL15 8LY   Cornwall
Tel: (01566) 781232   Fax 01566 781232   Open: FEB - NOV   Map Ref No. 12

Tregondale Farm

| £22.50 to £25.00 | Y | Y | N |

Nearest Road: A.390, A.38

Feeling like a break? Relax in style in this charming, elegant farmhouse, beautifully set in an original walled garden. 3 delightful bedrooms, 2 en-suite & 1 with private bathroom, all with T.V., radio & tea/coffee. Log fires. Home produce a speciality. Play tennis, explore the woodland trail with its abundance of wild flowers & birds, through a 200-acre mixed farm. Find award-winning pedigree cattle, lambs in spring. Cycling, fishing from the pond. Plenty of information for walkers.

VISA: M'CARD:
E-mail: tregondale@connectfree.co.uk

Stephanie Rowe   Tregondale Farm   Menheniot   Liskeard PL14 3RG   Cornwall
Tel: (01579) 342407   Fax 01579 342407   Open: ALL YEAR   Map Ref No. 14

The Old Rectory

| £32.00 to £35.00 | N | N | Y |

Nearest Road: A.3083

Where buzzards mew & curlews call, this 200-year-old, listed former rectory lies hidden in a secluded valley on the upper reaches of the mystical Helford River. The elegant guest rooms with private bathrooms overlook south-facing gardens, bordered by a stream. The surrounding ancient woodland provides enchanting walks leading to the river, whilst the grandeur of the west coast is just 5 mins' drive away. A delightful home. Animals by arrangement.
E-mail: leith@euphony.net

Mrs Susan Leith   The Old Rectory   Mawgan   The Lizard TR12 6AD   Cornwall
Tel: (01326) 221261   Fax 01326 221797   Open: ALL YEAR   Map Ref No. 15

Landewednack House

| £39.00 to £46.00 | N | Y | N |

Nearest Road: A.3083

An elegant, Grade II listed, restored Georgian country house, idyllically positioned overlooking the sea, offering absolute peace & comfort. Delightful sea-view bedrooms, furnished with antiques; 4-poster & half-tester beds with private bathrooms (1 with jacuzzi). Relax in front of log fires, laze in the secluded walled garden by the swimming pool, play croquet or just step onto the Heritage coastal footpath of the beautiful Lizard Peninsula. A delightful home at England's most southerly point.

VISA: M'CARD:
E-mail: landewednack.house@virgin.net

Mr & Mrs Peter Stanley   Landewednack House   Church Cove   The Lizard TR12 7PQ   Cornwall
Tel: (01326) 290909   Fax 01326 290192   Open: ALL YEAR (Excl. Xmas)   Map Ref No. 16

Coombe Farm. Widegates.

rate £ from - to per person	children taken	evening meals	animals taken		

Coombe Farm Hotel

£35.00 to £38.00	Y	Y	Y

🚭 (no smoking)

see PHOTO over p. 62

Nearest Road: A.374

A lovely country house, beautifully furnished with antiques, set in 10 acres of lawns, meadows, woods, streams & ponds, with superb views down a wooded valley to the sea. The atmosphere is delightful, with open log fires, a candlelit dining room (in which to enjoy delicious home-cooking) & an informal, licensed bar. An old barn has been converted for indoor games. Croquet lawn, a swimming pool & many birds & animals, including peacocks & horses. All bedrooms are en-suite.
E-mail: coombe_farm@hotmail.com

VISA: M'CARD: AMEX:

Martin Eades   Coombe Farm Hotel   Widegates   Looe PL13 1QN   Cornwall
Tel: (01503) 240223   Fax 01503 240895   Open: APR - OCT   Map Ref No. 18

Trenance Lodge Hotel & Restaurant

£25.00 to £35.00	N	Y	N

Nearest Road: A.3075

An attractive house standing in its own grounds, overlooking the lakes & gardens of Trenance Valley, leading to the Gannel Estuary. The restaurant has a reputation for serving the finest fresh local food in elegant surroundings. Adjoining the restaurant is a spacious, relaxing bar lounge. Accommodation is in 5 comfortable en-suite bedrooms, with colour T.V., radio & tea/coffee-making facilities. An excellent base for touring Cornwall, with a warm welcome assured.
E-mail: info@trenance-lodge.co.uk

VISA: M'CARD:

Mr & Mrs Mackenzie Trenance Lodge Hotel/Restaurant 83 Trenance Rd Newquay TR7 2HW Cornwall
Tel: (01637) 876702   Fax 01637 878772   Open: ALL YEAR   Map Ref No. 20

Degembris Farmhouse

£22.00 to £25.00	Y	Y	N

🚭 (no smoking)

Nearest Road: A.3058

The original manor house of Degembris was built in the 16th century & is now used as a barn. The present-day house, surrounded by attractive gardens, was built 200 years ago, & its slate-hung exterior blends well with the rolling countryside. 5 bedrooms, 3 en-suite, each prettily decorated, with dried flowers enhancing the country atmosphere. Hearty breakfasts & traditional 4-course evening meals. Centrally situated in superb countryside, yet close to the sea, this is the perfect holiday base.
E-mail: kathy@degembris.co.uk

VISA: M'CARD:

Kathy Woodley   Degembris Farmhouse   St. Newlyn East   Newquay TR8 5HY   Cornwall
Tel: (01872) 510555   Fax 01872 510230   Open: ALL YEAR   Map Ref No. 22

The Old Mill House

£30.00 to £32.00	Y	N	N

Nearest Road: A.389

This delightful, 16th-century, converted corn mill, complete with water wheel, stands in its own grounds at the head of Little Petherick Creek. The house & bedrooms are furnished with antiques & collections of genuine artifacts, & each bedroom has an en-suite/private bathroom & tea/coffee-making facilities. Licensed, with a colour T.V. available for the guests' use. Also, a terraced sun garden. Light supper available on request. Children over 14 years welcome.
E-mail: dwalker@oldmillbandb.demon.co.uk

VISA: M'CARD:

David & Debbie Walker   The Old Mill House   Little Petherick   Nr. Padstow PL27 7QT   Cornwall
Tel: (01841) 540388   Fax 0870 0569360   Open: APR - OCT   Map Ref No. 24

Ednovean Farm   Perranuthnoe.

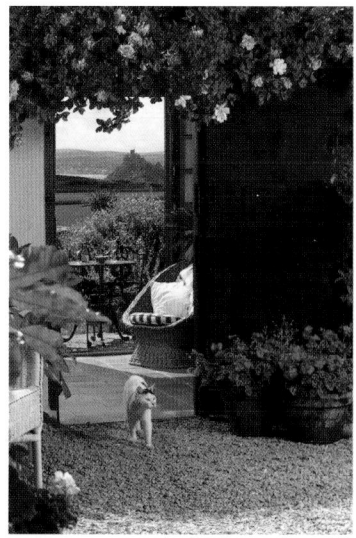

Cornwall

£23.00 to £23.00	Y	Y	N	**Boscean Country Hotel**

Nearest Road: A.3071

The Boscean Country Hotel is set in 3 acres of walled gardens in an Area of Outstanding Natural Beauty overlooking the sea & countryside. There are a wealth of oak beams in the downstairs rooms & a grand staircase. (Much of the wood is from HMS Camperdown.) All 12 en-suite bedrooms are attractively furnished & have tea/coffee-making facilities. A comfortable T.V. lounge, a well-stocked bar & a residents dining room. The Boscean has a reputation for excellent home-cooking.

E-mail: boscean@aol.com

VISA: M'CARD:

Mr & Mrs Wilson   Boscean Country Hotel   Boswedden Road   St. Just   Penzance   TR19 7QP   Cornwall
Tel: (01736) 788748   Fax 01736 788748   Open: ALL YEAR   Map Ref No. 28

£27.50 to £35.00	N	N	N	**Ednovean Farm**

Nearest Road: A.394

A small farm nestling above the peaceful village of Perranuthnoe, with glorious views towards St. Michael's Mount & Mounts Bay. A stunning 17th-century barn, lovingly renovated, with elegant, beautifully furnished, country-style en-suite bedrooms, some with private terraces or Four-Poster beds. All with little luxuries to spoil you. Stroll to the village, cliff-top walks, secluded coves or just enjoy the view. Ednovean Farm is the perfect spot for a peaceful & relaxing break.

E-mail: info@ednoveanfarm.co.uk

see PHOTO over p. 64

VISA: M'CARD: AMEX:

Christine Taylor   Ednovean Farm   Ednovean Lane   Perranuthnoe   Penzance   TR20 9LZ   Cornwall
Tel: (01736) 711883   Fax 01736 710480   Open: ALL YEAR (Excl. Xmas)   Map Ref No. 30

£25.00 to £35.00	N	N	N	**Trenderway Farm**

Nearest Road: A.387

Built in the late 16th-century, this attractive award-winning farmhouse is set in peaceful, beautiful countryside at the head of the Polperro valley, 5 mins' from the fishing ports of Looe & Polperro. Bedrooms here are superb, individually decorated with the flair of a interior designer. A wide choice of breakfasts are offered, including smoked salmon & scrambled egg. Excellent restaurants & inns are nearby. Perfectly located to visit historic houses, The Lost Gardens of Heligan & the Eden Project.

E-mail: trenderwayfarm@hotmail.com

see PHOTO over p. 66

VISA: M'CARD:

Lynne & Anthony Tuckett   Trenderway Farm   Pelynt   Polperro PL13 2LY   Cornwall
Tel: (01503) 272214   Fax 01503 272991   Open: ALL YEAR (Excl. Xmas)   Map Ref No. 32

£31.00 to £32.50	Y	Y	N	**Aviary Court**

Nearest Road: A.30

Aviary Court stands in 2 1/2 acres of grounds on the edge of Illogan Woods. This part-300-year-old house offers guests a choice of 6 comfortable bedrooms, all with en-suite facilities, overlooking the gardens. Each has radio, colour T.V., tea/coffee-making facilities & 'phone. The comfortable lounge has a bar &, in winter, a log fire. The restaurant serves delicious food with a selection of wine. Tennis court available. Children over 3.

E-mail: aviarycourt@connexions.co.uk

VISA: M'CARD:

The Studley Family   Aviary Court   Mary's Well   Illogan   Redruth TR16 4QZ   Cornwall
Tel: (01209) 842256   Fax 01209 843744   Open: ALL YEAR   Map Ref No. 34

Trenderway Farm. Pelynt.

Cornwall

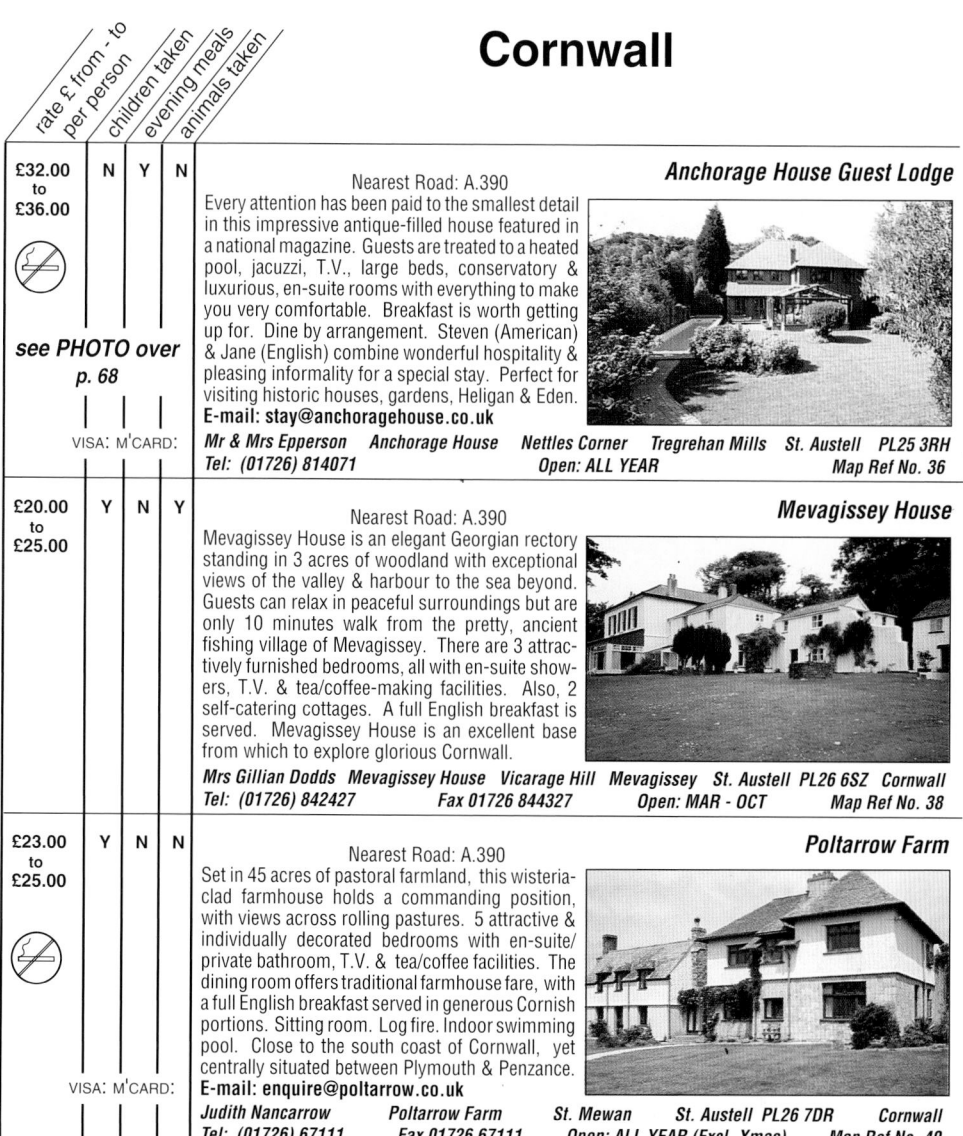

rate £ from - to per person	children taken	evening meals	animals taken		
£32.00 to £36.00	N	Y	N	Nearest Road: A.390	**Anchorage House Guest Lodge**

Anchorage House Guest Lodge

£32.00 to £36.00 — N Y N

see PHOTO over p. 68

VISA: M'CARD:

Nearest Road: A.390
Every attention has been paid to the smallest detail in this impressive antique-filled house featured in a national magazine. Guests are treated to a heated pool, jacuzzi, T.V., large beds, conservatory & luxurious, en-suite rooms with everything to make you very comfortable. Breakfast is worth getting up for. Dine by arrangement. Steven (American) & Jane (English) combine wonderful hospitality & pleasing informality for a special stay. Perfect for visiting historic houses, gardens, Heligan & Eden.
E-mail: stay@anchoragehouse.co.uk

Mr & Mrs Epperson Anchorage House Nettles Corner Tregrehan Mills St. Austell PL25 3RH
Tel: (01726) 814071 Open: ALL YEAR Map Ref No. 36

Mevagissey House

£20.00 to £25.00 — Y N Y

Nearest Road: A.390
Mevagissey House is an elegant Georgian rectory standing in 3 acres of woodland with exceptional views of the valley & harbour to the sea beyond. Guests can relax in peaceful surroundings but are only 10 minutes walk from the pretty, ancient fishing village of Mevagissey. There are 3 attractively furnished bedrooms, all with en-suite showers, T.V. & tea/coffee-making facilities. Also, 2 self-catering cottages. A full English breakfast is served. Mevagissey House is an excellent base from which to explore glorious Cornwall.

Mrs Gillian Dodds Mevagissey House Vicarage Hill Mevagissey St. Austell PL26 6SZ Cornwall
Tel: (01726) 842427 Fax 01726 844327 Open: MAR - OCT Map Ref No. 38

Poltarrow Farm

£23.00 to £25.00 — Y N N

VISA: M'CARD:

Nearest Road: A.390
Set in 45 acres of pastoral farmland, this wisteria-clad farmhouse holds a commanding position, with views across rolling pastures. 5 attractive & individually decorated bedrooms with en-suite/private bathroom, T.V. & tea/coffee facilities. The dining room offers traditional farmhouse fare, with a full English breakfast served in generous Cornish portions. Sitting room. Log fire. Indoor swimming pool. Close to the south coast of Cornwall, yet centrally situated between Plymouth & Penzance.
E-mail: enquire@poltarrow.co.uk

Judith Nancarrow Poltarrow Farm St. Mewan St. Austell PL26 7DR Cornwall
Tel: (01726) 67111 Fax 01726 67111 Open: ALL YEAR (Excl. Xmas) Map Ref No. 40

Visit our website at:
http://www.bestbandb.co.uk

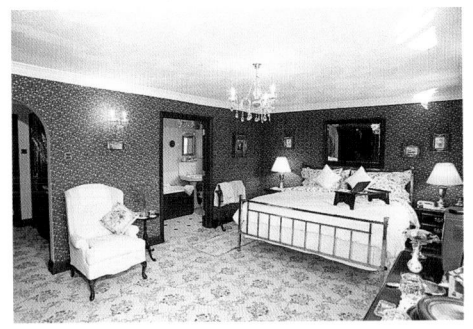

Anchorage House Guest Lodge. Tregrehan.

Nanscawen House. St. Blazey.

	rate £ from - to per person	children taken	evening meals	animals taken

Nanscawen Manor House

Nearest Road: A.390

A beautiful 15th-century manor house with an elegant, stately Georgian wing, set in 5 acres of grounds with stunning views across a romantic valley. Keith & Fiona offer you a relaxed welcome & friendly hospitality. You can enjoy the heated outdoor swimming pool, & the luxurious bedrooms are all en-suite, with spa baths. Breakfasts are a treat to the eye & the palette. Ideally situated for visiting the Heligan Gardens, Fowey, Lanhydrock & the Eden Project (2 miles.) Children over 12.
E-mail: keith@nanscawen.com

| £30.00 to £42.00 | Y | N | N |

🚭

see PHOTO over p. 69

VISA: M'CARD:

Mr & Mrs Martin   Nanscawen Manor House   Prideaux Road   Luxulyan Valley   St. Blazey   PL24 2SR
Tel: (01726) 814488   Open: ALL YEAR   Map Ref No. 42

Old Vicarage Hotel

Nearest Road: A.30

The Old Vicarage Hotel, set in its own wooded grounds on the edge of the moorlands to the west of St. Ives, is secluded & peaceful. Offering 8 bedrooms, 7 with an en-suite bath/shower, all with colour T.V. All rooms have tea/coffee-making facilities. Families well catered for. A delightful large garden for guests to relax in, & a safe recreation area for children. Convenient for beaches & places of interest.
E-mail: holidays@oldvicaragehotel.com

| £23.00 to £27.00 | Y | N | Y |

VISA: M'CARD:

Mr J. & Miss D. Sykes   Old Vicarage Hotel   Parc-an-Creet   St. Ives   TR26 2ES   Cornwall
Tel: (01736) 796124   Fax 01736 796343   Open: APR - OCT   Map Ref No. 44

Beckside Cottage

Nearest Road: A.30

'Beck' means stream in Celtic, so naturally there's one in the garden of Beckside Cottage, where butterflies visit from the adjacent nature reserve. Nearby, 400 acres of sand dunes nudge the Atlantic coast. Cornish gardens, charming St. Ives, the National Trust beach which inspired Virginia Woolf, helicopters for the Isles of Scilly ... all are accesible from this 200-year-old cottage with its 2 delightful en-suite bedrooms, guests' lounge & genuine friendly feel. Children over 12 welcome.
E-mail: enquiry@becksidecottage.demon.co.uk

| £23.50 to £30.00 | Y | N | N |

🚭

see PHOTO over p. 71

Suzanne Semmens   Beckside Cottage   Treeve Lane   Connor Downs   St. Ives   TR27 5BN   Cornwall
Tel: (01736) 756751   Open: ALL YEAR   Map Ref No. 46

Polkerr Guest House

Nearest Road: A.39

Polkerr has been converted from a farmhouse to a refurbished guest house of a very high standard. All rooms have an en-suite or private bathroom, T.V. & tea-making facilities. A recent addition has been a beautifully appointed sun lounge where guests can relax after viewing some of the most impressive coastal views of north Cornwall. Within easy reach of Tintagel village is the King Arthur Castle & other amenities such as golf, gardens, horse riding & much more. A charming home.

| £19.00 to £25.00 | Y | N | N |

Mrs J. A. Fry   Polkerr Guest House   Molesworth Street   Tintagel   PL34 0BY   Cornwall
Tel: (01840) 770382/770132   Open: ALL YEAR   Map Ref No. 48

Beckside Cottage.   Connor Down.

	rate £ from - to per person	children taken	evening meals	animals taken

Trebrea Lodge

Nearest Road: A.39

This lovely Grade II listed Georgian house, set in 4 1/2 acres of wooded hillside, has outstanding views of the north Cornish coast. The land was originally granted by the Black Prince to the Bray family, who lived here for 600 years. The beautiful bedrooms are individually decorated with antique furniture, & all have en-suite bathrooms. Award-winning, high-quality cooking, log fires & a relaxed atmosphere. Trebrea Lodge is a truly delightful home. Children over 12.

E-mail: trebrea-lodge@supanet.com

£43.00 to £48.00 — Y Y Y

VISA: M'CARD: AMEX:

Sean Devlin & John Charlick Trebrea Lodge Trenale Tintagel PL34 0HR Cornwall
Tel: (01840) 770410 Fax 01840 770092 Open: FEB - DEC Map Ref No. 50

The Old Rectory

Nearest Road: A.374

Regency-period, Grade II listed country house with subtropical garden & millpond located by tidal creek in this 'forgotten corner of Cornwall'. This home, full of interest, allows guests time to reflect; to enjoy its understated elegance with its beautifully appointed & romantic bedrooms, imaginative breakfasts & relaxing drawing room. Coastal path walks, beaches, moors, golf, sailing & National Trust properties close by. 4 miles from chain ferry. Children & animals by prior arrangement.

E-mail: clive@oldrectory-stjohn.co.uk

£32.50 to £47.50 — Y N Y

see PHOTO over p. 73

Clive & Button Poole The Old Rectory St. John-in-Cornwall Nr. Torpoint PL11 3AW Cornwall
Tel: (01752) 822275 Fax 01752 823322 Open: ALL YEAR Map Ref No. 52

Cliff House

Nearest Road: A.374

Cliff House is a Grade II listed, 17th-century building, converted from 2 cottages into 1 house around 150 years ago. Although modernised to include en-suite facilities, it still retains many of its original features. A drawing room, with wonderful views, log fires, T.V. etc. is available for guests' use. It has a large balcony through French windows overlooking Plymouth Sound, Cawsand Bay & the village. Ann is an enthusiastic wholefood cook, & meals (by arrangement) include home-made soups & bread.

E-mail: chkingsand@aol.com

£25.00 to £30.00 — Y Y N

Ann Heasman Cliff House Kingsand Torpoint PL10 1NJ Cornwall
Tel: (01752) 823110 Fax 01752 822595 Open: ALL YEAR Map Ref No. 54

Bissick Old Mill

Nearest Road: A.30, A.390

Bissick Old Mill, formerly a working corn mill, is conveniently situated in the village of Ladock (10 mins' drive from Truro), & provides exceptional standards of comfort, cuisine & hospitality. Its central position makes it an ideal base from which to visit all areas of Cornwall, whether it be on business or purely for pleasure. A chef proprietor (mostly English/French dishes). A residential licence. Children over 10 years welcome.

E-mail: sonia.v@bissickoldmill.ndo.co.uk

£27.00 to £34.50 — Y Y N

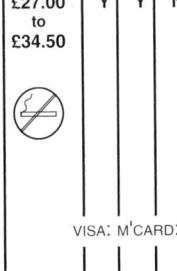

VISA: M'CARD:

Mikhail & Sonia Vichniakov Bissick Old Mill Ladock Nr. Truro TR2 4PG Cornwall
Tel: (01726) 882557 Fax 01726 884057 Open: ALL YEAR Map Ref No. 56

The Old Rectory. St. John-in-Cornwall.

Cornwall

Crugsillick Manor

Nearest Road: A.3078

A hidden treasure of the Roseland Peninsula, one of Cornwall's loveliest areas - meandering lanes, unspoilt fishing villages & sheltered coves. Find Crugsillick, a beautiful Grade II listed Queen Anne manor house, offering peace & comfort. Stroll down the smugglers' path below the house to glorious beaches & spectacular coastline, visit the historic houses & famous gardens - returning to dine, if you wish, on freshly caught seafood & home-grown vegetables. Children over 12.

E-mail: barstow@adtel.co.uk

| | £35.00 to £49.00 | Y | Y | Y |

VISA: M'CARD:

Oliver & Rosemary Barstow   Crugsillick Manor   Ruan High Lanes   Truro TR2 5LJ   Cornwall
Tel: (01872) 501214   Fax 01872 501228   Open: ALL YEAR   Map Ref No. 58

Apple Tree Cottage

Nearest Road: A.39

Apple Tree Cottage, set amid rolling countryside with delightful gardens & river, is furnished with country antiques & has a warm, welcoming atmosphere. The large lounge has a log fire, & traditional farmhouse breakfasts, cooked on the Aga, are taken in the sunlit dining room. The attractive bedrooms have pine double beds, tea/coffee facilities, washbasins & lovely views. Many National Trust gardens & the Trebah Gardens on the Helford River are only 15 mins' away. Children over 10.

E-mail: appletreecottage@talk21.com

| | £23.00 to £24.00 | Y | N | Y |

Ann Tremayne   Apple Tree Cottage   Laity Moor   Ponsanooth   Truro TR3 7HR   Cornwall
Tel: (01872) 865047   Open: ALL YEAR (Excl. Xmas)   Map Ref No. 60

Trevispian-Vean Farm Guest House

Nearest Road: A.39

A delightful farmhouse, dating back over 300 years, offering a very warm welcome & good accommodation in 6 pleasant & comfortably furnished en-suite guest rooms. Only 7 miles from the coast, & surrounded by beautiful countryside, it is a perfect base for everyone. Families will particularly enjoy it here, as children can look around the farm, & there are plenty of places to visit & things to do. There's even a donkey for the children. Trevispian-Vean Farm is a charming home.

| | £21.00 to £24.00 | Y | Y | N |

The Dymond Family   Trevispian-Vean Farm Guest House   St. Erme   Truro TR4 9BL   Cornwall
Tel: (01872) 279514   Fax 01872 263730   Open: ALL YEAR   Map Ref No. 62

When booking your accommodation please mention
The Best Bed & Breakfast

Cumbria

Cumbria

The Lake District National Park is deservedly famous for its magnificent scenery. Here, England's highest mountains & rugged fells surround shimmering lakes & green valleys. But there is more to Cumbria than the beauty of the Lake District. It also has a splendid coastline, easily accessible from the main lakeland centres, as well as a border region where the Pennines, the backbone of England, reach their highest point, towering over the Eden valley.

Formation of the dramatic Lakeland scenery began in the Caledonian period when earth movements raised & folded the already ancient rocks, submerging the whole mass underseas & covering it with limestone. During the ice age great glaciers ground out the lake beds & dales of todays landscape. There is tremendous variety, from the craggy outcrops of the Borrowdale Volcanics with Skiddaw at 3054 feet, to the gentle dales, the open moorlands & the lakes themselves. Each lake is distinctive, some with steep mountain sides sliding straight to the water's edge, others more open with sloping wooded hillsides. Ellerwater, the enchanting "lake of swans" is surrounded by reed & willows at the foot of Langdale. The charm of Ullswater inspired Wordsworth's famous poem "Daffodils". Whilst many lakes are deliberately left undisturbed for those seeking peace, there are others - notably Windermere - where a variety of water sports can be enjoyed. The changeable weather of the mountainous region can produce a sudden transformation in the character of a tranquil lake, raising choppy waves across the darkened surface to break along the shoreline. It is all part of the fascination of Lakeland.

Fell walking is the best way to appreciate the full beauty of the area. There are gentle walks along the dales, & the tops of the ridges are accessible to walkers with suitable footwear & an eye to the weather.

Ponytrekking is another popular way to explore the countryside & there are many centres catering even for inexperienced riders.

There are steamboats on lakes such as Coniston & Ullswater, where you can appreciate the scenery. On Windermere there are a variety of boats for hire, & facilities for water-skiing.

Traditional crafts & skills are on display widely. Craft centres at Keswick, Ambleside & Grasmere, & the annual exhibition of the Guild of Lakeland Craftsmen held in Windermere from mid-July to early September represent the widest variety of craft artistry.

Fairs & festivals flourish in Lakeland. The famous Appleby Horse Fair, held in June is the largest fair of its kind in the world & attracts a huge gypsy gathering. Traditional agriculture shows, sheep dog trials & local sporting events abound. The Grasmere Sports, held each August include gruelling fell races, Cumberland & Westmoreland wrestling, hound trails & pole-leaping.

The traditional custom of "Rush-bearing" when the earth floors of the churches were strewn with rushes still survives as a procession in Ambleside & Grasmere & many other villages in the summer months

The coast of Cumbria stretches from the estuaries of Grange-over-Sands & Burrow-in-Furness by way of the beautiful beaches between Bootle & Cardurnock, to the mouth of the Solway Firth. The coastal areas, especially the estuaries, are excellent for bird-watching. The sand dunes north of the Esk are famous for the colony of black-headed gulls which can be visited by arrangement, & the colony of seabirds at St. Bees Head is the largest in Britain.

Cumbria

Cumbria
Gazeteer

Area of outstanding natural beauty.
The Lake District National Park.

House & Castles

Carlisle Castle - Carlisle
12th century. Massive Norman keep -
half-moon battery - ramparts, portcullis &
gatehouse.
Brough Castle - Kirby Stephen
13th century - on site of Roman Station
between York & Carlisle.
Dacre Castle - Penrith
14th century - massive pele tower.
Sizergh Castle - Kendal
14th century - pele tower - 15th century
great hall. English & French furniture,
silver & china - Jacobean relics. 18th
century gardens.
Belle Island - Boweness-on-Windermere
18th century - interior by Adams Brothers,
portraits by Romney.
Swarthmoor Hall - Ulverston
Elizabethan house, mullioned windows,
oak staircase, panelled rooms. Home of
George Fox - birthplace of Quakerism -
belongs to Society of Friends.
Lorton Hall - Cockermouth
15th century pele tower, priest holes, oak
panelling, Jacobean furniture.
Muncaster Castle - Ravenglass
14th century with 15th & 19th century
additions - site of Roman tower.
Rusland Hall - Ulveston
Georgian mansion with period panelling,
sculpture, furniture, paintings.
Levens Hall - Kendal
Elizabethan - very fine panelling &
plasterwork - famous topiary garden.
Hill Top - Sawrey
17th century farmhouse home of Beatrix
Potter - contains her furniture, china &
some of original drawings for her
children's books.
Dove Cottage - Town End, Grasmere
William Wordsworth's cottage - still
contains his furnishing & his personal
effects as in his lifetime.
Brantwood
The Coniston home of John Ruskin, said
to be the most beautifully situated house
in the Lake District. Exhibition, gardens,
bookshops & tearooms.

Cathedrals & Churches

Carlisle Cathedral - Carlisle
1130. 15th century choir stalls with
painted backs - carved misericords, 16th
century screen, painted roof.
Cartmel Priory (St. Mary Virgin)
15th century stalls, 17th century screen,
large east window, curious central tower.
Lanercost Priory (St. Mary Magdalene)
12th century - Augustinian - north aisle
now forms Parish church.
Greystoke (St. Andrew)
14th/15th century. 19th century
misericords. Lovely glass in chancel.
Brougham (St. Wilfred)
15th century carved altarpiece.
Furness Abbey
12th century monastery beautiful setting.
Shap Abbey
12th century with 16th century tower.

Museums & Galleries

Abbot Hall - Kendal
18th century, Georgian house with period
furniture, porcelain, silver, pictures, etc.
Also contains modern galleries with
contemporary paintings, sculptures &
ceramics. Changing exhibitions on show.
Carlisle Museum & Art Gallery - Carlisle
Archaeological & natural history
collections. National centre of studies of
Roman Britain. Art gallery principally
exhibiting paintings & porcelain.
Hawkshead Courthouse - Kendal
Exhibition of domestic & working life
housed in mediaeval building.
Helena Thompson Museum - Workington
displays Victorian family life & objects of
the period.
Lakeland Motor Museum - Holker Hall -
Grange-over-Sands
Exhibits cars, bicycles, tricycles, motor
cycles, etc., & model cars.
Millom Folk Museum - St. George's
Road, Millom
Reconstructions of drift in iron ore mine,
miner's cottage kitchen, blacksmith's forge
& agricultural relics.
Ravenglass Railway Museum -
Ravenglass
History of railways
relics, models, etc.

Cumbria

Wordsworth Museum - Town End, Grasmere
Personal effects, first editions, manuscripts, & general exhibits from the time of William Wordsworth.
Border Regiment Museum - The Castle, Carlisle.
Collection of uniforms, weapons, trophies, documents, medals from 1702, to the present time.
Whitehaven Museum - Whitehaven
History & development of area show in geology, paleontology, archaeology, natural history, etc. Interesting maritime past.
Fitz Park Museum & Art Gallery - Keswick.

Collection of manuscripts - Wordsworth, Walpole, Coleridge, Southey.
The Beatrix Potter Gallery - Hawkshead

Things to see & do

Fell Walking - there is good walking throughout Cumbria, but check weather reports, clothing & footwear before tackling the heights.
Pony-trekking - opportunities for novice & experienced riders.
Watersports - Windermere is the ideal centre for sailing, waterskiing, windsurfing, scuba-diving.
Golf - championship course to the north at Silloth.

Grasmere.

CUMBRIA
Map reference

02 Rhone	27 R. Jones
04 Butcher	27 Coy
05 Hood	27 Russ
07 Hempstead	28 Briggs
08 Stobbart	29 Lowe
09 McKenzie	30 Skelton
10 Sisson	32 White
11 Cervetti	34 Whittam
13 Thompson	35 Sowerby
14 Denman	37 Clowes
15 Pettit	38 Harris
18 Clark	38 Holcroft
19 Kirby	38 Casey
20 Beale	38 Drinkall
22 Midwinter	38 Thomas
24 Miller	

Rowanfield Country House. Ambleside.

Cumbria

Riverside Lodge

Nearest Road: A.593

Riverside Lodge is a house of immense charm & character, superbly situated in a unique riverside setting, just a few mins' walk from the centre of Ambleside & Lake Windermere. The house has been refurbished throughout in keeping with its beamed ceilings & stone-flagged floors. Guests have access to the house without any restrictions in a very relaxed & informal atmosphere. There are 5 beautifully furnished en-suite bedrooms.

E-mail: alanrhone@riversidelodge.co.uk

£30.00 to £35.00	N	N	N

VISA: M'CARD

Alan Rhone   Riverside Lodge   Rothay Bridge   Ambleside LA22 0EH   Cumbria
Tel: (015394) 34208   Open: ALL YEAR   Map Ref No. 02

Rowanfield Country House

Nearest Road: A.591

Set in quiet countryside 3/4 of a mile outside Ambleside, Rowanfield enjoys breathtaking lake & mountain views. Superbly situated for exploring the whole Lake District area. A beautiful period house with Laura Ashley style decor. All bedrooms are en-suite with power showers, some have baths, queen & king-size beds. Certain weeks of the year chef/patron, Philip Butcher performs wizardry in the kitchen. His dinners are superb. Unlicensed but own wine welcome. Children over 8. Parking.

E-mail: mail@rowanfield.com

£32.50 to £50.00	Y	Y	N

see PHOTO over
p. 79

VISA: M'CARD

Philip & Jane Butcher Rowanfield Country House Kirkstone Road Ambleside LA22 9ET Cumbria
Tel: (015394) 33686   Fax 015394 31569   Open: MAR - DEC   Map Ref No. 04

The Fairfield

Nearest Road: A.591

Fairfield is a small, friendly, 200-year-old Lakeland hotel found in a peaceful garden setting, 200 metres from Bowness village, 400 metres from the shores of Lake Windermere & at the end of the Dales Way (an 81-mile walk from Ilkley to Bowness). The Beatrix Potter Exhibition is within easy walking distance. There are 9 well-appointed & tastefully furnished bedrooms with T.V., welcome tray & private showers/bathrooms. Breakfasts are a speciality. Leisure facilities available.

E-mail: Ray&barb@the-fairfield.co.uk

£26.00 to £33.00	Y	N	N

see PHOTO over
p. 81

VISA: M'CARD

Ray & Barbara Hood   The Fairfield   Brantfell Road   Bowness-on-Windermere LA23 3AE Cumbria
Tel: (015394) 46565   Fax 015394 46565   Open: FEB - NOV   Map Ref No. 05

Courtyard Cottages

Nearest Road: A.69

You won't be staying in someone else's home but in 1 of 2 comfortable double-bedded en-suite bedrooms in the lovely, but tiny, courtyard cottage of a Victorian mansion standing in 3 acres of grounds. Stone steps lead to the upper accommodation, providing total independence & privacy. Breakfast is served in your room. Enjoy the tranquillity or venture out to Hadrian's Wall, the lakes & Scottish borders, or just stay as a stop-over & be pampered as you travel north or south. (M.6 10 mins.)

E-mail: janet@warrenbank.demon.co.uk

£25.00 to £35.00	N	N	N

see PHOTO over
p. 82

Janet Hempstead Courtyard Cottages Warren Bank Station Road Brampton CA8 1EX Cumbria
Tel: (016977) 41818 Fax 016977 41398 Open: ALL YEAR (Excl. Xmas & New Year) Map Ref No. 07

The Fairfield. Bowness-on-Windermere.

Courtyard Cottages.   Brampton.

Cumbria

rate £ from - to per person	children taken	evening meals	animals taken		

£23.50 to £24.00 — Y N N

🚭 (no smoking)

VISA: M'CARD:

Hullerbank

Nearest Road: A.69

Attractive pink-washed Georgian style farmhouse dated 1635-1751 standing in its own grounds, near the picturesque village of Talkin, 2 1/2 miles from Brampton. Superb walking country & central for visiting Hadrian's Wall, the Lake District & the Borders. A friendly & relaxed atmosphere awaits. 3 bedrooms with private facilities. A T.V. lounge with open fire & comfortable dining room where excellent breakfasts are served. 2 inns with restaurant facilities in nearby Talkin. Children over 12.

E-mail: info@hullerbank.freeserve.co.uk

| Sheila Stobbart | Hullerbank | Talkin | Brampton CA8 1LB | Cumbria |
| Tel: (016977) 46668 | | Fax 016977 46668 | Open: FEB - DEC | Map Ref No. 08 |

£29.00 to £35.00 — N Y N

🚭 (no smoking)

see PHOTO over
p. 84

Wood House

Nearest Road: A.66

The view overlooking Wood House was chosen by J.M.W. Turner for his famous painting of Buttermere in 1798. A visitor describing the interior has written, "The furnishings & decor are serene & beautiful though completely unpretentious. The bedrooms reach similarly high standards & enjoy lovely views." Food is freshly prepared from carefully selected ingredients. Woodalls (Royal Warranty) are nearby & supply the house with their renowned meat products. Judy's home-baked bread is highly recommended.

| Michael & Judy McKenzie | Wood House | Buttermere CA13 9XA | Cumbria |
| Tel: (017687) 70208 | Fax 017687 70241 | Open: FEB - NOV | Map Ref No. 09 |

£25.00 to £35.00 — Y Y N

🚭 (no smoking)

VISA: M'CARD:

Bessiestown

Nearest Road: A.7

An award-winning country guest house, overlooking the Scottish borders, where a friendly, relaxing atmosphere is assured. 5 pretty, en-suite rooms with radio, T.V. & tea/coffee-making facilities. Delightfully decorated public rooms & conservatory. Also, ground-floor accommodation in extremely comfortable courtyard cottages. Delicious home-cooking. Residential drinks licence. Guests may use the indoor heated swimming pool (May-Sept). Stop-off to/from Scotland & N. Ireland.

E-mail: Bestbb2000@cs.com

| Jack & Margaret Sisson | Bessiestown | Catlowdy | Longtown | Carlisle CA6 5QP | Cumbria |
| Tel: (01228) 577219 | | Fax 01228 577019 | Open: ALL YEAR | | Map Ref No. 10 |

£25.00 to £28.00 — Y Y Y

🚭 (no smoking)

VISA: M'CARD:

Lightwood Country Guest House

Nearest Road: A.592

Lightwood is a 17th-century farmhouse built in approx. 1650. It possesses all modern amenities whilst retaining the charm of original oak beams & staircase. 2 acres of lovely gardens, with streams running through. Individually decorated rooms, with countryside views. The 6 bedrooms have en-suite bathrooms. A cosy lounge with T.V. & log fire. Only 2 miles from the southern end of Lake Windermere. Good English breakfast, with free-range eggs. Animals by arrangement.

E-mail: enquiries@lightwoodguesthouse.co.uk

| Mrs Evelyn Cervetti | Lightwood Country Guest House | Cartmell Fell LA11 6NP | Cumbria |
| Tel: (015395) 31454 | Fax 015395 31454 | Open: ALL YEAR (Excl. Xmas) | Map Ref No. 11 |

Wood House. Buttermere.

New House Farm. Lorton.

Cumbria

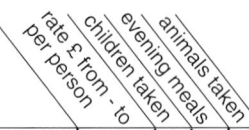

	rate £ from - to per person	children taken	evening meals	animals taken

New House Farm

Nearest Road: A.66
New House Farm is set superbly in the Lorton Vale, has its own 15 acres of fields, ponds, stream & woods & easy access to nearby fells & lakes. All bedrooms are tastefully furnished & en-suite, & there is a comfortable sitting room with open fire & a cosy dining room. Lots of personal attention is offered by the hosts. The cooking is fine traditional fare with a Cumbrian flavour. Children over 6. Animals by arrangement.
E-mail: hazel@newhouse-farm.co.uk

£40.00 to £44.00 — Y Y Y

see PHOTO over
p. 85

VISA: M'CARD:

Hazel Thompson   New House Farm   Lorton   Cockermouth CA13 9UU   Cumbria
Tel: (01900) 85404   Fax 01900 85404   Open: ALL YEAR   Map Ref No. 13

Winder Hall Country House

Nearest Road: A.66
This historic manor house has grounds to the River Cocker in possibly the most peaceful valley in the National Park, ideal for the Northern & Western Lakes. Mary & Derek provide 6 luxurious rooms with superb views, 2 with special 4-posters. Guests appreciate the attentive service, the wide breakfast choice & the 4-course dinner featuring local produce. Residential licence. Short breaks available. Children over 8 years welcome.
E-mail: stay@winderhall.com

£30.00 to £40.00 — Y Y N

see PHOTO over
p. 87

VISA: M'CARD:

Mary & Derek Denman   Winder Hall Country House   Lorton   Nr. Cockermouth CA13 9UP   Cumbria
Tel: 01900 85107   Fax 01900 85107   Open: ALL YEAR   Map Ref No. 14

Greenacres Country Guest House

Nearest Road: A.590
Greenacres is a charming 19th-century cottage ideally located for exploring the lakes & dales. Situated in the National Park, in the small village of Lindale at the foot of the beautiful Winster Valley, where you can walk in unspoilt countryside. All of the 4 bedrooms are luxury en-suite. There is a lovely lounge & conservatory, & cosy dining room where excellent home-cooking is served. A warm & friendly atmosphere awaits you. Greenacres is the perfect spot for a relaxing break.

£25.00 to £29.00 — Y Y N

VISA: M'CARD:

Mrs Barbara Pettit   Greenacres Country Guest House   Lindale   Grange-over-Sands   LA11 6LP Cumbria
Tel: (015395) 34578   Fax 015395 34578   Open: ALL YEAR   Map Ref No. 15

Banerigg Guest House

Nearest Road: A.591
Delightfully situated overlooking Grasmere Lake is this small, friendly guest house. The informal hospitality & relaxing atmosphere make this a super base for a holiday. All 6 comfortable rooms have modern amenities. A pleasant lounge with a cosy log fire. A delicious & plentiful breakfast is served. Ideally located for fell walking, sailing, canoeing & fishing. Angela & Martin ensure that guests have a memorable Lakeland holiday.
E-mail: banerigg2001@hotmail.com

£21.50 to £27.00 — Y N N

Angela & Martin Clark   Banerigg Guest House   Lake Road   Grasmere LA22 9PW   Cumbria
Tel: (015394) 35204   Open: ALL YEAR   Map Ref No. 18

Winder Hall. Low Lorton.

Blaven Homestay. Old Hutton.

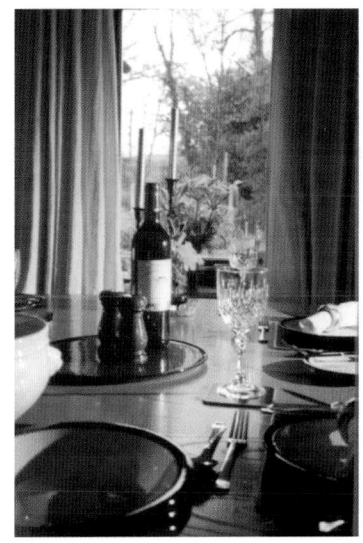

rate £ from - to per person | children taken | evening meals taken | animals taken

---

| £25.00 to £27.50 | Y | N | Y |

VISA: M'CARD: AMEX:

Buckle Yeat

Nearest Road: A.591

Buckle Yeat is famous for its connections with Beatrix Potter. Although over 200 years old, it has been sympathetically & tastefully refurbished. There is a large lounge with log fire & an attractive dining room which also serves morning coffee & afternoon teas. There are 6 comfortable en-suite bedrooms. Many good local pubs & restaurants offer excellent meals. Buckle Yeat is in an ideal position for touring Lakeland, with walks, fishing & birdwatching all nearby. Animals by arrangement.

E-mail: info@buckle-yeat.co.uk

Robert & Helen Kirby   Buckle Yeat   Nr. Sawrey   Hawkshead LA22 0LF   Cumbria
Tel: (015394) 36446   Fax 015394 36446   Open: ALL YEAR   Map Ref No. 19

| £27.50 to £32.50 | Y | Y | Y |

see PHOTO over p. 88

VISA: M'CARD:

Blaven Homestay

Nearest Road: A.65

Blaven Homestay, peacefully located beside a pretty Lakeland trout stream is close to the village of Old Hutton & convenient for the M.6 & touring the glorious Lake District & Yorkshire Dales. This lovely Cumbrian house, in a recently converted barn is seriously comfortable & beautifully appointed with delicious cooking by chef owners. Guests are welcomed as though friends & the hospitality offered is informal, warm & genial. Local walks. Drying facilities. Wood fires in cool weather. Animals by arrangement.

Janet Beale & Barry Green   Blaven Homestay   Middleshaw   Old Hutton   Kendal LA8 0LZ   Cumbria
Tel: (01539) 734894   Fax 01539 727447   Open: ALL YEAR   Map Ref No. 20

| £23.50 to £29.00 | Y | Y | Y |

VISA: M'CARD:

Low Jock Scar

Nearest Road: A.6

A charming country guest house. A relaxing & friendly atmosphere with genuine warmth. In an idyllic setting with 6 acres of garden & woodland, it is a peaceful base from which to explore the Lakes & Yorkshire Dales. There are 6 comfortable bedrooms (3 en-suite, 2 on the ground floor) & a lounge well-stocked with books & maps. Excellent freshly prepared dinners - vegetarians catered for. Residential licence. Single supplement. Children over 12. Animals by arrangement.

E-mail: ljs@avmail.co.uk

Philip & Alison Midwinter   Low Jock Scar   Selside   Kendal LA8 9LE   Cumbria
Tel: (01539) 823259   Fax 01539 823259   Open: Mid MAR - NOV   Map Ref No. 22

| £28.00 to £37.50 | Y | N | N |

see PHOTO over p. 90

VISA: M'CARD:

The Grange Country House

Nearest Road: A.66

Grange Country House is situated in its own grounds, with excellent parking, overlooking Keswick-on-Derwentwater & the surrounding mountains. Lovely bedrooms with those extra touches together with comfort, care, quality furnishings & relaxed hospitality make this award-winning home a perfect holiday base. The exceptional breakfast menu will give you an ideal start to your day in Lakeland. Somewhere special for lovers of the countryside. Children over 7.

E-mail: duncan.miller@btconnect.com

Duncan & Jane Miller   The Grange Country House   Manor Brow   Keswick CA12 4BA   Cumbria
Tel: 017687 72500   Fax 017687 72500   Open: FEB - NOV   Map Ref No. 24

The Grange Country House Hotel. Manor Brow.

Greystones. Keswick.

rate £ from - to per person
children taken
evening meals
animals taken

Greystones Hotel

Nearest Road: A.66

Greystones enjoys an enviable position overlooking the grounds of St. John's Church, & has excellent fell views. It is just a short walk to the market square & Lake Derwentwater. Accommodation is in 8 delightful & attractively furnished en-suite rooms, each with T.V., hot drinks tray & a folder of suggested walks & tours. Private parking available. Greystones is an excellent base for a relaxing break. Children over 10 years welcome.
E-mail: greystones@keslakes.freeserve.co.uk

£23.00 to £26.00 | Y | N | N

see PHOTO over
p. 91

VISA: M'CARD:

Robert & Janet Jones   Greystones Hotel   Ambleside Road   Keswick CA12 4DP   Cumbria
Tel: (017687) 73108   Open: JAN - NOV   Map Ref No. 27

Scales Farm Country Guest House

Nearest Road: A.66

Stunning open views & a warm friendly welcome await you at Scales Farm, a traditional 17th-century fells farmhouse sensitively modernised to provide accommodation of the highest standard. All bedrooms are en-suite, centrally heated, with tea/coffee-making facilities, colour T.V. & fridges. Separate entrance from private car park allows guests access to rooms & traditional lounge. Lakeland Inn/Restaurant next door. Scales Farm is a lovely base for touring or walking.
E-mail: scales@scalesfarm.com

£26.00 to £28.00 | Y | N | Y

VISA: M'CARD:

Chris & Caroline Briggs   Scales Farm Country Guest House   Scales   Threlkeld   Keswick CA12 4SY
Tel: (017687) 79660   Fax 017687 79660   Open: ALL YEAR (Excl. Xmas)   Map Ref No. 28

Dale Head Hall Lakeside Hotel

Nearest Road: A.591

Lose yourself in the ancient woodlands & mature gardens of an Elizabethan country manor, set serenely on the shores of Lake Thirlmere. Delicious dinners prepared by mother & daughter, using fresh produce from the Victorian kitchen garden, served with fine wines in the oak-beamed dining room. 12 individually decorated bedrooms, some with 4-posters, each with bath/shower rooms. Together with the lounge & bar, there are unspoilt views across lawns, lakes & fells.
E-mail: onthelakeside@dale-head-hall.co.uk

£30.00 to £50.00 | Y | Y | N

see PHOTO over
p. 93

VISA: M'CARD: AMEX:

Alan & Shirley Lowe   Dale Head Hall Lakeside Hotel   Lake Thirlmere   Keswick CA12 4TN   Cumbria
Tel: (017687) 72478   Fax 017687 71070   Open: FEB - DEC   Map Ref No. 29

The Ravensworth Hotel

Nearest Road: A.66

Ravensworth Hotel is ideally situated near the town centre & all its amenities. The lake & lower fells are just a short walk away. All rooms are tastefully furnished & all are en-suite with T.V. & beverage tray. Starting with a wholesome breakfast you may enjoy the lakes by day & then relax in the splendid lounge or enjoy a drink in the Herdwick Bar. (Evening meals by arrangement.) Personally run by proprietors Tony & Tina, the Ravensworth ranks amongst the top small hotels in Keswick. Children over 6.
E-mail: info@ravensworth-hotel.co.uk

£22.50 to £29.50 | Y | N | N

VISA: M'CARD: AMEX:

A. Russ   The Ravensworth Hotel   29 Station Street   Keswick CA12 5HH   Cumbria
Tel: (017687) 72476   Fax 017687 75287   Open: ALL YEAR   Map Ref No. 27

Dale Head Hall.   Lake Thirlmere.

Cumbria

Lairbeck Hotel

Nearest Road: A.66

On the outskirts of Keswick, yet less than 10 mins' walk from the centre, Lairbeck is a delightful, family-run hotel built in 1875 of Lakeland stone, within a secluded garden setting. All 14 bedrooms are en-suite, non-smoking, each with its own individual character. The atmosphere is welcoming & informal. Featured on a national T.V. programme, Lairbeck offers excellent home-cooking. Log fires, spacious car parking. Children over 5.
E-mail: bbb@lairbeckhotel-keswick.co.uk

£32.00 to £40.00 — Y Y N

VISA: M'CARD:

Roger & Irene Coy   Lairbeck Hotel   Vicarage Hill   Keswick CA12 5QB   Cumbria
Tel: (017687) 73373   Fax 017687 73144   Open: MAR - DEC   Map Ref No. 27

Hipping Hall

Nearest Road: A.65

Hipping Hall is a 17th-century country house set in 3 acres of walled gardens on the edge of the Yorkshire Dales National Park, 2 miles from pretty Kirkby Lonsdale & only 30 mins' from Windermere. The 5 bedrooms are all en-suite & for non-smokers & the 2 cottages are attractively furnished & fully equipped. Guests may dine in the Great Hall or in the separate dining room. All dishes are freshly prepared from home & local produce. Reduced rates for 3 nights or more. Single supplement.
E-mail: hippinghal@aol.com

£48.00 to £57.00 — Y Y Y

VISA: M'CARD: AMEX:

Richard & Jean Skelton   Hipping Hall   Cowan Bridge   Kirkby Lonsdale LA6 2JJ   Cumbria
Tel: (015242) 71187   Fax 015242 72452   Open: Easter - DEC   Map Ref No. 30

Beckfoot Country House

Nearest Road: A.6

A fine old residence featuring a half-panelled hall, staircase & attractive panelled dining room. Set in 3 acres of grounds in the delightful Lake District, it is a quiet, peaceful retreat for a holiday base, & is within easy reach of the many pleasure spots in the area. Offering 6 rooms, all with private shower/bathroom & tea/coffee-making facilities. A dining room, drawing & reading room. This is a delightful base for a touring holiday.
E-mail: info@beckfoot.co.uk

£31.00 to £40.00 — Y Y Y

VISA: M'CARD: AMEX:

Lesley & David White   Beckfoot Country House   Helton   Penrith CA10 2QB   Cumbria
Tel: (01931) 713241   Fax 01931 713391   Open: MAR - NOV   Map Ref No. 32

Netherdene Guest House

Nearest Road: A.5091

A traditional Lakeland house set in its own quiet grounds, with extensive mountain views. Offering a warm welcome & personal attention. There are 5 attractively furnished bedrooms, all en-suite, each with central heating, T.V. & tea/coffee facilities. A cosy lounge with log fire & T.V. is available throughout the day, & a dining room with excellent home cooking. Private parking. An ideal location from which to explore the Lake District. Traditional inns/restaurants close-by. Children over 8.
E-mail: info@netherdene.co.uk

£20.00 to £25.00 — Y N N

Mrs Marjorie Whittam   Netherdene Guest House   Troutbeck   Penrith CA11 0SJ   Cumbria
Tel: (01768) 483475   Fax 01768 483475   Open: ALL YEAR (Excl. Xmas)   Map Ref No. 34

rate £ from - to per person	children taken	evening meals	animals taken		

Brandelhow Guest House

£18.00 to £21.50	Y	N	Y

Nearest Road: A.6, A.66, M.6

Brandelhow is a very pleasant Victorian house situated in the lovely market town of Penrith. Accommodation is in 5 tastefully decorated & furnished, bright & comfortable rooms, including 3 en-suite rooms, & all with modern amenities, central heating, colour T.V. & tea/coffee-making facilities. Penrith is an ideal base for touring the Lake District & enjoying the usual outdoor sporting activities. A warm & friendly welcome is assured. Animals by arrangement.

Peter Sowerby & Eileen Reid Brandelhow Guest House 1 Portland Place Penrith CA11 7QN Cumbria
Tel: (01768) 864470   Open: ALL YEAR   Map Ref No. 35

The Cross Keys

£32.50 to £32.50	Y	Y	N

(no smoking)

VISA: M'CARD:

Nearest Road: A.683

For those looking for an inn full of character situated in one of the most magnificent of Dales settings the Cross Keys offers excellent food & accommodation. The restaurant provides wonderful home-produced food with a wide choice to suit all tastes, and although a Temperance Inn guests are invited to bring along the drink of their choice. The bedrooms, recently totally refurbished, offer full en-suite facilities.
E-mail: clowes@freeuk.com

Alan & Chris Clowes   The Cross Keys   Cautley   Sedbergh LA10 5NE   Cumbria
Tel: (015396) 20284   Fax 015396 21966   Open: ALL YEAR   Map Ref No. 37

The Archway

£20.00 to £30.00	Y	Y	N

(no smoking)

Nearest Road: A.591

An impeccable Victorian home, beautifully decorated throughout with antiques, pictures & fresh flowers, where good food & comfort of guests is the priority. 4 en-suite bedrooms, with colour T.V.. & beverage tray. A breakfast well worth getting up for, which includes homemade granola & yoghurt, a selection of dried & fresh fruits, followed by a choice of cooked breakfast - the decision is hard. Superb mountain views, easy access to the lakes & surrounding places of interest. Children over 10.
E-mail: archway@btinternet.com

Sarah & Jonathan Harris The Archway   13 College Road   Windermere LA23 1BU   Cumbria
Tel: (015394) 45613   Fax 015394 45328   Open: ALL YEAR   Map Ref No. 38

Lynwood Guest House

£15.00 to £25.00	Y	N	N

(no smoking)

Nearest Road: A.591

A Victorian Lakeland stone house built in 1865, offering 9 centrally heated bedrooms, each with en-suite bathrooms, all with modern amenities including colour T.V. & tea/coffee-making facilities. Guests may relax in the T.V. lounge available throughout the day. Centrally located, only 150 yards from village shops & restaurants, & only 5 mins from the bus & railway station. The host is a Lakeland tour guide, & is happy to assist in planning your stay. Children over 5 years.

Brian & Frances Holcroft Lynwood Guest House   Broad Street   Windermere LA23 2AB   Cumbria
Tel: (015394) 42550   Fax 015394 42550   Open: ALL YEAR   Map Ref No. 38

Beaumont Hotel. Windermere.

Column headers (rotated): rate £ from - to per person | children taken | evening meals | animals taken

---

The Beaumont

£28.00 to £48.00 — Y N N — 🚭 — *see PHOTO over p. 96* — VISA: M'CARD:

Nearest Road: A.591

This elegant Victorian house hotel combines all the grace & charm of its time with all the comforts of today. Ideal for Windermere & Bowness, & for touring the lakes. 9 attractive en-suite bedrooms with tea-making facilities, T.V. & hairdryers. Two 4-poster bedrooms are available for that special occasion, & a 'Romantic Presentation' of wine, chocolates & flowers may be ordered. The standards are high, breakfasts are hearty & the hospitality is warm & sincere. Parking. Children over 10.

E-mail: THEBEAUMONTHOTEL@BTINTERNET.COM

James & Barbara Casey   The Beaumont   Holly Road   Windermere LA23 2AF   Cumbria
Tel: (015394) 47075   Fax 015394 47075   Open: FEB - NOV   Map Ref No. 38

Fir Trees

£24.00 to £32.00 — Y N N — 🚭 — VISA: M'CARD: AMEX:

Nearest Road: A.591

Situated mid-way between Windermere village & the lake, & built in the traditional Lakeland style, Fir Trees offers delightful accommodation of exceptional quality & charm. The dining room has been extensively refurbished & similarly, the 8 en-suite bedrooms are now beautifully appointed to offer T.V., tea/coffee-making facilities & bath robes. A full English breakfast is served using the best of local produce with vegetarian catered for. Parking. Also, guests have free use of a local leisure club.

E-mail: firtreeshotel@msn.com

Mark & Jill Drinkall   Fir Trees   Lake Road   Windermere LA23 2EQ   Cumbria
Tel: (015394) 42272   Fax 015394 42512   Open: ALL YEAR   Map Ref No. 38

Rosemount

£20.00 to £35.00 — Y N N — 🚭 — *see PHOTO over p. 98* — VISA: M'CARD: AMEX:

Nearest Road: A.591

Rosemount is an attractive Victorian house halfway between Windermere & the lake. Accommodation is in 17 comfortable & attractively furnished bedrooms (including 3 singles & 3 spacious family rooms), each with an en-suite or private bathroom, colour T.V. & tea/coffee-making facilities. An excellent breakfast is served. Rosemount is the perfect base for a relaxing break or for touring this lovely region & affords first-class accommodation.

E-mail: enquiries@lakedistrictguesthouse.com

Steve Thomas   Rosemount   Lake Road   Windermere LA23 2EQ   Cumbria
Tel: (015394) 43739   Fax 015394 48978   Open: ALL YEAR   Map Ref No. 38

Visit our website at:
http://www.bestbandb.co.uk

Rosemount. Windermere.

Derbyshire & Staffordshire

Derbyshire
(East Midlands)

A county with everything but the sea, this was Lord Byron's opinion of Derbyshire, & the special beauty of the Peak District was recognised by its designation as Britain's first National Park.

Purple heather moors surround craggy limestone outcrops & green hills drop to sheltered meadows or to deep gorges & tumbling rivers.

Derbyshire's lovely dales have delightful names too - Dove Dale, Monk's Dale, Raven's Dale, Water-cum-Jolly-Dale, & they are perfect for walking. The more adventurous can take up the challenge of the Pennine Way, a 270 mile pathway from Edale to the Scottish border.

The grit rock faces offer good climbing, particularly at High Tor above the River Derwent, & underground there are extensive & spectacular caverns. There are show caves at the Heights of Abraham, which you reach by cable-car, & at Castleton, source of the rare Blue John mineral, & at Pole's Cavern in Buxton where there are remarkable stalactites & stalagmites.

Buxton's splendid Crescent reflects the town's spa heritage, & the Opera House is host to an International Festival each summer.

The waters at Matlock too were prized for their curative properties & a great Hydro was built there in the last century, to give treatment to the hundreds of people who came to "take the waters".

Bakewell is a lovely small town with a fascinating market, some fine buildings & the genuine Bakewell Pudding, (known elsewhere as Bakewell tart).

Well-dressing is a custom carried on throughout the summer in the villages & towns. It is a thanksgiving for the water, that predates the arrival of Christianity in Britain. Flower-petals, leaves, moss & bark are pressed in

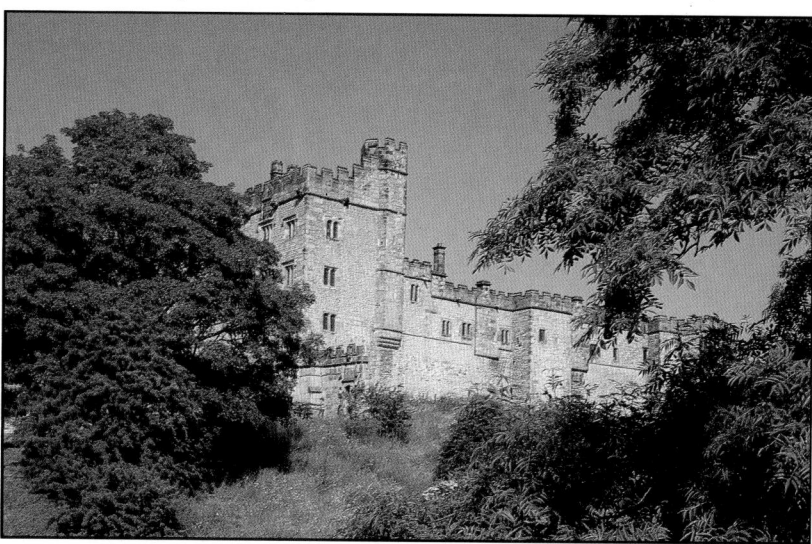

Haddon Hall; Derby.

Derbyshire & Staffordshire

intricate designs into frames of wet clay & erected over the wells, where they stay damp & fresh for days.

The mining of lead & the prosperity of the farms brought great wealth to the landowning families who were able to employ the finest of architects & craftsmen to design & build their great houses. Haddon Hall is a perfectly preserved 12th century manor house with with terraced gardens of roses & old-fashioned flowers. 17th century Chatsworth, the "Palace of the Peak", houses a splendid collection of paintings, drawings, furniture & books, & stands in gardens with elaborate fountains.

Staffordshire
(Heart of England)

Staffordshire is a contrast of town & county. Miles of moorland & dramatic landscapes lie to the north of the country, & to the south is the Vale of Trent & the greenery of Cannock Chase. But the name of Staffordshire invokes that of the Potteries, the area around Stoke-on-Trent where the world-renowned ceramics are made.

The factories that produce the Royal Doulton, Minton, Spode & Coalport china will arrange tours for visitors, & there is a purpose-built visitor centre at Barlaston displaying the famous Wedgwood tradition.

The Gladstone Pottery Museum is set in a huge Victorian potbank, & the award-winning City museum in Stoke-on-Trent has a remarkable ceramics collection.

There is lovely scenery to be found where the moorlands of Staffordshire meet the crags & valleys of the Peak District National Park. From the wild & windy valleys of The Roaches (from the French 'roche') you can look across the county to Cheshire & Wales. Drivers can take high moorland roads that are marked out as scenic routes.

The valleys of the Dove & Manifold are beautiful limestone dales & ideal for walking or for cycling. Sir Izzak Walton, author of 'The Compleat Angler', drew his inspiration, & his trout, from the waters here.

The valley of the River Churnet is both pretty & peaceful, being largely inaccessible to cars. The Caldon Canal, with its colourful narrowboats, follows the course of the river & there are canal-side pubs, picnic areas, boat rides & woodland trails to enjoy. The river runs through the grounds of mock-Gothic Alton Towers, now a leisure park.

The Vale of Trent is largely rural with small market towns, villages, river & canals.

Cannock Chase covers 20 square miles of heath & woodland & is the home of the largest herd of fallow deer in England. Shugborough Hall stands in the Chase. The ancestral home of Lord Lichfeld, it also houses the Stafforshire County Museum & a farm for rare breeds including the famous Tamworth Pig.

Burton-on-Trent is known as the home of the British brewery industry & there are two museums in the town devoted to the history of beer.

Lichfield is a small & picturesque city with a cathedral which dates from the 12th century & has three graceful spires known as the 'Ladies of the Vale'. Dr. Samuel Johnson was born in the city & his house is now a museum dedicated to his life & work.

One of the Vale's villages retains its mediaeval tradition by performing the Abbot's Bromley Horn Dance every September.

Derbyshire & Staffordshire

Derbyshire

Gazeteer

Areas of outstanding natural beauty.
Peak National Park. The Dales.

Houses & Castles

Chatsworth - Bakewell
17th century, built for 1st. Duke of Devonshire. Furniture, paintings & drawings, books, etc. Fine gardens & parklands.
Haddon Hall - Bakewell
Mediaeval manor house - complete. Terraced rose gardens.
Hardwick Hall - Nr. Chesterfield
16th century - said to be more glass than wall. Fine furniture, tapestries & furnishings. Herb garden.
Kedleston Hall - Derby
18th century - built on site of 12th century Manor house. Work of Robert Adam - has world famous marble hall. Old Master paintings. 11th century church nearby.
Melbourne Hall - Nr. Derby
12th century origins - restored by Sir John Coke. Fine collection of pictures & works of art. Magnificent gardens & famous wrought iron pagoda
Sudbury Hall - Sudbury
Has examples of work of the greatest craftsmen of the period-Grinling Gibbons,Pierce and Laguerre.
Winster Market House Nr. Matlock
17th century stone built market house.

Cathedrals & Churches

Chesterfield (St. Mary & All Saints)
13th & 14th centuries.
4 chapels, polygonal apse, mediaeval screens, Jacobean pulpit.
Derby (All Saints)
Perpendicular tower - classical style - 17th century plate, 18th century screen.
Melbourne (St. Michael & St. Mary)
Norman with two west towers & crossing tower.
Splendid plate, 18th century screen.
Normbury (St. Mary & St. Barloke)
14th century - perpendicular tower.
Wood carving & brasses.
Wirksworth (St. Mary)
13th century, restored & enlarged.

Staffordshire

Gazeteer

Houses & Castles

Ancient High House - Stafford
16th century - largest timber-framed town house in England.
Shugborough - Nr. Stafford
Ancestral home of the Earl of Lichfield. Mansion house, paintings, silver, ceramics, furniture. County Museum. Rare Breeds Farm.
Moseley Old Hall - Nr. Wolverhampton
Elizabethan house formerly half-timbered.
Stafford Castle
Large & well-preserved Norman castle in grounds with castle trail.
Tamworth Castle
Norman motte & bailey castle with later additions. Museum.

Cathedrals & Churches

Croxden Abbey
12th century foundation Cistercian abbey. Ruins of 13th century church.
Ingestre (St. Mary the Virgin)
A rare Wren church built in1676.
Lichfield Cathedral
Unique triple-spired 12th century cathedral.
Tamworth (St. Editha's)
Founded 963, rebuilt 14th century. Unusual double spiral staircase.
Tutbury (St. Mary's)
Norman church with impressive West front.

Museums & Galleries

City Museum & Art Gallery - Stoke-on-Trent
Modern award-winning museum. Ceramics, decorative arts, etc.
Dr. Johnson Birthplace Museum - Lichfield
Gladstone Pottery Museum - Longton
Izaak Walton Cottage & Museum - Shallowfield, Nr. Stafford
National Brewery Museum & the Bass Museum of Brewing-both in Stoke-on-Trent
Stafford Art Gallery & Craft Shop - Stafford
Major gallery for the visual arts & centre for quality craftsmanship.

DERBYSHIRE & STAFFORDSHIRE

Map reference

- 00 Chambers
- 01 Moore
- 02 Foster
- 04 Moffett
- 05 Lewis
- 06 Taylor
- 07 Rowlands
- 08 Wilkins
- 09 Sutcliffe
- 10 Egerton-Orme
- 10 Ball

rate £ from - to per person | children taken | evening meals | animals taken

---

£25.00 to £40.00	Y	Y	N

Stanshope Hall

Nearest Road: A.515

Stanshope Hall, with its informal feel but with every comfort, stands in splendid isolation among the dry stone walls of the southern Peak District. Walks from the door lead to verdant Dovedale or the undiscovered seclusion of the Manifold Valley. The attractive en-suite rooms have hand-painted walls & frescos in the bathrooms. Candle-lit dinners (by arrangement) are prepared using uncomplicated but imaginative recipes with local & garden produce. A charming home.

VISA: M'CARD:

E-mail: naomi@stanshope.demon.co.uk

Naomi Chambers & Nicholas Lourie   Stanshope Hall   Stanshope   Ashbourne DE6 2AD   Derbyshire
Tel: (01335) 310278   Fax 01335 310470   Open: ALL YEAR (Excl. Xmas)   Map Ref No. 00

£25.00 to £27.00	Y	N	N

(non-smoking symbol)

Rose Cottage

Nearest Road: A.515

A mid-Victorian house in 6 acres, Rose Cottage is a family home in quiet, unspoilt, beautiful & peaceful countryside. Bedrooms have panoramic views over Dove Valley towards Weaver Hills (George Eliot's 'Adam Bede' country). Ideal for visiting Dales, walking, country houses (Chatsworth, Haddon Hall etc.), potteries & Alton Towers (9 miles). Comfortable double rooms, private bathrooms, 1 en-suite, T.V., tea-making facilities in rooms. Children over 12.

E-mail: pjmoore@beeb.net

Mrs Cynthia Moore   Rose Cottage   Snelston   Ashbourne DE6 2DL   Derbyshire
Tel: (01335) 324230   Fax 01335 324651   Open: ALL YEAR   Map Ref No. 01

£23.00 to £24.00	Y	N	N

(non-smoking symbol)

Shirley Hall

Nearest Road: A.52

Shirley Hall is a lovely, peaceful old farmhouse, just to the south of Ashbourne, close to the village of Shirley. In the centre of rolling pastureland enjoy the tranquillity of this part-moated, timbered farmhouse, surrounded by a lawned garden. 2 attractive bedrooms with en-suite/private bathrooms, T.V. & tea/coffee facilities. The full English breakfast with homemade bread & preserves is renowned. The village pub is excellent for evening meals. Coarse-fishing available. Woodland walks.

E-mail: sylviafoster@shirleyhallfarm.com

Sylvia Foster & Ruth Crabtree   Shirley Hall   Shirley   Ashbourne DE6 3AS   Derbyshire
Tel: (01335) 360346/360820   Fax 01335 360346   Open: ALL YEAR   Map Ref No. 02

£25.00 to £50.00	Y	Y	Y

see PHOTO over p. 104

VISA: M'CARD: AMEX:

Biggin Hall Hotel

Nearest Road: A.515, A.52

A delightful 17th-century stone house, completely restored & keeping all the character of its origins, with massive oak beams. 19 comfortable rooms, all charmingly furnished, 1 with a 4-poster bed, all with en-suite facilities & modern amenities. Guests have the choice of 2 sitting rooms, 1 with a log fire, 1 with colour T.V. & library, & there is a lovely garden. The house is beautifully furnished, with many antiques. Non-smoking areas. Children over 12. Animals by arrangement.

E-mail: bigginhall@compuserve.com

James Moffett   Biggin Hall Hotel   Biggin-by-Hartington   Buxton SK17 0DH   Derbyshire
Tel: (01298) 84451   Fax 01298 84681   Open: ALL YEAR   Map Ref No. 04

Biggin Hall. Biggin by Hartington.

rate £ from - to per person | **children taken** | **evening meals** | **animals taken**

| £25.00 to £35.00 | Y | N | N |

🚭

Delf View House

Nearest Road: A.623

Beautiful & tranquil accommodation in an elegant listed Georgian country house in historic Eyam village in the magnificent Peak National Park. Guests are warmly welcomed in the drawing room, delightfully furnished with antiques & pictures. 3 bedrooms, 1 en-suite, include a Sheraton 4-poster & 18th-century French twin beds. Sumptuous breakfasts served in the oak-beamed dining room. Restaurants nearby. Ideal for visiting Chatsworth, Haddon & Eyam Hall. Children over 12.
E-mail: lewis@delfview.demon.co.uk

David & Meirlys Lewis   Delf View House   Church Street   Eyam S32 5QH   Derbyshire
Tel: (01433) 631533   Fax 01433 631972   Open: ALL YEAR   Map Ref No. 05

| £30.00 to £33.00 | Y | N | N |

🚭

see PHOTO over p. 106

VISA: M'CARD:

Underleigh House

Nearest Road: A.6187

Set in an idyllic & peaceful location amidst glorious scenery, this extended cottage & barn conversion (dating from 1873) is the perfect base for exploring the Peak District. Underleigh is in the heart of magnificent walking country & offers 6 en-suite rooms, furnished to a high standard with many thoughtful extras included. Delicious breakfasts in the flagstoned dining hall feature local & home-made specialities. The beamed lounge with log fire is the perfect place to relax. Children over 12.
E-mail: underleigh.house@btinternet.com

Philip & Vivienne Taylor Underleigh House Off Edale Road Hope Hope Valley S33 6RF Derbyshire
Tel: (01433) 621372   Fax 01433 621324 Open: ALL YEAR (Excl. Xmas & New Year) Map Ref No. 06

| £30.00 to £40.00 | Y | N | Y |

🚭

VISA: M'CARD:

Uppertown Farmhouse

Nearest Road: A.6

Uppertown Farmhouse, formerly a 17th-century coaching inn, is a Grade II listed farmhouse complete with its own walled courtyard & village stocks. Standing in the heart of the Peak National Park it commands a panoramic view over the Dales. It is furnished with antiques & retains many original features. Bedrooms are en-suite. Good restaurants & antique shops abound in the area together with historic houses & castles, including Chatsworth House. Children & animals by arrangement.
E-mail: jonliz@hudrow.enterprise-plc.com

Mr & Mrs J. Rowlands   Uppertown Farmhouse   Birchover   Matlock DE4 2BH   Derbyshire
Tel: (01629) 650112   Fax 01629 650112   Open: ALL YEAR   Map Ref No. 07

| £27.50 to £30.00 | Y | Y | N |

🚭

The Old Hall

Nearest Road: A.444

A particularly peaceful Grade II listed manor house set in 18 acres of gardens & woodland, overlooking a lake. The house, dating from 1644, incorporates part of a medieval monastery & despite all modern conveniences retains its unique character, original features & panelling. 3 bedrooms with en-suite/ private bathrooms, T.V., etc. Traditional English food is served by arrangement. Convenient for Lichfield, Shugborough, Calke Abbey, Kedleston, Castle Donington & the N.E.C.. Children over 12.
E-mail: clemencywilkins@hotmail.com

Mrs Clemency Wilkins   The Old Hall   Netherseal   Swadlincote DE12 8DF   Derbyshire
Tel: (01283) 760258 Fax 01283 762991 Open: ALL YEAR (Excl. Xmas & New Year) Map Ref No. 08

Underleigh House. Hope.

rate £ from - to per person	children taken	evening meals	animals taken		
£27.50 to £30.00 🚭	Y	Y	N	Nearest Road: A.520 This 17th-century stone cottage, once a resting place for ostlers, now provides beautifully appointed bedrooms, with full en-suite facilities, central heating, colour T.V., tea/coffee tray & telephone. The Pine Room & Rose Room have 4-poster beds, & 1 is suitable as a family suite. Quiet location convenient for the Peak District, potteries & Alton Towers. Excellent food & careful attention to detail is assured. **E-mail: enquiries@choircottage.co.uk**	**Choir Cottage & Choir House**
				William & Elaine Sutcliffe Choir Cottage & Choir House Ostlers Lane Cheddleton Leek ST13 7HS **Tel: (01538) 360561**　　　　　　**Open: ALL YEAR**　　　　　**Map Ref No. 09**	
£30.00 to £39.00 🚭 VISA: M'CARD:	Y	N	Y	Nearest Road: A.50 A handsome house, overlooking the picturesque Churnet Valley. This elegantly furnished home provides superb en-suite/private accommodation which is also, well-equipped. The aim at Bank House is to create a relaxed & friendly 'house party' ambience for guests, & the facilities are all that one might expect from a friend's country house that has all the comforts of a quality hotel. Wonderful centre for touring this region. Animals by arrangement. Single supplement. **E-mail: john.orme@dial.pipex.com**	**Bank House**
				Mrs M. Egerton-Orme Bank House Farley Lane Oakamoor Stoke-on-Trent ST10 3BD Staffordshire **Tel: (01538) 702810**　　　　**Fax 01538 702810**　　　　**Open: ALL YEAR**　　　**Map Ref No. 10**	
£22.50 to £26.00 VISA: M'CARD:	Y	N	N	Nearest Road: A.50 A beautiful Grade II listed farmhouse, set amid rolling hills & rivers. Accommodation is in 3 attractive bedrooms, all with 4-poster beds & an en-suite bathroom. (1 can be used as a twin.) Tastefully furnished with antiques & retaining traditional features including an oak-panelled breakfast room. Guests may relax in the extensive gardens with grass tennis court & Victorian summer house. Ideal for visiting Alton Towers, the Peak District or the potteries. **E-mail: cm_ball@yahoo.co.uk**	**Manor House Farm**
				Christopher Ball Manor House Farm Quixhill Lane Prestwood Denstone Uttoxeter ST14 5DD **Tel: (01889) 590415**　　　　　**Fax 01335 342198**　　　　**Open: ALL YEAR**　　　**Map Ref No. 10**	

When booking your accommodation please mention
The Best Bed & Breakfast

Devon

Devon
(West Country)

Here is a county of tremendous variety. Two glorious & contrasting coastlines with miles of sandy beaches, sheltered coves & rugged cliffs. There are friendly resorts & quiet villages of cob & thatch, two historic cities, & a host of country towns & tiny hamlets as well as the wild open spaces of two national parks.

From the grandeur of Hartland Point east to Foreland Point where Exmoor reaches the sea, the north Devon coast is incomparable. At Westward Ho!, Croyde & Woolacombe the rolling surf washes the golden beaches & out to sea stands beautiful Lundy Island, ideal for bird watching, climbing & walking. The tiny village of Clovelly with its cobbled street tumbles down the cliffside to the sea. Ilfracombe is a friendly resort town & the twin towns of Lynton & Lynmouth are joined by a cliff railway.

The south coast is a colourful mixture of soaring red sandstone cliffs dropping to sheltered sandy coves & the palm trees of the English Riviera. This is one of England's great holiday coasts with a string of popular resorts; Seaton, Sidmouth, Budleigh Salterton, Exmouth, Dawlish, Teignmouth & the trio of Torquay, Paignton & Brixham that make up Torbay. To the south, beyond Berry Head are Dartmouth, rich in navy tradition, & Salcombe, a premiere sailing centre in the deep inlet of the Kingsbridge estuary. Plymouth is a happy blend of holiday resort, tourist centre, historic & modern city, & the meeting-point for the wonderful old sailing vessels for the Tall Ships Race.

Inland the magnificent wilderness of Dartmoor National Park offers miles of sweeping moorland, granite tors, clear streams & wooded valleys, ancient stone circles & clapper bridges. The tors, as the Dartmoor peaks, are called are easily climbed & the views from the tops are superb. Widecombe-in-the-Moor, with its imposing church tower, & much photographed Buckland-in-the-Moor are only two of Dartmoor's lovely villages.

The Exmoor National Park straddles the Devon/Somerset border. It is a land of wild heather moorland above deep wooded valleys & sparkling streams, the home of red deer, soaring buzzards & of legendary Lorna Doone from R.D. Blackmore's novel. The south west peninsula coastal path follows the whole of the Exmoor coastline affording dramatic scenery & spectacular views, notably from Countisbury Hill.

The seafaring traditions of Devon are well-known. Sir Walter Raleigh set sail from Plymouth to Carolina in 1584; Sir Francis Drake began his circumnavigation of the world at Plymouth in the "Golden Hind" & fought the Spanish Armada off Plymouth Sound. The Pilgrim Fathers sailed from here & it was to here that Sir Francis Chichester returned having sailed around the world in 1967.

Exeter's maritime tradition is commemorated in an excellent museum located in converted riverside warehouses but the city's chief glory is the magnificent 13th century cathedral of St. Mary & St. Peter, built in an unusual decorated Gothic style, with its west front covered in statues.

The River Dart near Dittisham.

Devon

Devon
Gazeteer
Areas of outstanding natural beauty.
North, South, East Devon.

Houses & Castles
Arlington Court - Barnstaple
Regency house, collection of shell, pewter & model ships.
Bickleigh Castle - Nr. Tiverton
Thatched Jacobean wing. Great Hall & armoury. Early Norman chapel, gardens & moat.
Buckland Abbey - Nr. Plymouth
13th century Cistercian monastery - 16th century alterations. Home of Drake - contains his relics & folk gallery.
Bradley Manor - Newton Abbot
15th century Manor house with perpendicular chapel.
Cadhay - Ottery St. Mary
16th century Elizabethan Manor house.
Castle Drogo - Nr.Chagford
Designed by Lutyens - built of granite, standing over 900 feet above the gorge of the Teign river.
Chambercombe Manor - Illfracombe
14th-15th century Manor house.
Castle Hill - Nr. Barnstaple
18th century Palladian mansion - fine furniture of period, pictures, porcelain & tapestries.
Hayes Barton - Nr. Otterton
16th century plaster & thatch house. Birthplace of Walter Raleigh.
Oldway - Paignton
19th century house having rooms designed to be replicas of rooms at the Palace of Versailles.
Powederham Castle - Nr. Exeter
14th century mediaeval castle much damaged in Civil War. Altered in 18th & 19th centuries. Fine music room by Wyatt.
Saltram House - Plymouth
Some remnants of Tudor house built into George II house, with two rooms by Robert Adam. Excellent plasterwork & woodwork.
Shute Barton - Nr. Axminster
14th century battlemented Manor house with Tudor & Elizabethan additions.
Tiverton Castle - Nr. Tiverton
Fortress of Henry I. Chapel of St. Francis. Gallery of Joan of Arc.

Torre Abbey Mansion - Torquay
Abbey ruins, tithe barn. Mansion house with paintings & furniture.

Cathedrals & Churches
Atherington (St. Mary)
Perpendicular style - mediaeval effigies & glass, original rood loft. Fine screens, 15th century bench ends.
Ashton (St. John the Baptist)
15th century - mediaeval screens, glass & wall paintings. Elizabethan pulpit with canopy, 17th century altar railing.
Bere Ferrers (St. Andrew)
14th century rebuilding - 14th century glass, 15th century benches, Norman font.
Bridford (St. Thomas a Becket)
Perpendicular style - mediaeval glass & woodwork. Excellent rood screen c.1530.
Cullompton (St. Andrew)
15th century perpendicular - Jacobean west gallery - fan tracery in roof, exterior carvings.
Exeter Cathedral
13th century decorated - Norman towers. Interior tierceron ribbed vault (Gothic) carved corbels & bosses, moulded piers & arches. Original pulpitum c.1320. Choir stalls with earliest misericords in England c.1260.
Haccombe (St. Blaize)
13th century effigies, 14th century glass, 17th century brasses, 19th century screen, pulpit & reredos.
Kentisbeare (St. Mary)
Perpendicular style - checkered tower. 16th century rood screen.
Ottery St. Mary (St. Mary)
13th century, 14th century clock, fan vaulted roof, tomb with canopy, minstrel's gallery, gilded wooded eagle. 18th century pulpit.
Parracombe (St. Petrock)
Unrestored Georgian - 16th century benches, mostly perpendicular, early English chancel.
Sutcombe (St. Andrew)
15th century - some part Norman. 16th century bench ends, restored rood screen, mediaeval glass & floor tiles.
Swimbrige (St. James)
14th century tower & spire - mediaeval stone pulpit, 15th century rood screen, font cover of Renaissance period.

Devon

Tawstock (St. Peter)
14th century, Italian plasterwork ceiling, mediaeval glass, Renaissance memorial pew, Bath monument.

Buckfast Abbey
Living Benedictine monastery, built on mediaeval foundation. Famous for works of art in church, modern stained glass, tonic wine & bee-keeping.

Museums & Galleries

Bideford Museum - Bideford
Geology, maps, prints, shipwright's tools, North Devon pottery.

Burton Art Gallery - Bideford
Hubert Coop collection of paintings etc.

Butterwalk Museum - Dartmouth
17th century row of half timbered buildings, nautical museum. 140 model ships.

Newcomen Engine House - Nr. Butterwalk Museum
Original Newcomen atmospheric/pressure steam engine c.1725.

Royal Albert Memorial Museum Art Gallery - Exeter
Collections of English watercolours, paintings, glass & ceramics, local silver, natural history & anthropology.

Rougemont House Museum - Exeter
Collections of archaeology & local history. Costume & lace collection

Guildhall - Exeter
Mediaeval structure with Tudor frontage - City regalia & silver.

Exeter Maritime Museum - Exeter
Largest collection in the world of working boats, afloat, ashore & under cover.

The Steam & Countryside Museum - Exmouth
Very large working layout - hundreds of exhibits.
Including Victorian farmhouse - farmyard pets for children.

Shebbear - North Devon
Alcott Farm Museum with unique collections of agricultural implements & photographs, etc.

The Elizabethan House - Totnes
Period costumes & furnishings, tools, toys, domestic articles, etc.

The Elizabethan House - Plymouth
16th century house with period furnishings.

City Museum & Art Gallery - Plymouth
Collections of pictures & porcelain, English & Italian drawing. Reynolds' family portraits, early printed books, ship models.

Cookworthy Museum - Kingsbridge
Story of china clay. Local history, shipbuilding tools, rural life.

Honiton & Allhallows Public Museum - Honiton
Collection of Honiton lace, implements etc. Complete Devon Kitchen.

Lyn & Exmoor Museum - Lynton
Life & history of Exmoor.

Torquay & Natural History Society Museum - Torquay
Collection illustrating Kent's Cavern & other caves - natural history & folkculture.

Historic Monuments

Okehampton Castle - Okehampton
11th -14th century chapel, keep & hall.

Totnes Castle - Totnes
13th - 14th century ruins of Castle.

Blackbury Castle - Southleigh
Hill fort - well preserved.

Dartmouth Castle - Dartmouth
15th century castle - coastal defence.

Lydford Castle - Lydford
12th century stone keep built upon site of Saxon fortress town.

Hound Tor - Manaton
Ruins of mediaeval hamlet.

Other things to see & do

The Big Sheep - Abbotsham
Sheep-milking parlour, with gallery, dairy & production rooms. Exhibition & play area.

Dartington Crystal - Torrington
Watch skilled craftworkers make lead crystalware. Glass centre & exhibition.

Dartmoor Wildlife Park - Sparkwell Nr. Plymouth
Over 100 species, including tigers, lions, bears, deer, birds of prey & waterfowl.

The Devon Guild of Craftsmen - Riverside Mill, Bovey Tracey
Series of quality exhibitions throughout the year.

Paignton Zoological & Botanical Gardens - Paignton
Third largest zoo in England. Botanical gardens, tropical house, "The Ark" family activity centre.

DEVON

Map reference

02 Payne
03 Laugharne
04 Jones
06 Pearce
09 Daniel
11 Butt
12 Farrington
13 Campbell
15 Hyde
16 Wroe
17 Jennings
19 Lancaster
20 Howard
21 Kamp
22 Pile
23 Chilcott
24 Cuming
25 Merchant
26 Williams
27 Oakey
28 Wiemeyer
29 Bell
30 Gregson
31 Pakenham
32 Steele-M.
33 Turner
35 Scharenguivel
36 Sampson
37 Rowlatt
38 Wright
39 Tucker
40 Scull
44 Graeme
45 Allan
45 Brown
46 Pugsley
48 Ayres
49 Burke
50 Allnut
51 Clapp
52 Worth
53 Frost
54 Gozzard

	rate £ from - to per person	children taken	evening meals	animals taken

Huxtable Farm

Nearest Road: A.361

Enjoy a memorable candlelit dinner of farm/local produce with complimentary home-made wine in this wonderful medieval longhouse with original oak panelling, beams & bread ovens. This secluded sheep farm with abundant wildlife & panoramic views is ideally situated on the Tarka Trail for exploring Exmoor & N. Devon's coastline. Tennis court, sauna, fitness & games room. Log fires in winter. 5 en-suite bedrooms & 1 with a private bathroom, each with T.V. & tea/coffee facilities.

E-mail: info@huxtablefarm.co.uk

£25.00 to £26.00 — Y Y N

VISA: M'CARD:

Jackie & Antony Payne   Huxtable Farm   West Buckland   Barnstaple EX32 0SR   Devon
Tel: (01598) 760254   Fax 01598 760254   Open: FEB - NOV & New Year   Map Ref No. 02

The Mount

Nearest Road: A.39

The Mount is a small interesting Georgian house which is full of character & charm. It is set in a pretty garden with large handsome trees. A peaceful haven yet, only 5 minutes walk from the town centre with its quay, narrow streets & medieval bridge. The 7 bedrooms are tastefully furnished & have en-suite facilities & T.V.. (1 ground-floor room.) Conveniently situated for Exmoor, Dartmoor, Clovelly, Lundy & the beautiful North Devon coastline with its sandy beaches & rugged cliffs.

E-mail: andrew@themountbideford.fsnet.co.uk

£25.00 to £28.00 — Y N N

VISA: M'CARD: AMEX:

Andrew & Heather Laugharne   The Mount   Northdown Road   Bideford EX39 3LP   Devon
Tel: (01237) 473748   Fax 01271 373813   Open: ALL YEAR   Map Ref No. 03

The Pines at Eastleigh

Nearest Road: A.39, A.386

Rediscover peace & relaxation at this Grade II listed Georgian home. Set in 7 acres of gardens & paddocks with views of Bideford, Lundy & Hartland Point. Licensed. Books & maps to borrow & an audio system for guest use. Generous farmhouse-style cooking featuring fresh local produce by arrangement. Special diets catered for. There are 6 attractive bedrooms with en-suite facilities. Colour T.V., 'phones, tea/coffee, hairdryers. Ground-floor courtyard rooms & king-size beds.

E-mail: barry@thepinesateastleigh.co.uk

£35.00 to £45.00 — Y Y Y

VISA: M'CARD:

Jenny & Barry Jones   The Pines at Eastleigh   Eastleigh   Bideford EX39 4PA   Devon
Tel: (01271) 860561   Fax 01271 861248   Open: ALL YEAR   Map Ref No. 04

Brookfield House

Nearest Road: A.38, A.382

A spacious early Edwardian residence situated on the edge of Bovey Tracey & Dartmoor National Park. Set in 2 acres with panoramic views of the moor & bounded by the gently flowing waters of the Pottery Leat, Brookfield House offers the best of everything; secluded tranquillity yet within walking distance of the town, attractions & moorland. Easy access to South Devon's glorious countryside & coast. 3 bedrooms with en-suite/private bathrooms. Dinner by arrangement. Children over 12.

E-mail: brookfieldh@tinyworld.co.uk

£25.00 to £32.00 — Y Y N

VISA: M'CARD: AMEX:

Frances & Laurence Pearce   Brookfield House   Challabrook Lane   Bovey Tracey TQ13 9DF   Devon
Tel: (01626) 836181   Fax 01626 836182   Open: FEB - NOV   Map Ref No. 06

The New Inn. Coleford.

Devon

	rate £ from - to per person	children taken	evening meals	animals taken

Parford Well

Nearest Road: A.382

Parford Well is a comfortable & cosy house, surrounded by its own walled garden, set in the tiny hamlet of Sandy Park in the Dartmoor National Park. It is the ideal place to stay if you want to get away from it all, relax & be well looked after. Accommodation is in 3 charming & attractively furnished bedrooms, each with an en-suite/private bathroom. There are wonderful walks on the doorstep both in the wooded valley of the River Teign & on the open moor.

E-mail: parfordwell@guestbeds.com

£25.00 to £30.00	N	N	N

Tim Daniel   Parford Well   Sandy Park   Chagford TQ13 8JW   Devon
Tel: (01647) 433353   Open: FEB - DEC   Map Ref No. 09

The New Inn

Nearest Road: A.377

The New Inn is a 13th-century thatched inn nestling in a quiet valley by the side of a brook. Accommodation in this attractive property includes 6 en-suite bedrooms with 'phone, T.V. & tea/coffee-making facilities. There is also an extensive menu, using fresh local produce whenever possible. Local amenities include several golf courses, fishing, horse riding & sport & leisure facilities. Easy access to Dartmoor, Exmoor & the north & south Devon coasts.

E-mail: NEW-INN@reallyreal-group.com

£34.00 to £39.00	Y	Y	N

see PHOTO over
p. 113

VISA: M'CARD: AMEX:

Paul & Irene Butt   The New Inn   Coleford   Crediton EX17 5BZ   Devon
Tel: 01363 84242   Fax 01363 84646   Open: ALL YEAR   Map Ref No. 11

Lydgate House

Nearest Road: A.30

In the heart of Dartmoor National Park, this charming Victoian country house nestles in its own private valley beside the East Dart River, amidst 36 acres of natural wildlife. Refurbished this year, the house offers 7 delightful en-suite bedrooms, lounge with log fire, conservatory & terrace; all with superb views over the valley. Enjoy delicious home-cooked breakfasts & evening meals using fresh local produce. A beautiful & peaceful haven for exploring Dartmoor & beyond. Children over 12.

E-mail: lydgatehouse@email.com

£38.00 to £45.00	Y	Y	Y

see PHOTO over
p. 115

VISA: M'CARD:

Peter & Cindy Farrington   Lydgate House   Postbridge   Dartmoor PL20 6TJ   Devon
Tel: (01822) 880209   Fax 01822 880202   Open: ALL YEAR   Map Ref No. 12

Campbells

Nearest Road: A.3122

Set in a quiet location with a lovely garden, Campbells is only a few minutes walk from the centre of Dartmouth. Both bedrooms have stunning panoramic views; they are beautifully furnished with comfortable double beds, T.V. & are fully en-suite. The accent is on friendliness & comfort with many added extras. Flexible breakfasts, with West Country food & home-baking. Off-road parking. Children & evening meals by arrangement. A delightful home & the perfect spot for a relaxing break.

£30.00 to £30.00	Y	Y	Y

Mrs Angela Campbell   Campbells   5 Mount Boone   Dartmouth TQ6 9PB   Devon
Tel: (01803) 833438   Fax 01803 833438   Open: ALL YEAR   Map Ref No. 13

Lydgate House.   Postbridge.

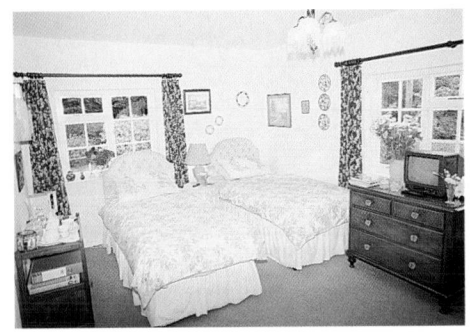

Leworthy Farmhouse B & B.   Lower Loworthy.

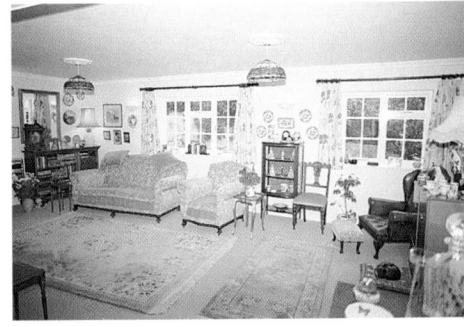

Devon

£25.00 to £26.00	Y	Y	Y

VISA : M'CARD : AMEX :

Raffles

Nearest Road: M.5

Imagine a large Victorian town house, furnished with antiques, tastefully decorated, a delightful walled garden yet minutes from the town centre, then come to Raffles the home of Richard & Sue. Their aim is to offer high-quality accommodation with friendly personal service. All bedrooms are en-suite with tea/coffee-making facilities, colour T.V. & central heating. Lock-up garages are also available on request. Raffles is an excellent base from which to explore Devon.

E-mail: raffleshtl@btinternet.com

Rick & Sue Hyde	Raffles	11 Blackall Road	Exeter EX4 4HD	Devon
Tel: (01392) 270200	Fax 01392 270200	Open: ALL YEAR	Map Ref No. 15	

£23.00 to £26.00	Y	N	Y

(no smoking)

see PHOTO over p. 118

Lower Marsh Farm

Nearest Road: A.30

Charming 17th-century Grade II listed farmhouse set in 5 acres of gardens & paddocks with orchard, pond, stream & stable courtyard on the edge of a pretty East Devon hamlet. Easy access to Exeter, coast, Exmoor & Dartmoor. This is a beautiful family home, tastefully furnished with antiques. There are 3 comfortable guest bedrooms, each with an en-suite bathroom, colour T.V. & hospitality tray. Guest sitting room with log fire. Excellent country pubs nearby.

E-mail: lowermarshfarm@talk21.com

Mrs Sian Wroe	Lower Marsh Farm	Marsh Green	Exeter EX5 2EX	Devon
Tel: (01404) 822432	Fax 01404 823330	Open: ALL YEAR	Map Ref No. 16	

£20.00 to £25.00	Y	Y	N

(no smoking)

see PHOTO over p. 116

Leworthy Farmhouse

Nearest Road: A.388, A.3072

A charming Georgian farmhouse nestling in an unspoilt backwater with lawns, meadow & a fishing lake. The inviting guest rooms are beautifully furnished with antiques or pine & have en-suite/private facilities, T.V., fresh flowers & hospitality tray. A peaceful lounge in which to relax with chiming clocks & sparkling Victoriana china. A traditional farmhouse breakfast with free-range eggs is served or kippers, prunes etc. Good walking, cycling & fishing nearby & only 20 mins' from the spectacular north Cornish coast.

Mrs Patricia Jennings	Leworthy Farmhouse	Lower Leworthy	Nr. Pyworthy	Holsworthy EX22 6SJ
Tel: (01409) 259469		Open: ALL YEAR		Map Ref No. 17

£23.00 to £25.00	Y	N	N

(no smoking)

Helliers Farm

Nearest Road: A.379

Set in the heart of the South Hams countryside, this recently modernised farmhouse offers accommdation in 5 pleasant & comfortably furnished bedrooms with tea/coffee-making facilities. Also. a spacious dining room where good farmhouse breakfasts are served, a comfortable lounge with T.V. & a games room. Situated close to the beaches, moors, golf courses, National Trust walks & the city of Plymouth.

E-mail: helliersfarm@ukonline.co.uk

Mrs C. M. Lancaster	Helliers Farm	Ashford	Aveton Gifford	Kingsbridge TQ7 4ND	Devon
Tel: (01548) 550689	Fax 01548 550689	Open: All Year (Excl. Xmas & New Year)			Map Ref No. 19

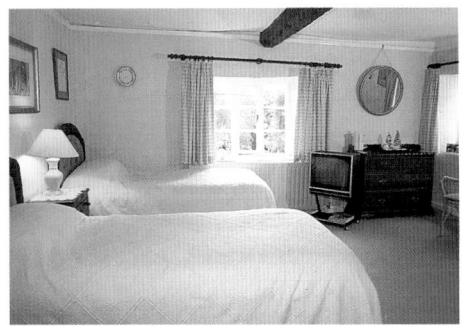

Lower Marsh Farm. Marsh Green.

Devon

rate £ from - to per person / children taken / evening meals taken / animals taken

£23.00 to £35.00	N	Y	N

(no smoking symbol)

VISA: M'CARD:

Highcliffe House Hotel

Nearest Road: A.39

Highcliffe House Hotel is a superb, warm & friendly Victorian house with everything provided for your comfort. Situated in an elevated position, only 5 minutes walk from Lynton & commanding stunning woodland & sea views over Lynmouth Bay to South Wales; which can be enjoyed from the bedrooms, lounge & candlelit conservatory restaurant. There are 6 spacious & attractively furnished, en-suite bedrooms. Excellent walks from the front door. An ideal base for touring picturesque Devon.
E-mail: HIGHCLIFFE.hotel@excite.co.uk

Brian & Pam Howard *Highcliffe House Hotel* *Sinai Hill* *Lynton EX35 6AR* *Devon*
Tel: (01598) 752235 *Fax 01598 752235* *Open: Mid JAN - Mid DEC* *Map Ref No. 20*

£20.00 to £25.00	Y	N	Y

(no smoking symbol)

VISA: M'CARD:

Southcliffe

Nearest Road: A.39

A Listed Victorian gentleman's residence with characteristic pitch-pine staircase & doors & Swiss-style balconies. Beautifully appointed, comfortable bedrooms, all with private bathrooms, colour T.V. & tea/coffee-making facilities. June & Adrian Kamp have been at Southcliffe since 1978, & have a reputation for good food, comfort, cleanliness & value for money. Children over 10 years welcome. Animals by arrangement.
E-mail: june.kamp@tesco.net

June & Adrian Kamp *Southcliffe* *Lee Road* *Lynton EX35 6BS* *Devon*
Tel: (01598) 753328 *Fax 01598 753328* *Open: MAR - OCT* *Map Ref No. 21*

£20.00 to £25.00	Y	N	N

(no smoking symbol)

VISA: M'CARD:

Coombe Farm

Nearest Road: A.39

Coombe is a 365-acre, hill-sheep farm, with an early-17th-century farmhouse set betwixt Lynmouth & the legendary Doone Valley. The coast path runs through the farm at Desolate. All within the spectacular Exmoor National Park. The bedrooms are 2 doubles, en-suite, 1 twin & 2 family. All have hot-drink facilities, shaver points, & bath & hand towels. Central heating. A lounge with woodburner fire & colour T.V..
E-mail: coombefarm@freeuk.com

Susan Pile *Coombe Farm* *Countisbury* *Lynton EX35 6NF* *Devon*
Tel: (01598) 741236 *Fax 01598 741236* *Open: MAR - NOV* *Map Ref No. 22*

£29.00 to £55.00	Y	Y	N

(no smoking symbol)

VISA: M'CARD:

Wigham Organic Farm & Guesthouse

Nearest Road: A.377

Wigham is a 16th-century Devon longhouse, with a 30-acre farm which provides fresh fruit, vegetables & dairy produce for imaginative meals. There are 5 double rooms, including a 4-poster suite. All with T.V., video & full en-suite bathroom. There are 2 sitting rooms in which guests may relax, & a snooker lounge & outdoor heated pool for pleasure. Licensed. Full S.A. organic symbol Sept. 1999. (Kitchen certified organic Jan. 2000.) Children & evening meals by arrangement.
E-mail: info@wigham.co.uk

Stephen & Dawn Chilcott *Wigham Organic Farm & Guesthouse* *Morchard Bishop EX17 6RJ* *Devon*
Tel: (01363) 877350 *Open: ALL YEAR* *Map Ref No. 23*

Devon

Great Wooston Farm

Nearest Road: B.3212, A.30

Great Wooston Farm, once part of the Manor House Estate owned by Lord Hambledon. Situated high above the Teign Valley in the Dartmoor National Park, with views across the moors. Plenty of walks, golf, fishing & riding nearby. The farmhouse is surrounded by a delightful garden of 1/2 an acre, also barbeque & picnic area. 3 bedrooms, 2 en-suite, 1 with 4-poster bed, 1 with private bathroom, with every facility. Excellent breakfasts are served. Also, a guests' lounge for your relaxation after a day exploring the magical Dartmoor. Children over 8.

	£20.00 to £23.00	Y	N	N

VISA: M'CARD:

Mrs Mary Cuming	Great Wooston Farm	Moretonhampstead TQ13 8QA	Devon
Tel/Fax: (01647) 440367	Mobile 07798 670590	Open: ALL YEAR	Map Ref No. 24

Great Sloncombe Farm

Nearest Road: A.382

Great Sloncombe Farm is a listed, granite-&-cob-built, 13th-century farmhouse. Set in a peaceful Dartmoor valley, the rambling house has a magical atmosphere, & is furnished with oak & pine, antique china & interesting old photographs. The 3 warm & pleasant bedrooms are all en-suite, with every facility included. Delicious breakfasts, with home-made bread & plentiful Devonshire suppers, are served. Children over 8 yrs.
E-mail: hmerchant@sloncombe.freeserve.co.uk

	£23.00 to £25.00	Y	Y	Y

Trudie Merchant	Great Sloncombe Farm	Moretonhampstead TQ13 8QF	Devon
Tel: (01647) 440595	Fax 01647 440595	Open: ALL YEAR	Map Ref No. 25

Gate House

Nearest Road: A.30, A.38

North Bovey is an historic village set within the Dartmoor National Park. Gate House, near the village green, is a listed 500-year-old thatched medieval longhouse with beamed ceilings, old granite fireplaces & bread oven. An acre of gardens with a swimming pool. The charming bedrooms combine country-style elegance with en-suite/private bathrooms. Lovely walks amidst breathtaking scenery & National Trust properties within easy reach. Animals by arrangement. Children over 15 years.
E-mail: gatehouseondartmoor@talk21.com

	£29.00 to £29.00	N	Y	Y

see PHOTO over p. 121

John & Sheila Williams	Gate House	North Bovey	Moretonhampstead TQ13 8RB	Devon
Tel: (01647) 440479		Fax 01647 440479	Open: ALL YEAR	Map Ref No. 26

Great Doccombe Farm

Nearest Road: A.30

Great Doccombe Farm is situated in the pretty hamlet of Doccombe, within the Dartmoor National Park, on the B.3212 from Exeter. An ideal base for walking in the Teign Valley & nearby moors, with golf, riding & fishing nearby. This lovely 16th-century granite farmhouse is surrounded by gardens & fields. The bedrooms (1 ground-floor) are all en-suite, & have shower, T.V. & tea/coffee facilities. A traditional English breakfast is served. Great Doccombe Farm is a perfect place to relax.

	£19.00 to £20.00	Y	N	N

Gill & David Oakey	Great Doccombe Farm	Doccombe	Moretonhampstead TQ13 8SS	Devon
Tel: (01647) 440694		Open: ALL YEAR		Map Ref No. 27

Gate House.   North Bovey.

	rate £ from - to per person	children taken	evening meals	animals taken

The Thatched Cottage Restaurant

Nearest Road: A.380

A beautiful 400-year-old, Grade II listed, thatched longhouse where old oak beams & a large open fireplace lend a cosy & welcoming atmosphere. There are 2 en-suite bedrooms, both with colour T.V. & tea/coffee-making facilities. A full English breakfast is served. Character bar & restaurant, where table d'hote & a la carte menus are available each evening. A pretty garden for guests' use. An ideal base for touring, with a warm welcome.
E-mail: thatched@globalnet.co.uk

| £25.00 to £30.00 | Y | Y | N |

VISA: M'CARD: AMEX:

Janice Wiemeyer   The Thatched Cottage Restaurant   9 Crossley Moor Road   Kingsteignton
Newton Abbot TQ12 3LE   Tel: (01626) 365650   Open: ALL YEAR   Map Ref No. 28

Sampsons Thatch Hotel & Restaurant

Nearest Road: A.38, A.380

Sampsons is a welcoming thatched farmhouse, set in its own grounds in a tiny, sleepy village & yet it is only 5 mins from the A.38 & A.380. There are a wealth of oak beams, log fires, history & tranquillity & a renowned (award-winning) restaurant serving delicious country produce. Pretty en-suite rooms are available in barn conversions. A disabled en-suite room & an apartment for groups & families. Also, charming en-suite rooms in the farmhouse. Lovely river & meadow walks. Dartmoor views.
E-mail: nigel@sampsonsfarm.com

| £25.00 to £50.00 | Y | Y | Y |

VISA: M'CARD:

Nigel Bell   Sampsons Thatch Hotel & Restaurant   Preston   Newton Abbot TQ12 3PP   Devon
Tel: (01626) 354913   Fax 01626 354913   Open: ALL YEAR   Map Ref No. 29

Penpark

Nearest Road: A.38

In the Dartmoor National Park, with secluded, beautiful woodland gardens, tennis court & glorious panoramic views, Penpark is an elegant country house, a gem of its period, designed by Clough Williams Ellis of Portmeirion fame. 3 charming rooms: a spacious double/twin with balcony; a single next door & a further double - all with wonderful views; private facilities; tea/coffee & T.V.. Dinner by arrangement. The Gregsons offer you a truly relaxed stay in beautiful surroundings.
E-mail: gregson.penpark@ukgateway.net

| £25.00 to £28.00 | Y | Y | N |

Mrs M. J. Gregson   Penpark   Bickington   Newton Abbot TQ12 6LH   Devon
Tel: (01626) 821314   Fax 01626 821101   Open: ALL YEAR   Map Ref No. 30

Tor Down House

Nearest Road: A.30

A 14th-century thatched Dartmoor longhouse (Grade II) set in lovely secluded gardens within Dartmoor National Park. Hidden away from a quiet lane, 100 paces from the moor, but only a mile from the A.30 giving fast access to all the West Country. Old oak beams, granite fireplaces, cats on Persian rugs, 4-poster beds, en-suite facilities, etc. Sumptuous breakfasts. National Trust properties, gardens, Bronze Age stone circles, character pubs & restaurants. Children over 14. Single supplement.
E-mail: info@tordownhouse.co.uk

| £35.00 to £35.00 | Y | N | N |

VISA: M'CARD:

Maureen & John Pakenham   Tor Down House   Belstone   Okehampton EX20 1QY   Devon
Tel: (01837) 840731 Fax 01837 840731   Open: ALL YEAR (Excl. Xmas & New Year) Map Ref No. 31

rate £ from - to per person	children taken	evening meals taken	animals taken		

Holme Down

£31.00 to £36.00 — Y | Y | N

VISA: M'CARD:

Nearest Road: A.30

Situated in 100 acres of private pasture & woodland, Holme Down, a Victorian manor house, offers a tranquil & secluded hide-a-way. The spacious rooms have stunning views over Dartmoor & are attractively furnished throughout. Private fishing available on a mile stretch of peaceful river plus a stocked lake with large Rainbow trout. Sarah can create imaginative dinners with special emphasis on organic & locally grown & reared produce. A property well-worth a visit! Children over 12.
E-mail: sarah@holmedown.co.uk

Sarah & Peter Steele-Mortimer   Holme Down   Exbourne   Okehampton EX20 3QY   Devon
Tel: (01837) 851485   Fax 01837 851585   Open: ALL YEAR   Map Ref No. 32

Westways

£22.00 to £££ — Y | N | N

VISA: M'CARD:

Nearest Road: A.38

Situated approx. 3 1/2 miles from Plymouth city centre, this attractive detached house offers pleasant accommodation in 3 well-furnished (non-smoking) rooms, with tea/coffee facilities. Excellent breakfasts are served in the elegant dining room. Guests may choose to relax & plan their excursions in the comfortable sitting room. Also, a small T.V. room. A homely & friendly base both for visitors wishing to make the most of the many attractions in the area, & for touring Devon. Children over 12.
E-mail: westways@cwcom.net

John & Daphne Turner   Westways   706 Budshead Road   Crownhill   Plymouth PL6 5DY   Devon
Tel: (01752) 776617   Fax 01752 776617   Open: ALL YEAR   Map Ref No. 33

Coombe House

£25.00 to £40.00 — Y | Y | N

see PHOTO over p. 124

Nearest Road: A.38

Coombe House is a gracious Georgian residence set in a tranquil & beautiful valley in a designated Area of Outstanding Natural Beauty. 4 en-suite bedrooms & a single with private bathroom. T.V., radio, hairdryer & tea/coffee tray. Elegant dining room & guest lounge. Enjoy delicious home-cooked food prepared using fresh local produce (by arrangement.) The coast, Dartmoor, Totnes, Salcombe, Plymouth & Exeter are all within easy reach. 4 barn conversions for self-catering.
E-mail: coombehouse@hotmail.com

Faith & John Scharenguivel   Coombe House   North Huish   South Brent TQ10 9NJ   Devon
Tel: (01548) 821277   Fax 01548 821277   Open: ALL YEAR   Map Ref No. 35

Kerscott Farm

£22.00 to £22.00 — N | Y | N

Nearest Road: A.361

Kerscott Farm offers quality accommodation at a sensible price. This peaceful Exmoor working farm & olde worlde farmhouse is mentioned in the Domesday Book (1086). It has an absolutely fascinating interior with many antiques, pictures & china - a rare find. There are beautiful, extensive views. There are 3 pretty & tastefully furnished en-suite bedrooms with colour T.V. & tea/coffee-making facilities. Wholesome country cooking, pure spring water. An elegant home.
E-mail: kerscott.farm@virgin.net

Mrs Theresa Sampson   Kerscott Farm   Ash Mill   South Molton EX36 4QG   Devon
Tel: (01769) 550262 Fax 01769 550910 Open: ALL YEAR (Excl. Xmas & New Year) Map Ref No. 36

Coombe House.   North Huish.

rate £ from - to per person	children taken	evening meals taken	animals taken

---

Tor Cottage

| £57.50 to £57.50 | N | N | N |

see PHOTO over p. 126

VISA: M'CARD:

Nearest Road: A.30

Award-winning Tor Cottage has a warm & relaxed atmosphere & nestles in its own private valley. 18 acres of wildlife hillsides. Lovely gardens & a streamside setting. Beautifully appointed en-suite bed/sitting rooms with log fires & a private terrace. Sumptuous breakfasts. Dinner booking service at local restaurants. Heated outdoor pool (summer). Tranquil base adjacent Dartmoor Valley. Central for touring Devon & Cornwall. Easy 45 min drive to New Eden Project. Special autumn/spring breaks.
E-mail: info@torcottage.co.uk

Mrs Maureen Rowlatt   Tor Cottage   Chillaton   Tavistock PL16 0JE   Devon
Tel: (01822) 860248 Fax 01822 860126 Open: ALL YEAR (Excl. Xmas & New Year) Map Ref No. 37

Quither Mill

| £35.00 to £35.00 | N | Y | N |

VISA: M'CARD:

Nearest Road: A.30

Quither Mill is situated in a sleepy hamlet & is Grade II listed, being of architectural & historical interest. Dating from the 18th century, the mill wheel & workings are intact. Guests enjoy the comfort of beamed en-suite bedrooms & full English breakfast. The hosts are proud of their reputation for fine cooking drawn from 20 years in the hotel world, which makes dinner a memorable experience. Animals by arrangement.
E-mail: quither.mill@virgin.net

David & Jill Wright   Quither Mill   Quither   Chillaton   Tavistock PL19 0PZ   Devon
Tel: Tel: (01822) 860160   Fax 01822 860160   Open: ALL YEAR   Map Ref No. 38

Beera Farm

| £20.00 to £25.00 | Y | Y | N |

VISA: M'CARD:

Nearest Road: A.30

Beera is a large, traditional stone built Victorian farmhouse set in an Area of Outstanding Natural Beauty. The farm is a 160-acre beef & sheep farm on the bank of the river Tamar. Guests may walk on the farm & take in the beautiful scenery. 3 attractive en-suite bedrooms (1 with 4-poster), each with T.V. & tea/coffee facilities. Evening meals by arrangement. Ideal for touring the West Country & within easy reach of the coast, Dartmoor National Park, National Trust properties & the Eden Project.
E-mail: robert.tucker@farming.co.uk

Hilary Tucker   Beera Farm   Milton Abbot   Tavistock PL19 8PL   Devon
Tel: (01822) 870216   Fax 01822 870216   Open: ALL YEAR   Map Ref No. 39

Ringmore House

| £25.00 to £40.00 | Y | Y | N |

Nearest Road: A.379

Dating from the 17th-century, this beautiful home is a few metres from the River Teign & within walking distance of Shaldon's beaches. Recently restored & refurbished, Ringmore House offers every comfort, from a tray of tea brought to your room when you wake, to homemade bread & jams, & a huge breakfast menu served in the garden conservatory. Partly arranged with 1 bedroom in its own cottage & garden. Also, 3 other beautiful bedrooms. Children over 12. Dinner by arrangemnt.
E-mail: hscull@aol.com

Robert & Helen Scull   Ringmore House   Brook Lane Shaldon   Teignmouth TQ14 0AJ   Devon
Tel: (01626) 873323   Fax 01626 873353   Open: ALL YEAR (Excl. Xmas)   Map Ref No. 40

Tor Cottage. Chillaton.

Thomas Luny House. Teignmouth.

Devon

Fonthill

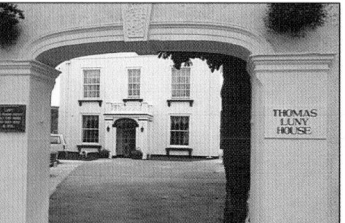

Nearest Road: A.379

Visitors are warmly welcomed to this lovely Georgian house, for a peaceful holiday in charming & very comfortable accommodation. Fonthill stands in 20 acres of beautiful gardens, woodland & fields on the edge of Shaldon, a pretty village on the South Devon coast. 2 delightful rooms, with en-suite/private bathrooms & every comfort. The lovely garden is for guests' enjoyment, & there is also a tennis court in the grounds. Several sandy beaches nearby & an 18-hole golf course.

E-mail: swanphoto2@aol.com

| | £28.00 to £30.00 | Y | N | N |

Anthony & Jenny Graeme   Fonthill   Torquay Road   Shaldon   Teignmouth TQ14 0AX   Devon
Tel: (01626) 872344   Fax 01626 872344   Open: MAR - NOV   Map Ref No. 44

Thomas Luny House

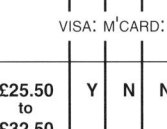

Nearest Road: A.381

A Grade II listed Georgian house, built by the marine artist Thomas Luny. Tucked away in the old quarter of Teignmouth, it forms a quiet oasis surrounded by its own high walls. Each superb, en-suite bedroom is individual in style, some with views over the River Teign. Alison & John & their family love to share their home, & they spare no effort in preparing the delicious breakfasts & attending to their guests' general well-being. Licensed. Children over 12 yrs. Single supplement.

E-mail: alisonandjohn@thomas-luny-house.co.uk

| | £27.50 to £37.50 | Y | N | N |

see PHOTO over
p. 127

VISA: M'CARD:

Alison & John Allan   Thomas Luny House   Teign Street   Teignmouth TQ14 8EG   Devon
Tel: (01626) 772976   Open: ALL YEAR   Map Ref No. 45

Wytchwood

Nearest Road: A.381

Award-winning Wytchwood has an outstanding reputation for lavish hospitality & traditional home-cooking. To stay here is to be truly pampered! Panoramic views, beautiful garden, stylish interior design & the prettiest en-suite bedrooms, all combine to fulfil every expectation. Home-made bread & rolls, jams, preserves, orchard honey & garden produce. Delicious Devonshire cream teas, sponges & cakes. Many culinary awards. A warm welcome is always assured at Wytchwood.

E-mail: wytchwood@yahoo.com

| | £25.50 to £32.50 | Y | N | N |

see PHOTO over
p. 129

VISA: M'CARD:

Jennifer Richardson Brown   Wytchwood   West Buckeridge   Teignmouth TQ14 8NF   Devon
Tel: (01626) 773482   Mobile 07971 783454   Open: ALL YEAR   Map Ref No. 45

Hornhill

Nearest Road: A.361

Hornhill, originally a coaching inn, has panoramic views over the beautiful Exe valley. Set in a large garden & surrounded by farmland. The charming hosts offer guests comfort, delicious home-cooking & a happy atmosphere. The house, furnished with antiques, has 3 attractive bedrooms (1 with a Victorian 4-poster), each with private bathroom, T.V. etc. 1 is suitable for the partially disabled. The drawing room has plenty of books & a log fire. Children over 10. Dinner/animals by arrangement.

E-mail: hornhill@tinyworld.co.uk

| | £22.00 to £26.00 | Y | Y | Y |

VISA: M'CARD:

Barbara Pugsley   Hornhill   Exeter Hill   Tiverton EX16 4PL   Devon
Tel: (01884) 253352   Fax 01884 253352   Open: ALL YEAR   Map Ref No. 46

Wytchwood. West Buckeridge.

Manor Mill House. Bampton.

Column headers (rotated):
- rate £ from - to per person
- children taken
- evening meals
- animals taken

Manor Mill House

£22.00 to £25.00	Y	N	N

see PHOTO over p. 130

VISA: M'CARD:

Nearest Road: A.396, B.3227

Manor Mill House is a relaxing & welcoming 17th-century home with inglenooks, beams, log fires & delicious breakfasts using local produce. There are 3 double/twin rooms, 2 with 4-poster beds (1 ground floor) & all are en-suite & have T.V. & tea/coffee facilities. A pleasant garden with views over water meadows, yet close to the amenities of historic Bampton. An ideal base for exploring moors, coasts & N. T. properties & walks. Good places to eat locally. Parking. Children over 12.
E-mail: stay@manormill.demon.co.uk

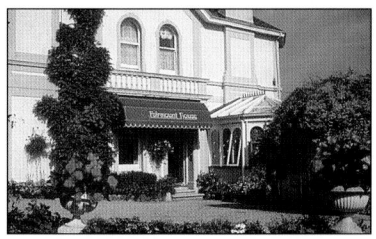

Mrs K. Ayres   Manor Mill House   Bampton   Tiverton EX16 9LP   Devon
Tel: (01398) 332211   Fax 01398 332009   Open: ALL YEAR   Map Ref No. 48

Fairmount House Hotel

£27.00 to £32.00	Y	Y	Y

VISA: M'CARD:

Nearest Road: A.380

Experience somewhere special & feel completely at home in the tranquillity, warmth & informal atmosphere of this small hotel. Offering 8 comfortable en-suite bedrooms, unhurried breakfasts & undisturbed evenings. (2 lower-ground floor rooms have private doors opening onto the garden.) Renowned for its mild climate, Torquay boasts a profusion of sub-tropical plants & miles of beaches & sheltered coves. Nestling away from the busy seafront, Fairmount offers quality, comfort & genuine friendly service.

Shaun & Carole Burke   Fairmount House Hotel   Herbert Road   Chelston   Torquay TQ2 6RW   Devon
Tel: (01803) 605446   Fax 01803 605446   Open: ALL YEAR   Map Ref No. 49

The Old Forge at Totnes

£27.00 to £37.00	Y	N	N

see PHOTO over p. 132

VISA: M'CARD:

Nearest Road: A.381, A.384

A delightfully converted, working, 600-year-old smithy. This family-run hotel, located in the centre of Totnes, offers visitors a choice of 10 comfortable, well-equipped bedrooms, 9 en-suite, all with radio, T.V., 'phone & tea/coffee-making facilities. A cottage suite also available for families. There is a pleasant walled garden for guests' use, where delicious cream teas are served. The Old Forge is ideally located for touring the Torbay coast & Dartmoor. Golf breaks a speciality. Licensed. Leisure lounge with whirlpool spa.

The Old Forge at Totnes   Seymour Place   Totnes TQ9 5AY   Devon
Tel: (01803) 862174   Fax 01803 865385   Open: ALL YEAR   Map Ref No. 50

Manor Farm

£24.00 to £26.00	Y	N	Y

Nearest Road: A.381

Manor Farm is an elegant Georgian farmhouse built in 1774 with a walled garden & cider orchard, situated in the picturesque village of Broadhempston, with 2 excellent pubs. There are 2 rooms, 1 double with en-suite bath/shower & 1 twin with private bath/shower. There are colour T.V.'s & tea/coffee facilities in each room. Situated on the edge of the South Hams & Dartmoor, excellent for walking, sailing, fishing & golf. Children over 12. Animals by arrangement.
E-mail: clappfamily@members.shines.net

Sarah Clapp   Manor Farm   Broadhempston   Totnes TQ9 6BD   Devon
Tel: (01803) 813260   Fax 01803 813260   Open: ALL YEAR   Map Ref No. 51

The Old Forge at Totnes.   Totnes.

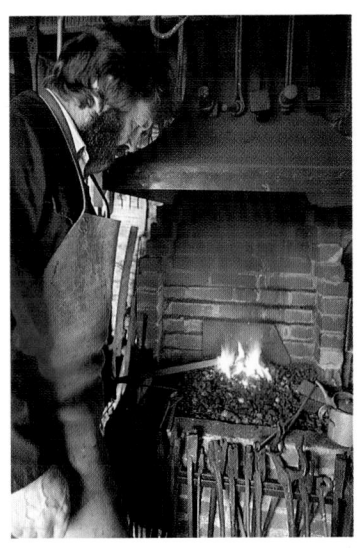

rate £ from - to per person	children taken	evening meals taken	animals taken		

£20.00 to £23.00 — Y N N — 🚭 *see PHOTO over p. 134*

Orchard House

Nearest Road: A.381

Tucked away in a rural hamlet of the South Hams, between Totnes & Kingsbridge, Orchard House nestles within an old cider orchard. It offers superb accommodation: all bedrooms are en-suite with colour T.V., radio, tea/coffee-making facilities & beautiful furnishings. Breakfasts are ample, with cereals, juice, yoghurts & grapefruit, followed by a cooked platter with toast & croissants. Also, guests' own sitting & dining room, with a log fire. Large garden & private parking. Children over 3.

Mrs Helen Worth	Orchard House	Horner	Halwell	Totnes TQ9 7LB	Devon
Tel: (01548) 821448		Open: MAR - NOV			Map Ref No. 52

£26.00 to £32.00 — Y N N — 🚭

Lower Grimpstonleigh

Nearest Road: A.381

Idyllic rural retreat situated at the end of a quiet Devon lane, 4 miles from Kingsbridge. The ideal location for both Dartmoor & the South Devon coastline. Old stone house with spacious & very comfortably furnished bedrooms with vaulted ceilings, country antiques & en-suite bath/shower. Colour T.V., tea/coffee-making facilities, sofas, clock/radios & hairdryers provided. Breakfasts include the Frosts' own free-range eggs, home-made preserves & other local produce.
E-mail: grimpstonleigh@ukgateway.net

Petrina & Kevin Frost	Lower Grimpstonleigh	East Allington	Totnes TQ9 7QH	Devon
Tel: (01548) 521258	Fax 01548 521258	Open: ALL YEAR (Excl. Xmas)		Map Ref No. 53

£22.50 to £25.00 — Y N N — 🚭

Stokehill Farmhouse

Nearest Road: A.386

Stokehill Farmhouse is a beautiful Victorian country house, set in lovely grounds in a peaceful hamlet on the edge of the Dartmoor National Park. The house is richly furnished with large, attractive, well-equipped rooms & commands stunning views across rolling fields. An elegant drawing room, conservatory & the lovely gardens are available for use by the residents. Secure parking. The house is ideally situated for enjoying the many & varied delights of Devon & Cornwall. Children over 10.
E-mail: gozzard@compuserve.com

Ruth & John Gozzard	Stokehill Farmhouse	Stokehill	Yelverton PL20 7PP	Devon
Tel: (01822) 853791	Fax 01822 853791	Open: ALL YEAR		Map Ref No. 54

Visit our website at:
http://www.bestbandb.co.uk

Orchard House.   Horner.

Dorset

Dorset
(West Country)

The unspoilt nature of this gem of a county is emphasised by the designation of virtually all of the coast & much of the inland country as an Area of Outstanding Natural Beauty. Along the coast from Christchurch to Lyme Regis there are a fascinating variety of sandy beaches, towering cliffs & single banks, whilst inland is a rich mixture of downland, lonely heaths, fertile valleys, historic houses & lovely villages of thatch & mellow stone buildings.

Thomas Hardy was born here & took the Dorset countryside as a background for many of his novels. Few writers can have stamped their identity on a county more than Hardy on Dorset, forever to be known as the "Hardy Country". Fortunately most of the area that he so lovingly described remains unchanged, including Egdon Heath & the county town of Dorchester, famous as Casterbridge.

In the midst of the rolling chalk hills which stretch along the Storr Valley lies picturesque Cerne Abbas, with its late mediaeval houses & cottages & the ruins of a Benedictine Abbey. At Godmanstone is the tiny thatched "Smiths Arms" claiming to be the smallest pub in England.

The north of the county is pastoral with lovely views over broad Blackmoor Vale. Here is the ancient hilltop town of Shaftesbury, with cobbled Gold Hill, one of the most photographed streets in the country.

Coastal Dorset is spectacular. Poole harbour is an enormous, almost circular bay, an exciting mixture of 20th century activity, ships of many nations & beautiful building of the 15th, 18th & early 19th centuries.

Westwards lies the popular resort of Swanage, where the sandy beach & sheltered bay are excellent for swimming. From here to Weymouth is a marvellous stretch of coast with scenic wonders like Lulworth Cove & the arch of Durdle Door.

Chesil Beach is an extraordinary bank of graded pebbles, as perilous to shipping today as it was 1,000 years ago. It is separated from the mainland by a sheltered lagoon known as the Fleet. From here a range of giant cliffs rises to 617 feet at Golden Gap & stretches westwards to Lyme Regis, beloved by Jane Austen who wrote "Persuasion" whilst living here.

Dorset has many interesting archaeological features. Near Dorchester is Maiden Castle, huge earthwork fortifications on a site first inhabited 6,000 years ago. The Badbury rings wind round a wooded hilltop near Wimborne Minster; legend has it that King Arthur's soul, in the form of a raven, inhabited this "dread" wood. The giant of Cerne Abbas is a figure of a man 180 feet high carved into the chalk hillside. Long associated with fertility there is still speculation about the figures' origins, one theory suggesting it is a Romano-British depiction of Hercules. A Roman amphitheatre can be seen at Dorchester, & today's road still follows the Roman route to Weymouth.

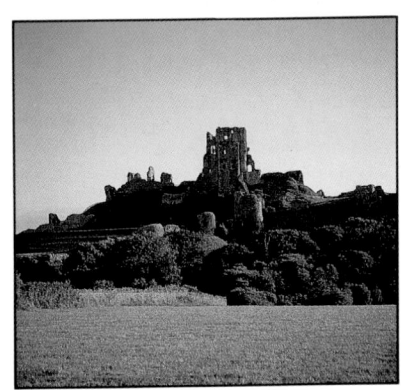

Corfe Castle.

Dorset

Dorset
Gazeteer

Areas of outstanding natural beauty.
The Entire County.

Houses & Castles

Athelthampton
Mediaeval house - one of the finest in all England. Formal gardens.

Barneston Manor - Nr. Church Knowle
13th - 16th century stone built manor house.

Forde Abbey - Nr. Chard
12th century Cistercian monastery - noted Mortlake tapestries.

Manor House - Sandford Orcas
Mansion of Tudor period, furnished with period furniture, antiques, silver, china, glass, paintings.

Hardy's Cottage - Higher Bockampton
Birthplace of Thomas Hardy, author (1840-1928).

Milton Abbey - Nr. Blandford
18th century Georgian house built on original site of 15th century abbey.

Purse Caundle Manor - Purse Caundle
Mediaeval Manor - furnished in style of period.

Parnham House - Beaminster
Tudor Manor - some later work by Nash. Leaded windows & heraldic plasterwork. Home of John Makepeace & the International School for Craftsmen in Wood. House, gardens & workshops.

Sherborne Castle - Sherborne
16th century mansion - continuously occupied by Digby family.

No. 3 Trinity Street - Weymouth
Tudor cottages now converted into one house, furnished 17th century.

Smedmore - Kimmeridge
18th century manor.

Wolfeton House - Dorchester
Mediaeval & Elizabethan Manor. Fine stone work, great stair. 17th century furniture - Jacobean ceilings & fireplaces.

Cathedrals & Churches

Bere Regis (St. John the Baptist)
12th century foundation - enlarged in 13th & 15th centuries.
Timber roof & nave, fine arcades. 16th century seating.

Blandford (St. Peter & St. Paul)
18th century - ashlar - Georgian design. Galleries, pulpit, box pews, font & mayoral seat.

Bradford Abbas (St. Mary)
14th century - parapets & pinnacled tower, panelled roof. 15th century bench ends, stone rood screen. 17th century pulpit.

Cerne Abbas (St. Mary)
13th century - rebuilt 15th & 16th centuries, 14th century wall paintings, 15th century tower, stone screen, pulpit possibly 11th century.

Chalbury (dedication unknown)
13th century origin - 14th century east windows, timber bellcote. Plastered walls, box pews, 3-decker pulpit, west gallery.

Christchurch (Christ Church)
Norman nave - ribbed plaster vaulting - perpendicular spire. Tudor renaissance Salisbury chantry - screen with Tree of Jesse: notable misericord seats.

Milton Abbey (Sts. Mary, Michael, Sampson & Branwaleder)
14th century pulpitum & sedilia, 15th century reredos & canopy, 16th century monument, Milton effigies 1775.

Sherborne (St. Mary)
Largely Norman but some Saxon remains - excellent fan vaulting, of nave & choir. 12th & 13th century effigies - 15th century painted glass.

Studland (St. Nicholas)
12th century - best Norman church in the country. 12th century font, 13th century east windows.

Whitchurch Canonicorum (St. Candida & Holy Cross)
12th & 13th century. 12th century font, relics of patroness in 13th century shrine, 15th century painted glass, 15th century tower.

Wimbourne Minster (St. Cuthberga)
12th century central tower & arcade, otherwise 13th-15th century. Former collegiate church. Georgian glass, some Jacobean stalls & screen. Monuments & famed clock of 14th century.

Yetminster (St. Andrew)
13th century chancel - 15th century rebuilt with embattled parapets. 16th century brasses & seating.

Dorset

Museums & Galleries

Abbey Ruins - Shaftesbury
Relics excavated from Benedictine
Nunnery founded by Alfred the Great.
Russell-Cotes Art Gallery & Museum -
Bournemouth
17th-20th century oil paintings,
watercolours, sculptures, ceramics,
miniatures, etc.
Rothesay Museum - Bournemouth
English porcelain, 17th century furniture,
collection of early Italian paintings, arms &
armour, ethnography, etc.
**Bournemouth Natural Science
Society's Museum**
Archaeology & local natural history.
Brewery Farm Museum - Milton Abbas
Brewing & village bygones from Dorset.
Dorset County Museum - Dorchester
Geology, natural history, pre-history.
Thomas Hardy memorabilia
Philpot Museum - Lyme Regis
Old documents & prints, fossils, lace & old
fire engine.
Guildhall Museum - Poole
Social & civic life of Poole during 18th &
19th centuries displayed in two-storey
Georgian market house.
Scapolen's Court - Poole
14th century house of local merchant

exhibiting local & archaeological history of
town, also industrial archaeology.
Sherborne Museum - Sherborne
Local history & geology - abbey of AD
705, Sherborne missal AD 1400, 18th
century local silk industry.
Gallery 24 - Shaftesbury
Art exhibitions - paintings, pottery, etc.
Red House Museum & Art Gallery -
Christchurch
Natural history & antiques of the region.
Georgian house with herb garden.
Priest's House Museum - Wimbourne
Minster
Tudor building in garden exhibiting local
archaeology & history.

Other things to see & do

Abbotsbury Swannery - Abbotsbury
Unique colony of Swans established by
monks in the 14th century. 16th century
duck decoy, reed walk, information centre.
Dorset Rare Breeds Centre - Park Farm,
Gillingham
Poole Potteries - the Quay, Poole
Sea Life Centre - Weymouth
Variety of displays, including Ocean
Tunnel, sharks, living "touch" pools.

West Bay.

DORSET

Map reference

03	Edwards	16	Lake	
03	Cattell	17	Bradley-Watson	
04	Hardy	18	Pow	
05	Davies	19	Kunnath	
06	Diment	20	Benjamin	
07	Tennant	22	Partridge	
08	Modley-W.	23	Hookham-Bassett	
11	Millorit	26	Hipwell	
12	McCarthy	27	Brachi	
13	Angell	29	Dale	
14	Adeney	31	Turnbull	
16	T. Norman			

Dorset

£23.00 to £35.00	Y	N	N	Nearest Road: A.338	**Gervis Court Hotel**

Nearest Road: A.338

Gervis Court is a charming detached Victorian villa, set in its own grounds amongst the pine trees. Centrally located for all amenities. It is just a very short walk to the beach, shops, theatres, clubs & Conference Centre. Bedrooms are en-suite, tastefully furnished with comfort in mind & all have T.V. & coffee/tea-making facilities. Many rooms are on the ground floor. It is ideally located for visiting the beautiful Dorset coast & the New Forest.
E-mail: enquiries@gerviscourthotel.co.uk

VISA: M'CARD:

Mr & Mrs A. Edwards   Gervis Court Hotel   38 Gervis Road   Bournemouth BH1 3DH   Dorset
Tel: (01202) 556871   Fax 01202 467066   Open: ALL YEAR   Map Ref No. 03

£22.00 to £22.00	Y	Y	N	Nearest Road: A.35, A.3060	**Sandhurst Hotel**

Nearest Road: A.35, A.3060

Guests' comfort is a priority at this friendly, welcoming hotel. There's a choice of 5 comfortable bedrooms (incl. a ground-floor one), each with en-suite facilities. All have colour T.V. & tea/coffee makers. Good home-cooked breakfasts, & evening meals available. Situated only 2 mins' from the beach in a quiet suburb of Bournemouth. An ideal centre for touring, with Christchurch, Beaulieu, the New Forest, Salisbury & Dorchester a short drive away. Private parking.
E-mail: sandhursthotel@lineone.net

Brian & Jane Cattell   Sandhurst Hotel   16 Southern Rd   Southbourne   Bournemouth BH6 3SR   Dorset
Tel: (01202) 423748   Open: APR - OCT   Map Ref No. 03

£20.00 to £32.00	Y	N	Y	Nearest Road: A.35	**Britmead House**

Nearest Road: A.35

A friendly welcome in a relaxed & comfortable atmosphere. Renowned for good food, a high standard of facilities & personal service. Situated between Bridport, the fishing harbour of West Bay, Chesil Beach & the Dorset Coastal Path. 7 en-suite bedrooms, 1 on the ground floor, all with T.V., tea facilities & hairdryer. South-facing lounge & dining room overlook the garden & open countryside beyond. Optional dinner, incorporating local fish & produce. Licensed. Parking.
E-mail: britmead@talk21.com

VISA: M'CARD:

Mr A. Hardy   Britmead House   154 West Bay Road   Bridport DT6 4EG   Dorset
Tel: (01308) 422941   Fax 01308 422516   Open: ALL YEAR   Map Ref No. 04

£32.50 to £40.00	Y	Y	Y	Nearest Road: A.35	**Innsacre Farmhouse**

Nearest Road: A.35

17th-century farmhouse & barn in a magical & peaceful setting. Hidden midway between Lyme Regis & Dorchester, 3 miles from the sea & National Trust coastal path. South-facing, 10 acres of spinneys, steep hillsides, orchard & lawns in a beautiful setting. A mix of French rustic style, English comfort & a genuine, warm welcome. All rooms en-suite (with T.V. & tea tray). Large, cosy sitting-room, log fires, beams & delicious breakfasts. Private parking. Licensed. Children over 9. Single supplement.

VISA: M'CARD:

Sydney Davies   Innsacre Farmhouse   Shipton Gorge   Bridport DT6 4LJ   Dorset
Tel: (01308) 456137   Fax 01308 456137   Open: ALL YEAR (Excl. Xmas & New Year)   Map Ref No. 05

	rate £ from - to per person	children taken	evening meals	animals taken

Rudge Farm

Nearest Road: A.35

Rudge Farm is peacefully situated on a gentle south-facing slope overlooking the beautiful Bride Valley, just over 2 miles from the sea. After a day spent exploring the lovely West Dorset country-side, relax in this comfortable Victorian farmhouse before trying one of the excellent local pubs or restaurants. The large, attractively furnished rooms are all en-suite, with T.V., tea/coffee-making facilities & far-reaching views. A charming home.

E-mail: sue@rudgefarm.co.uk

£26.00 to £28.00 — Y — N — N

VISA: M'CARD:

Sue Diment	Rudge Farm	Chilcombe	Bridport DT6 4NF	Dorset
Tel: (01308) 482630		Open: ALL YEAR (Excl. Xmas & New Year)		Map Ref No. 06

Champ's Land

Nearest Road: A.35

Champ's Land is a pretty 17th-century former farmhouse. It is in a beautiful, rural setting, with an attractive walled garden & orchard leading to a stream. It is tastefully decorated throughout with antiques & offers 2 comfortable guest rooms with tea/coffee-making facilities. A delicious breakfast is served. Several good pubs & restaurants locally for dinner. A number of gardens & historic houses within easy reach. Champ's Land is situated only 1 1/2 miles from the sea. Children over 12. Single supplement. Animals by arrangement.

£28.00 to £35.00 — N — N — Y

Mrs Miranda Tennant	Champ's Land	North Chideock	Bridport DT6 6JZ	Dorset
Tel: (01297) 489314		Open: ALL YEAR (Excl. Xmas & New Year)		Map Ref No. 07

Springbrook Cottage

Nearest Road: A.351

Springbrook Cottage is a beautiful house which is set in an acre of garden, lawn & shrubs including mature trees. There is an attractive conservatory in which guests may choose to relax, which boasts lovely views down to the valley beyond. Tradition-ally furnished with antiques, the property offers attractive accommodation in 2 charming bedrooms. The light & airy rooms are very comfortable. A delicious breakfast is served. Evening meals are available by prior arrangement. A lovely base from which to explore the beautiful Dorset countryside.

£25.00 to £30.00 — Y — Y — N

Mrs G. Modley-Wingfield	Springbrook Cottage	Springbrook Close	Corfe Castle BH20 5HS	Dorset
Tel: (01929) 480509		Open: ALL YEAR		Map Ref No. 08

Brambles

Nearest Road: A.37

Set in beautiful, tranquil countryside, Brambles is a pretty thatched cottage offering every comfort, superb views & a friendly welcome. There is a choice of en-suite twin, double or single rooms, all very comfortable & with colour T.V. & tea/coffee-making facilities. Pretty garden available for relax-ing. A full English or Continental breakfast is served. Evening meals available by prior arrange-ment. There are many interesting places to visit & wonderful walks for enthusiasts.

£18.00 to £25.00 — Y — Y — N

see PHOTO over
p. 141

Andre & Anita Millorit	Brambles	Woolcombe	Melbury Bubb	Dorchester DT2 0NJ	Dorset
Tel: (01935) 83672		Open: ALL YEAR (Excl. Xmas)			Map Ref No. 11

Brambles. Woolcombe.

Dorset

Rew Cottage

Nearest Road: A.35, A.37
A warm welcome awaits you in a peaceful cottage in the heart of Hardy's Dorset. Surrounded by green farmland with lovely views on all sides. An ideal centre for walking & within easy reach of Sherborne, Dorchester & the sea. Bedrooms are comfortably furnished; double, twin & single rooms (with tea/coffee-making facilities & T.V.). 2 private bathrooms adjacent. Attractive pubs within easy reach for evening meals. Children & animals by arrangement.

	rate	Y	N	N
	£20.00 to £26.00	Y	N	N

Annette & Rupert McCarthy   Rew Cottage   Buckland Newton   Dorchester DT2 7DN   Dorset
Tel: (01300) 345467   Fax 01300 345467   Open: Mid JAN - Mid DEC   Map Ref No. 12

Peony Cottage

Nearest Road: A.35
Peony Cottage, Grade II listed, is an annexe to the main family home & was built in the 17th century. Nearby is the historic Athelhampton House & Gardens. A short drive away is Ringstead Bay, breathtaking coastal walks & beaches. Tastefully decorated with a mediterranean feel, 2 twin bedrooms (1 suitable only for children (over 6 & only £10.00 per child), private bathroom, own sitting room with T.V. & video. Organic & local produce used.
E-mail: peony.cottage@virgin.net

£25.00 to £30.00   Y N Y

Harriet & Colin Angell   Peony Cottage   Affpuddle   Dorchester DT2 7HH   Dorset
Tel: (01305) 849162   Fax 01305 848783   Open: ALL YEAR   Map Ref No. 13

Whites Dairy House

Nearest Road: A.35, A.352
Nestling in the lovely Piddle Valley, a warm welcome awaits guests at the oldest house in the village (1622) with its ancient beams & interesting features. Outside a charming stream runs at the bottom of the garden. The old stables have recently been converted to provide high-quality en-suite rooms, each with T.V., radio & tea/coffee-making facilities. 4 pubs with excellent restaurants within 3 1/2 miles, 1 within walking easy distance. Children over 12. Animals by arrangement.
E-mail: robin.adeney@care4free.net

£25.00 to £30.00   Y N Y

see PHOTO over
p. 143

VISA: M'CARD: AMEX:

Liz & Robin Adeney   Whites Dairy House   16 High Street   Piddlehinton   Dorchester DT2 7TD   Dorset
Tel: (01300) 348386   Fax 01300 348386   Open: ALL YEAR (Excl. Xmas & New Year)   Map Ref No. 14

The Red House

Nearest Road: A.3052
This distinguished house, set in mature grounds, enjoys spectacular coastal views, & yet is only a short walk to the centre of Lyme Regis. The 3 en-suite bedrooms (1 for family use; 2 are especially spacious) are furnished with every comfort, including tea/coffee makers, T.V., clock-radio, desk, armchairs, a drink refrigerator, central heating & electric heaters. Fresh flowers & magazines are among the little extras. Breakfast can be taken on the garden balcony. Parking. Children over 8.
E-mail: red.house@virgin.net

£22.00 to £27.00   Y N N

VISA: M'CARD:

Tony & Vicky Norman   The Red House   Sidmouth Road   Lyme Regis DT7 3ES   Dorset
Tel: (01297) 442055   Fax 01297 442055   Open: Mid MAR - Early NOV   Map Ref No. 16

Whites Dairy House.   Piddlehinton.

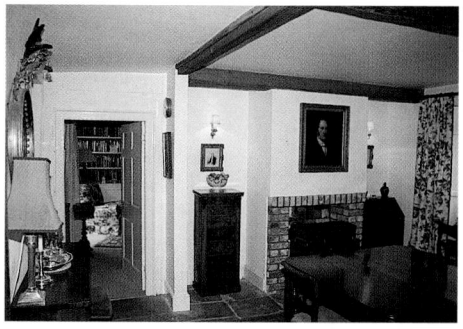

Dorset

Rashwood Lodge

Nearest Road: A.3052, A.35

Rashwood Lodge is an unusual octagonal house, located on the western hillside with views over Lyme Bay. Just a short walk away is the coastal footpath & Ware Cliff, famed for its part in 'The French Lieutenant's Woman'. The bedrooms have their own facilities & benefit from their south-facing aspect overlooking a large & colourful garden set in peaceful surroundings. Golf course 1 mile. A charming home. Children over 4 years.

| £22.00 to £26.00 | Y | N | N |

Mrs Diana Lake   *Rashwood Lodge*   *Clappentail Lane*   **Lyme Regis DT7 3LZ**   *Dorset*
Tel: (01297) 445700   *Open: FEB - NOV*   **Map Ref No. 16**

Melbury Mill

Nearest Road: A.350

Mr & Mrs Bradley-Watson offer a warm welcome at this old working mill, set in 9 acres of meadows & overlooking a mill pond abounding with waterfowl. All bedrooms are large & centrally heated, & have en-suite facilities. Located just south of Shaftesbury, famous for its Gold Hill, it is in picturesque Thomas Hardy countryside. Ideal for walkers, with National Trust downland & the properties of Stourhead & Kingston Lacy close by. Melbury Mill is an ideal base for a short-break holiday.
E-mail: richardbradleywatson@hotmail.com

| £25.00 to £30.00 | Y | N | N |

see PHOTO over p. 145

Richard & Tavy Bradley-Watson   *Melbury Mill*   *Melbury Abbas*   **Shaftesbury SP7 0DB**   *Dorset*
Tel: (01747) 852163   *Open: ALL YEAR*   **Map Ref No. 17**

Cliff House

Nearest Road: A.30, A.350

Cliff House is a spacious Regency Grade II listed property set in an acre of peaceful mature garden. Within walking distance of the historic Saxon town with magnificent views & the famous Gold Hill. An ideal position for visiting the surrounding countryside, historic houses, towns & villages with cathedrals & abbeys. Both bedrooms are attractive with en-suite bathrooms. A full English breakfast is served with home-made jams, or choose kippers or haddock for a change. Children over 5.
E-mail: dianaepow@aol.com

| £27.50 to £30.00 | Y | N | N |

Diana Pow   *Cliff House*   *Breach Lane*   **Shaftesbury SP7 8LF**   *Dorset*
Tel: (01747) 852548   *Fax 01747 852548*   *Open: ALL YEAR*   **Map Ref No. 18**

The Old Vicarage

Nearest Road: A.30

The Old Vicarage is a gothic Victorian building, set in 3 1/2 acres of grounds on the edge of a charming village. It is 2 miles from the historic town of Sherborne & affords magnificent views of open country. All of the 7 bedrooms are stylishly decorated & have en-suite facilities. The large lounge is beautifully furnished with antiques. On Friday & Saturday evenings, one of the owners, a highly acclaimed chef, prepares dinner. All inclusive weekend breaks are available. Children over 5.
E-mail: theoldvicarage@milborneport.freeserve.co.uk

| £27.00 to £48.00 | Y | Y | Y |

VISA: M'CARD: AMEX:

Jorgen Kunath & Anthony Ma   *The Old Vicarage*   *Sherborne Road*   *Milborne Port*   **Sherborne DT9 5AT**
Tel: (01963) 251117   *Fax 01963 251515*   *Open: FEB - DEC*   **Map Ref No. 19**

Melbury Mill. Melbury Abbas.

	rate £ from - to per person	children taken	evening meals	animals taken

Munden House

Nearest Road: A.3030

A warm welcome awaits you at Munden House. 6 attractively decorated & tastefully furnished bedrooms & a studio annex. Each room has its own bathroom, T.V., tea/coffee-making facilities etc. It is located in the picturesque Blackmore Vale on the outskirts of Sherborne with its historic castle, Abbey & Almshouses. Golf & tennis closeby. Horse-riding a short drive away. Excellent pubs & restaurants. Reflexology, shiatsu & aromatherapy massage available from visiting therapists.
E-mail: sylvia@mundenhouse.demon.co.uk

£27.50 to £42.50 — Y N N

VISA: M'CARD:

Sylvia & Joe Benjamin   Munden House   Munden Lane   Alweston   Sherborne DT9 5HU   Dorset
Tel: (01963) 23150   Fax 01963 23153   Open: ALL YEAR   Map Ref No. 20

Manor Farmhouse

Nearest Road: A.37

This 17th-century farmhouse, with oak panelling, beams & inglenook fireplaces, offers every comfort to the discerning visitor. 4 bedrooms, all with en-suite facilities & modern amenities, including T.V. & tea/coffee. Delicious meals served, made from traditional recipes & using fresh local produce. The village is described as the best 17th-century stone-built village in the south of England. An excellent centre for visiting Sherborne, Glastonbury, New Forest & Hardy's Dorset.
E-mail: anneparty@aol.com

£35.00 to £35.00 — N Y N

VISA: M'CARD:

Mrs Ann C. Partridge   Manor Farmhouse   High Street   Yetminster   Sherborne DT9 6LF   Dorset
Tel: (01935) 872247   Fax 01935 872247   Open: ALL YEAR   Map Ref No. 22

Stourcastle Lodge

Nearest Road: A.357

Stourcastle Lodge is a family-run business, offering a very high standard of accommodation, with personal service & excellent cuisine. A superb breakfast is served in the attractive dining room. All the elegant bedrooms are south-facing & overlook the delightful garden, which is stocked full of herbaceous & perennial borders. Stourcastle Lodge is a beautiful home, & an ideal base for exploring Dorset & its many attractions.
E-mail: enquiries@stourcastle-lodge.co.uk

£32.00 to £39.00 — Y Y N

see PHOTO over p. 147

VISA: M'CARD:

Mr & Mrs Hookham-Bassett   Stourcastle Lodge   Gough's Close   Sturminster Newton   DT10 1BU Dorset
Tel: (01258) 472320   Fax 01258 473381   Open: ALL YEAR   Map Ref No. 23

Gold Court House

Nearest Road: A.351

Gold Court House is a charming Georgian house with walled garden on a small square on the south-side of Wareham. It offers 3 light & airy double or twin rooms with private bathrooms & all facilities at hand, at your request. Wareham is ideally situated for exploring the magnificent coastline of South Dorset & the Isle of Purbeck. Anthea & Michael are always pleased to help & advise on the numerous places of interest, sporting activities & where to dine. (Evening meals are available during the winter only.) Children over 10 years.

£25.00 to £25.00 — Y N N

Anthea & Michael Hipwell   Gold Court House   St. John's Hill   Wareham BH20 4LZ   Dorset
Tel: (01929) 553320   Fax 01929 553320   Open: ALL YEAR (Excl. Xmas & New Year)   Map Ref No. 26

Stourcastle Lodge. Sturminster Newton.

Dorset

West Coombe Farmhouse

Nearest Road: A.352

Discover a peaceful way of life when you stay at this restored Georgian farmhouse in the delightful village of Coombe Keynes. In summer, unwind in the beautiful garden & in winter linger by the open fire in the private sitting room. There are 3 attractive guest bedrooms. Lulworth is only 3 miles away & many traditional outdoor activities can be found locally, or explore the glorious countryside on your hosts' mountain bikes. Children over 12. Special winter are breaks available, which include dinner.
E-mail: west.coombe.farmhouse@barclays.net

	£ from - to	children taken	evening meals	animals taken
West Coombe Farmhouse	£25.00 to £25.00	Y	N	N

Rachel & Peter Brachi   West Coombe Farmhouse   Coombe Keynes Wareham BH20 5PS Dorset
Tel: (01929) 462889   Fax 01929 405863   Open: ALL YEAR (Excl. Xmas)   Map Ref No. 27

Gatton House

Nearest Road: A.352

Spectacularly positioned, quiet & comfortable, this small hotel is set amongst the Purbeck Hills, yet only a strolling distance from famous Lulworth Cove. There are 8 attractive bedrooms (all en-suite) & a lounge with colour T.V.. Outside, the terrace provides a perfect venue for morning coffee or afternoon tea. Gatton House is an ideal location for walking or touring Dorset's beauty spots, & it is within easy reach of Bournemouth, Poole, Swanage, Dorchester & Weymouth.
E-mail: mike@gattonhouse.co.uk

	£ from - to	children taken	evening meals	animals taken
Gatton House	£20.00 to £33.00	Y	N	Y

VISA: M'CARD:

Mike & Avril Dale   Gatton House   Main Road   West Lulworth   Wareham BH20 5RU Dorset
Tel: (01929) 400252   Fax 01929 400252   Open: MAR - OCT   Map Ref No. 29

Thornhill

Nearest Road: A.31

Visitors are warmly welcomed to this large, thatched family house located in rural surroundings 3 1/2 miles from Wimborne. Large garden. Hard tennis court available. Accommodation includes double, twin & single rooms. 1 private bathroom, & another which may be shared. Sitting room with colour T.V. & coffee/tea-making & laundry facilities. Plenty of good local pubs. Well situated for exploring the coast, New Forest & Salisbury area.
E-mail: sct@gardener.com

	£ from - to	children taken	evening meals	animals taken
Thornhill	£22.00 to £25.00	N	N	N

John & Sara Turnbull   Thornhill   Holt   Wimborne BH21 7DJ   Dorset
Tel: (01202) 889434   Open: ALL YEAR   Map Ref No. 31

When booking your accommodation please mention
The Best Bed & Breakfast

Essex

Essex
(East Anglia)

Essex is a county of commerce, busy roads & busier towns, container ports & motorways, yet it is also a landscape of mudflats & marshes, of meadows & leafy lanes, villages & duckponds. Half timbered buildings & thatched & clapboard cottages stand among rolling hills topped by orange brick windmills.

The coast on the east, now the haunt of wildfowl, sea-birds, sailors & fishermen has seen the arrival of Saxons, Romans, Danes, Vikings & Normans. The names of their settlements remain - Wivenhoe, Layer-de-la-Haye, Colchester & Saffron Walden - the original Saxon name was Walden, but the Saffron was added when the crocus used for dyes & flavouring was grown here in the 15th century.

The seaside resorts of Southend & Clacton are bright & cheery, much-loved by families for safe beaches. Harbours here are great favourites with anglers & yachtsmen.

Inland lie the watermeadows & windmills, willows & cool green water which shaped the life & work of John Constable, one of the greatest landscape painters. Scenes are instantly recognisable today as you walk to Dedham along the banks of the swiftly flowing River Stour.

Colchester is England's oldest recorded town, once the Roman capital of Britain trading in corn & cattle, slaves & pearls. Roman remains are still to be seen & their original street plan is the basis of much of modern Colchester. A great feast is held here annually to celebrate the famous oyster - the "Colchester native".

South Essex, though sliced through by the M.25 motorway is still a place of woodland & little rivers. The ancient trees of Epping Forest, hunting ground for generations of monarchs, spread 6,000 acres of leafy glades & heathland into the London suburbs.

Audley End. Saffron Walden.

Essex

Essex
Gazeteer

Areas of outstanding natural beauty.
Dedham Vale (part), Epping Forest.

Houses & Castles
Audley End House - Saffron Walden
1603 - Jacobean mansion on site of
Benedictine Abbey. State rooms & Hall.
Castle House - Dedham
Home of the late Sir A. Munnings.
President R.A. Paintings & other works.
Hedingham Castle - Castle Hedingham
Norman keep & Tudor bridge.
Layer Marney Tower - Nr. Colchester
1520 Tudor brick house. 8 storey gate
tower. Formal yew hedges & lawns.
Payecock's - Coggeshall
1500 - richly ornamented - merchant's
house - National Trust.
St. Osyth's Priory - St. Osyth
Was Augustinian Abbey for 400 years until
dissolution in 1537, 13th-18th century
buildings. 13th century chapel. Wonderful
gatehouse containing works of art
including ceramics & Chinese Jade.
Spains Hall - Finchingfield
Elizabethan Manor incorporating parts of
earlier timber structure. Paintings,
furniture & tapestries.

Cathedrals & Churches
Brightlingsea (All Saints)
15th century tower - some mediaeval
painting fragments. Brasses.
Castle Hedingham (St. Nicholas)
12th century doorways, 14th century rood
screen, 15th century stalls, 16th century
hammer beams, altar tomb.
Copford (St. Michael & All Angels)
12th century wall paints. Continuous
vaulted nave & chancel
.**Finchingfield** (St. John the Baptist)
Norman workmanship. 16th century tomb
-18th centuary tower & cupola.
Layer Marney (St. Mary)
Tudor brickwork, Renaissance
monuments, mediaeval screens, wall
paintings.
Little Maplestead (St. John the Baptist)
14th century, one of the five round

churches in England, having hexagonal
nave, circular aisle, 14th century arcade.
Newport (St. Mary the Virgin)
13th century. Interesting 13th century
altar (portable) with top which becomes
reredos when opened. 15th century
chancel screen. Pre-Reformation Lectern.
Some old glass.

Museums & Galleries
Dutch Cottage Museum - Canvey Island
17th century thatched cottage of octagonal
Dutch design. Exhibition of models of
shipping used on the Thames through the
ages.
Ingatestone Hall - Ingatestone
Documents & pictures of Essex.
The Castle - Colchester
Norman Keep now exhibiting
archeological material from Essex &
especially Roman Colchester.
Southchurch Hall - Southend-on-Sea
14th century moated & timber framed
manor house - Tudor wing, furnished as
meiaeval manor.
Thurrock - Grays
Prehistoric, Romano-British & pagan
Saxon archaeology.

Other things to see & do
Colchester Oyster Fishery - Colchester
Tour showing cultivating, harvesting,
grading & packing of oysters. Talk, tour
& sample.

Burnham on Crouch.

ESSEX

Map reference

01 Hodge
02 Larcom
03 Westerhuis

151

Essex

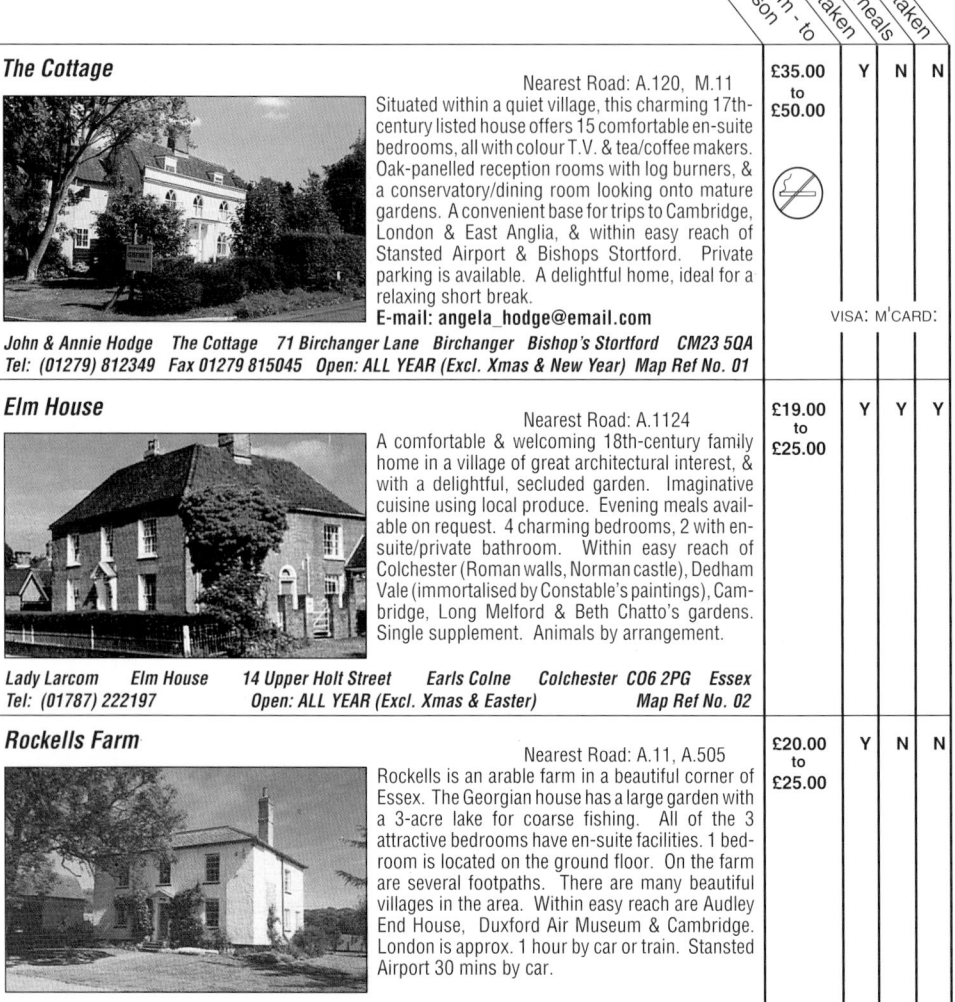

	rate £ from - to per person	evening meals children taken	animals taken

The Cottage

Nearest Road: A.120, M.11

Situated within a quiet village, this charming 17th-century listed house offers 15 comfortable en-suite bedrooms, all with colour T.V. & tea/coffee makers. Oak-panelled reception rooms with log burners, & a conservatory/dining room looking onto mature gardens. A convenient base for trips to Cambridge, London & East Anglia, & within easy reach of Stansted Airport & Bishops Stortford. Private parking is available. A delightful home, ideal for a relaxing short break.
E-mail: angela_hodge@email.com

£35.00 to £50.00 — Y N N

VISA: M'CARD:

John & Annie Hodge   The Cottage   71 Birchanger Lane   Birchanger   Bishop's Stortford   CM23 5QA
Tel: (01279) 812349   Fax 01279 815045   Open: ALL YEAR (Excl. Xmas & New Year)   Map Ref No. 01

Elm House

Nearest Road: A.1124

A comfortable & welcoming 18th-century family home in a village of great architectural interest, & with a delightful, secluded garden. Imaginative cuisine using local produce. Evening meals available on request. 4 charming bedrooms, 2 with en-suite/private bathroom. Within easy reach of Colchester (Roman walls, Norman castle), Dedham Vale (immortalised by Constable's paintings), Cambridge, Long Melford & Beth Chatto's gardens. Single supplement. Animals by arrangement.

£19.00 to £25.00 — Y Y Y

Lady Larcom   Elm House   14 Upper Holt Street   Earls Colne   Colchester CO6 2PG   Essex
Tel: (01787) 222197   Open: ALL YEAR (Excl. Xmas & Easter)   Map Ref No. 02

Rockells Farm

Nearest Road: A.11, A.505

Rockells is an arable farm in a beautiful corner of Essex. The Georgian house has a large garden with a 3-acre lake for coarse fishing. All of the 3 attractive bedrooms have en-suite facilities. 1 bedroom is located on the ground floor. On the farm are several footpaths. There are many beautiful villages in the area. Within easy reach are Audley End House, Duxford Air Museum & Cambridge. London is approx. 1 hour by car or train. Stansted Airport 30 mins by car.

£20.00 to £25.00 — Y N N

Mrs Tineke Westerhuis   Rockells Farm   Duddenhoe End   Saffron Walden CB11 4UY   Essex
Tel: (01763) 838053   Fax 01763 837001   Open: ALL YEAR   Map Ref No. 03

Visit our website at:
http://www.bestbandb.co.uk

Gloucestershire

Gloucestershire
(Heart of England)

The landscape is so varied the people speak not of one Gloucestershire but of three - Cotswold, Vale & Forest. The rounded hills of the Cotswolds sweep & fold in graceful compositions to form a soft & beautiful landscape in which nestle many pretty villages. To the east there are wonderful views of the Vale of Berkeley & Severn, & across to the dark wooded slopes of the Forest of Dean on the Welsh borders.

Hill Forts, ancient trackways & long barrows of neolithic peoples can be explored, & remains of many villas from late Roman times can be seen. A local saying "Scratch Gloucester & find Rome" reveals the lasting influence of the Roman presence. Three major roads mark the path of invasion & settlement. Akeman street leads to London, Ermine street & the Fosse Way to the north east. A stretch of Roman road with its original surface can be seen at Blackpool Bridge in the Forest of Dean, & Cirencester's museum reflects its status as the second most important Roman city in the country.

Offa's Dyke, 80 miles of bank & ditch on the Welsh border was the work of the Anglo-Saxons of Mercia who invaded in the wake of the Romans. Cotswold means "hills of the sheepcotes" in the Anglo-Saxon tongue, & much of the heritage of the area has its roots in the wealth created by the wool industry here.

Fine Norman churches such as those at Tewkesbury & Bishops Cleeve were overshadowed by the development of the perpendicular style of building made possible by the growing prosperity. Handsome 15th century church towers crown many wool towns & villages as at Northleach, Chipping Camden & Cirencester, & Gloucester has a splendid 14th century cathedral. Detailing on church buildings gives recognition to the source of the wealth-cloth-workers shears are depicted on the north west buttresses of Grantham church tower & couchant rams decorate church buttresses at Compton Bedale.

Wool & cloth weaving dominated life here in the 14th & 15th centuries with most families dependent on the industry. The cottage craft of weaving was gradually overtaken by larger looms & water power. A water mill can be seen in the beautiful village of Lower Slaughter & the cottages of Arlington Row in Bibury were a weaving factory.

The Cotswold weaving industry gave way to the growing force of the Lancashire mills but a few centres survive. At Witney you can still buy the locally made blankets for which the town is famous.

From the 16th century the wealthy gentry built parks & mansions. Amongst the most notable are the Jacobean Manor house at Stanway & the contrasting Palladian style mansion at Barnsley Park. Elizabethan timber frame buildings can be seen at Didbrook, Dymock & Deerhurst but houses in the local mellow golden limestone are more common, with Chipping Camden providing excellent examples.

Cheltenham was only a village when, in 1716 a local farmer noticed a flock of pigeons pecking at grains of salt around a saline spring in his fields. He began to bottle & sell the water & in 1784 his son-in-law, Henry Skillicorne, built a pump room & the place received the name of Cheltenham Spa. Physicians published treatises on the healing qualities of the waters, visitors began to flock there & Cheltenham grew in style & elegance.

Gloucestershire

Gloucestershire Gazeteer

Areas of outstanding natural beauty
The Cotswolds, Malvern Hills & the Wye Valley.

Houses & Castles

Ashleworth Court - Ashleworth
15th century limestone Manor house.
Badminton House - Badminton
Built in the reign of Charles II.
Stone newel staircase.
Berkeley Castle - Berkeley
12th century castle - still occupied by the Berkeley family. Magnificent collections of furniture, paintings, tapestries & carved timber work. Lovely terraced gardens & deer park.
Chavenage - Tetbury
Elizabethan Cotswold Manor house, Cromwellian associations.
Clearwell Castle - Nr. Coleford
A Georgian neo-Gothic house said to be oldest in Britain, recently restored.
Court House - Painswick
Cotswold Manor house - has original court room & bedchamber of Charles I.
Splendid panelling & antique furniture.
Dodington House - Chipping Sodbury
Perfect 18th century house with superb staircase.   Landscape by Capability Brown.
Horton Court - Horton
Cotswold manor house altered & restored in 19th century.
Kelmscott Manor - Nr. Lechlade
16th century country house - 17th century additions. Examples of work of William Morris, Rosetti & Burne-Jones.
Owlpen Manor - Nr. Dursley
Historic group of traditional Cotswold stone buildings. Tudor Manor house with church, barn, court house & a grist mill.
Holds a rare set of 17th century painted cloth wall hangings.
Snowshill Manor - Broadway
Tudor house with 17th century facade.
Unique collection of musical instruments & clocks, toys, etc. Formal garden.
Sudeley Castle - Winchcombe
12th century - home of Katherine Parr, is rich in historical associations, contains art treasures & relics of bygone days.

Cathedrals & Churches

Bishops Cleeve (St. Michael & All Saints)
12th century with 17th century gallery.
Magnificent Norman west front & south porch. Decorated chancel.   Fine window.
Bledington (St.Leonards)
15th century glass in this perpendicular church, Norman bellcote. Early English east window.
Buckland (St. Michael)
13th century nave arcades. 17th century oak panelling, 15th century glass.
Cirencester (St. John the Baptist)
A magnificent church - remarkable exterior, 3 storey porch, 2 storey oriel windows, traceries & pinnacles. Wine-glass pulpit c.1450. 15th century glass in east window, monuments in Lady chapel.
Gloucester Cathedral
Birthplace of Perpendicular style in 14th century. Fan vaulting, east windows commemorate Battle of Crecy - Norman Chapter House.
Hailes Abbey - Winchcombe
14th century wall paintings, 15th century tiles, glass & screen, 17th century pulpit.
Elizabethan benches.
Iron Acton (St. James the Less)
Perpendicular - 15th century memorial cross. 19th century mosaic floors, Laudian alter rails, Jacobean pulpit, effigies.
Newland (All Saints)
13th century, restored 18th century.
Pinnacled west tower, effigies.
Prinknash Abbey - Gloucester
14th & 16th century - Benedictine Abbey.
Tewkesbury Abbey - Tewkesbury
Dates back to Norman times, contains Romanesque & Gothic styles. 14th century monuments.
Yate (St. Mary)
Splendid perpendicular tower.

Museums & Galleries

Bishop Hooper's Lodgings - Gloucester
3 Tudor timber frame buildings - museum of domestic life & agriculture in Gloucester since 1500.
Bourton Motor Museum - Bourton-on-the-Water
Collection of cars & motor cycles.
Cheltenham Art Gallery - Cheltenham.

Gloucestershire

Lower Slaughter.

Gallery of Dutch paintings, collection of oils, watercolours, pottery, porcelain, English & Chinese; furniture.
City Wall & Bastion - Gloucester
Roman & mediaeval city defences in an underground exhibition room.
Stroud Museum - Cirencester
Depicts earlier settlements in the area & has a very fine collection of Roman antiquities.

Historic Monuments

Chedworth Roman Villa - Yanworth
Remains of Romano-British villa.
Belas Knap Long Barrow - Charlton Abbots
Neolithic burial ground - three burial chambers with external entrances.
Hailes Abbey - Stanway
Ruins of beautiful mediaeval abbey built by son of King John, 1246.
Witcombe Roman Villa - Nr. Birdlip

Large Roman villa - Hypocaust & mosaic pavements preserved.
Ashleworth Tithe Barn - Ashleworth
15th century tithe barn - 120 feet long - stone built, interesting roof timbering.
Odda's Chapel - Deerhurst
Rare Saxon chapel dating back to 1056.
Hetty Pegler's Tump - UleLong Barrow-fairly complete, chamber is 120 feet long.

Other things to see & do

Cheltenham International Festival of Music & Literature - Annual event.
Cotswolds Farm Park - dozens of rare breeds of farm animals.
The Three Choirs Festival - music festival staged in alternating years at Gloucester, Hereford & Worcester Cathedrals.
Slimbridge - Peter Scott's Wildfowl Trust.

GLOUCESTERSHIRE

Map reference

01	Nesbitt	22	Annis
01	Bolton	23	Rodger
01	Wright	24	Parkes
02	Thornely	25	Helm
03	Moodie	27	Anderson
06	Hazell	28	Dean
09	Gamez	29	Ritchie
10	Gisby	30	Peacock
13	Powell	31	Digby
14	Wilson	32	Walsh
15	Yardley	33	Solomon
16	Langton	34	Brunsdon
18	Keyser	35	Sayers
20	Parsons	36	Brown

Church House.   Clapton on the Hill.

Gloucestershire

Church House

Nearest Road: A.429, A.40

Church House is a completely restored 17th-century Cotswold stone house in the small village of Clapton-on-the-Hill. The 2 lovely bedrooms, each with sloping ceilings, beams, T.V. & an en-suite bathroom, offer seclusion & privacy plus full use of guests' private drawing room & dining room downstairs. Wonderful views over the Windrush Valley & the church, newly designed & planted gardens & brilliantly located for visiting the Cotswolds.
E-mail: bill.nesbitt@ukf.net

| £30.00 to £35.00 | Y | N | N |

see PHOTO over
p. 157

Mrs Caroline Nesbitt   Church House   Clapton-on-the-Hill   Bourton-on-the-Water GL54 2LG
Tel: (01451) 822532   Fax 01451 822472   Open: ALL YEAR (Excl. Xmas)   Map Ref No. 01

Clapton Manor

Nearest Road: A.40, A.429

Clapton Manor dates from the 16th-century & stands at the top of a quiet village with stunning views over the Windrush valley. It is an informal, very comfortable & welcoming family home with massive inglenook fireplaces & old oak beams. Guests have the use of a private sitting room with log fire, a dining room with a Tudor fireplace & 2 delightful, light & airy en-suite rooms, 1 of which has a secret door to its bathroom. The other bedroom has views over the garden, which was recently featured in 'The English Garden' magazine.

| £35.00 to £40.00 | Y | N | N |

see PHOTO over
p. 159

VISA: M'CARD:

Mrs Karin Bolton   Clapton Manor   Clapton-on-the-Hill   Bourton-on-the-Water GL54 2LG
Tel: (01451) 810202   Fax 01451 821804   Open: ALL YEAR (Excl. Xmas & New Year) Map Ref No. 01

Farncombe

Nearest Road: A.429

Come & share the peace, tranquillity & superb views of Farncombe, & eat, drink & sleep - smoke-free - 700ft above sea level & only 2 miles from Bourton-on-the-Water. 2 attractive doubles with showers, & 1 twin en-suite. A spacious dining room, with tea/coffee-making facilities, & a comfortable T.V. lounge. Tourist information, maps & books, & current menus for your choice when eating out. Numerous walks & drives, with easy access to all attractions & places of interest.
E-mail: jwrightbb@aol.com

| £20.00 to £25.00 | N | N | N |

Mrs Julia Wright   Farncombe   Clapton   Bourton-on-the-Water GL54 2LG   Gloucestershire
Tel/Fax: (01451) 820120   Mobile 07714 703142   Open: ALL YEAR   Map Ref No. 01

Eastcote Cottage

Nearest Road: A.38

Eastcote is a charming 200-year-old stone house located in a lovely rural setting, with splendid views across open countryside. Guests have a choice of 2 comfortable bedrooms with modern amenities. A colour-T.V. lounge is available for guests' use. Eastcote Cottage is an ideal base for touring being conveniently situated for the M.4/M.5 interchange for the Cotswolds, with Bristol, Bath, Cheltenham & the Wye Valley easily accessible. Private parking.
E-mail: nickthornely@cwcom.net

| £25.00 to £25.00 | Y | N | N |

Mrs Ann Thornely   Eastcote Cottage Knapp Road East   Thornbury   Bristol BS35 2HJ   Gloucestershire
Tel: (01454) 413106   Fax 01454 281812   Open: ALL YEAR (Excl. Xmas)   Map Ref No. 02

Clapton Manor. Clapton on the Hill.

The Elms. Olveston.

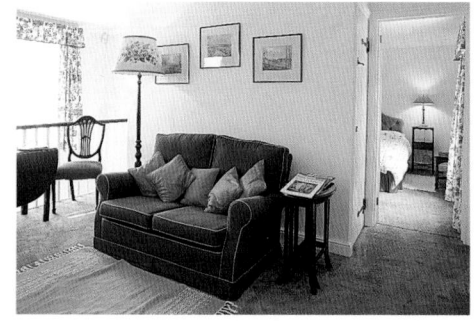

rate £ from - to per person	children taken	evening meals	animals taken

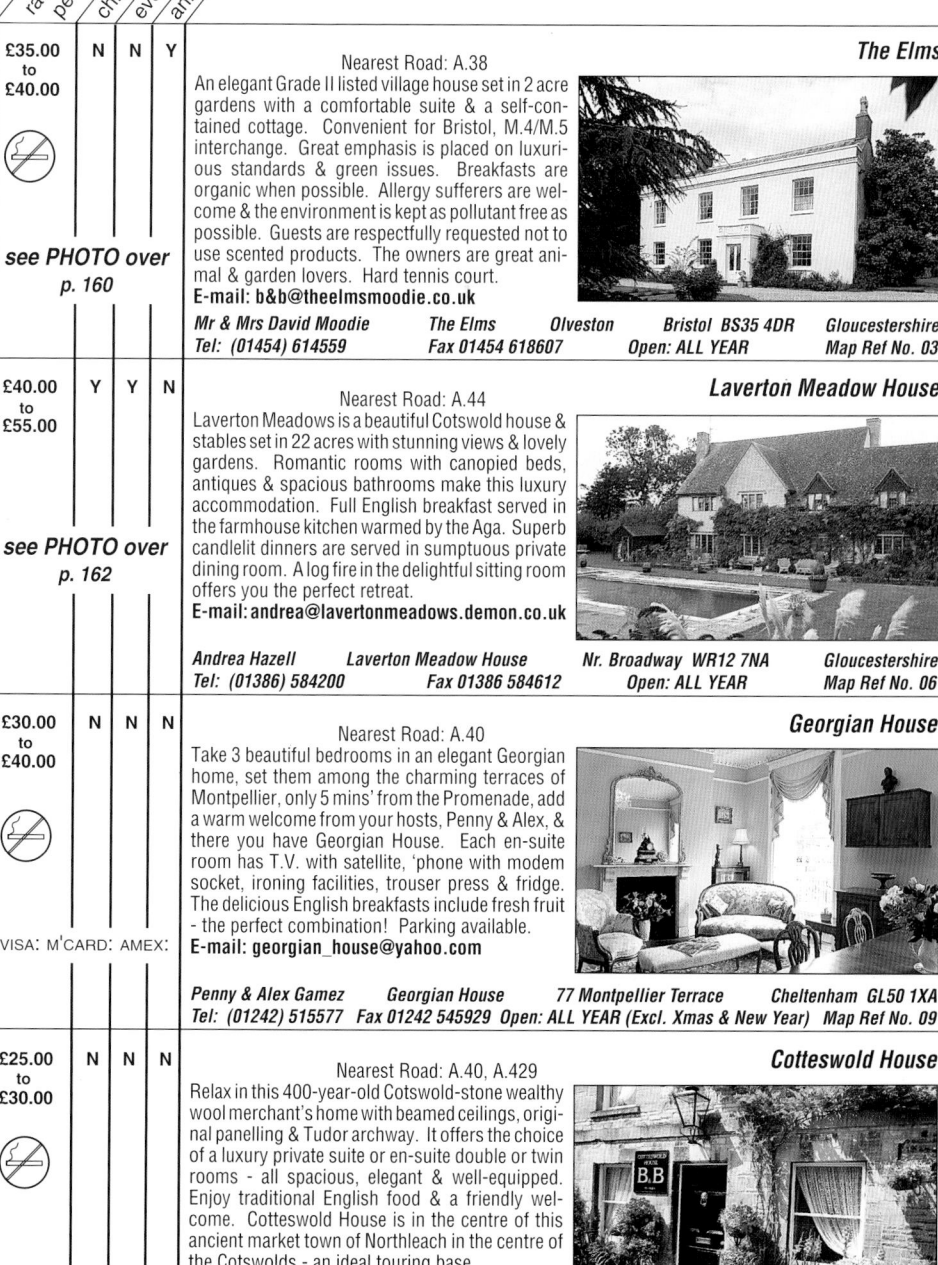

£35.00 to £40.00 | N | N | Y

(no smoking)

see PHOTO over p. 160

The Elms

Nearest Road: A.38

An elegant Grade II listed village house set in 2 acre gardens with a comfortable suite & a self-contained cottage. Convenient for Bristol, M.4/M.5 interchange. Great emphasis is placed on luxurious standards & green issues. Breakfasts are organic when possible. Allergy sufferers are welcome & the environment is kept as pollutant free as possible. Guests are respectfully requested not to use scented products. The owners are great animal & garden lovers. Hard tennis court.
E-mail: b&b@theelmsmoodie.co.uk

Mr & Mrs David Moodie   *The Elms*   *Olveston*   *Bristol BS35 4DR*   *Gloucestershire*
Tel: (01454) 614559   *Fax 01454 618607*   *Open: ALL YEAR*   *Map Ref No. 03*

£40.00 to £55.00 | Y | Y | N

see PHOTO over p. 162

Laverton Meadow House

Nearest Road: A.44

Laverton Meadows is a beautiful Cotswold house & stables set in 22 acres with stunning views & lovely gardens. Romantic rooms with canopied beds, antiques & spacious bathrooms make this luxury accommodation. Full English breakfast served in the farmhouse kitchen warmed by the Aga. Superb candlelit dinners are served in sumptuous private dining room. A log fire in the delightful sitting room offers you the perfect retreat.
E-mail: andrea@lavertonmeadows.demon.co.uk

Andrea Hazell   *Laverton Meadow House*   *Nr. Broadway WR12 7NA*   *Gloucestershire*
Tel: (01386) 584200   *Fax 01386 584612*   *Open: ALL YEAR*   *Map Ref No. 06*

£30.00 to £40.00 | N | N | N

(no smoking)

VISA: M'CARD: AMEX:

Georgian House

Nearest Road: A.40

Take 3 beautiful bedrooms in an elegant Georgian home, set them among the charming terraces of Montpellier, only 5 mins' from the Promenade, add a warm welcome from your hosts, Penny & Alex, & there you have Georgian House. Each en-suite room has T.V. with satellite, 'phone with modem socket, ironing facilities, trouser press & fridge. The delicious English breakfasts include fresh fruit - the perfect combination! Parking available.
E-mail: georgian_house@yahoo.com

Penny & Alex Gamez   *Georgian House*   *77 Montpellier Terrace*   *Cheltenham GL50 1XA*
Tel: (01242) 515577   Fax 01242 545929   Open: ALL YEAR (Excl. Xmas & New Year)   Map Ref No. 09

£25.00 to £30.00 | N | N | N

(no smoking)

VISA: M'CARD:

Cotteswold House

Nearest Road: A.40, A.429

Relax in this 400-year-old Cotswold-stone wealthy wool merchant's home with beamed ceilings, original panelling & Tudor archway. It offers the choice of a luxury private suite or en-suite double or twin rooms - all spacious, elegant & well-equipped. Enjoy traditional English food & a friendly welcome. Cotteswold House is in the centre of this ancient market town of Northleach in the centre of the Cotswolds - an ideal touring base.
E-mail: cotteswoldhouse@talk21.com

Pauline & Frank Powell   *Cotteswold House*   *Market Place   Northleach   Cheltenham   GL54 3EG*
Tel: (01451) 860493   Fax 01451 860493   Open: ALL YEAR (Excl. Xmas & New Year)   Map Ref No. 13

Laverton Meadow House. Broadway.

Rectory Farmhouse.   Lower Swell.

Gloucestershire

Rectory Farmhouse

Nearest Road: A.429

Rectory Farmhouse is an historic 17th-century traditional Cotswold farmhouse located in the quiet hamlet of Lower Swell, which lies 1 mile to the west of Stow-on-the-Wold. It is elegantly furnished throughout & boasts superb double bedrooms with luxury en-suite bathrooms, enjoying stunning views over open countryside. Chipping Campden & Bourton-on-the-Water are just a short drive away. Cheltenham, Oxford & Stratford-upon-Avon are all easily accessible. Children over 16.
E-mail: rectory.farmhouse@cw-warwick.co.uk

| £35.00 to £40.00 | N | N | N |

see PHOTO over
p. 163

Sybil Gisby   Rectory Farmhouse   Lower Swell   Nr. Stow-on-the-Wold   Cheltenham GL54 1LH
Tel: (01451) 832351   Open: ALL YEAR   Map Ref No. 10

Westward

Nearest Road: A.40

The Wilson families share this beautiful Grade II listed Georgian house on the scarp of the Cotswolds above Sudeley Castle, sitting within its own 600-acre estate with spectacular views to the Malverns. The heart of the Cotswolds is very close, with Broadway, Oxford & Stratford within easy reach. The Wilsons combine good food - Susie trained at Prue Leith's - with elegance & comfort in a relaxed family home. 3 delightful en-suite rooms available. Children over 12 & animals by arrangement.
E-mail: jimw@haldon.co.uk

| £35.00 to £42.50 | Y | Y | Y |

see PHOTO over
p. 165

VISA: M'CARD:

Jim & Susie Wilson   Westward   Sudeley   Winchcombe   Cheltenham GL54 5JB   Gloucestershire
Tel: (01242) 604372   Fax 01242 604640   Open: ALL YEAR (Excl. Xmas)   Map Ref No. 14

Ninevah Farm

Nearest Road: A.44

This fine Georgian farmhouse with flagstone floors, beams & antique furnishings, is set in large gardens surrounded by open countryside, close to Mickleton village. Comfortable bedrooms with en-suite/private bath/shower rooms, all have T.V. & tea/coffee tray. Ideally placed for Stratford-upon-Avon & the Cotswolds, Kiftsgate & Hidcote Gardens & other N. T. properties. Warwick Castle, Blenheim Palace, Sudeley Castle & the NEC (40 mins' drive). Children over 5. Single supplement.
E-mail: stay@ninevahfarm.co.uk

| £27.50 to £27.50 | Y | N | N |

VISA: M'CARD:

Alison & Michael Yardley   Ninevah Farm   Campden Road   Mickleton   Chipping Campden GL55 6PS
Tel: (01386) 438923   Open: ALL YEAR   Map Ref No. 15

Old Court

Nearest Road: A.417, A.419

Old Court welcomes you with its spaciousness & old world atmosphere. This former wool merchants mansion, with 4 en-suite guest rooms, lies in the heart of this historic Cotswold town. Cirencester has a fascinating museum of Roman antiquities, a celebrated church & excellent shopping & restaurants. Walkers enjoy the 3000 acre park which starts from the front door. Bath, Oxford & Stratford are all about an hours drive. Private parking is available for 4 cars.
E-mail: langton@cripps.f9.co.uk

| £35.00 to £35.00 | Y | N | Y |

VISA: M'CARD: AMEX:

Stephen & Anna Langton   Old Court   Coxwell Street   Cirencester GL7 2BQ   Gloucestershire
Tel: (01285) 653164   Fax 01285 642803   Open: ALL YEAR (Excl. Xmas)   Map Ref No. 16

Westward.   Sudeley.

Gloucestershire

	rate £ from - to	children taken	evening meals	animals taken

Lady Lamb Farm

Nearest Road: A.417

Lady Lamb Farm is a Cotswold-stone farmhouse, surrounded by countryside & situated less than a mile from the small market town of Fairford. 2 charming bedrooms, each with T.V. & tea/coffee facilities. (1 is en-suite.) Swimming pool & tennis court available. Set on the edge of the Cotswolds, Bath, Oxford & Cotswold towns & lovely gardens are within easy reach. Cotswold Water Park offers a wide range of watersports. Golf, riding & fishing nearby. Animals by arrangement.

E-mail: jekeyser1@aol.com

Rate	Children	Evening	Animals
£30.00 to £30.00	Y	N	Y

VISA: M'CARD:

Mrs J. Keyser   Lady Lamb Farm   Meysey Hampton   Cirencester GL7 5LH   Gloucestershire
Tel: (01285) 712206   Fax 01285 712206   Open: ALL YEAR   Map Ref No. 18

Winstone Glebe

Nearest Road: A.417

A small Georgian rectory overlooking a Saxon church in a Domesday-listed village, & enjoying spectacular rural views. Ideally situated for exploring Cotswold market towns, with their medieval churches, antique shops & rich local history. 3 charming rooms, with private/en-suite bathrooms. Being an Area of Outstanding Natural Beauty, there are well-signposted walks. The more energetic can borrow a bicycle & explore, or just enjoy warm hospitality & good food. Single supplement.

E-mail: sparsons@cableinet.co.uk

Rate	Children	Evening	Animals
£30.00 to £36.00	Y	Y	Y

see PHOTO over p. 167

VISA: M'CARD:

Shaun & Susanna Parsons   Winstone Glebe   Winstone   Cirencester GL7 7JU   Gloucestershire
Tel: (01285) 821451   Fax 01285 821451   Open: ALL YEAR (Excl. Xmas)   Map Ref No. 20

Evington Hill Farm

Nearest Road: A.38

Crown your Gloucestershire visit at this lovely 16th-century house. Take tea & homemade cake in the sunny conservatory, stay in the antique pine furnished bedrooms with their beautiful new spacious bathrooms. 1 has a 4-poster bed, all have T.V. & hostess tray. The old beamed sitting room with log burning fire is perfect for a relaxing drink. Set in 4 acres with ample parking. Licensed bar. Games room. Evening meals by arrangement. 2 holiday cottages available for extended stays.

Rate	Children	Evening	Animals
£30.00 to £37.00	Y	Y	N

Keith & Joyce Annis   Evington Hill Farm   Tewkesbury Road   The Leigh GL19 4AQ   Gloucestershire
Tel: (01242) 680255   Open: ALL YEAR   Map Ref No. 22

The Old Farm

Nearest Road: A.40, M.50

Treat yourself to a stay in this charming 16th-century farmhouse with its wealth of beams, fireplaces & character. Relax with afternoon tea infront of the fire or in the south-facing garden. Luxuriate in your well-equipped en-suite bedroom (one 4-poster.) Sumptuous English breakfasts made from local produce include free-range eggs. Ideal for visiting the Royal Forest of Dean, Wye Valley, Gloucester, Cheltenham & Ross-on-Wye. Choice of good pubs & restaurants. Children over 10.

E-mail: BBB@the-old-farm.co.uk

Rate	Children	Evening	Animals
£20.00 to £26.00	Y	N	Y

VISA: M'CARD:

Lucy Rodger   The Old Farm   Barrel Lane   Longhope GL17 0LR   Gloucestershire
Tel: (01452) 830252   Fax 01452 830255   Open: ALL YEAR   Map Ref No. 23

Winstone Glebe. Winstone.

Hunters Lodge. Minchinhampton.

Gloucestershire

rate £ from - to per person	children taken	evening meals taken	animals taken		

£23.00 to £28.50	Y	Y	Y		*Edale House*

Nearest Road: A.48

Edale House is a fine Georgian residence facing the cricket green in the village of Parkend at the heart of the Royal Forest of Dean. Once the home of local G.P. Bill Tandy, author of 'A Doctor in the Forest', the house has been tastefully restored to provide comfortable en-suite accommodation with every facility for guests. Enjoy delicious & imaginative cuisine prepared by your hosts. Fully licensed. Children over 12. Animals by arrangement.

VISA: M'CARD:

E-mail: edale@lineone.net

Alan & Christine Parkes   Edale House   Folly Road   Parkend   Lydney   GL15 4JF   Gloucestershire
Tel: (01594) 562835   Fax 01594 564488   Open: ALL YEAR (Excl. New Year)   Map Ref No. 24

£23.00 to £25.00	Y	N	N		*Hunters Lodge*

Nearest Road: A.46, B.419

A friendly and helpful welcome is assured for guests at this beautifully furnished Cotswold stone country house situated adjoining 600 acres of National Trust common land and a golf course. Central heating throughout. All bedrooms have T.V., tea/coffee-making facilities & en-suite/private bathrooms. A visitors' lounge, with colour T.V., adjoins a delightful conservatory overlooking a large garden. An ideal centre for Bath, Cheltenham, Cirencester & the Cotswolds. Peter is a registered tourist guide. Children over 10.

see PHOTO over p. 168

Margaret Helm   Hunters Lodge   Dr. Browns Road   Minchinhampton   GL6 9BT   Gloucestershire
Tel: (01453) 883588   Fax 01453 731449   Open: ALL YEAR (Excl. Xmas)   Map Ref No. 25

£25.00 to £40.00	Y	Y	Y		*Gunn Mill House*

Nearest Road: A.48

Bounded by its mill stream & the Royal Forest of Dean, the Andersons' Georgian home stands in 5 acres of gardens & meadows. Refurbished to a high standard, the galleried sitting room & 8 large en-suite bedrooms & suites (4-poster, doubles, twins, family) are filled with antiques & collectables from around the world. Share your hosts' love of good food, home-made breads & preserves. Vegetarians catered for. Liquor licence. Overseas visitors especially welcomed.

see PHOTO over p. 170

E-mail: info@gunnmillhouse.co.uk

VISA: M'CARD: AMEX:

David & Caroline Anderson   Gunn Mill House   Lower Spout Lane   Mitcheldean   GL17 0EA   Glos.
Tel: (01594) 827577   Fax 01594 827577   Open: ALL YEAR   Map Ref No. 27

£22.50 to £25.00	Y	N	N		*Treetops Guest House*

Nearest Road: A.44

A beautiful family home offering traditional bed & breakfast. There are 6 attractive bedrooms, all with a bathroom en-suite, & 2 of which are on the ground floor and thus suitable for disabled persons or wheelchair users. All rooms have T.V., radio and tea/coffee-making facilities. Cots and high chairs available. Delightful secluded gardens to relax in. Ideally situated for exploring the Cotswolds. A warm and homely atmosphere awaits you here.

E-mail: treetops1@talk21.com

VISA: M'CARD:

Mrs E. M. Dean   Treetops Guest House   London Road   Moreton-in-Marsh   GL56 0HE   Gloucestershire
Tel: (01608) 651036   Fax 01608 651036   Open: ALL YEAR   Map Ref No. 28

Gunn Mill House. Mitcheldean.

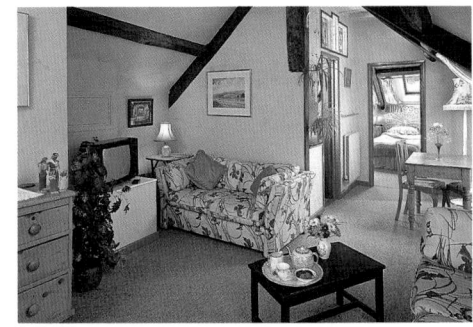

rate £ from - to per person	children taken	evening meals taken	animals taken		

The Fox Inn

£29.00 to £42.50	Y	Y	Y

VISA: M'CARD:

Nearest Road: A.436

The Fox Inn is set in one of the most idyllic Cotswold villages. This 16th-century Cotswold stone Inn with its flagstone floors, beams, fireplaces & antiques is perfect for a stay in a quintessential British pub. The pretty cottage garden has a covered terrace for summer eating "al fresco". The menu uses local produce. The 3 bedrooms are furnished with fine antiques & character beds. Good food, fine wines & well-kept beers make a visit to the award-winning Fox Inn essential.
E-mail: info@foxinn.net

Mr & Mrs Kirk Ritchie The Fox Inn Lower Oddington Moreton-in-Marsh LG56 0UR Gloucestershire
Tel: (01451) 870555 Fax 01451 870669 Open: ALL YEAR (Excl. Xmas & New Year) Map Ref No. 29

Cinderhill House

£31.00 to £45.00	Y	Y	N

see PHOTO over
p. 172

Nearest Road: A.466

A pretty, 14th-century house tucked into the hill below the castle in St. Briavels, with magnificent views across the Wye Valley to the Brecon Beacons & Black Mountains. A lovingly restored & tastefully furnished house with 4 beautiful bedrooms, all with king or queen-size beds & a private or en-suite bathroom. Gillie is a professional cook, & takes delight in ensuring that all meals are well cooked using local produce. Also, in the grounds is a romantic cottage hideaway. Licensed.
E-mail: cinderhill.house@virgin.net

Gillie Peacock   Cinderhill House   St. Briavels GL15 6RH   Gloucestershire
Tel: (01594) 530393   Fax 01594 530098   Open: ALL YEAR   Map Ref No. 30

South Hill Lodge

£25.00 to £30.00	N	N	N

Nearest Road: A.429

South Hill Lodge was built in 1880 as the gatelodge to the local manor, & is just 4 minutes level walk from Stow centre with its restaurants, cafes, art & antique galleries. There is ample private parking & the garden enjoys wonderful views over the surrounding Cotswold Hills. Elegantly furnished & decorated & serving superb full English breakfasts, South Hill Lodge is a relaxing base for touring this Area of Outstanding Natural Beauty.
E-mail: digby@southilllodge.freeserve.co.uk

Linda & Barry Digby   South Hill Lodge   Fosseway Stow-on-the-Wold GL54 1JU   Gloucestershire
Tel: (01451) 831083   Open: ALL YEAR   Map Ref No. 31

The Firs

£25.00 to £27.50	Y	N	N

Nearest Road: A.46

The Firs is set in a quiet village location. A fine Georgian house with many period features & panoramic views over the Cotswold escarpment. Within walking distance of several pubs & restaurants. Ideally situated for exploring the north Cotswolds, Bath, Cheltenham, Westonbirt Arboretum, Gatcomb, Badminton, Cirencester, Gloucester Docks & Bristol. 2 attractive en-suite rooms. Your hosts put great emphasis on guest comfort & strive to make each guest's stay memorable.
E-mail: CWalsh3088@aol.com

Carol & Gerry Walsh   The Firs   Selsley Road   Woodchester   Stroud GL5 5NQ   Gloucestershire
Tel: (01453) 873088   Fax 01453 873053   Open: ALL YEAR (Excl. Xmas)   Map Ref No. 32

Cinderhill House. St. Briavels.

rate £ from - to per person	children taken	evening meals taken	animals taken

---

£22.00 to £22.00

🚭 (No smoking)

Y	Y	N

Pretoria Villa

Nearest Road: A.419

Enjoy luxurious bed & breakfast in a relaxed family country house set in peaceful secluded gardens. Spacious bedrooms, with en-suite/private facilities. Hospitality trays, hairdryers & bathrobes in all rooms. Guests have their own comfortable lounge & delicious breakfasts are served in the dining room. Evening meals by prior arrangement, although many good eating places nearby. An excellent base from which to explore the Cotswolds. Personal service & your comfort is guaranteed.
E-mail: glynis@gsolomon.freeserve.co.uk

Glynis Solomon   Pretoria Villa   Wells Road   Eastcombe   Stroud GL6 7EE   Gloucestershire
Tel: (01452) 770435   Fax 01452 770435   Open: ALL YEAR (Excl. Xmas)   Map Ref No. 33

£25.00 to £30.00

🚭 (No smoking)

see PHOTO over p. 174

Y	N	N

Hope Cottage

Nearest Road: A.46, A.419

For peace & tranquillity, this charming, undiscovered village 10 miles from Cirencester is unrivalled. Box is in an Area of Outstanding Natural Beauty enjoying glorious Cotswold views. Here, you can savour the charm of this delightful country house, set in 3 acres of landscaped gardens & with a heated pool. Lovely en-suite rooms all with king-size bed, settee, T.V. & hospitality tray. Sumptuous English breakfasts. Good local restaurants & pubs. Strategic base for walking & touring.
E-mail: garth.brunsdon@virgin.net

Sheila & Garth Brunsdon   Hope Cottage   Box   Nr. Stroud GL6 9HD   Gloucestershire
Tel: (01453) 832076   Open: FEB - NOV   Map Ref No. 34

£25.00 to £25.00

N	N	N

The Old Rectory

Nearest Road: A.433

The Old Rectory (Grade II listed) is a charming home, where a happy & relaxed atmosphere prevails. The friendly hosts offer very comfortable accommodation in 2 attractively furnished bedrooms, each with an en-suite/private bathroom & T.V.. Also, a cosy lounge with T.V. & a pretty garden in which guests may choose to relax. A delicious breakfast is served. The Old Rectory is an ideal base from which to explore this beautiful region & its many attractions.

Mrs Marie-Teresa Sayers   The Old Rectory   Didmarton   Tetbury GL9 1DS   Gloucestershire
Tel: (01454) 238233   Fax 01454 238909   Open: ALL YEAR (Excl. Xmas)   Map Ref No. 35

£35.00 to £40.00

VISA: M'CARD: AMEX:

Y	Y	N

Wesley House

Nearest Road: A.438

Wesley House is a delightful medieval half-timbered house dating from c.1435. John Wesley, the Methodist, is believed to have stayed here in 1779. 5 cosy, individually designed en-suite bedrooms. An elegant lounge with log fire which conveys a sense of old world intimacy. Head Chef, Alex Breach, has acquired an excellent reputation for fine cuisine at Wesley House. A perfect spot from which to explore the Cotswolds; Cheltenham, Oxford & Stratford are also within easy reach by car.
E-mail: enquiries@wesleyhouse.co.uk

Matthew Brown   Wesley House   High Street   Winchcombe GL54 5LJ   Gloucestershire
Tel: (01242) 602366   Fax 01242 609046   Open: ALL YEAR   Map Ref No. 36

Hope Cottage. Box.

Hampshire & Isle of Wight

Hampshire (Southern)

Hampshire is located in the centre of the south coast of England & is blessed with much beautiful & unspoilt countryside. Wide open vistas of rich downland contrast with deep woodlands. Rivers & sparkling streams run through tranquil valleys passing nestling villages. There is a splendid coastline with seaside resorts & harbours, the cathedral city of Winchester & the "jewel" of Hampshire, the Isle of Wight.

The north of the county is known as the Hampshire Borders. Part of this countryside was immortalised by Richard Adams & the rabbits of 'Watership Down'. Beacon Hill is a notable hill-top landmark. From its slopes some of the earliest aeroplane flights were made by De Haviland in 1909. Pleasure trips & tow-path walks can be taken along the restored Basingstoke Canal.

The New Forest is probably the area most frequented by visitors. It is a landscape of great character with thatched cottages, glades & streams & a romantic beauty. There are herds of deer & the New Forest ponies wander at will. To the N.W. of Beaulieu are some of the most idyllic parts of the old forest, with fewer villages & many little streams that flow into the Avon. Lyndhurst, the "capital" of the New Forest offers a range of shops & has a contentious 19th century church constructed in scarlet brickwork banded with yellow, unusual ornamental decoration, & stained glass windows by William Morris.

The Roman city of Winchester became the capital city of Saxon Wessex & is today the capital of Hampshire. It is famous for its beautiful mediaeval cathedral, built during the reign of William the Conquerer & his notorious son Rufus. It contains the great Winchester Bible.

William completed the famous Domesday Book in the city, & Richard Coeur de Lion was crowned in the cathedral in 1194.

Portsmouth & Southampton are major ports & historic maritime cities with a wealth of castles, forts & Naval attractions from battleships to museums.

The channel of the Solent guarded by Martello towers, holds not only Southampton but numerous yachting centres, such as Hamble, Lymington & Bucklers Hard where the ships for Admiral Lord Nelson's fleet were built.

The River Test.

The Isle of Wight

The Isle of Wight lies across the sheltered waters of the Solent, & is easily reached by car or passenger ferry. The chalk stacks of the Needles & the multi-coloured sand at Alum Bay are among the best known of the island's natural attractions & there are many excellent beaches & other bays to enjoy. Cowes is a famous international sailing centre with a large number of yachting events throughout the summer. Ventnor, the most southerly resort is known as the "Madeira of England" & has an exotic botanic garden. Inland is an excellent network of footpaths & trails & many castles, manors & stately homes.

May Cottage. Thruxton.

rate £ from - to per person	children taken	evening meals	animals taken

---

| £25.00 to £35.00 | Y | Y | N |

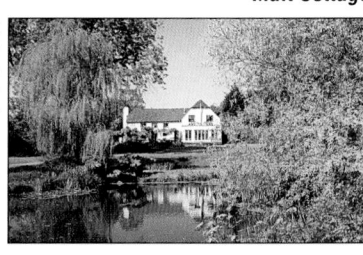

Malt Cottage

Nearest Road: A.303

Walk around the beautiful 6-acre garden with chalk stream & lakes, or sit by the fire in the charming beamed sitting room. Malt Cottage, an ideal stop en-route from London Heathrow to the West Country, is situated in a picturesque village with many thatched cottages & offers 3 attractively furnished bedrooms with en-suite/private facilities. During the summer, evening barbecues are held. Places to visit include Stonehenge, Salisbury & Winchester. Fly fishing & airport collection can be arranged.
E-mail: info@maltcottage.co.uk

see PHOTO over
p. 180

| Richard & Patricia Mason | Malt Cottage | Upper Clatford | Andover SP11 7QL | Hampshire |
| Tel: (01264) 323469 | Fax 01264 334100 | Open: ALL YEAR (Excl. Xmas) | Map Ref No. 02 |

| £30.00 to £35.00 | Y | N | N |

VISA: M'CARD:

Broadwater

Nearest Road: A.303

Broadwater is a 17th-century, listed, thatched cottage situated in a peaceful unspoilt village just off the A.303. It is an ideal base for sightseeing in Hampshire, with easy access to the West Country & London. The cottage offers 2 delightful, double/ twin-bedded rooms, both with en-suite facilities. Guests have a private & very comfortable sitting/ dining room with a traditional open log fire & a very pretty garden to enjoy. Homemade bread. T.V..
E-mail: carolyn@dmac.co.uk

| Mrs Carolyn Mallam | Broadwater | Amport | Andover SP11 8AY | Hampshire |
| Tel: (01264) 772240 | Fax 01264 772240 | Open: ALL YEAR | Map Ref No. 03 |

| £25.00 to £25.00 | Y | Y | Y |

VISA: M'CARD:

Gunville House

Nearest Road: A.303

Gunville House is a charming thatched, beamed family house, dating from the 18th-century in a secluded, rural situation, 5 mins from the A.303. The house offers 1 twin bedroom & 1 single, both with en-suite bath & shower, colour T.V. & tea trays. Ideally situated for Salisbury, Winchester, Stonehenge, Marlborough & many famous Hampshire/Wiltshire attractions. Fly fishing, golf, clay pigeon shooting can all be arranged locally. Good pub within easy walking distance.
E-mail: pct@onetel.net.uk

| Mrs Sarah Chetwynd-Talbot | Gunville House | Grateley | Andover SP11 8JQ | Hampshire |
| Tel: (01264) 889206 | Fax 01264 889060 | Open: ALL YEAR | Map Ref No. 04 |

| £25.00 to £35.00 | Y | N | N |

May Cottage

Nearest Road: A.303

May Cottage dates back to 1740 & is situated in the heart of this picturesque tranquil village with Post Office & old inn. A most comfortable home with 2 doubles & 1 twin room with en-suite/private bathrooms, 1 on the ground floor. All with colour T.V. & tea trays. Guests' own sitting/dining room with T.V.. An ideal base for visiting ancient cities, stately homes & gardens, yet within easy reach of ports & airports. Excellent home-cooking & dinner by prior arrangement. Parking. Children over 6. (Hosts can be contacted on mobile 07768 242166).

see PHOTO over
p. 178

| Tom & Fiona Biddolph | May Cottage | Thruxton | Andover SP11 8LZ | Hampshire |
| Tel: (01264) 771241 | Fax 01264 771770 | Open: ALL YEAR (Excl. Xmas) | Map Ref No. 05 |

Malt Cottage. Upper Clatford.

Land of Nod. Headley.

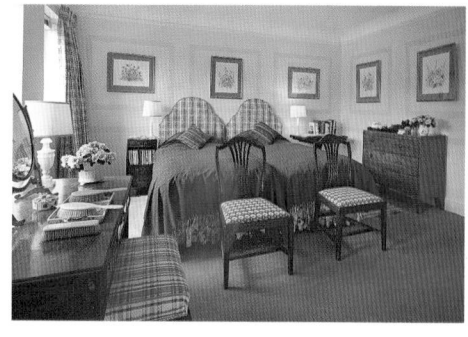

	rate £ from - to per person	evening meals children taken	animals taken

Land of Nod

Nearest Road: A.3

A large neo-Georgian house set in 7 acres of garden in the centre of 100 acres of a private woodland estate. This attractive home has 2 twin-bedded rooms with private or en-suite bathroom, T.V. & tea/coffee-making facilities. Situated just 1 hour from London, Heathrow, Gatwick & Portsmouth, & within easy reach of many fine gardens & historic houses in the south of England, the Land of Nod is the perfect spot for a relaxing break. A car, though, is essential for maximum enjoyment. Evening meals by arrangement. Children over 12.

£30.00 to £30.00 — Y Y N

see PHOTO over p. 181

Jeremy & Philippa Whitaker   Land of Nod   Headley   Bordon GU35 8SJ   Hampshire
Tel: (01428) 713609   Fax 01428 717698   Open: ALL YEAR (Excl. Xmas Day)   Map Ref No. 06

Tothill House

Nearest Road: A.35

An Edwardian country house set in 12 acres of woodland. An Area of Outstanding Natural Beauty noted for its flora & fauna. 5 mins' from Burley village, a popular New Forest tourist attraction. Offering good food & 3 attractive rooms, 2 with en-suite facilities & 1 with a private bathroom. Each individually decorated, with T.V. & tea-making facilities. Very secluded, with peace & tranquillity. Local sporting & recreational activities, & a variety of places to visit. The perfect spot for a relaxing break. Children over 16.

£30.00 to £35.00 — N N N

Mrs Wendy Buckley   Tothill House   Black Lane   Thorney Hill   Burley   Christchurch BH23 8DZ
Tel: (01425) 674414   Fax 01425 672235   Open: FEB - NOV   Map Ref No. 08

Merry Hall Hotel

Nearest Road: A.259

Situated in a delightful fishing village mid-way between Chichester & Portsmouth. A modern hotel with a cosy relaxed atmosphere. All of the bedrooms are non-smoking & have T.V. & tea/coffee facilities & most are en-suite with a view of the pretty garden & fields beyond. Goodwood House, H.M.S. Victory & the Mary Rose are closeby, with easy access to the Isle of Wight & the Continental ferries. Highly acclaimed restaurants & excellent village pubs. Animals by arrangement.
E-mail: merryhall@ltwine.fsnet.co.uk

£22.50 to £35.00 — Y N Y

VISA: M'CARD:

Mrs Marx   Merry Hall Hotel   73 Horndean Road   Emsworth PO10 7PU   Hampshire
Tel: (01243) 431377   Fax 01243 431411   Open: ALL YEAR   Map Ref No. 09

Rudge House

Nearest Road: A.287, A.3

Elegant, spacious family home, dating from the 1850s, featuring a 4-acre garden with tennis court & croquet lawn. Edging an historic village, the house is quiet & secluded, bordering farmland, yet within 45 mins' of Heathrow, Gatwick & London. Windsor, Ascot, Winchester & Oxford highly accessible. Extremely comfortable accommodation, offering en-suite/private facilities & pump showers, plus T.V. lounge & tea/coffee. Evening meal & packed lunches by arrangement. Children over 12.

£33.00 to £39.00 — Y N N

see PHOTO over p. 183

Mr & Mrs Nigel Tose   Rudge House   Itchel Lane   Crondall   Farnham GU10 5PR   Hampshire
Tel: (01252) 850450   Fax 01252 850829   Open: ALL YEAR (Excl. Xmas)   Map Ref No. 10

Rudge House. Crondall.

Hampshire

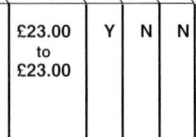
Cottage Crest

Nearest Road: A.338

Woodgreen is a typical New Forest village, with cottages surrounded by thick hedges to keep out the cattle & ponies. Cottage Crest is a Victorian drover's cottage set high in its own 4 acres, & enjoying superb views of the River Avon & valley below. The guest bedrooms are spacious & attractively decorated to a very high standard. All have an en-suite bathroom/shower & W.C.. Children over 8 yrs welcome. Cottage Crest is an ideal base from which to explore Hampshire.

| £23.00 to £23.00 | Y | N | N |

Mrs G. Cadman   Cottage Crest   Castle Hill   Woodgreen   Fordingbridge SP6 2AX   Hampshire
Tel: (01725) 512009   Open: ALL YEAR   Map Ref No. 11

Hendley House

Nearest Road: A.338, A.354

Overlooking water meadows, a beautiful, south-facing, 16th-century house with a wealth of beams, elegantly decorated & a relaxed family atmosphere. So much to visit & do in surrounding countryside & south coast. Walking & cycling in New Forest, returning to relax by log fires in winter or swimming pool in spacious garden in summer. Riding, fishing, golf & racing nearby. Discounts for 3 nights or more. 2 charming bedrooms with en-suite shower or private bathroom. Children over 12.

| £25.00 to £30.00 | Y | N | N |

Mrs P. A. Ratcliffe   Hendley House   Rockbourne   Fordingbridge SP6 3NA   Hampshire
Tel: (01725) 518303   Fax 01725 518546   Open: APR - OCT   Map Ref No. 12

Under Rock Country House B & B

Nearest Road: A.3055

Historical Georgian house set in large secluded gardens near Horseshoe Bay & southern coastal paths, with isolated coves, narrow ravines or chines, soaring cliffs & high chalk downland, & country walks. There are 3 bedrooms - single/double, double & twin. T.V., tea/coffee trays. Most have their own bath/shower & W.C.. A guest lounge & terrace, a peaceful, relaxed setting. Picturesque Bonchurch village has literary associations including Thackeray, Dickens & Swinburne.
E-mail: enquiries@under-rock.co.uk

| £22.00 to £26.00 | N | N | N |

J. Pritchett Under Rock Country House B & B   Shore Rd Bonchurch   Ventnor Isle of Wight PO38 1RF
Tel: (01983) 855274   Open: FEB - NOV   Map Ref No. 14

Briantcroft

Nearest Road: A.337

Enjoy the grace & elegance of this Edwardian house with its spacious & luxurious rooms. Set in peaceful surroundings, at the edge of the New Forest, Briantcroft is 10 mins' walk to the beach. The 3 large bedroom suites are individually themed, with en-suite/private facilities, T.V. 3-seater sofas & a refreshment tray. Breakfast is a gourmet experience with traditional & other tempting choices using fresh & local produce. Full colour brochure/ menu on request. Children over 12.
E-mail: florence.iles@lineone.net

| £30.00 to £35.00 | Y | N | N |

Florence Iles   Briantcroft   George Road   Milford-on-Sea   Lymington SO41 0RS   Hampshire
Tel: (01590) 644355   Fax 01590 644355   Open: ALL YEAR   Map Ref No. 15

rate £ from - to per person	children taken	evening meals taken	animals taken

---

| £50.00 to £50.00 | Y | Y | Y |

(non-smoking) VISA: M'CARD: AMEX:

The Nurse's Cottage

Nearest Road: A.337, A.35

The former tiny cottage home of Sway's District Nurses has been lovingly refurbished by Tony Barnfield & is now one of the New Forest's premier properties. The en-suite bedrooms, situated on the ground floor, feature T.V./video, cd player, refrigerator, 'phone, & many little extras. The award-winning restaurant (open to the public) offers a seasonally changing dinner menu, with over 60 wines. Ideal touring centre, with reduced half-board rates for 2+ nights. Children over 10.
E-mail: nurses.cottage@lineone.net

R. A. Barnfield   The Nurse's Cottage   Station Road   Sway   Lymington SO41 6BA   Hampshire
Tel: (01590) 683402   Fax 01590 683402   Open: ALL YEAR   Map Ref No. 16

| £35.00 to £40.00 | N | N | N |

(non-smoking)

Wheatsheaf House

Nearest Road: A.337

A beautifully appointed early 17th-century former tavern, Wheatsheaf House is close to the centre of this charming Georgian market town, & only 3 mins' walk from the historic town quay. Offering 2 large, comfortable, en-suite rooms with tea/coffee facilities & there is an attractive drawing room with T.V.. The house is ideally placed for sailing, the New Forest & for touring the whole region, with many restaurants within walking distance. (Reductions for longer stays.) Dogs by arrangement.
E-mail: wheatsheaf@cutmore.com

Peter & Jennifer Cutmore   Wheatsheaf House   Gosport Street   Lymington SO41 9BG   Hampshire
Tel: (01590) 679208   Open: MAR - DEC (Excl. Xmas)   Map Ref No. 17

| £25.00 to £50.00 | Y | Y | Y |

see PHOTO over p. 186

VISA: M'CARD: AMEX:

Ormonde House Hotel

Nearest Road: A.35

Ormonde House is set back from the main road opposite the open forest; easy for an early morning walk. Lyndhurst village is just 5 mins' walk & Exbury Gardens & the National Motor Museum, Beaulieu 20 mins' drive. The popular licensed restaurant offers freshly prepared dishes. Accommodation is in 19 pretty en-suite bedrooms, all with satellite T.V., 'phone & tea-making facilities. Delightful rooms with huge king-size beds & whirlpool baths for that special treat.
E-mail: info@ormondehouse.co.uk

Mr. Paul Ames   Ormonde House Hotel   Southampton Road   Lyndhurst SO43 7BT   Hampshire
Tel: (023) 8028 2806   Fax 023 8028 2004   Open: ALL YEAR (Excl. Xmas)   Map Ref No. 18

| £27.50 to £30.00 | Y | N | Y |

(non-smoking)

Holmans

Nearest Road: A.35, A.31

Holmans is a charming country house in the heart of the New Forest, set in 4 acres with stabling available for guests' own horses. Superb walking, horse riding & carriage driving, with a golf course nearby. A warm, friendly welcome is assured at this elegant home, which is ideal for a relaxing break. All bedrooms are tastefully furnished & en-suite with tea/coffee-making facilities, radio & hairdryers. Colour T.V. in guests' lounge with adjoining orangery & log fires in winter.

Robin & Mary Ford   Holmans   Bisterne Close   Burley   New Forest BH24 4AZ   Hampshire
Tel: (01425) 402307   Fax 01425 402307   Open: ALL YEAR (Excl. Xmas)   Map Ref No. 21

Ormonde House Hotel. Lyndhurst.

rate £ from - to per person	children taken	evening meals taken	animals taken

Trotton Farm

£20.00 to £30.00 — Y N Y

Nearest Road: A.272

This charming home, set in 200 acres of farmland, offers comfortable accommodation in 2 twin-bedded rooms & 1 double-bedded room each with en-suite shower & modern amenities, including tea/coffee-making facilities. A residents' lounge is available throughout the day. Games room & pretty garden for guests' relaxation. Ideally situated for visiting many local, historical & sporting attractions, & only 1 hour from Gatwick & Heathrow Airports. Single supplement.

E-mail: baigentfarms@farmsweekly.net

Mrs J. E. Baigent   Trotton Farm   Trotton   Petersfield GU31 5EN   Hampshire
Tel: (01730) 813618   Fax 01730 816093   Open: ALL YEAR   Map Ref No. 22

Crofton Country Accommodation

£22.50 to £25.00 — Y N N

VISA: M'CARD:

Nearest Road: A.27

Nestling in 2 acres of garden, including a vineyard, Crofton offers quality accommodation within the tranquil setting of a small hamlet in the beautiful Test Valley. A large family room & a twin room, both tastefully decorated & each with tea/coffee-making facilities, T.V., hairdryer, trouser press & toiletries. Delicious breakfasts are served in the Breakfast Hall & a small conservatory is also available for guests' use. Located just 4 miles north of Romsey making Salisbury, Winchester, New Forest & the south coast resorts very accessible.

Mrs Pauline Lightfoot Crofton Country Accommodation Kents Oak Awbridge Romsey SO51 0HH
Tel: (01794) 340333 Fax 01794 340333 Open: ALL YEAR (Excl. Xmas & New Year) Map Ref No. 23

Ranvilles Farm House

£25.00 to £27.50 — Y N Y

Nearest Road: A.3090

Ranvilles Farm House dates from the 13th century when Richard De Ranville came from Normandy & settled with his family. Now this Grade II listed house provides a peaceful setting surrounded by 5 acres of gardens & paddock. All rooms, with extra large beds, are attractively decorated & furnished with antiques, & each room has its own en-suite bathroom/shower room. Only 3 miles from the New Forest & just over a mile from Romsey, a small town equidistant from the 2 cathedral cities of Winchester & Salisbury. Single supplement.

Bill & Anthea Hughes   Ranvilles Farm House   Romsey SO51 6AA   Hampshire
Tel: (02380) 814481   Fax 02380 814481   Open: ALL YEAR   Map Ref No. 24

Montrose

£23.00 to £26.00 — N N N

VISA: M'CARD:

Nearest Road: A.32

Montrose offers accommodation of a high standard in tasteful surroundings. There are 3 delightful bedrooms, 1 is en-suite. Comfort & personal attention has helped to build a superb reputation. Situated in the Meon Valley between the historical villages of Wickham & Bishops Waltham, & yet close to the M.27, M.3 & continental ferry ports, thus providing an ideal base for exploring the towns of Winchester, Portsmouth & Southampton, & the lovely Hampshire countryside & coastline.

E-mail: bb@montrose78.fsnet.co.uk

Mrs Y. Chivers Montrose Solomons Lane Shirrell Heath Nr. Southampton SO32 2HU Hampshire
Tel: (01329) 833345   Fax 01329 833345   Open: ALL YEAR   Map Ref No. 26

Hampshire

	rate £ from - to per person	evening meals children taken	animals taken

Church Farm

Nearest Road: A.303, A.30

Church Farm is a 15th-century tithe barn with Georgian & modern additions. It features an adjacent coach house & groom's cottage, recently converted, where guests may be totally self-contained, or be welcomed to the log-fired family drawing room & dine on locally produced fresh food. There are 6 beautiful bedrooms for guests, all with a private bathroom, T.V. & tea/coffee-making facilities. Horses are kept. Swimming pool & croquet. Tennis court adjacent.

£22.00 to £40.00   Y Y Y

VISA: M'CARD:

James & Jean Talbot   *Church Farm*   *Barton Stacey*   *Winchester SO21 3RR*   *Hampshire*
Tel: (01962) 760268   *Fax 01962 761825*   *Open: ALL YEAR*   *Map Ref No. 27*

Moortown Farm

Nearest Road: A.32

A friendly atmosphere is found at Moortown in the heart of the Meon Valley, an Area of Outstanding Natural Beauty, crossed by both the Wayfayers Walk & Southdowns Way. There is 1 twin en-suite & 1 four-bedded room, with a private bathroom each with T.V. & tea-making facilities. Situated in a peaceful village within easy reach of Winchester, home of King Arthur's Round Table, Portsmouth with the Mary Rose & Nelson's Flagship, the New Forest & Southampton. Good places to eat nearby.
E-mail: rosemarytaylor@lineone.net

£25.00 to £30.00   N N N

Dick & Rosemary Taylor   *Moortown Farm*   *Station Road*   *Soberton*   *Winchester SO32 3QU*
Tel: (01489) 877256   *Fax 01489 877256*   *Open: ALL YEAR*   *Map Ref No. 28*

All the establishments mentioned in this guide are members of
The Worldwide Bed & Breakfast Association

When booking your accommodation please mention
The Best Bed & Breakfast

Hereford & Worcester

Hereford & Worcester
(Heart of England)

Hereford is a beautiful ancient city standing on the banks of the River Wye, almost a crossing point between England & Wales. It is a market centre for the Marches, the border area which has a very particular history of its own.

Hereford Cathedral has a massive sandstone tower & is a fitting venue for the Three Choirs festival which dates from 1727, taking place yearly in one or the other of the three great cathedrals of Hereford, Worcester & Gloucester.

The county is fortunate in having many well preserved historic buildings. Charming "black & white" villages abound here, romantically set in a soft green landscape.

The Royal Forest of Dean spreads its oak & beech trees over 22,000 acres. When people first made their homes in the woodlands it was vaster still. There are rich deposits of coal & iron mined for centuries by the foresters, & the trees have always been felled for charcoal. Ancient courts still exist where forest dwellers can & do claim their rights to use the forest's resources.

The landscape alters dramatically as the land rises to merge with the great Black Mountain range at heights of over 2,600 feet. It is not possible to take cars everywhere but a narrow mountain road, Gospel Pass, takes traffic from Hay-on-Wye to Llanthony with superb views of the upper Wye Valley.

The Pre-Cambrian Malvern Hills form a natural boundary between Herefordshire & Worcestershire & from the highest view points you can see over 14 counties. At their feet nestle pretty little villages such as Eastonor with its 19th century castle in revived Norman style that looks quite mediaeval amongst the parklands & gardens.

There are, in fact, five Malverns. The largest predictably known as Great Malvern was a fashionable 19th century spa & is noted for the purity of the water which is bottled & sold countrywide.

The Priory at Malvern is rich in 15th century stained glass & has a fine collection of mediaeval tiles made locally. William Langland, the 14th century author of "Piers Ploughman", was educated at the Priory & is said to have been sleeping on the Malvern Hills when he had the visionary experience which led to the creation of the poem. Sir Edward Elgar was born, lived & worked here & his "Dream of Gerontius" had its first performance in Hereford Cathedral in 1902.

In Worcestershire another glorious cathedral, with what remains of its monastic buildings, founded in the 11th century, stands beside the River Severn. College Close in Worcester is a lovely group of buildings carefully preserved & very English in character.

The Severn appears to be a very lazy waterway but flood waters can reach astonshing heights, & the "Severn Bore" is a famous phenomenon.

A cruise along the river is a pleasant way to spend a day seeing villages & churches from a different perspective, possibly visiting a riverside inn. To the south of the county lie the undulating Vales of Evesham & Broadway - described as the show village of England.

The Malvern Hills.

Hereford & Worcester

Hereford & Worcester Gazeteer

Areas of outstanding natural beauty.
The Malvern Hills, The Cotswolds, The Wye Valley.

Historic Houses & Castles

Berrington Hall - Leominster
18th century - painted & plastered ceilings. Landscape by Capability Brown.

Brilley - Cwmmau Farmhouse - Whitney-on-Wye
17th century timber-framed & stone tiled farmhouse.

Burton Court - Eardisland
14th century great hall. Exhibition of European & Oriental costume & curios. Model fairground.

Croft Castle - Nr. Leominster
Castle on the Welsh border - inhabited by Croft family for 900 years.

Dinmore Manor - Nr. Hereford
14th century chapel & cloister.

Eastnor Castle - Nr. Ledbury
19th century - Castellated, containing pictures & armour. Arboretum.

Eye Manor - Leominster
17th century Carolean Manor house - excellent plasterwork, paintings, costumes, books, secret passage. Collection of dolls.

Hanbury Hall - Nr. Droitwich
18th century red brick house - only two rooms & painted ceilings on exhibition.

Harvington Hall - Kidderminster
Tudor Manor house with moat, priest's hiding places.

The Greyfriars - Worcester
15th century timber-framed building adjoins Franciscan Priory.

Hellen's - Much Marcle
13th century manorial house of brick & stone. Contains the Great hall with stone table - bedroom of Queen Mary. Much of the original furnishings remain.

Kentchurch Court - Hereford
14th century fortified border Manor house. Paintings & Carvings by Grinling Gibbons.

Moccas Court - Moccas
18th century - designed by Adam - Parklands by Capability Brown - under restoration.

Pembridge Castle - Welsh Newton
17th century moated castle.

Sutton Court - Mordiford
Palladian mansion by Wyatt, watercolours, embroideries, china.

Cathedrals & Churches

Amestry (St. John the Baptist & St.Alkmund)
16th century rood screen.

Abbey Dore (St. Mary & Holy Trinity)
17th century glass & great oak screen - early English architecture.

Brinsop (St. George)
14th century, screen & glass, alabaster reredos, windows in memory of Wordsworth, carved Norman tympanum.

Bredon (St. Giles)
12th century - central tower & spire. Mediaeval heraldic tiles, tombs & early glass.

Brockhampton (St. Eadburgh)
1902. Central tower & thatched roof.

Castle Frome (St. Michael & All Angles)
12th century carved font, 17th century effigies in alabaster.

Chaddesley Corbett (St. Cassian)
14th century monuments, 12th century font.

Elmley (St. Mary)
12th century & 15th century font, tower, gargoyles, mediaeval.

Great Witley (St. Michael)
Baroque - Plasterwork, painted ceiling, painted glass, very fine example.

Hereford (All Saints)
13th-14th centuries, spire, splendid choir stalls, chained library.

Hereford Cathedral
Small cathedral.
Fine central tower c.1325, splendid porch, brasses, early English Lady Chapel with lancet windows. Red sandstone.

Kilpeck (St. Mary & St. David)
Romanesque style - mediaeval windows - fine carvings.

Leominster (St. Peter & St. Paul)
12th century doorway, fine Norman arches, decorated windows.

Much Marcle (St. Bartholomew)
13th century. 14th & 17th century monuments.

Hereford & Worcester

Worcester Cathedral
11th -16th centry. Fine cloisters & crypt.
Tomb of King John
Worcester (St. Swithun)
18th century - furnishings untouched.
Ceiling vaulted in plaster.

Museums& Galleries

Hereford City Museum & Art Gallery
Collections of natural history & archeology,
costumes, textiles embroideries, toys,
agricultural l bygones.
Paintings by local artists, examples of
applied art, silver, pottery & porcelain.
The Old House - Hereford
Jacobean period museum with furnishings
of time.
Churchill Gardens Museum -   Hereford
Extensive costume collection, fine
furniture, work by local artists.
Almonry Museum - Evesham
Anglo-British. Roman-British, mediaeval -
monastic remains.

Avoncroft Museum of Buildings -
Stoke Heath.
Open air museum showing buildings of
reconstructed iron-age dwellings to 15th
century merchants homes.
City Museum & Art Gallery
Local History, archaeology, natural history,
environmental studies.
Dyson Perins Museums of Worcester
Porcelain - Worcester
Most comprehensive collection of old
Worcester in the world.
The Commandery   - Sidbury
15th century timber-framed building, was
originally a hospital. Royalist H.Q. during
battle of Worcester 1651.

Other things to see & do

Three choirs Festival - an annual event,
held in the cathedrals of Hereford,
Worcester & Gloucestershire, alternately.

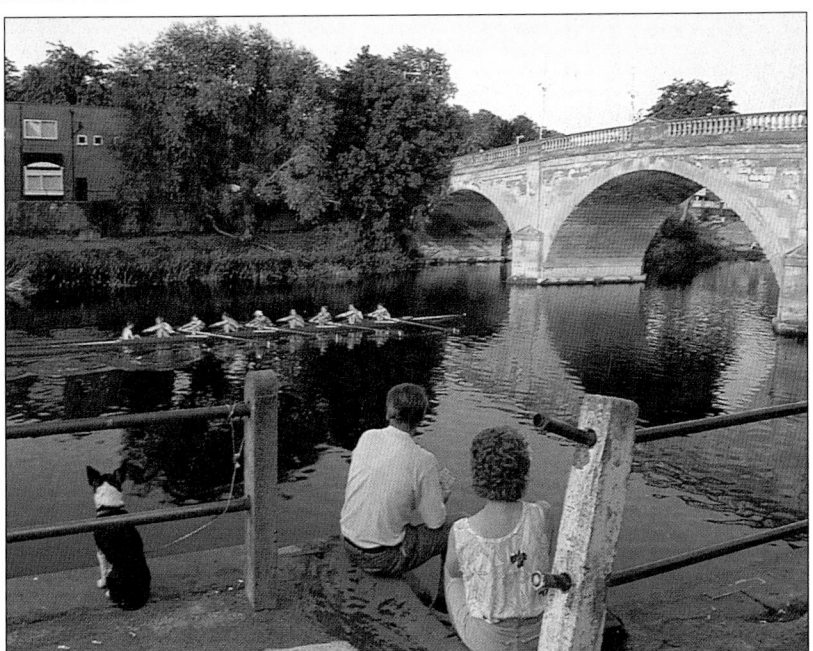

The River Severn at Bewdley.

HEREFORD & WORCESTER

Map reference

02 Bengry
03 Lee
04 Watson
07 Conolly
08 Fothergill
10 Robertson
12 Kemp
14 Beach
15 Stringer
16 Williams

192

rate £ from - to per person	children taken	evening meals taken	animals taken

| £25.00 to £35.00 | N | Y | N |

The Vauld Farm

Nearest Road: A.49, A.417

The Vauld Farm is a delightful 16th-century black-&-white former farmhouse, set in a beautiful garden. It retains many period features throughout & affords attractive accommodation. There are 4 charming & elegantly furnished bedrooms, each with an en-suite bathroom, T.V. & tea/coffee-making facilities. (1 with 4-poster.) Hearty breakfasts & delicious evening meals are served in the tastefully decorated dining room. A beautiful home & the perfect location for a relaxing break.

Mr & Mrs J. Bengry   The Vauld Farm   The Vauld   Marden   Hereford HR1 3HA   Herefordshire
Tel: (01568) 797898   Open: ALL YEAR   Map Ref No. 02

| £18.00 to £19.00 | Y | N | N |

Cwm Craig Farm

Nearest Road: A.49

Spacious Georgian farmhouse, surrounded by superb unspoilt countryside. Situated between the cathedral city of Hereford & Ross-on-Wye, & just a few mins' drive from the Wye Valley. An ideal base for touring the Forest of Dean. All 3 bedrooms are comfortably furnished & have modern amenities, shaver points, tea/coffee-making facilities & an en-suite bathroom. There is a lounge & separated dining room, both with colour T.V.. A delicious full English breakfast is served.

Mrs G. W. Lee   Cwm Craig Farm   Little Dewchurch   Hereford HR2 6PS   Herefordshire
Tel: (01432) 840250   Fax 01432 840250   Open: ALL YEAR   Map Ref No. 03

| £18.00 to £22.00 | Y | Y | N |

Hall's Mill House

Nearest Road: A.438, A.44

Hall's Mill House has recently been restored & is situated in peaceful, idyllic countryside overlooking the River Arrow. Offering 3 attractively furnished rooms with en-suite/private bathrooms available. A comfortable lounge in which guests may choose to relax. An excellent base from which to explore the area. Easy access to Offa's Dyke, the Black Mountains, Hay-on-Wye, black-&-white villages, Welsh border country, churches & castles. Many excellent pubs & restaurants locally. Evening meals by prior arrangement. Children over 4.

Grace Watson   Hall's Mill House   Huntington   Kington HR5 3QA   Herefordshire
Tel: (01497) 831409   Open: ALL YEAR   Map Ref No. 04

| £29.00 to £31.00 | N | Y | N |

The Hills Farm

Nearest Road: A.4112

Magnificent views & a splendid welcome await you at this 15th-century farmhouse on the edge of the village of Leysters betwixt Ludlow & Leominster. Delightful en-suite bedrooms have T.V. & beverage-making facilities. 3 are in charming barn conversions offering complete seclusion. Scrumptious dinners, traditional or vegetarian, are available (excluding Tues.) in the individually tabled dining room - the dairy in days gone by - which is unlicensed, so bring your own wine.

VISA: M'CARD:

E-mail: conolly@bigwig.net

Peter & Jane Conolly   The Hills Farm   Leysters   Leominster HR6 0HP   Herefordshire
Tel: (01568) 750205   Fax 01568 750306   Open: MAR - OCT   Map Ref No. 07

Cowley House. Broadway.

rate £ from - to per person	children taken	evening meals	animals taken		
£18.50 to £24.00	N	Y	N	Nearest Road: A.44, A.49	**Highfield**

Twins Catherine & Marguerite are eager to make you feel welcome & at home in their elegant Edwardian house, set in a rural, tranquil location. You will be very comfortable in any of the 3 attractive bedrooms, all with a bathroom (1 being en-suite) & tea/coffee-making facilities. There is a large garden & a T.V. lounge with a crackling fire in which guests may relax, & the home-made food is absolutely delicious. Residential licence.
E-mail: info@stay-at-highfield.co.uk

C. & M. Fothergill	**Highfield**	**Newtown**	**Ivington Road**	**Leominster HR6 8QD**	**Herefordshire**
Tel: (01568) 613216			**Open: ALL YEAR**		**Map Ref No. 08**

£22.00 to £26.00	Y	Y	N	Nearest Road: A.40, A.49	**Sunnymount Hotel**

Quietly situated on the edge of the town, this attractive Edwardian house is warm & inviting. Offering 6 well-appointed bedrooms, with en-suite bathrooms, T.V. & tea/coffee-making facilities. The sitting rooms (1 with colour T.V.) & dining room overlook the pretty garden. A wide choice of breakfasts using home & local produce freshly prepared for each meal. English/French cooking. Licensed. Ample private parking. An ideal base from which to explore this fascinating area. E-mail: sunnymount@tinyworld.co.uk

VISA: M'CARD:

Mrs D. Robertson	**Sunnymount Hotel**	**Ryefield Road**	**Ross-on-Wye HR9 5LU**	**Herefordshire**
Tel: (01989) 563880	**Fax 01989 566251**		**Open: ALL YEAR**	**Map Ref No. 10**

£25.00 to £37.50	Y	N	N	Nearest Road: A.44	**Cowley House**

Cowley House is a delightful 17th-century Cotswold stone house set in a 3/4-acre garden, situated just off Broadways village green in a central but secluded position. It has beautiful antiques, and a wealth of charm & character with exposed stone walls, stone-flagged floors & ceiling beams. Bedrooms have private facilities & hairdryers. Complementary beverages are available. Ample car parking. Children over 5 years.
E-mail: kemp@cowleyhouse.fs.net.co.uk

see PHOTO over p. 194

Mrs Mary Kemp	**Cowley House**	**Church Street**	**Broadway WR12 7AE**	**Worcestershire**
Tel: (01386) 853262			**Open: ALL YEAR**	**Map Ref No. 12**

£30.00 to £35.00	Y	Y	N	Nearest Road: A.46	**Salford Farm House**

Salford Farm House dates back to the 19th century & has many original features including beams, flagstones & fireplaces. It is traditionally decorated with antiques. The outstanding en-suite bedrooms have large beds, T.V.s, etc. Delicious Aga cooked dinners are available & include fresh local produce when in season. Situated on the outskirts of the Vale of Evesham, it is ideally placed for visiting Stratford-upon-Avon, the Cotswolds & many attractions & places of interest. Children over 8.
E-mail: salford@wside.globalnet.co.uk

Richard Beach & Jane Gibson	**Salford Farm House**	**Salford Priors**	**Evesham WR11 5SG**	**Worcs.**
Tel: (01386) 870000	**Fax 01386 870300**		**Open: ALL YEAR**	**Map Ref No. 14**

Worcestershire

		rate £ from - to per person	children taken	evening meals	animals taken
Cowleigh Park Farm This beautifully restored & historic listed farmhouse is peacefully situated at the foot of the Malvern hills, creating a tranquil setting for a relaxing & friendly stay. 3 comfortable rooms, all with en-suite facilities, T.V. & period furnishings. Excellent parking within the attractive landscaped gardens. Also available is a self-catering 3 bedroom cottage & a 1 bedroom apartment. Ideally situated to enjoy the walks & countryside of this lovely area. Children over 7 years. E-mail: cowleighparkfarm@talk21.com	Nearest Road: A.449, A.4103	£28.00 to £29.00	Y	Y	Y

Mrs Sue Stringer Cowleigh Park Farm Cowleigh Road Malvern WR13 5HJ Worcestershire
Tel: (01684) 566750 Fax 01684 566750 Open: ALL YEAR Map Ref No. 15

		rate £ from - to per person	children taken	evening meals	animals taken
Wyche Keep Wyche Keep is a unique arts-&-crafts castle-style house, perched high on the Malvern Hills, built by the family of Sir Stanley Baldwin, Prime Minister, to enjoy spectacular 60-mile views, with a long history of elegant entertaining. 3 large double suites, including a 4-poster. Traditional English cooking is a speciality, & guests can savour memorable 4-course candle-lit dinners, selected from fresh local vegetables & game, served in a 'house party' atmosphere. Private parking. Licensed. E-mail: Wychekeep@aol.com *see PHOTO over p. 197*	Nearest Road: B.4218	£30.00 to £35.00	N	Y	N

Jon & Judith Williams Wyche Keep 22 Wyche Road Malvern WR14 4EG Worcestershire
Tel: (01684) 567018 Fax 01684 892304 Open: ALL YEAR Map Ref No. 16

All the establishments mentioned in this guide are members of
The Worldwide Bed & Breakfast Association

WORLDWIDE BED & BREAKFAST ASSOCIATION

When booking your accommodation please mention
The Best Bed & Breakfast

Wyche Keep. Malvern.

Kent

Kent
(South East)

Kent is best known as "the garden of England". At its heart is a tranquil landscape of apple & cherry orchards, hop-fields & oast-houses, but there are also empty downs, chalk sea-cliffs, rich marshlands, sea ports, castles & the glory of Canterbury Cathedral.

The dramatic chalk ridgeway of the North Downs links the White Cliffs of Dover with the north of the county which extends into the edge of London. It was a trade route in ancient times following the high downs above the Weald, dense forest in those days. It can be followed today & it offers broad views of the now agricultural Weald.

The pilgrims who flocked to Canterbury in the 12th-15th centuries, (colourfully portrayed in Chaucer's Canterbury Tales), probably used the path of the Roman Watling Street rather than the high ridgeway.

Canterbury was the cradle of Christianity in southern England & is by tradition the seat of the Primate of All England. This site, on the River Stour, has been settled since the earliest times & became a Saxon stonghold under King Ethelbert of Kent. He established a church here, but it was in Norman times that the first great building work was carried out, to be continued in stages until the 15th century. The result is a blending of styles with early Norman work, a later Norman choir, a vaulted nave in Gothic style & a great tower of Tudor design. Thomas Becket was murdered on the steps of the Cathedral in 1170. The town retains much of its mediaeval character with half-timbered weavers' cottages, old churches & the twin towers of the west gate.

Two main styles of building give the villages of Kent their special character. The Kentish yeoman's house was the home of the wealthier farmers & is found throughout the county. It is a timber-frame building with white lath & plaster walls & a hipped roof of red tiles. Rather more modest in style is a small weatherboard house, usually painted white or cream. Rolvenden & Groombridge have the typical charm of a Kentish village whilst Tunbridge Wells is an attractive town, with a paved parade known as the Pantiles & excellent antique shops.

There are grand houses & castles throughout the county. Leeds Castle stands in a lake & dates back to the 9th century. It has beautifully landscaped parkland. Knowle House is an impressive Jacobean & Tudor Manor House with rough ragstone walls, & acres of deer-park & woodland.

Kent is easily accessible from the Channel Ports, Gatwick Airport & London.

Leeds Castle.

Kent

Kent Gazeteer

Areas of outstanding natural beauty.
Kent Downs.

Historic Houses & Castles

Aylesford, The Friars - Nr. Maidstone
13th century Friary & shrine of Our Lady,
(much restored), 14th century cloisters -
original.

Allington Castle -Nr. Maidstone
13th century. One time home of Tudor
poet Thomas Wyatt. Restored early 20th
century. Icons & Renaissance paintings.

Black Charles - Nr. Sevenoaks
14th century Hall house - Tudor fireplaces,
beautiful panelling.

Boughton Monchelsea Place - Nr.
Maidstone
Elizabethan Manor House - grey stone
battlements - 18th century landscaped
park, wonderful views of Weald of Kent.

Chartwell - Westerham
Home of Sir Winston Churchill.
Chiddingstone Castle - Nr. Edenbridge
18th century Gothic revival building
encasing old remains of original Manor
House - Royal Stuart & Jacobite
collection.
Ancient Egyptian collection - Japanese
netsuke, etc.

Eyehorne Manor - Hollingbourne
15th century Manor house with 17th
century additions.

Cobham Hall - Cobham
16th century house - Gothic &
Renaissance - Wyatt interior. Now school
for girls.

Fairfield - Eastry, Sandwich
13th-14th centuries - moated castle. Was
home of Anne Boleyn. Beautiful gardens
with unique collection of classical statuary.

Knole - Sevenoaks
15th century - splendid Jacobean interior -
17th & 18th century furniture. One of the
largest private houses in England.

Leeds Castle- Nr. Maidstone
Built in middle of the lake, it was the home
of the mediaeval Queens of England.

Lullingstone Castle - Eynsford
14th century mansion house - frequented
by Henry VIII & Queen Anne.
Still occupied by descendants of the
original owners

Long Barn - Sevenoaks
14th century house - said to be home of
William Caxton. Restored by Edwin
Lutyens; 16th century barn added to
enlarge house. Galleried hall - fine
beaming & fireplaces. Lovely gardens
created by Sir Harold Nicholson & his wife
Vita Sackville-West.

Owletts - Cobham
Carolean house of red brick with
plasterwork ceiling & fine staircase.

Owl House - Lamberhurst
16th century cottage, tile hung; said to be
home of wool smuggler. Charming
gardens.

Penshurst Place - Tonbridge
14th century house with mediaeval Great
Hall perfectly preserved.English Gothic.
Birthplace of Elizabethan poet, Sir Philip
Sidney
Fine staterooms, splendid picture gallery,
famous toy museum. Tudor gardens &
orchards.

Saltwood Castle - Nr. Hythe
Mediaeval - very fine castle & is privately
occupied. Was lived in by Sir Ralph de
Broc, murderer of Thomas a Becket.

Squerreys Court - Westerham
Manor house of William & Mary period,
with furniture, paintings & tapestries of
time. Connections with General Wolfe.

Stoneacre - Otham
15th century yeoman's half-timbered
house.

Cathedrals & Churches

Brook (St. Mary)
11th century paintings in this unaltered
early Norman church.

Brookland (St. Augustine)
13th century & some later part. Crown-
post roofs, detached wooden belfry with
conical cap. 12th century lead font.

Canterbury Cathedral
12th century wall paintings, 12th & 13th
century stained glass. Very fine Norman
crypt. Early perpendicular nave &
cloisters which have heraldic bosses.
Wonderful central tower.

Charing (St. Peter & St. Paul)
13th & 15th century interior with 15th
century tower. 17th century restoration.

Kent

Cobham (St. Mary)
16th century carved & painted tombs - unequalled collection of brasses in county.
Elham (St. Mary the Virgin)
Norman wall with 13th century arcades, perpendicular clerestory. Restored by Eden.
Lullingstone (St. Botolph)
14th century mainly - 16th century wood screen. Painted glass monuments.
Newington-on-the-Street (St. Mary the Virgin)
13th & 14th century - fine tower. 13th century tomb. Wall paintings.
Rochester Cathedral
Norman facade & nave, otherwise early English.
12th century west door. 14th century doorway to Chapter room.
Stone (St. Mary)
13th century - decorated - paintings, 15th century brass, 16th century tomb.
Woodchurch (All Saints)
13th century, having late Norman font & priest's brass of 1320. Arcades alternating octagonal & rounded columns. Triple lancets with banded marble shafting at east end.

Museums & Galleries

Royal Museums - Canterbury
Archaeological, geological, mineralogical exhibits, natural history, pottery & porcelain. Engravings, prints & pictures.
Westgate - Canterbury
Museum of armour, etc. in 14th century gatehouse of city.
Dartford District Museum - Dartford
Roman, Saxon & natural history.
Deal Museum - Deal
Prehistoric & historic antiquities.
Dicken's House Museum - Broadstairs
Personalia of Dickens; prints, costume & Victoriana.
Down House - Downe
The home of Charles Darwin for 40 years, now his memorial & museum.
Dover Museum - Dover
Roman pottery, ceramics, coins, zoology, geology, local history, etc.
Faversham Heritage Society - Faversham
1000 years of history & heritage.
Folkestone Museum & Art Gallery - Folkestone
Archeology, local history & sciences.

Herne Bay Museum - Herne Bay
Stone, Bronze & Early Iron Age specimens. Roman material from Reculver excavations. Items of local & Kentish interest.
Museum & Art Gallery - Maidstone
16th century manor house exhibiting natural history & archaeolgical collections. Costume Gallery, bygones, ceramics, 17th century works by Dutch & Italian painters. Regimental museum

Historic Monuments

Eynsford Castle - Eynsford
12th century castle remains.
Rochester Castle - Rochester
Storied keep - 1126-39
Roman Fort & Anglo-Saxon Church - Reculver
Excavated remains of 3rd century fort & Saxon church.
Little Kit's Coty House - Aylesford
Ruins of burial chambers from 2 long barrows.
Lullingstone Roman Villa - Lullingstone
Roman farmstead excavations.
Roman Fort & Town - Richborough
Roman 'Rutupiae' & fort
Tonbridge Castle - Tonbridge
12th century curtain walls, shell of keep & 14th century gatehouse.
Dover Castle - Dover
Keep built by Henry II in 1180. Outer curtain built 13th century.

Gardens

Chilham Castle Gardens - Nr. Canterbury
25 acre gardens of Jacobean house, laid out by Tradescant.
Lake garden, fine trees & birds of prey. Jousting & mediaeval banquets.
Great Comp Gardens - Nr. Borough Green
Outstanding 7 acre garden with old brick walls.
Owl House Gardens - Lamberhurst
16th century smugglers cottage with beautiful gardens of roses, daffodils & rhododendrons.
Sissinghurst Castle Gardens - Sissinghurst
Famous gardens created by Vita Sackville-West around the remains of an Elizabethan mansion.

KENT
Map reference

02 Leadbeater	20 C.Turner
05 Williams	21 Latham
06 Rishworth	22 Martin
07 Gunn	23 Sargent
08 Wilkinson	26 Piper
09 Stevens	27 Barr
10 Tennent	28 Earl
11 Wilson	29 Lindasy
12 A.Parker	30 Watson
13 H.Parker	31 Burnett
14 Rodger	32 A.Turner
15 Evison	33 Rogers
16 Popple	34 Dakin
17 Chesterfield	34 Carrell
19 Scutt	35 Douche

Kent

rate £ from - to per person *children taken* *evening meals* *animals taken*

Shirkoak Farm

Nearest Road: A.28
Lovingly restored 18th-century Georgian farmhouse in 2 acres of beautiful gardens with tennis court. 3 en-suite bedrooms, (2 queen-size doubles & 1 twin). All with T.V. & tea/coffee tray. Elegant dining-room overlooking small lake, drawing-room with oak beams & an inglenook fireplace. Furnished throughout with antiques. Situated in quiet rural setting ideal for Kentish Weald, Sissinghurst Castle, Tenterden, Canterbury & Dover. (M.20 at Ashford only 10 mins' drive.) Children over 10.
E-mail: shirkoakfarm@aol.com

£25.00 to £25.00   Y   N   N

VISA: M'CARD:

| Mrs Tessa Leadbeater | Shirkoak Farm | Woodchurch | Ashford TN26 3PZ | Kent |
| Tel: (01233) 860056 | Fax 01233 861402 | Open: MAR-DEC | | Map Ref No. 02 |

Clare Ellen Guest House

Nearest Road: A.28
A warm welcome & bed & breakfast in style. Large, elegant en-suite/private rooms, all with colour T.V., clock/radio, hairdryer & tea/coffee-making facilities. Ironing centre with trouser press for guests' convenience. Vegetarians & special diets catered for on request. A cosy residents' lounge. Numerous restaurants/pubs close by. 6 mins' walk to the town centre/cathedral. 4 mins' walk to Canterbury East Station. Private car park & garage available.
E-mail: loraine.williams@clareellenguesthouse.co.uk

£24.00 to £27.00   Y   N   N

VISA: M'CARD:

| Mrs Loraine Williams | Clare Ellen Guest House | 9 Victoria Road | Canterbury CT1 3SG | Kent |
| Tel: (01227) 760205 | Fax 01227 784482 | Open: ALL YEAR | | Map Ref No. 05 |

Oriel Lodge

Nearest Road: A.2, M.2
In a tree-lined residential avenue, 5 mins' walk from the city centre & restaurants, Oriel Lodge is an attractive Edwardian detached house, retaining a warm & restful period character. Accommodation is in 6 well-furnished bedrooms with clean, up-to-date facilities. Afternoon tea is served in the garden, or in the attractive lounge, with a log fire in winter. Smoking in lounge area only. Private parking. Children over 6 years.
E-mail: info@oriel-lodge.co.uk

£22.00 to £33.00   Y   N   N

VISA: M'CARD:

| Keith & Anthea Rishworth | Oriel Lodge | 3 Queens Avenue | Canterbury CT2 8AY | Kent |
| Tel: (01227) 462845 | Fax 01227 462845 | Open: ALL YEAR | | Map Ref No. 06 |

Great Weddington

Nearest Road: A.257
A fine Regency Grade II listed country house. The stunning hallway welcomes you into an elegant but cosy atmosphere & the bedrooms are prettily furnished. Delicious dinners & a log fire in the drawing room, make for a perfect place to unwind. Surrounded by farmland & extensive gardens, Neil runs a library of 'Talking Books' from the stables. Well-situated for Canterbury cathedral & the medieval town of Sandwich, Dover & Walmer castles & the gardens of Goodnestone Park. Children over 8.
E-mail: traveltale@aol.com

£37.50 to £37.50   Y   Y   N

VISA: M'CARD:

| Kate & Neil Gunn | Great Weddington | Ash | Canterbury CT3 2AR | Kent |
| Tel: (01304) 813407 | Fax 01304 812531 | Open: All Year (Excl. Xmas & New Year) | Map Ref No. 07 |

Kent

Chislet Court Farm

£25.00 to £30.00	Y	N	N

🚭

Nearest Road: A.28, A.299

A listed Queen Anne farmhouse, set in mature gardens with views overlooking the surrounding countryside & the ancient village church. There are 2 double en-suite bedrooms, which are large & comfortable with tea/coffee-making facilities & T.V.. Guests are welcome to wander round the garden or relax in the conservatory - where breakfast is served. An ideal base for exploring Canterbury & the Kent countryside. Children over 12.
E-mail: chisletcourtfarm@dial.pipex.com

Kathy & Mike Wilkinson — Chislet Court Farm — Chislet — Canterbury CT3 4DU — Kent
Tel: (01227) 860309 — Fax 01227 860444 — Open: ALL YEAR (Excl. Xmas) — Map Ref No. 08

Iffin Farmhouse

£25.00 to £30.00	Y	N	N

🚭

see PHOTO over
p. 204

Nearest Road: A.2

A warm welcome awaits you in this old 18th-century farmhouse, renovated to a very high standard. 3 large double bedrooms, each with views to the garden & orchards, T.V., tea/coffee-making facilities & an en-suite/private bathroom. Enjoy a full English breakfast, served in a lovely dining room. Set in 10 acres of gardens, paddocks & orchards, Iffin Farmhouse (only 6 mins' drive from historic Canterbury) is a delightful spot for touring Kent. Children over 5 years.
E-mail: iffinfarmhouse@btinternet.com

Rosemary Stevens — Iffin Farmhouse — Iffin Lane — Canterbury CT4 7BE — Kent
Tel: (01227) 462776 — Fax 01227 462776 — Open: ALL YEAR — Map Ref No. 09

Little Mystole

£35.00 to £35.00	Y	Y	Y

🚭

Nearest Road: A.28

Small Gerogian house of great charm with pretty secluded walled garden. Set amidst parkland, orchards & hop gardens in an area of unspoilt natural beauty, 41/2 miles from Canterbury & 30 mins' from the Dover ferries & Channel Tunnel. Several beautiful castles & gardens nearby including Hever, Leeds & Sissinghurst. 2 comfortable en-suite bedrooms with T.V. & tea/coffee facilities. A sitting room is available for guests' use. Children over 13. Evening meals & animals by arrangement.

Mrs Patricia Tennent — Little Mystole — Mystole Park — Canterbury CT4 7DB — Kent
Tel: (01227) 738210 — Fax 01227 738210 — Open: ALL YEAR — Map Ref No. 10

Stour Farm

£25.00 to £25.00	Y	N	N

🚭

VISA: M'CARD:

Nearest Road: A.28

Stour Farm, overlooking the River Stour on the edge of Chartham village is ideal for visiting Canterbury. Also, convenient for channel ports, castles, gardens, walks & golf courses. 2 attractively furnished en-suite double bedrooms, each with colour T.V. & tea/coffee-making facilities. Breakfast is served in the guests' own dining room or weather permitting on the sun terrace overlooking the river. Good restaurants & pubs nearby. Ample parking. Children over 12.
E-mail: info@stourfarm.co.uk

Mr & Mrs J. Wilson — Stour Farm Riverside — Chartham — Canterbury CT4 7NX — Kent
Tel: (01227) 731977 — Fax 01227 731977 — Open: ALL YEAR — Map Ref No. 11

Iffin Farmhouse. Canterbury.

Kent

rate £ from - to per person | children taken | evening meals taken | animals taken

£25.00 to £35.00	Y	N	Y

West Winchet

Nearest Road: A.262

West Winchet is an elegant Victorian house surrounded by parkland in a secluded & peaceful setting. 2 beautifully decorated rooms, 1 double with private bathroom & 1 twin with en-suite shower. Each with T.V. & tea/coffee, etc. Both rooms are on the ground floor, & the twin-bedded room has French windows onto the terrace & into the garden. A magnificent drawing room. An ideal touring centre for Kent & East Sussex. 2 1/2 miles mainline station (London 55 mins). Children over 5.

E-mail: annieparker@jpa-ltd.co.uk

Mrs Annie Parker   *West Winchet*   *Winchet Hill*   *Goudhurst*   *Cranbrook TN17 1JX*   *Kent*
Tel: (01580) 212024   Fax 01580 212250   Open: ALL YEAR   Map Ref No. 12

£38.00 to £38.00	Y	Y	N

VISA: M'CARD:

Maplehurst Mill

Nearest Road: A.229

Maplehurst Mill is a beautiful water mill, attached to a medieval mill house & standing in 11 acres of landscaped gardens. Offering 5 attractively furnished guest rooms (incl. 1 4-poster), with en-suite bathroom, T.V., etc.. Each has views over the water & the surrounding countryside. A breakfast & candlelit dinner are served in the medieval miller's house, in the beamed dining room with inglenook, antiques & silver. A delightful home, where a warm welcome awaits you. Children over 12.

E-mail: maplehurst@clara.net

Heather & Kenneth Parker   *Maplehurst Mill*   *Mill Lane*   *Frittenden*   *Cranbrook TN17 2DT*   *Kent*
Tel: (01580) 852203   Fax 01580 852117   Open: ALL YEAR   Map Ref No. 13

£27.50 to £27.50	Y	N	N

The Wren's Nest

Nearest Road: A.21

Built in traditional Kentish style, with oak beams & vaulted ceilings, The Wren's Nest suites have been designed specifically for the comfort & pleasure of guests. The suites are spacious & beautifully furnished & are well-equipped with T.V., tea/coffee facilities, tourist information literature, etc. & excellent en-suite bathrooms. The suites are entered via their own front door allowing absolute privacy. Hearty English breakfasts are served in the main house. An idyllic rural setting, well-placed for touring, walking & birdwatching. Children over 8.

Lynne Rodger   *The Wren's Nest*   *Hastings Road*   *Hawkhurst*   *Cranbrook TN18 4RT*   *Kent*
Tel: (01580) 754919   Fax 01580 754919   Open: APR - DEC   Map Ref No. 14

£32.50 to £45.00	Y	N	N

VISA: M'CARD:

The Old Vicarage

Nearest Road: A.20

Many guests are totally surprised by the peaceful atmosphere & commanding position of this house, given its closeness to Dover. This is a beautiful country house built around 1870 & now totally restored, yet retaining many original features. It is elegantly furnished with antiques & provides everything for your stay to the very highest standards, 2 en-suite bedrooms & 1 with private bathroom. Excellent base for touring east Kent. 2 miles ferry ports/9 miles Channel Tunnel. Parking.

E-mail: vicarage@csi.com

Mrs Judith P. Evison   *The Old Vicarage*   *Chilverton Elms*   *Hougham*   *Dover CT15 7AS*   *Kent*
Tel: (01304) 210668   Fax 01304 225118   Open: ALL YEAR   Map Ref No. 15

Kent

Sunshine Cottage

Nearest Road: A.2

A 17th-century, Grade II listed cottage, overlooking Shepherdswell village green, with a wealth of beams, an inglenook fireplace & 2 lounges. Tastefully furnished, & with a homely atmosphere. 6 attractive bedrooms. A pretty garden & courtyard. Good home-cooking & home-made preserves. Good food also available at a nearby pub. Shepherdswell is situated halfway between Canterbury & Dover, 25 mins' from the Channel Tunnel. BR station 5 mins' walk away.
E-mail: sunshinecottage@shepherdswell.fsnet.co.uk

| £24.00 to £28.00 | Y | N | N |

VISA: M'CARD: AMEX:

Barry & Lyn Popple   Sunshine Cottage   The Green   Mill Lane   Shepherdswell   Dover CT15 7LQ   Kent
Tel: (01304) 831359   Open: ALL YEAR   Map Ref No. 16

Frith Farm House

Nearest Road: A.20, A.2

This lovingly restored Georgian farmhouse with orchards, gardens & indoor swimming pool is situated on the North Downs. Extremely peaceful & well-positioned for visiting the historic houses, castles & cathedrals of Kent. Accommodation in beautifully furnished en-suite rooms together with breakfasts that include homemade bread & preserves. 3 nights or more - 10% discount. Self-catering cottage available. A warm welcome awaits all to this delightful home. Children over 10.
E-mail: enquiries@frithfarmhouse.co.uk

| £28.00 to £32.00 | Y | Y | N |

see PHOTO over p. 207

VISA: M'CARD:

Markham & Susan Chesterfield   Frith Farm House   Otterden   Faversham ME13 0DD   Kent
Tel: (01795) 890701   Fax 01795 890009   Open: ALL YEAR   Map Ref No. 17

Leaveland Court

Nearest Road: A.251

Guests are warmly welcomed to this enchanting 15th-century timbered farmhouse, & its delightful gardens with heated swimming pool. Situated in a quiet rural setting, between 13th-century Leaveland church & woodlands, & surrounded by a 300-acre downland farm. All of the attractive bedrooms have en-suite facilities, colour T.V. & tea/coffee tray. Conveniently placed only 5 mins' from M.2 & Faversham, 20 mins' Canterbury & 30 mins' Channel ports. A charming home.
E-mail: leaveland@mail.com

| £25.00 to £27.00 | Y | N | N |

VISA: M'CARD:

Mrs Corrine Scutt   Leaveland Court   Leaveland   Faversham ME13 0NP   Kent
Tel: (01233) 740596   Fax 01233 740015   Open: FEB - NOV   Map Ref No. 19

Preston Lea

Nearest Road: A.2

A warm welcome & tea on arrival are guaranteed in this beautiful, elegant private house, set in secluded gardens on the edge of Faversham. Spacious en-suite bedrooms with garden views, antique furniture & offering every comfort. The lovely drawing-rooms, pannelled dining-room & gardens are available to guests. Help & advice is on hand from your caring hosts. Delicious breakfasts. Good restaurants nearby, beautiful countryside, beaches & places of interest to visit, ensure enjoyable stays.
E-mail: preston.lea@which.net

| £27.00 to £30.00 | Y | N | N |

VISA: M'CARD:

Alan & Catherine Turner   Preston Lea   Canterbury Road   Faversham ME13 8XA   Kent
Tel: (01795) 535266   Fax 01795 533388   Open: ALL YEAR   Map Ref No. 20

Frith Farm House.   Otterden.

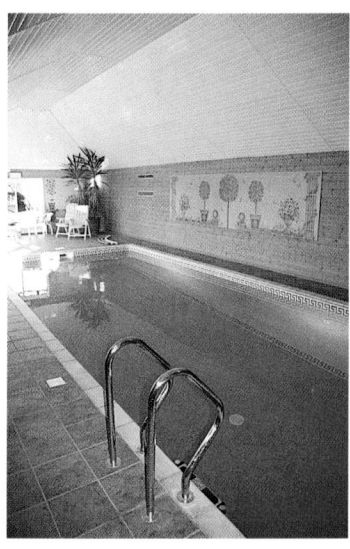

rate £ from – to per person | *children taken* | *evening meals* | *animals taken*

Tenterden House

Nearest Road: A.2, M.2

Stay in one of the en-suite bedrooms (1 double, 1 twin) in this delightful gardener's cottage & stroll through the shrubbery to the 16th-century dining room in the main house, for a traditional English breakfast, beneath the dragon beam. Close to Canterbury, Whitstable & the Channel Ports, it makes an ideal base for exploring Kent, then walk to one of the historic inns in the village for your evening meal. Tea/coffee-making facilities are provided as well as secure off-road parking.

£21.00 to £23.00 — Y N N

Prudence Latham   Tenterden House   209 The Street   Boughton   Faversham ME13 9BL   Kent
Tel: (01227) 751593   Open: ALL YEAR   Map Ref No. 21

Pigeonwood House

Nearest Road: A.260

Pigeonwood House is the original, 18th-century farmhouse of the surrounding area, positioned in rural tranquillity in chalk downland. The 2 guest bedrooms have beautiful panoramic views over the surrounding countryside & many guests return for the homely, relaxing atmosphere. Pigeonwood House is ideally situated for touring historic Kent as well as having the channel tunnel & ports close by. Children over 5 years.
E-mail: samandmary@aol.com

£22.00 to £25.00 — Y N N

Mrs Mary Martin   Pigeonwood House   Arpinge   Folkestone CT18 8AQ   Kent
Tel: (01303) 891111   Fax 01303 891019   Open: ALL YEAR   Map Ref No. 22

Mount House

Nearest Road: A.262

Mount House is an 18th-century Grade II listed country house, which is surrounded by 2 acres of gardens. The house has been sympathetically restored & is tastefully decorated in keeping with its period character. It is set in unspoilt countryside within the designated High Weald conservation area. 2 elegantly furnished bedrooms, each with an en-suite/private bathroom, T.V. & tea/coffee-making facilities. Sissinghurst, Scotney & Great Dixter gardens are within easy reach. Children over 12.
E-mail: davidmargaretsargent@compuserve.com

£27.50 to £27.50 — Y N N

David & Margaret Sargent   Mount House   Ranters Lane   Goudhurst TN17 1HN   Kent
Tel: (01580) 211230   Open: APR - SEPT   Map Ref No. 23

Conghurst Farm

Nearest Road: A.268

Set in peaceful, totally unspoilt countryside, Conghurst Farm offers a perfect spot for a restful holiday. Within easy reach of all the marvellous houses & gardens that this part of the country has to offer. Accommodation is in 3 very comfortable bedrooms, all with en-suite/private bathrooms. There is an attractive drawing room, a separate T.V. room &, in the summer, a delightful garden for guests to enjoy. An ideal base from which to explore Kent. Children over 12.
E-mail: rosa@conghurst.co.uk

£26.00 to £28.00 — Y Y N

see PHOTO over
p. 209

VISA: M'CARD:

Mrs Rosemary Piper   Conghurst Farm   Hawkhurst TN18 4RW   Kent
Tel: (01580) 753331   Fax 01580 754579   Open: FEB - NOV   Map Ref No. 26

Conghurst Farm.   Hawkhurst.

Kent

East Lenham Farm

Nearest Road: A.20

This spacious old farmhouse is set at the end of an avenue of 100 year old lime & horse chesnut trees on a 1400 acre farm. Enjoy the view from the ground-floor en-suite bedroom & lounge, across the lake to fields grazed by Romney sheep. This charming home is only 1 mile from the thriving medieval village of Lenham, 5 miles from Leeds Castle & 25 mins to the Channel Tunnel. Tennis court & garden available for guests' use. Ideal base for exploring Kent. Good restaurants nearby.
E-mail: eastlenham@farmline.com

	£	children	evening	animals
	£30.00 to £32.50	N	N	N

Andrew & Catherine Barr   East Lenham Farm   Lenham   Maidstone ME17 2DP   Kent
Tel: (01622) 859686   Fax 01622 859474   Open: MAR - JAN   Map Ref No. 27

The Greswolde Hotel

Nearest Road: A.28

The Greswolde is a 5-bedroomed Victorian hotel retaining much of its original character & charm. All rooms have en-suite facilities, with colour T.V. & tea makers. There is a quiet, relaxing lounge/ reading room. Located 100 yds from the prom-enade, & close to championship indoor & outdoor bowling greens. Many golf courses also within easy reach. Pubs & eating places are nearby. Ideal for touring, with Channel ports close by. Children over 10 years welcome.

£20.00 to £20.00   Y   N   Y

VISA: M'CARD:

Mrs Ann Earl   The Greswolde Hotel   20 Surrey Road   Cliftonville   Margate CT9 2LA   Kent
Tel: (01843) 223956   Fax 01843 223956   Open: ALL YEAR   Map Ref No. 28

Jordans

Nearest Road: A.227

Beautiful, picture-postcard, 15th-century Tudor house (awarded a 'Historic Building of Kent' plaque) in the picturesque village of Plaxtol, among or-chards & parkland. It is beautifully furnished, & has leaded windows, inglenook fireplaces, massive oak beams & an enchanting old English garden with rambler roses & espalier trees. Within easy reach are Ightham Mote, Leeds & Hever Castle, Penshurst, Chartwell & Knole. 3 lovely rooms, 2 with en-suite/ private facilities. London 35 mins by train, & easy access to airports. Children over 12.

£26.00 to £34.00   Y   N   N

see PHOTO over
p. 211

Mrs Jo Lindsay N.D.D., A.T.D.   Jordans   Sheet Hill Plaxtol   Sevenoaks TN15 0PU   Kent
Tel: (01732) 810379   Open: Mid JAN - Mid DEC   Map Ref No. 29

Wittersham Court

Nearest Road: A.28, A.259

This 300-year-old house offers a peaceful retreat in delightful gardens with much to explore close by. Ideally located under 1 hr from Dover & less from the Eurostar/Shuttle terminus, it is mid-way be-tween Rye & Tenterden with its numerous antique shops. Also close by are the gardens of Sissinghurst & Great Dixter & castles of Leeds, Bodiam & Scotney. The Romney Marsh with its unique churches and the sea is 6 miles away. 2 bedrooms with en-suite/private facilities. Children over 14.
E-mail: watsoni5@aol.com

£40.00 to £40.00   Y   Y   N

VISA: M'CARD:

Mr & Mrs I. Watson   Wittersham Court   The Street   Wittersham   Tenterden TN30 7EA   Kent
Tel: (01797) 270425 Fax 01797 270425 Open: ALL YEAR (Excl. Xmas & New Year) Map Ref No. 30

Jordans. Plaxtol.

Kent

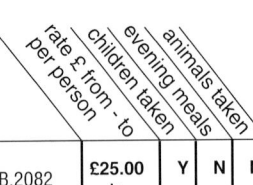

Oxney Farm

Nearest Road: A.28, B.2082

A warm welcome awaits you at award-winning Oxney Farm. Convenient for the Channel Tunnel, ports & Gatwick Airport. The spacious, well-furnished, comfortable farmhouse, with luxurious indoor pool, lies between Tenterden & Rye (2km from B.2082) in peaceful, rural surroundings; ideal for a relaxing break. The area is steeped in history, scenery & culture. The miniature ponies add their charm to the friendly country-house atmosphere. Children by arrangement.
E-mail: oxneyf@globalnet.co.uk

£25.00 to £30.00	Y	N	N

VISA: M'CARD:

Mrs Eve Burnett   Oxney Farm   Moons Green   Wittersham   Tenterden TN30 7PS   Kent
Tel: (01797) 270558   Fax 01797 270958   Open: ALL YEAR   Map Ref No. 31

Leavers Oast

Nearest Road: A.26

A warm, friendly welcome & imaginative cooking is to be found in this beautiful 19th-century oast. An en-suite bedroom in the barn & 2 roundel bedrooms provide very comfortable accommodation. The house is furnished with interesting antiques, & the lovely garden overlooks open country. Excellent communications make it an ideal base for visiting many historic houses & gardens. London 40 mins by rail. Children over 12 years welcome. Evening meals by arrangement.
E-mail: denis@leavers-oast.freeserve.co.uk

£27.50 to £32.00	Y	Y	N

Mrs Anne Turner   Leavers Oast   Stanford Lane   Hadlow   Tonbridge TN11 0JN   Kent
Tel: (01732) 850924   Fax 01732 850924   Open: ALL YEAR   Map Ref No. 32

Ash Tree Cottage

Nearest Road: A.21

Ashtree Cottage is situated in a quiet private road just above the famous Pantiles, & within a few minutes' walk of the high street & station. There are 2 charming & attractively furnished bedrooms with en-suite bathrooms, radio, T.V., tea/coffee-making facilities & plenty of tourist information. There is an excellent choice of restaurants & country pubs nearby, & many places of interest are within easy reach. Children over 8.
E-mail: rogersashtree@excite.co.uk

£23.50 to £27.00	Y	N	N

Richard & Sue Rogers   Ash Tree Cottage   Eden Road   Tunbridge Wells TN1 1TS   Kent
Tel: (01892) 541317 Fax 01892 616770 Open: ALL YEAR (Excl. Xmas & New Year) Map Ref No. 33

The Old Parsonage

Nearest Road: A.267

This magnificent award-winning country house, built by Lord Abergavenny 200 years ago, is quietly situated by the church in pretty Frant village with its 2 character pubs closeby. It offers superb accommodation in luxury en-suite bedrooms, antique-furnished reception rooms, plus a flower-filled conservatory. Short drive to more than 15 major historic houses, castles & gardens. Gatwick 40 mins. Heathrow 70 mins. London 45 mins by train. Children over 7 years.
E-mail: Oldparson@aol.com

£34.00 to £40.00	Y	N	Y

VISA: M'CARD:

Mary & Tony Dakin   The Old Parsonage   Church Lane   Frant   Tunbridge Wells TN3 9DX   Kent
Tel: (01892) 750773   Fax 01892 750773   Open: ALL YEAR   Map Ref No. 34

rate £ from - to per person	children taken	evening meals taken	animals taken		
£25.00 to £27.00	Y	N	N	Nearest Road: A.267 A delightful Elizabethan house, listed as of architectural interest, standing in 20 acres, with sheep, horses, dogs & chickens. Surrounded by the beautiful, rolling, wooded countryside of Sussex, it is perfectly placed for visiting the stately homes & towns of Kent & Sussex. There is1 twin-bedded room, with private bathroom, & 2 singles with washbasins. All have tea/coffee-making facilities & are non-smoking. An attractive drawing room, with T.V.. Gatwick 1 hour, London 1 1/4 hours. Children over 10.	**Rowden House Farm**

Carolyn Carrell   **Rowden House Farm**   *Front*   *Tunbridge Wells*   *TN3 9HS*   *Kent*
Tel: (01892) 750259   *Open: APR - OCT*   *Map Ref No. 34*

| £27.50 to £32.50 | Y | N | N | Nearest Road: A.264 This fine early Georgian house, listed Grade II, stands in its' own grounds surrounded by the famous Tunbridge Wells Common. Guests can enjoy the superb interior decoration & take breakfast in the library. Your hosts can offer you a choice of double/twin rooms or a ground floor suite. Ephraim Lodge is a 5 mins' walk to the railway station, shopping centre & restaurants. An ideal centre for visiting the wealth of lovely gardens & historic buildings. Children over 15. | **Ephraim Lodge** |

Glyn & John Douche   *Ephraim Lodge*   *The Common*   *Mount Ephraim*   *Tunbridge Wells*   *TN4 8BX*   *Kent*
Tel: (01892) 523053   *Fax 01892 543582*   *Open: ALL YEAR*   *Map Ref No. 35*

All the establishments mentioned in this guide are members of
The Worldwide Bed & Breakfast Association

When booking your accommodation please mention
The Best Bed & Breakfast

Leicestershire, Nottinghamshire & Rutland

Leicestershire (East Midlands)

Rural Leicestershire is rich in grazing land, a peaceful, undramatic landscape broken up by the waterways that flow through in the south of the county.

The River Avon passes on its way to Stratford, running by 17th century Stanford Hall & its motorcycle museum. The Leicester section of the Grand Union Canal was once very important for the transportation of goods from the factories of the Midlands to London Docks. It passes through a fascinating series of multiple locks at Foxton. The decorative barges, the 'narrow boats' are pleasure craft these days rather than the lifeblood of the closed community of boat people who lived & worked out their lives on the canals.

Rutland was formerly England's smallest county, but was absorbed into East Leicestershire in the 1970's. Recently, once again, it has become a county in its' own right. Rutland Water, is one of Europe's largest reservoirs & an attractive setting for sailing, fishing or enjoying a trip on the pleasure cruiser. There is also the Rutland Theatre at Tolethorpe Hall, where a summer season of Shakespeare's plays is presented in the open air.

Melton Mowbray is famous for its pork pies & it is also the centre of Stilton cheese country. The "King of Cheeses" is made mainly in the Vale of Belvoir where Leicestershire meets Nottinghamshire, & the battlements & turrets of Belvoir Castle overlook the scene from its hill-top.

To the north-west the Charnwood Forest area is pleasantly wooded & the deer park at Bradgate surrounding the ruined home of Lady Jane Grey, England's nine-day queen, is a popular attraction.

Nottinghamshire (East Midlands)

Nottinghamshire has a diversity of landscape from forest to farmland, from coal mines to industrial areas.

The north of the county is dominated by the expanse of Sherwood Forest, smaller now than in the time of legendary Robin Hood & his Merry Men, but still a lovely old woodland of Oak & Birch.

The Dukeries are so called because of the numerous ducal houses built in the area & there is beautiful parkland on these great estates that can be visited. Clumber Park, for instance has a huge lake & a double avenue of Limes.

Newstead Abbey was a mediaeval priory converted into the Byron family home in the 16th century. It houses the poet Byron's manuscripts & possessions & is set in wonderful gardens.

More modest is the terraced house in Eastwood, where D.H. Lawrence was born into the mining community on which his novels are based.

Nottingham was recorded in the Domesday Book as a thriving community & that tradition continues. It was here that Arkwright perfected his cotton-spinning machinery & went on to develop steam as a power source for industry.

Textiles, shoes, bicycles & tobacco are all famous Nottingham products, & the story of Nottingham Lace can be discovered at the Lace Hall, housed in a former church.

Nottingham Castle, high on Castle Rock, was built & destroyed & rebuilt many times during its history. It now houses the city's Art Gallery & Museum. The Castle towers over the ancient 'Trip to Jerusalem' Inn, said to be so named because crusaders stopped there for a drink on their way to fight in the Holy Land.

Leicestershire, Nottinghamshire & Rutland

Leicestershire Gazeteer

Areas of outstanding natural beauty.
Charnwood Forest, Rutland Water.

Historic Houses & Castles

Belvoir Castle - Nr. Grantham
Overlooking the Vale of Belvoir, castle rebuilt in 1816, with many special events including jousting tournaments. Home of the Duke of Rutland since Henry VIII. Paintings, furniture, historic armoury, military museums, magnificent stateroom.

Belvoir Castle

Belgrave Hall - Leicester
18th century Queen Anne house - furnishing of 18th & 19th centuries.
Langton Hall - Nr. Market Harborough
Privately occupied - perfect English country house from mediaeval times - drawing rooms have 18th century Venetian lace.

Oakham Castle - Oakham
Norman banqueting hall of late 12th C.
Stanford Hall - Nr Lutterworth
17th century William & Mary house - collection of Stuart relics & pictures, antiques & costumes of family from Elizabeth I onward. Motor cycle museum.
Stapleford Park - Nr. Melton Mowbray
Old wing dated 1500, restored 1663. Extended to mansion in 1670. Collection of pictures, tapestries, furniture & Balston's Staffordshire portrait figures of Victorian age.

Cathedrals & Churches

Breedon-on-the-Hill (St. Mary & St. Hardulph)
Norman & 13th century. Jacobean canopied pew, 18th century carvings.
Empingham (St. Peter)
14th century west tower, front & crocketed spire. Early English interior - double piscina, triple sedilla.
Lyddington (St. Andrew)
Perpendicular in the main - mediaeval wall paintings & brasses.
Staunton Harol (Holy Trinity)
17th century - quite unique Cromwellian church - painted ceilings.

Museums & Galleries

Bosworth Battlefield Visitor Centre - Nr Market Bosworth
Exhibitions, models, battlefield trails at site of 1485 Battle of Bosworth where Richard III lost his life & crown to Henry.
Leicestershire Museum of Technology - Leicester
Beam engines, steam shovel, knitting machinery & other aspects of the county's industrial past.
Leicester Museum & Art Gallery - Leicester
Painting collection.
18th & 19th century, watercolours & drawings, 20th century French paintings, Old Master & modern prints.
English silver & ceramics, special exhibitions.
Jewry Wall Museum & Site - Leicester
Roman wall & baths site adjoining museum of archaeology.

Leicestershire, Nottinghamshire & Rutland

Melton Carnegie Museum-Melton Mowbray
Displays of Stilton cheese, pork pies & other aspects of the past & present life of the area.

Rutland County Museum - Oakham
Domestic & agricultural life of Rutland, England's smallest county.

Donnington Collection of Single-Seater Racing Cars - Castle Donington
Large collection of grand prix racing cars & racing motorcycles, adjoining Donington Park racing circuit..

Wygson's House Museum of Costume - Leicestershire
Costume, accessories & shop settings in late mediaeval buildings.

The Bellfoundry Museum - Loughborough
Moulding, casting, tuning & fitting of bells, with conducted tours of bellfoundry.

Historic Monuments

The Castle - Ashby-de-la-Zouch
14th century with tower added in 15th century.

Kirby Muxloe Castle - Kirby Muxloe
15th century fortified manor house with moat ruins.

Other things to see & do

Rutland Farm Park - Oakham
Rare & commercial breeds of livestock in 18 acres of park & woodland, with early 19th century farm buildings.

Stoughton Farm Park - Nr. Leicester
Shire horses, rare breeds, small animals & modern 140 dairy herd. Milking demonstrations, farm museum, woodland walks. Adventure playground.

Twycross Zoo - Nr. Atherstone
Gorillas, orang-utans, chimpanzees, gibbons, elephants, giraffes, lions & many other animals.

The Battlefield Line Nr. Market Bosworth
Steam railway & collection of railway relics, adjoining Bosworth Battlefield.

Great Central Railway - Loughborough
Steam railway over 5-mile route in Charnwood Forest area, with steam & diesel museum.

Rutland Railway Museum - Nr. Oakham
Industrial steam & diesel locomotives.

Nottinghamshire Gazeteer
Historic Houses & Castles

Holme Pierrepont Hall - Nr. Nottingham
Outstanding red brick Tudor manor, in continuous family ownership, with 19th century courtyard garden.

Newark Castle - Newark
Dramatic castle ruins on riverside site, once one of the most important castles of the north.

Newstead Abbey - Nr. Mansfield
Priory converted to country mansion, home of poet Lord Byron with many of his possessions & manuscripts on display. Beautiful parkland, lakes & gardens.

Nottingham Castle - Nottingham
17th century residence on site of mediaeval castle.
Fine collections of ceramics, silver, Nottingham alabaster carvings, local historical displays. Art gallery. Special exhibitions & events.

Wollaton Hall - Nottingham
Elizabethan mansion now housing natural history exhibits. Stands in deer park, with Industrial Museum in former stables, illustrating the city's bicycle, hosiery, lace, pharmaceutical & other industries.

Cathedrals & Churches

Egmanton (St. Mary)
Magnificent interior by Comper. Norman doorway & font. Canopied rood screen, 17th century altar.

Newark (St. Mary Magdalene)
15th century. 2 painted panels of "Dance of Death". Reredos by Comper.

Southwell Cathedral
Norman nave, unvaulted, fine early English choir. Decorated pulpitum, 6 canopied stalls, fine misericords. Octagonal chapter house..

Terseval (St. Catherine)
12th century - interior 17th century unrestored.

Museums & Galleries

Castlegate Museum - Nottingham
Row of Georgian terraced houses showing costume & textile collection.
Lace making equipment & lace collection.

Leicestershire, Nottinghamshire & Rutland

Nottingham Castle Museum - Nottingham
Collections of ceramics, glass & silver. Alabaster carvings.
D.H. Lawrence Birthplace - Eastwood
Home of the novelist & poet, as it would have been at time of his birth, 1885.
Millgate Museum of Social & Folk Life - Newark
Local social & folk life, with craft workshops.
Brewhouse Yard Museum - Nottingham
Daily life in Nottingham, displayed in 17th century cottages & rock-cut cellars.
The Lace Hall - Nottingham
The story of Nottingham Lace audio-visual display & exhibition with lace shops, in fine converted church.
Museum of Costume & Textiles - Nottingham
Costumes, lace & textiles on display in fine Georgian buildings.
Bassetlaw Museum - Retford
Local history of north Nottinghamshire.
Canal Museum - Nottinghamshire
History of the River Trent & canal history, in former canal warehouse.
Ruddington Framework Knitters' Museum - Ruddington
Unique complex of early 19th-century framework knitters' buildings with over 20 hand frames in restored workshop.

Other things to see & do

The Tales of Robin Hood - Nottingham
A 'flight to adventure' from mediaeval Nottingham to Sherwood Forest through the tales of the world's most famous outlaw.
Clumber Park - Nr. Worksop
Landscaped parkland, with double avenue of limes, lake, chapel. One of the Dukeries' estates, though the house no longer remains.
Rufford - Nr. Ollerton
Parkland, lake & gallery with fine crafts, around ruin of Cistercian abbey.
Sherwood Forest Visitor Centre - Nr. Edwinstowe
Robin Hood exhibition.
450 acres of ancient oak woodland associated with the outlaw & his merry men.
Sherwood Forest Farm Park - Nr. Edwinstowe
Rare breeds of cattle, sheep, pigs & goats. Lake with wildfowl.
White Post Farm Centre - Farnsfield, Nr Newark
Working modern farm with crops & many animals, including cows, sheep, pigs, hens, geese, ducks, llamas, horses. Indoor displays & exhibits.

Newark Castle.

LEICESTERSHIRE, NOTTINGHAMSHIRE & RUTLAND

Map reference

01 White
02 Goodwin
03 Shipside
04 Hinchley
05 Ibbotson
06 Spratt
07 Kay
08 Kinder

NOTTINGHAMSHIRE
RUTLAND
LEICESTERSHIRE

rate £ from - to per person	children taken	evening meals	animals taken		

Abbots Oak Country House

£30.00 to £40.00 — Y Y Y

Nearest Road: A.511, M.1

A Grade II listed building with a wealth of oak panelling, & including the staircase reputedly from Nell Gwynn's town house. Set in mature gardens & woodland, with natural granite outcrops. There are 4 delightful rooms, all with en-suite/private bathroom. Open fires create a warm & welcoming atmosphere, & Carolyn's superb dinners are served in the candlelit dining room. Stratford, Belvoir Castle & Rutland Water can all be reached within the hour. Tennis court, billiard room. Children over 6 years welcome.

Mr & Mrs White Abbots Oak Country House Warren Hills Road Coalville LE67 4UY Leicestershire
Tel: (01530) 832328   Fax 01530 832328   Open: ALL YEAR   Map Ref No. 01

Hillside House

£18.50 to £21.00 — Y N N

Nearest Road: A.606

Charmingly converted farm buildings with superb views over open countryside, in the small village of Burton Lazars. Comfortable accommodation is offered in 1 double & 2 twin-bedded rooms, each with an en-suite/private bathroom. All have tea/coffee facilities & colour T.V.. A pleasant garden to relax in. Close to Melton Mowbray, famous for its pork pies & Stilton cheese, & with Burghley House, Belvoir Castle & Rutland Water within easy reach. Children over 10. Single supplement.
E-mail: hillhs27@aol.com

Sue Goodwin Hillside House 27 Melton Road Burton Lazars Melton Mowbray LE14 2UR Leics.
Tel: (01664) 566312 Fax 01664 501819 Open: ALL YEAR (Excl. Xmas & New Year) Map Ref No. 02

Holly Lodge

£25.00 to £28.00 — Y N N

see PHOTO over p. 220

VISA: M'CARD: AMEX:

Nearest Road: A.60

Holly Lodge is situated just off the A.60, 10 miles north of Nottingham. This attractive former hunting lodge stands in 15 acres of grounds. The 4 comfortable & attractive, en-suite guest rooms are housed within the converted stables. There are panoramic countryside views on all sides, with woodland walks, tennis, golf & riding nearby. Ideally situated for a peaceful, rural holiday base with a relaxed & friendly atmosphere.
E-mail: ann.hollylodge@ukonline.co.uk

Ann Shipside   Holly Lodge   Ricket Lane   Blidworth NG21 0NQ   Nottinghamshire
Tel: (01623) 793853   Fax 01623 490977   Open: ALL YEAR   Map Ref No. 03

Titchfield Guest House

£18.00 to £19.00 — Y N Y

VISA: M'CARD: AMEX:

Nearest Road: A.617

This is 2 houses converted into 1 family-run guest house, offering 8 comfortable rooms, a lounge with T.V., a kitchen for guests' use, a bathroom & showers. It also has an adjoining garage. Near to Mansfield, which is a busy market town. Sherwood Forest & the Peak District are both easily accessible. Titchfield Guest House is a very handy location for touring this lovely area, & for onward travel. A warm & friendly welcome is assured at this charming home. Animals by arrangement.

Mrs B. Hinchley Titchfield Guest House 300/302 Chesterfield Rd North Mansfield NG19 7QU Notts.
Tel: (01623) 810356/810921   Fax 01623 810356   Open: ALL YEAR   Map Ref No. 04

Holly Lodge. Blidworth.

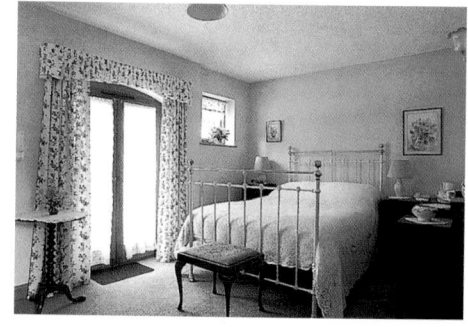

Nottinghamshire & Rutland

Blue Barn Farm

£20.00 to £22.00 | Y | N | N

Nearest Road: A.616, A.632

An enjoyable visit is guaranteed at this family-run, 250-acre farm, set in tranquil countryside on the edge of Sherwood Forest (Robin Hood country). 3 guest bedrooms, each with modern amenities including h&c, tea/coffee-making facilities & a guest bathroom with shower. 1 bedroom is en-suite. A colour-T.V. lounge & garden are also available. Guests are very welcome to walk around the farm. Many interesting places, catering for all tastes, only a short journey away.
E-mail: ibbotsonbluebarn@netscapeonline.co.uk

June M. Ibbotson   Blue Barn Farm   Langwith   Mansfield NG20 9JD   Nottinghamshire
Tel: (01623) 742248 Fax 01623 742248 Open: ALL YEAR (Excl. Xmas & New Year) Map Ref No. 05

Greenwood Lodge City Guest House

£29.00 to £33.00 | Y | N | Y

Nearest Road: A.60

A warm, welcoming Victorian house situated in a quiet cul-de-sac, 1 mile from the city centre. The home of Sheila & Michael Spratt, The Lodge is furnished mainly with antiques, & boasts a fine 4-poster bed. All rooms are en-suite, non-smoking & individually decorated & furnished to a high standard, with T.V., hairdryer, trouser press & hospitality tray. An ideal base from which to explore Nottingham & its many places of interest. Animals by arrangement.
E-mail: coolspratt@aol.com

VISA: M'CARD:

Mr & Mrs Spratt   Greenwood Lodge City Guest House   Third Avenue   Sherwood Rise   Nottingham
NG7 6JH   Notts.   Tel: (0115) 9621206   Fax 0115 9621206   Open: ALL YEAR   Map Ref No. 06

The Barns Country Guest House

£22.00 to £30.00 | Y | N | N

Nearest Road: A.1

A welcoming & pleasant, relaxed atmosphere awaits you at The Barns. This beautifully converted 18th-century barn, furnished in antiques & pine, boasts open fires & oak beams. Prettily decorated en-suite bedrooms, including a 4-poster bedroom, all with T.V., tea/coffee trays, etc. Enjoy a delicious Aga cooked breakfast & why not sample the home-made muesli? The Barns is an interesting base for touring, located at Babworth, home of the Pilgrim Fathers, Robin Hood country & Clumber Park.
E-mail: harry@thebarns.co.uk

VISA: M'CARD:

Mr & Mrs Kay   The Barns Country Guest House   Morton Farm   Babworth   Retford DN22 8HA   Notts.
Tel: (01777) 706336   Fax 01777 709773   Open: ALL YEAR   Map Ref No. 07

Torr Lodge

£23.50 to £25.00 | Y | Y | Y

Nearest Road: A.1

A warm welcome awaits you at Torr Lodge, Barrow, in the heart of scenic Rutland, England's smallest county. Belvoir Castle, Burghley House & Geoff Hamilton's infamous gardens are all within easy reach, as is Rutland Water. Georgiana has been in the hospitality business for many years & offers tastefully furnished en-suite accommodation, delicious home-cooking on an Aga & hearty breakfasts. Dinner is available by arrangement. Children over 12 years.

Mrs Georgiana Kinder   Torr Lodge   Main Street   Barrow   Oakham LE15 7PE   Rutland
Tel: (01572) 813396   Fax 01572 813396   Open: ALL YEAR   Map Ref No. 08

Lincolnshire

Lincolnshire
(East Midlands)

Lincolnshire is an intriguing mixture of coast & country, of flat fens & gently rising wolds.

There are the popular resorts of Skegness & Mablethorpe as well as quieter coastal regions where flocks of wild birds take food & shelter in the dunes. Gibraltar Point & Saltfleetby are large nature reserves.

Fresh vegetables for much of Britain are produced in the rich soil of the Lincolnshire fens, & windmills punctuate the skyline. There is a unique 8-sailed windmill at Heckington. In spring the fields are ablaze with the red & yellow of tulips. The bulb industry flourishes around Spalding & Holbeach, & in early May tulip flowers in abundance decorate the huge floats of the Spalding Flower Parade.

The city of Lincoln has cobbled streets & ancient buildings & a very beautiful triple-towered Cathedral which shares its hill-top site with the Castle, both dating from the 11th century. There is a 17th century library by Wren in the Cathedral, which has amongst its treasures one of the four original copies of Magna Carta.

Boston has a huge parish church with a distincive octagonal tower which can be seen for miles across the surrounding fenland, & is commonly known as the 'Boston Stump'. The Guildhall Museum displays many aspects of the town's history, including the cells where the early Pilgrim Fathers were imprisioned after their attempt to flee to the Netherlands to find religious freedom. They eventually made the journey & hence to America.

One of England's most outstanding towns is Stamford. It has lovely churches, ancient inns & other fine buildings in a mellow stone.

Sir Isaac Newton was born at Woolsthorpe Manor & educated at nearby Grantham where there is a museum which illustrates his life & work.

The poet Tennyson was born in the village of Somersby, where his father was Rector.

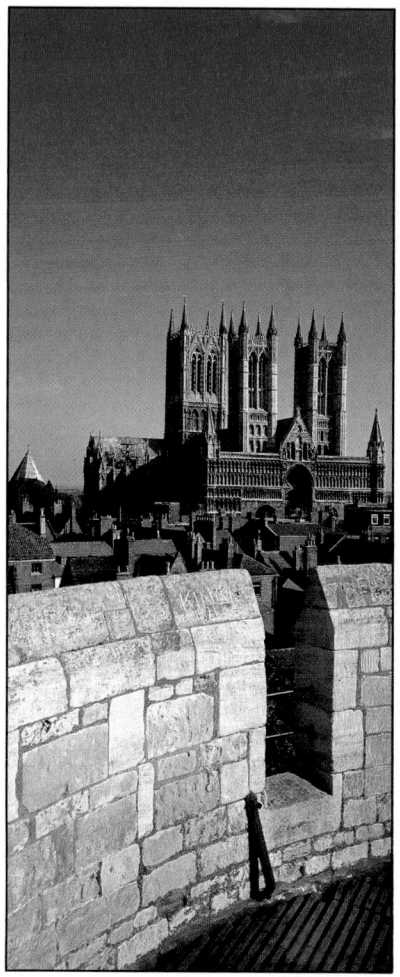

Lincoln Cathedral.

Lincolnshire

Lincolnshire Gazeteer

Areas of outstanding natural beauty.
Lincolnshire Wolds.

Historic Houses & Castles

Auborn House - Nr. Lincoln
16th century house with imposing carved staircase & panelled rooms.

Belton House - Grantham
House built 1684-88 - said to be by Christopher Wren - work by Grinling Gibbons & Wyatt also. Paintings, furniture, porcelain, tapestries, Duke of Windsor mementoes. A great English house with formal gardens & extensive grounds with orangery.

Doddington Hall - Doddington, Nr. Lincoln
16th century Elizabethan mansion with elegant Georgian rooms & gabled Tudor gatehouse. Fine furniture, paintings, porcelain, etc. Formal walled knot gardens, roses & wild gardens.

Burghley House - Stamford
Elizabethan - England's largest & grandest house of the era. Famous for its beautiful painted ceilings, silver fireplaces & art treasures.

Gumby Hall - Burgh-le-Marsh
17th century manor house. Ancient gardens.

Harrington Hall - Spilsby
Mentioned in the Domesday Book - has mediaeval stone base - Carolinean manor house in red brick. Some alterations in 1678 to mullioned windows. Panelling, furnishings of 17th & 18th century.

Marston Hall - Grantham
16th century manor house. Ancient gardens.

The Old Hall - Gainsborough
Fine mediaeval manor house built in 1480's with original kitchen, rebuilt after original hall destroyed during Wars of the Roses. Tower & wings, Great Hall. It was the first meeting place of the "Dissenters", later known as the Pilgrim Fathers.

Woolsthorpe Manor - Grantham
17th century house. Birthplace of Sir Isaac Newton.

Fydell House - Boston
18th century house, now Pilgrim College.

Lincoln Castle - Lincoln
William the Conqueror castle, with complete curtain wall & Norman shell keep. Towers & wall walk. Unique prisoners' chapel.

Tattershall Castle - Tattershall
100 foot high brick keep of 15th century moated castle, with fine views over surrounding country.

Cathedrals & Churches

Addlethorpe (St. Nicholas)
15th century - mediaeval stained glass - original woodwork.

Boston (St. Botolph)
14th century decorated - very large parish church. Beautiful south porch, carved stalls.

Brant Broughton (St. Helens)
13th century arcades - decorated tower & spire - perpendicular clerestory. Exterior decoration.

Ewerby (St. Andrew)
Decorated - splendid example of period - very fine spire. 14th century effigy.

Fleet (St. Mary Magdalene)
14th century - early English arcades - perpendicular windows - detached tower & spire.

Folkingham (St. Andrew)
14th century arcades - 15th century windows - perpendicular tower - early English chancel.

Gedney (St. Mary Magdalene)
Perpendicular spire (unfinished). Early English tower. 13th-14th century monuments, 14th-15th century stained glass.

Grantham (St. Wulfram)
14th century tower & spire - Norman pillars - perpendicular chantry - 14th century vaulted crypt.

Lincoln Cathedral - Lincoln
Magnificent triple-towered Gothic building on fine hill-top site.
Norman west front,
13th century - some 14th century additions. Norman work from 1072. Angel choir - carved & decorated pulpitum - 13th century chapter house - 17th century library by Wren (containing one of the four original copies of Magna Carta).

Lincolnshire

St. Botolph's Church - Boston
Fine parish church, one of the largest in the country, with 272 foot octagonal tower dominating the surrounding fens.
Long Sutton (St. Mary)
15th century south porch, mediaeval brass lectern, very fine early English spire.
Louth (St. James)
Early 16th century - mediaeval Gothic - wonderful spire.
Scotter (St. Peter)
Saxon to perpendicular - early English nave - 15th century rood screen.
Stow (St. Mary)
Norman - very fine example, particularly west door. Wall painting.
Silk Willoughby (St. Denis)
14th century - tower with spire & flying buttresses. 15th-17th century pulpit.
Stainfield (St. Andrew)
Queen Anne - mediaeval armour & early needlework.
Theddlethorpe (All Saints)
14th century - 15th century & reredos of 15th century, 16th century parcloses, 15th century brasses - some mediaeval glass.
Wrangle (St. Mary the Virgin & St. Nicholas)
Early English - decorated - perpendicular - Elizabethan pulpit. 14th century east window & glass.

Museums & Galleries
Alford Manor House - Alford
Tudor manor house - thatched - folk museum. Nearby windmill.
Boston Guildhall Museum - Boston
15th century building with mayor's parlour, court room & cells where Pilgrim Fathers were imprisoned in 1607. Local exhibits.
Lincoln Cathedral Library - Lincoln
Built by Wren housing early printed books & mediaeval manuscripts.
Lincoln Cathedral Treasury - Lincoln
Diocesan gold & silver plate.
Lincoln City & Country Museum - Lincoln
Prehistoric, Roman & mediaeval antiquities with local associations. Armour & local history.
Museum of Lincolnshire Life - Lincoln
Domestic, agricultural, industrial & social history of the county. Edwardian room settings, shop settings, agricultural machinery.

Usher Gallery - Lincoln
Paintings, watches, miniatures, porcelain, silver, coins & medals. Temporary exhibitions. Tennyson collection. Works of English watercolourist Peter de Wint.
Grantham Museum - Grantham
Archeology, prehistoric, Saxon & Roman. Local history with special display about Sir Isaac Newton, born nearby & educated in Grantham.
Church Farm Museum - Skegness
Farmhouse & buildings with local agricultural collections & temporary exhibitions & special events.
Stamford Museum - Stamford
Local history museum, with temporary special exhibitions.
Battle of Britain Memorial Flight - Coningsby
Lancaster bomber, five Spitfires & two Hurricanes with other Battle of Britain memorabilia.
National Cycle Museum - Lincoln
Development of the cycle.
Stamford Steam Brewery Museum - Stamford
Complete Victorian steam brewery with 19th century equipment.

Other things to see & do
Springfield - Spalding
Show gardens of the British bulb industry, & home of the Spalding Flower Parade each May. Summer bedding plants & roses.
Butlins Funcoast World - Skegness
Funsplash Water World with amusements & entertainments
Castle Leisure Park - Tattershall
Windsurfing, water-skiing, sailing, fishing & other sports & leisure facilities.
Long Sutton Butterfly Park - Long Sutton
Walk-through tropical butterfly house with outdoor wildflower meadows & pets corner.
Skegness Natureland Marine Zoo - Skegness
Seal sanctuary with aquaria, tropical house, pets corner & butterfly house.
Windmills - at Lincoln (Ellis Mill - 4 sails), Boston (Maud Foster - 5 sails), Burgh-le-Marsh (5 sails), Alford (5 sails), Sibsey (6 sails), Heckington (8 sails).

LINCOLNSHIRE
Map reference

01 Armstrong
02 Ramsay
03 Honnor
04 Woods
04 Baumber
06 Rook

Lincolnshire

Cawthorpe Hall

Nearest Road: A.15

This fine, old, listed house is surrounded by a large pretty garden & fields of roses supplying the rose distillery with fragrant blooms. The rooms are bright, spacious & comfortably furnished & have bathrooms en-suite. A full English breakfast will be served in a family country kitchen. Country lovers can enjoy beautiful woodland walks. Horse riding or golf, Grimsthorpe Castle & Park are all within easy reach. A charming home.
E-mail: bandb@rosewater.co.uk

| | £30.00 to £35.00 | Y | N | Y |

Mrs Chantal Armstrong   Cawthorpe Hall   Cawthorpe   **Bourne PE10 0AB**   Lincolnshire
Tel: (01778) 423830   Fax 01778 426620   *Open: ALL YEAR*   *Map Ref No. 01*

Church Farm

Nearest Road: A.15

Tucked away in unspoilt countryside, the Ramsays guarantee you a friendly welcome. Expect to enjoy good food, conversation, laughter & log fires on chilly evenings. Walk around the beautiful village lake or relax in the garden on sunny days & listen to the birdsong. Hemswell Antique Centre, Lincolnshire Showground, Lincoln & Gainsborough are nearby. Evening meals by arrangement & afternoon teas served. 2 attractive bedrooms with en-suite/private facilities. Children over 5.
E-mail: Fillinghambandb@lineone.net

| | £22.50 to £22.50 | Y | Y | N |

Christine B. Ramsay   Church Farm   Fillingham   **Gainsborough DN21 5BS**   Lincolnshire
Tel: (01427) 668279   Fax 01427 668025   *Open: ALL YEAR (Excl. Xmas)*   *Map Ref No. 02*

Pipwell Manor

Nearest Road: A.17

Pipwell Manor is a Grade II listed Georgian manor house, built in around 1740, set in paddocks & gardens in a small quiet village in the Lincolnshire Fens, just off the A.17. Beautifully restored & decorated in English-country style, but retaining many original features, Pipwell Manor is a delightful place to stay. 4 comfortably furnished & attractive bedrooms, each with an en-suite/private bathroom & tea/coffee-making facilities. Guests are welcomed with tea & home-made cake. Parking. Children over 10 years.

| | £22.00 to £24.00 | Y | N | N |

Mrs Lesley Honnor   Pipwell Manor   Washway Road   Saracens Head   Holbeach PE12 8AL   Lincs.
Tel: (01406) 423119   Fax 01406 423119   *Open: ALL YEAR*   *Map Ref No. 03*

Carline Guest House

Nearest Road: A.57, A.46, A.15

Barrie & Jackie Woods extend a warm welcome. Excellent accommodation, in 6 comfortable & attractively furnished bedrooms, each with en-suite facilities, T.V., radio, tea/coffee-making facilities, hairdryers & trouser press. The Carline is a short, pleasant stroll from the Lawns Tourism & Conference Centre, & from the historic Uphill area of Lincoln. There are several restaurants & public houses nearby for your lunch or evening meal. Ask for your hosts recommendations.

| | £22.00 to £22.00 | Y | N | N |

Barrie & Jackie Woods   Carline Guest House   1-3 Carline Road   **Lincoln LN1 1HL**   Lincolnshire
Tel: (01522) 530422 Fax 01522 530422 *Open: ALL YEAR (Excl. Xmas & New Year)* *Map Ref No. 04*

Lincolnshire

rate £ from - to per person	children taken	evening meals taken	animals taken	
£35.00 to £45.00	Y	N	N	**Minster Lodge**

Nearest Road: A.15

A delightful family-run town house, refurbished to a high standard. This lovely Victorian residence offers 6 attractive en-suite bedrooms with radio, T.V., 'phone & beverage facilities. Ideally situated within 50 yds of the only remaining Roman arch still in use & 5 mins' walk from historic Lincoln's major attractions of cathedral, castle & colourful mixture of restaurants & antique & gift shops. John & Margaret extend a very warm welcome!
E-mail: info@minsterlodge.co.uk

John & Margaret Baumber	Minster Lodge	3 Church Lane	Lincoln LN2 1QJ	Lincolnshire
Tel: (01522) 513220	Fax 01522 513220		Open: ALL YEAR (Excl. Xmas)	Map Ref No. 04

£35.00 to £45.00	Y	Y	N	**Stragglethorpe Hall**

see PHOTO over p. 228

Nearest Road: A.17

Situated just off the A.1, Stragglethorpe Hall is a haven of peace between Cambridge & York, offering unique Tudor elegance & modern amenities. Furnished with antiques & Grade II listed, its stone-mullioned windows & leaded windows overlook formal gardens with ancient yew hedges surrounded by open countryside. The large, elegant double bedrooms are all en-suite, & one is a 4-poster. Evening meals are available by arrangement for groups of 6 persons or more.
E-mail: stragglethorpe@compuserve.com

Mr & Mrs Michael Rook	Stragglethorpe Hall	Stragglethorpe LN5 0QZ	Lincolnshire
Tel: (01400) 272308	Fax 01400 273816	Open: FEB - NOV	Map Ref No. 06

All the establishments mentioned in this guide are members of
The Worldwide Bed & Breakfast Association

WORLDWIDE BED & BREAKFAST ASSOCIATION

When booking your accommodation please mention
The Best Bed & Breakfast

Stragglethorpe Hall.   Stragglethorpe.

Norfolk

Norfolk
(East Anglia)

One of the largest of the old counties, Norfolk is divided by rivers from neighbouring counties & pushes out into the sea on the north & east sides. This is old East Anglia.

Inland there is great concentration on agriculture where fields are hedged with hawthorn which blossoms like snow in summer. A great deal of land drainage is required & the area is crisscrossed by dykes & ditches - some of them dating back to Roman times.

Holkham Hall.

The Norfolk Broads were formed by the flooding of mediaeval peat diggings to form miles & miles of inland waterways, navigable & safe. On a bright summer's day, on a peaceful backwater bounded by reed & sedge, the Broads seem like paradise. Here are hidden treasures like the Bittern, that shyest of birds, the Swallowtail butterfly & the rare Marsh orchid.

Contrasting with the still inland waters is a lively coastline which takes in a host of towns & villages as it arcs around The Wash. Here are the joys of the seaside at its best, miles of safe & sandy golden beaches to delight children, dunes & salt marshes where birdlife flourishes, & busy ports & fishing villages with pink-washed cottages.

Cromer is a little seaside town with a pier & a prom, cream teas & candy floss, where red, white & blue fishing boats are drawn up on the beach.

Hunstanton is more decorous, with a broad green sweeping down to the cliffs. Great Yarmouth is a boisterous resort. It has a beach that runs for miles, with pony rides & almost every amusement imaginable.

It is possible to take a boat into the heart of Norwich, past warehouses, factories & new penthouses, & under stone & iron bridges. Walking along the riverbank you reach Pulls Ferry where a perfectly proportioned grey flint gateway arcs over what was once a canal dug to transport stone to the cathedral site. Norwich Cathedral is magnificent, with a sharply soaring spire, beautiful cloisters & fine 15th century carving preserved in the choir stalls. Cathedral Close is perfectly preserved, as is Elm Hill, a cobbled street from mediaeval times. There are many little shops & narrow alleys going down to the river.

Norfolk is a county much loved by the Royal family & the Queen has a home at Sandringham. It is no castle, but a solid, comfortable family home with red brick turrets & French windows opening onto the terrace.

Norfolk

Norfolk Gazeteer

Areas of outstanding beauty.
Norfolk coast (part)

Historic Houses & Castles

Anna Sewell House - Great Yarmouth
17th century Tudor frontage. Birthplace of writer Anna Sewell.

Blicking Hall - Aylsham
Great Jacobean house. Fine Russian tapestry, long gallery with exceptional ceiling. Formal garden.

Felbrigg Hall - Nr. Cromer
17th century, good Georgian interior. Set in wooded parklands.

Holkham Hall - Wells
Fine Palladian mansion of 1734. Paintings, statuary, tapestries, furnishings & formal garden by Berry.

Houghton Hall - Wells
18th century mansion. Pictures, china & staterooms.

Oxburgh Hall - Swafftham
Late 15th century moated house. Fine gatehouse tower. Needlework by Mary Queen of Scots.

Wolterton Hall - Nr. Norwich
Built in 1741 contains tapestries, porcelain, furniture.

Trinity Hospital - Castle Rising
17th century, nine brick & tile almshouses, court chapel & treasury.

Cathedrals & Churches

Attleborough (St. Mary)
Norman with late 14th century. Fine rood screen & frescoes.

Barton Turf (St. Michael & All Angles)
Magnificent screen with painting of the Nine Orders of Angles.

Beeston-next-Mileham (St. Mary)
14th century. Perpendicular clerestory tower & spire. Hammer Beam roof, parclose screens, benches, front cover. Tracery in nave & chancel windows.

Cawston (St. Agnes)
Tower faced with freestone. Painted screens, wall paintings, tower, screen & gallery. 15th century angel roof.

East Harding (St. Peter & St. Paul)
14th century, some 15th century alterations. Monuments of 15th-17th century. Splendid mediaeval glass.

Erpingham (St. Mary)
14th century military brass to John de Erpingham, 16th century Rhenish glass. Fine tower.

Gunton (St. Andrew)
18th century. Robert Adam - classical interior in dark wood - gilded.

King's Lynn (St. Margaret)
Norman foundation. Two fine 14th century Flemish brasses, 14th century screens, reredos by Bodley, interesting Georgian pulpit with sounding board.

Norwich Cathedral
Romanesque & late Gothic with 15th century spire. Perpendicular lierne vaults in nave, transeptsand presbytery.

Ranworth (St. Helens)
15th century screen, very fine example. Sarum Antiphoner, 14th century illuminated manuscript - East Anglian work.

Salle (St. Peter & St. Paul)
15th century. Highly decorated west tower & porches. Mediaeval glass, pulpit with 15th century panels & Jacobean tester. Stalls, misericords, brasses & monuments, sacrament font.

Terrington (St. Clement)
Detached perpendicular tower. Western front has fire-light window & canopied niches. Georgian panelling west of nave. 17th century painted font cover. Jacobean commandment boards.

Trunch (St. Botolph)
15th century screen with painted panels, mediaeval glass, famous font canopy with fine carving & painting, ringer's gallery, Elizabethan monument.

Wiggenhall (St. Germans)
17th century pulpit, table, clerk's desk & chair, bench ends 15th century.

Wymondham (St. Mary & St. Thomas of Canterbury)
Norman origins including arcades & triforium windows, 13th century font fragments, complete 15th century font. 15th century clerestory & roof. Comper reredos, famous Corporas Case, rare example of 13th century Opus Anglicanum.

Museums & Galleries

Norwich Castle Museum
Art collection, local & natural history,

Norfolk

Strangers Hall - Norwich
Mediaeval mansion furnished as museum of urban domestic life in 16th-19th centuries.

St. Peter Hungate Church Museum - Norwich
15th century church for the exhibition of ecclesiastical art & East Anglican antiquities.

Sainsbury Centre for Visual Arts - University, Norwich
Collection of modern art, ancient, classical & mediaeval art, Art Nouveau, 20th century constructivist art.

Bridewell Museum of Local Industries - Norwich
Crafts, industries & aspects of city life.

Museum of Social History - King's Lynn
Exhibition of domestic life & dress, etc., noted glass collection.

Bishop Bonner's Cottages
Restored cottages with coloured East Anglia pargetting, c. 1502, museum of archaeological discoveries, exhibition of rural crafts.

The Guildhall - Thetford
Duleep Singh Collection of Norfolk & Suffolk portraits.

Shirehall Museum - Walsingham
18th century court room having original fittings, illustrating Walsingham life.

Historic Monuments

Binham Priory & Cross - Binham
12th century ruins of Benedictine foundation.

Caister Castle - Great Yarmouth
15th century moated castle - ruins. Now motor museum.

The Castle - Burgh Castle
3rd century Saxon fort - walls - ruin.

Mannington Hall - Saxthorpe
Saxon church ruin in gardens of 15th century moated house.

Castle Rising - Castle Rising
Splendid Norman keep & earthworks.

Castle Acre Priory & Castle Gate - Swaffham

Other things to see & do

African Violet Centre - Terrington St. Clements.
60 varieties of African Violets. Talks & Tours.

Norfolk Lavender Centre - Heacham
Open to the public in July & August. Demonstrations of harvesting & distilling the oil.

Thetford Forest
Forest walks, rides & picnic places amongst conifers, oak, beech & birch.

The Broads.

NORFOLK
Map reference

01 Gillam
02 Bartlett
03 Tweedy Smith
04 Luddington
05 Franklin
06 Douglas
07 Lock
08 Collins

Felbrigg Lodge. Aylmerton.

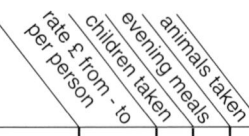

	rate £ from - to per person	children taken	evening meals	animals taken

Felbrigg Lodge

Nearest Road: A.148, A.140

Set in beautiful countryside 2 miles from the coast, Felbrigg Lodge is hidden in 8 acres of spectacular woodland gardens. Time has stood still since Edwardian ladies came here in their carriages to take tea & play croquet. Great care has been taken to preserve this atmosphere with comfortable en-suite rooms, luxuriously decorated with every facility. A true haven of peace & tranquillity. A nature lover's paradise. Candlelit dinners & copious breakfast. Indoor heated pool/gym. Children over 10.
E-mail: info@felbrigglodge.co.uk

£40.00 to £55.00	Y	Y	N

see PHOTO over
p. 233

VISA: M'CARD:

Jill & Ian Gillam	Felbrigg Lodge	Aylmerton NR11 8RA	Norfolk
Tel: (01263) 837588	Fax 01263 838012	Open: ALL YEAR	Map Ref No. 01

Bartles Lodge

Nearest Road: A.47, A.1067

Bartles Lodge is in the peaceful, unspoilt village of Elsing, set in 12 acres of landscaped meadows inhabited by plenty of wildlife. The rooms, which are centred around the patio, pond & fountain, are beautifully furnished in country style, & most overlook the Bartletts' own lakes. All of the bedrooms are en-suite with colour T.V.s, etc. & are very comfortable. Although Bartles Lodge is licensed, the local village inn is nearby. An ideal base from which to explore Norfolk.

£21.00 to £23.00	N	N	Y

VISA: M'CARD:

David & Annie Bartlett	Bartles Lodge	Church Street	Elsing	Dereham NR20 3EA	Norfolk
Tel: (01362) 637177		Open: ALL YEAR			Map Ref No. 02

Fieldsend House

Nearest Road: A.147

Come & stay at Fieldsend & enjoy the comfort of a large Edwardian carrstone house, close to the town centre & the sea with panoramic views over the Wash. Guests have a choice of 3 rooms, 2 en-suite, 1 with a private bathroom, all individually decorated by the owner who specialises in rag rolling & making the drapes & pelmets, as well as upholstery & collecting coloured glass. 1 bedroom has a 4-poster. Delicious breakfasts are served by a Cordon Bleu cook. Parking in the grounds.

£22.50 to £25.00	Y	N	N

see PHOTO over
p. 235

Sheila Tweedy Smith	Fieldsend House	Homefields Road	Hunstanton PE36 5HL	Norfolk
Tel: (01485) 532593	Fax 01485 532593	Open: ALL YEAR		Map Ref No. 03

Wallington Hall

Nearest Road: A.10

Wallington Hall is a magnificent, early 16th-century Grade I listed house, situated within a beautiful 600-acre family estate. The attractive accommodation comprises 3 superb & well-equipped double, twin & family en-suite rooms. Each of the guest rooms is spacious, furnished with antiques & of delightful character. Andrew & Miranda Luddington offer swimming (heated outdoor pool), tennis, stabling, course fishing & superb walks. Wallington Hall is the perfect spot for a relaxing break.
E-mail: luddington@wallingtonhall.co.uk

£40.00 to £50.00	Y	N	N

see PHOTO over
p. 236

VISA: M'CARD:

Miranda Luddington	Wallington Hall	King's Lynn PE33 0EP	Norfolk
Tel: (01553) 811567	Fax 01553 810661	Open: ALL YEAR	Map Ref No. 04

Fieldsend House. Hunstanton.

Wallington Hall.   Kings Lynn.

Norfolk

Le Grys Barn

| £25.00 to £35.00 | Y | Y | N |

Nearest Road: A.140

A stunning 17th-century barn conversion with tasteful oriental furnishings, which has been featured in several design magazines. Guests are accommodated in the luxuriously appointed en-suite Stable Room, with private entrance & patio. There are fresh flowers, T.V. & fresh cafetiere coffee/tea-making facilities. Breakfast made with local produce is served in the barn overlooking summer pastureland. Ideal for exploring East Anglia, with riding, fishing & golf close by. Evening meals & packed lunches can be arranged. Children over 12.

Julie Franklin   Le Grys Barn   Wacton Common   Wacton   Long Stratton NR15 2UR   Norfolk
Tel: (01508) 531576   Fax 01508 532124   Open: ALL YEAR (Excl. Xmas)   Map Ref No. 05

Greenacres Farmhouse

| £22.50 to £27.50 | N | N | N |

Nearest Road: A.140

A period 17th-century farmhouse on a 30-acre common with ponds & wildlife, only 10 miles from Norwich. All of the en-suite/private bedrooms (2 double/1 twin) are tastefully furnished to complement the oak beams & period furniture, with tea/coffee & T.V., etc. Relax in the beamed sitting room with inglenook fireplace & enjoy a leisurely breakfast in the sunny dining room. Snooker table & tennis court. Therapeutic massage, aromatherapy & reflexology service available.
E-mail: greenacresfarm@tinyworld.co.uk

Joanna Douglas   Greenacres Farmhouse   Woodgreen   Long Stratton   Norwich NR15 2RR   Norfolk
Tel: (01508) 530261   Fax 01508 530261   Open: ALL YEAR   Map Ref No. 06

Greenbanks Country Hotel

| £30.00 to £40.00 | Y | Y | Y |

Nearest Road: A.47

Charming, small, 18th-century hotel, with delightful country restaurant, situated in 9 acres of meadows & lakes. Spectacular gardens. Elegant en-suite rooms, including 3 ground-floor level access suites, offering peace & comfort. Superb cuisine, with excellent choice from varied menu: special diets catered for. Greenbanks is 15 mins' from Norwich, & within easy reach of the coast, the Broads & many stately homes. Walking, fishing & golfing breaks available. Pets by arrangement.
E-mail: greenbanks@skynow.net

VISA: M'CARD:

Jennie Lock   Greenbanks Country Hotel   Swaffham Road   Wendling   Nr. Swaffham   NR19 2AB
Tel: (01362) 687742   Fax 01362 687742   Open: ALL YEAR   Map Ref No. 07

Cedar Lodge

| £24.00 to £24.00 | Y | Y | Y |

Nearest Road: A.134

A warm welcome awaits you at Cedar Lodge, which stands on the edge of Thetford Forest. There are 2 attractive double bedrooms overlooking farmland & big log fires in a lovely sitting room. Food is the password - Christine owns a useful catering company & is a member of The Master Chefs of Great Britain & delights in preparing candlelit dinners for her guests. Children over 12 years welcome. Animals by arrangement.

Mrs Christine Collins   Cedar Lodge   West Tofts   Thetford IP26 5DB   Norfolk
Tel: (01842) 878281   Fax 01842 878281   Open: ALL YEAR   Map Ref No. 08

237

Northumbria

Northumbria

Mountains & moors, hills & fells, coast & country are all to be found in this Northern region which embraces four counties - Northumberland, Durham, Cleveland & Tyne & Wear.

Saxons, Celts, Vikings, Romans & Scots all fought to control what was then a great wasteland between the Humber & Scotland.

Northumberland

Northumberland is England's Border country, a land of history, heritage & breathtaking countryside. Hadrian's Wall, stretching across the county from the mouth of the Tyne in the west to the Solway Firth, was built as the Northern frontier of the Roman Empire in 122 AD. Excavations along the Wall have brought many archaeological treasures to light. To walk along the wall is to discover the genius of Roman building & engineering skill. They left a network of roads, used to transport men & equipment in their attempts to maintain discipline among the wild tribes.

Through the following centuries the Border wars with the Scots led to famous battles such as Otterburn in 1388 & Flodden in 1513, & the construction of great castles including Bamburgh & Lindisfarne. Berwick-on-Tweed, the most northerly town, changed hands between England & Scotland 13 times.

Northumberland's superb countryside includes the Cheviot Hills in the Northumberland National Park, the unforgettable heather moorlands of the Northern Pennines to the west, Kielder Water (Western Europe's largest man-made lake), & 40 miles of glorious coastline.

Holy Island, or Lindisfarne, is reached by a narrow causeway that is covered at every incoming tide. Here St. Aidan of Iona founded a monastery in the 7th century, & with St. Cuthbert set out to Christianise the pagan tribes. The site was destroyed by the Danes, but Lindisfarne Priory was built by the monks of Durham in the 11th century to house a Benedictine community. The ruins are hauntingly beautiful.

Durham

County Durham is the land of the Prince Bishops, who with their armies, nobility, courts & coinage controlled the area for centuries. They ruled as a virtually independent State, holding the first line of defence against the Scots.

In Durham City, the impressive Norman Castle standing proudly over the narrow mediaeval streets was the home of the Prince Bishops for 800 years.

Durham Cathedral, on a wooded peninsula high above the River Wear, was built in the early 12th century & is undoubtably one of the world's finest buildings, long a place of Christian pilgrimage.

The region's turbulent history led to the building of forts & castles. Some like Bowes & Barnard Castle are picturesque ruins whilst others, including Raby, Durham & Lumley still stand complete.

The Durham Dales of Weardale, Teesdale & the Derwent Valley cover about one third of the county & are endowed with some of the highest & wildest scenery. Here are High Force, England's highest waterfall, & the Upper Teesdale National Nature Reserve.

The Bowes Museum at Barnard Castle is a magnificent French-style chateau & houses an important art collection.

In contrast is the award-winning museum at Beamish which imaginatively recreates Northern life at the turn of the century.

Northumbria

Cleveland

Cleveland, the smallest 'shire' in England, has long been famous for its steel, chemical & shipbuilding industries but it is also an area of great beauty. The North Yorkshire National Park lies in the south, & includes the cone-shaped summit of Roseberry Topping, "Cleveland's Matterhorn".

Cleveland means 'land of cliffs', & in places along the magnificent coastline, cliffs tower more than 600 feet above the sea, providing important habitat for wild plants & sea-birds.

Pretty villages such as Hart, Elwick & Staithes are full of steep, narrow alleys. Marton was the birthplace of Captain James Cook & the museum there traces the explorer's early life & forms the start of the 'Cook Heritage Trail'.

The Tees estuary is a paradise for birdwatchers, whilst walkers can follow the Cleveland Way or the 38 miles of the Langbaurgh Loop. There is surfing, windsurfing & sailing at Saltburn, & for the less energetic, the scenic Esk Valley Railway runs from Middlesbrough to Whitby.

Tyne & Wear

Tyne & Wear takes its name from the two rivers running through the area, & includes the large & lively city of Newcastle-on-Tyne.

Weardale lies in a beautiful valley surrounded by wild & bleak fells. Peaceful now, it was the setting for a thriving industry mining coal & silver, zinc & lead. Nature trails & recreation areas have been created among the old village & market towns.

The county was the birthplace of George Stephenson, railway engineer, who pioneered the world's first passenger railway on the Stockton to Darlington Line in 1825.

Durham Cathedral.

Northumbria

Northumbria Gazeeter

Areas of Outstanding Natural Beauty
The Heritage Coast, the Cheviot Hills, the North Pennine chain.

Historic Houses & Castles

Alnwick Castle - Alnwick
A superb mediaeval castle of the 12th century.
Bamburgh Castle-Bamburgh
A restored 12th century castle with Norman keep.
Callaly Castle - Whittingham
A 13th century Pele tower with 17th century mansion. Georgian additions.
Durham Castle - Durham
Part of the University of Durham - a Norman castle.
Lindisfarne Castle - Holy Island
An interesting 14th century castle.
Ormesby Hall - Nr. Middlesbrough
A mid 18th century house.
Raby Castle - Staindrop, Darlington
14th century with some later alteration . Fine art & furniture. Large gardens.
Wallington Hall -Combo
A 17th century house with much alteration & addition.
Washington Old Hall-Washington
Jacobean manor house, parts of which date back to 12th century.

Cathedrals & Churches

Brancepeth (St. Brandon)
12th century with superb 17th century woodwork. Part of 2 mediaeval screens. Flemish carved chest.
Durham Cathedral
A superb Norman cathedral. A unique Galilee chapel & early 12th century vaults.
Escombe
An interesting Saxon Church with sundial.
Hartlepool (St. Hilda)
Early English with fine tower & buttresses.
Hexham (St. Andrews)
Remains of a 17th century church with Roman dressing. A unique night staircase & very early stool. Painted screens.
Jarrow (St. Pauls)
Bede worshipped here. Strange in that it was originally 2 churches until 11th century. Mediaeval chair.

Newcastle (St. Nicholas)
14th century with an interesting lantern tower.
Heraldic font. Roundel of 14th century glass.
Morpeth (St. Mary the Virgin)
Fine mediaeval glass in east window - 14th century.
Pittington (St. Lawrence)
Late Norman nave with wall paintings. Carved tombstone - 13th century.
Skelton (St. Giles)
Early 13th century with notable font, gable crosses, bell-cote & buttresses.
Staindrop (St. Mary)
A fine Saxon window.
Priests dwelling.
Neville tombs & effigies.

Museums & Galleries

Aribea Roman Fort Museum - South Shields
Interesting objects found on site.
Berwick-on-Tweed Museum - Berwick
Special exhibition of interesting local finds.
Bowes Museum - Bernard Castle
European art from mediaeval to 19th century.
Captain Cook Birthplace Museum - Middlesbrough
Cook's life & natural history relating to his travels.
Clayton Collection - Chollerford
A collection of Roman sculpture, weapons & tools from forts.
Corbridge Roman Station - Corbridge
Roman pottery & sculpture.
Dormitory Musuem - Durham Cathedral
Relics of St. Cuthbert.
Mediaeval seats & manuscripts.
Gray Art Gallery - Hartlepool
19th-20th century art & oriental antiquities.
Gulbenkian Museum of Oriental Art - University of Durham
Chinese pottery & porcelain, Chinese jade & stone carvings, Chinese ivories, Chinese textiles, Japenese & Tibetan art. Egyptian & Mesopotamian antiquities.
Jarrow Hall - Jarrow
Excavation finds of Saxon & mediaeval monastery.
Fascinating information room dealing with early Christian sites in England.

Northumbria

Keep Museum - Newcastle-upon-Tyne
Mediaeval collection.
Laing Art Gallery - Newcastle-upon-Tyne
17th-19th century British arts, porcelain,
glass & silver.
National Music Hall Museum -
Sunderland
19th-20th century costume & artefacts
associated with the halls.
Preston Hall Museum - Stockton-on-Tees
Armour & arms, toys, ivory period room
University - New Castle -Upon -Tyne
The Hatton Gallery - housing a fine
collection of Italian paintings.
Museum of Antiquities
Prehistoric, Roman & Saxon collection
with an interesting reconstruction of a
temple.
**Beamish North of England Open Air
Museum** - European Museum of the Year
Chantry Bagpipe Museum - Morpeth
Darlington Museum & Railway Centre.

Historic Monuments

Ariiea Roman Fort - South Shields
Remains which include the gateways &
headquarters.
Barnard Castle - Barnard Castle
17th century ruin with interesting keep.
Bowes Castle - Bowes
Roman Fort with Norman keep.
The Castle & Town Walls - Berwick-on-
Tweed
12th century remains, reconstructed later.
Dunstanburgh Castle - Alnwick
14th century remains.
Egglestone Abbey - Barnard Castle
Remains of a Poor House.
Finchdale Priory - Durham
13 th century church with much
remaining.
Hadrian's Wall - Housesteads
Several miles of the wall including castles
& site museum.
Mithramic Temple - Carrawbrough
Mithraic temple dating back to the 3rd
century.
Norham Castle - Norham
The partial remains of a 12th century
castle.
Prudhoe Castle - Prudhoe
Dating from the 12th century with
additions. Bailey & gatehouse well
preserved.

The Roman Fort - Chesters
Extensive remains of a Roman bath
house.
Tynemouth Priory & Castle - Tynemouth
11th century priory - ruin - with 16th
century towers & keep.
Vindolanda - Barton Mill
Roman fort dating from 3rd century.
Warkworth Castle - Warkworth
Dating from the 11th century with
additions.
A great keep & gatehouse.
Warkworth Hermitage - Warkworth
An interesting 14th century Hermitage.
Lindisfarne Priory - Holy Island
(Lindisfarne)
11th century monastery. Island accessible
only at low tide.

Other things to see & do

Botanical Gardens - Durham University
Bird & Seal Colonies - Farne Islands
Conducted tours by boat
Marine Life Centre & Fishing Museum -
Seahouses
Museum of sealife, & boat trips to the
Farne Islands.
Tower Knowe Visitor Centre - Keilder
Water

Saltburn Victorian Festival.

NORTHUMBERLAND, DURHAM & TYNE & WEAR

Map reference

05 Jackson
06 Clyde
07 Courage
09 Gay
10 Reed
11 Close
12 Booth

242

rate £ from - to per person	children taken	evening meals	animals taken		

| £22.00 to £27.00 | Y | Y | N | **Bilton Barns Farmhouse**
Nearest Road: A.1
This beautifully furnished & spacious farmhouse has magnificent panoramic views over Alnmouth & Warkworth Bay, only 1 1/2 miles away. Set in lovely countryside, it is ideally situated for visiting superb beaches, castles, walks & recreational activities. A warm & relaxing log fire awaits you on chilly evenings. All rooms are en-suite with T.V. & tea/coffee facilities. Dorothy makes delicious meals with a distinctly local flavour. Brian is pleased to show interested visitors around the farm.
E-mail: dorothy@biltonbarns.co.uk | | |

Brian & Dorothy Jackson   Bilton Barns Farmhouse   Alnmouth   Alnwick NE66 2TB   Northumberland
Tel: (01665) 830427   Fax 01665 830063   Open: ALL YEAR (Excl. Xmas)   Map Ref No. 05

| £32.50 to £35.00 | Y | Y | Y | **Allerwash Farmhouse**
Nearest Road: A.69
Allerwash is an elegant Regency farm house which is full of character & has secluded gardens surrounded by rolling countryside. Bedrooms are stylishly decorated & include private facilities. Open fires in the 2 drawing rooms add to the warmth of the house & elegant furnishings plus antiques & paintings make this a real house of distinction. Meals are delicious & Angela has many cookery awards to her credit. The Roman Wall, the Lake District, the Northumberland coast & many castles, country houses & gardens are within easy reach. | | |

(non-smoking symbol)

Ian & Angela Clyde   Allerwash Farmhouse   Newbrough   Hexham NE47 5AB   Northumberland
Tel: (01434) 674574   Fax 01434 674574   Open: ALL YEAR   Map Ref No. 06

| £22.50 to £22.50 | Y | Y | Y | **Rye Hill Farm**
Nearest Road: A.68, A.69
Rye Hill Farm dates back some 300 years & is a traditional livestock unit in beautiful countryside just 5 miles south of Hexham. Recently, some of the stone barns adjoining the farmhouse have been converted into superb modern guest accommodation. There are 6 bedrooms, all with private facilities, & all have radio, T.V. & tea/coffee-making facilities. Delicious home-cooked meals. Perfect for a get-away-from-it-all holiday.
E-mail: enquiries@consult-courage.co.uk | | |

VISA: M'CARD: AMEX:

Elizabeth Courage   Rye Hill Farm   Slaley   Hexham NE47 0AH   Northumberland
Tel: (01434) 673259   Fax 01434 673259   Open: ALL YEAR   Map Ref No. 07

| £25.00 to £25.00 | Y | Y | Y | **Shieldhall**
Nearest Road: A.696, B.6342
Within acres of well-kept gardens, offering unimpeded views & overlooking the National Trust's Wallington estate, this meticulously restored 18th-century farmhouse is built around a pretty courtyard. All of the 4 bedrooms are beautifully furnished & have en-suite facilities & T.V.. There are very comfortable lounges & an extremely charming inglenooked dining room where home produce is often used for delicious meals which are specially prepared when booked in advance.
E-mail: Robinson.Gay@btinternet.com | | |

(non-smoking symbol)

VISA: M'CARD:

Stephen & Celia Gay   Shieldhall   Wallington   Morpeth NE61 4AQ   Northumberland
Tel: (01830) 540387   Fax 01830 540490   Open: MAR - NOV   Map Ref No. 09

Durham

rate £ from - to per person / children taken / evening meals / animals taken

Lands Farm

Nearest Road: A.689

You will be warmly welcomed to Lands Farm, an old stone-built farmhouse within walking distance of Westgate village. A walled garden with stream meandering by. Accommodation is in centrally heated double & family rooms with luxury en-suite facilities, T.V., tea/coffee-making facilities. Full English breakfast or Continental alternative served in an attractive dining room. This is an ideal base for touring (Durham, Hadrian's Wall, Beamish Museum, etc.) & for walking.

£23.00 to £23.00	Y	N	N

Mrs B. Reed   **Lands Farm**   **Westgate-in-Weardale**   **Bishop Auckland DL13 1SN**   **Durham**
Tel: (01388) 517210   Fax 01388 517210   **Open: ALL YEAR**   Map Ref No. 10

Grove House

Nearest Road: A.68

Grove House, once an aristocrat's shooting lodge, is tastefully furnished throughout, & is situated in an idyllic setting in the middle of Hamsterley Forest. A spacious lounge with log fire gives a warm & comfortable country-house atmosphere. The grandeur of the dining room reminds one of an age gone by. (Take note of the door handles!) 3 bedrooms, all en-suite or with private bathrooms. Helene does all the cooking herself to ensure freshness & quality to her evening meals. Children over 8 years.
E-mail: xov47@dial.pipex.com

£26.00 to £32.50	Y	Y	N

Helene & Russell Close   **Grove House**   **Hamsterley Forest**   **Bishop Auckland DL13 3NL**   **Durham**
Tel: (01388) 488203   Fax 01388 488174   **Open: ALL YEAR (Excl. Xmas & New Year)**   Map Ref No. 11

Ivesley

Nearest Road: A.68

Ivesley is an elegantly furnished country house set in 220 acres. Each of the 5 bedrooms is decorated to a high standard. 3 of the rooms are en-suite. Adjacent to an equestrian centre with first-class facilities. An ideal centre for walking, sightseeing & mountain biking. Collection arranged from Durham Station & Newcastle Airport. Durham 7 miles. Wine cellar. Dogs by arrangement. Babies & children over 8 years welcome.
E-mail: ivesley@msn.com

£29.50 to £45.00	Y	Y	Y

VISA: M'CARD:

Roger & Pauline Booth   **Ivesley**   **Waterhouses**   **Durham DH7 9HB**   **Durham**
Tel: (0191) 3734324   Fax 0191 3734757   **Open: ALL YEAR**   Map Ref No. 12

Visit our website at:
http://www.bestbandb.co.uk

Oxfordshire

Oxfordshire
(Thames & Chilterns)

Oxfordshire is a county rich in history & delightful countryside. It has prehistoric sites, early Norman churches, 15th century coaching inns, Regency residences, distinctive cottages of black & white chalk flints & lovely Oxford, the city of dreaming spires.

The countryside ranges from lush meadows with willow-edged river banks scattered with small villages of thatched cottages, to the hills of the Oxfordshire Cotswolds in the west, the wooded Chilterns in the east & the distinctive ridge of the Berkshire Downs in the south. "Old Father Thames" meanders gently across the county to Henley, home of the famous regatta.

The ancient track known as the Great Ridgeway runs across the shire, & a walk along its length reveals barrows, hill forts & stone circles. The 2,000 year old Uffington Horse cut into the chalk of the hillside below an ancient hill fort site, is some 360 feet in length & 160 feet high.

The Romans built villas in the county & the remains of one, including a magnificent mosaic can be seen at North Leigh. In later centuries lovely houses were built. Minster Lovell stands beside the Windrush; Rousham house with its William Kent gardens is situated near Steeple Aston & beside the Thames lies Elizabethan Mapledurham House with its working watermill.

At Woodstock is Blenheim Palace, the largest private house in Britain & birthplace of Sir Winston Churchill. King Alfred's statue stands at Wantage, commemorating his birth there, & Banbury has its cross, made famous in the old nursery rhyme.

Oxford is a town of immense atmosphere with fine college buildings around quiet cloisters, & narrow cobbled lanes. It was during the 12th century that Oxford became a meeting place for scholars & grew into the first established centre of learning, outside the monasteries, in England.

The earliest colleges to be founded were University College, Balliol & Merton. Further colleges were added during the reign of the Tudors, as Oxford became a power in the kingdom. There are now 35 university colleges & many other outstanding historic buildings in the city . Christ Church Chapel is now the Cathedral of Oxford, a magnificent building with a deservedly famous choir.

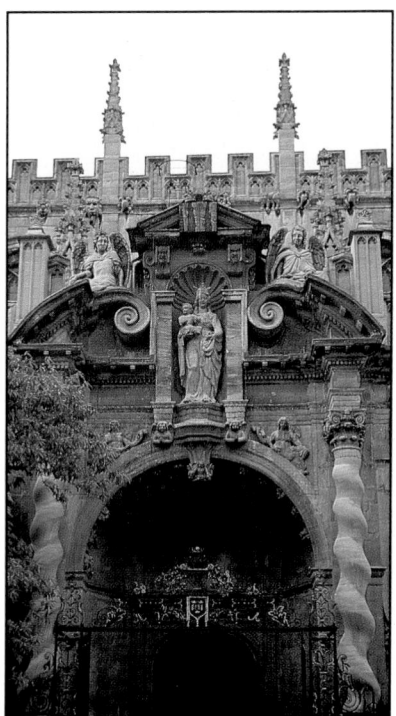

St. Mary's Church.

Oxfordshire

Oxfordshire Gazeteer

Areas of Oustanding Natural Beauty
The North Wessex Downs. The Chiltern Hills. The Cotswolds.

Historic Houses & Castles

Ashdown House - Nr. Lambourn
17th century, built for Elizabeth of Bohemia, now contains portraits associated with her. Mansard roof has cupola with golden ball.

Blenheim Palace - Woodstock
Sir John Vanbrugh's classical masterpiece. Garden designed by Vanbrugh & Henry Wise. Further work done by Capability Brown who created the lake. Collection of pictures & tapestries.

Broughton Castle- Banbury.
14th century mansion with moat - interesting plaster work fine panelling & fire places

Chaseton House-Morton in Marsh
17th century,fine examples of plaster work & panelling.Still has original furniture & tapestries. topiary garden from1700.

Grey Court - Henly-on-Thames
16th century house containing 18th century plasterwork & furniture. Mediaeval ruins. Tudor donkey-wheel for raising water from well.

Mapledurham House - Mapledurham
16th century Elizabethan house. Oak staircase, private chapel, paintings, original moulded ceilings. Watermill nearby.

Milton Manor House - Nr. Abingdon
17th century house designed by Inigo Jones - Georgian wings, walled garden, pleasure grounds.

Rousham House - Steeple Ashton
17th century - contains portraits & miniatures.

University of Oxford Colleges

University college ------------------1249
Balliol-------------------------------1263
Merton-------------------------------1264
Hertford-----------------------------1284
Oriel---------------------------------1326
New----------------------------------1379
All Souls-----------------------------1438
Brasenose---------------------------1509

Christ Church----------------------1546
St. John's----------------------------1555
Pembroke----------------------------1624
Worcester----------------------------1714
Nuffield ------------------------------1937
St. Edmund Hall--------------------1270
Exeter---------------------------------1314
The Queen's----------------------1340
Lincoln-------------------------------1427
Magdalen --------------------------1458
Corpus Christi --------------------1516
Trinity--------------------------------1554
Jesus--------------------------------1571
Wadham------------------------------1610
Keble---------------------------------1868

Cathedrals & Churches

Abingdon (St. Helen)
14th-16th century perpendicular. Painted roof. Georgian stained & enamelled glass.

Burford (St. John the Baptist)
15th century. Sculptured table tombs in churchyard.

Chislehampton (St. Katherine)
18th century. Unspoilt interior of Georgian period. Bellcote.

Dorchester (St. Peter & St. Paul)
13th century knight in stone effigy. Jesse window.

East Hagbourne (St. Andrew)
14th -15th century. Early glass, wooden roofs, 18th century tombs.

North Moreton (All Saints)
13th century with splendid 14th century chantry chapel - tracery.

Oxford Cathedral
Smallest of our English cathedrals. Stone spire form 1230. Norman arcade has double arches, choir vault.

Ryecote (St. Michael & All Angels)
14th century benches & screen base. 17th century altar-piece & communion rails, old clear glass, good ceiling.

Stanton Harcourt (St. Michael)
Early English - old stone & marble floor. Early screen with painting, monuments of 17th -19th century.

Yarnton (St. Bartholomew)
13th century - late perpendicular additions. Jacobean screen. 15th century alabaster reredos.

Oxfordshire

Museums & Galleries

The Ashmolean Museum of Art & Archaeology - Oxford
British ,European ,Mediterranean, Egyptian & Near Eastern archaeology. Oil paintings of Italian, Dutch, Flemish, French & English schools. Old Master watercolours, prints, drawings, ceramics, silver, bronzes & sculptures. Chinese & Japanese porcelain, lacquer & painting, Tibetan, Islamic & Indian art.

Christ Church Picture Gallery - Oxford
Old Master drawings & paintings.

Museum of Modern Art - Oxford
Exhibitiors of contemporary art.

Museum of Oxford
Many exhibits depicting the history of Oxford & its University.

The Rotunda - Oxford
Privately owned collection of dolls' houses 1700-1900, with contents such as furniture, china, silver, dolls, etc.

Oxford University Museum
Entomological, zoological, geological & mineralogical collections.

Pendon Museum of Miniature Landscape & Transport - Abingdon.
Showing in miniature the countryside & its means of transport in the thirties, with trains & thatched village. Railway relics.

Town Museum - Abingdon
17th century building exhibiting fossil, archaeological items & collection of charters & documents.

Tolsey Museum - Burford
Seals, maces, charters & bygones - replica of Regency room with period furnishings & clothing.

Historic Monuments

Uffington Castle & White Horse - Uffington
White horse cut into the chalk - iron age hill fort.

Rollright Stones - Nr. Chipping Norton
77 stones placed in circle - an isolated King's stone & nearby an ancient burial chamber.

Minster Lovell House - Minster Lovell
15th century mediaeval house - ruins.

Deddington Castle - Deddington

Other things to see & do

Didcot railway centre -a large collection of locomotives etc., from Brunel's Great Western Railway.

Filkins -a working wool mill where rugs & garments are woven in traditional way.

Blenheim Palace. Woodstock.

OXFORDSHIRE

Map reference

01 Canning
02 Allday
03 Dunipace
04 Alexander
05 Talfourd-Cook
07 Alden
08 Crofts
09 Anderson
09 Edwards
10 Hill
12 Wadsworth
14 Watsham
16 J. Simpson
17 Hamilton

Oxfordshire

La Madonette Country Guest House

£32.50 to £42.50	Y	N	N

Nearest Road: A.361

A peacefully situated 17th-century millhouse set in rural surroundings, where Patti & Michael offer a warm welcome to their guests. The 5 spacious double en-suite bedrooms are comfortably furnished with full facilities & are attractively decorated. Well located for the Cotswolds, Stratford-upon-Avon, Oxford & Blenheim. Good local pubs & restaurants offering evening meals nearby. An attractive lounge, gardens & swimming pool for guests' use. Licensed.
E-mail: lamadonett@aol.com

VISA: M'CARD: AMEX:

P. Ritter & M. Canning   La Madonette Country Guest House   North Newington   Banbury OX15 6AA
Tel: (01295) 730212   Fax 01295 730363   Open: ALL YEAR   Map Ref No. 01

College Farmhouse

£28.00 to £30.00	Y	Y	N

Nearest Road: A.4260

Fine period farmhouse, with lovely views, set in its own secluded grounds, which include a lake, tennis court & organic vegetable garden. Ideally located for visits to Oxford, Warwick, Stratford-upon-Avon & the Cotswolds. Excellent home-produced food - special diets catered for. Stephen & Sara have considerable local knowledge. They enjoy gardening, bridge & racing. You will be sure of a very comfortable & peaceful stay. Evening meals by arrangement.
E-mail: SEAllday@cs.com

see PHOTO over p. 250

VISA: M'CARD:

Stephen & Sara Allday   College Farmhouse   Astrop Road   Kings Sutton   Banbury OX17 3PS Oxon.
Tel: (01295) 811473   Fax 01295 812505   Open: ALL YEAR   Map Ref No. 02

The Glebe House

£28.00 to £34.00	Y	Y	Y

Nearest Road: A.40

The Glebe House is a pretty 18th-century Cotswold farmhouse on the edge of the beautiful village of Westwell, 2 miles from Burford, with stunning views over open countryside. It offers 3 double bedrooms, 2 with private bathrooms & 1 en-suite. Also, an elegantly furnished sitting room & a terrace in the secluded garden. Ideally located for Oxford, Blenheim Palace, Bath, Cirencester, Cheltenham & Stratford, you will enjoy a warm welcome, relaxed comfort & delicious food.
E-mail: info@oxford-cotswold-holidays.com

Mrs Clare Dunipace   The Glebe House   Westwell   By Burford OX18 4JT   Oxfordshire
Tel: (01993) 822171   Fax 01993 824125   Open: ALL YEAR   Map Ref No. 03

The Well Cottage

£15.00 to £25.00	Y	N	Y

Nearest Road: A.329

The Well Cottage is situated in a pretty garden, close to the River Thames, the historic town of Wallingford, the Berkshire Downs & the Ridgway. The cottage has been extended & now offers a secluded garden flat with 2 double/twin-bedded rooms, each with an en-suite bathroom, T.V. & tea/coffee-making facilities. Each room has its own private entrance. The Well Cottage is a charming home for a relaxing break. Within easy reach of Oxford & Henley-on-Thames.
E-mail: thewellcottage@talk21.com

Mrs J. Alexander   The Well Cottage   Caps Lane   Cholsey OX10 9HQ   Oxfordshire
Tel: (01491) 651959   Fax 01491 651675   Open: ALL YEAR   Map Ref No. 04

College Farmhouse. King Sutton.

Column headers (rotated):
- rate £ from - to per person
- children taken
- evening meals taken
- animals taken

Holmwood

£30.00 to £30.00	Y	N	N

see PHOTO over p. 252

VISA: M'CARD:

Nearest Road: A.4155

Holmwood is a large elegant Georgian country house, Grade II listed, furnished with antique, period furniture. There is a galleried hall, carved mahogany doors & marble fireplaces (wood fires in winter). All bedrooms are spacious & have en-suite facilities. The beautiful gardens extend to 3 1/2 acres & have extensive views over the Thames Valley. A good base for London & the South East. Heathrow Airport 30 mins', Reading 4 miles, Henley 2 1/2 miles. Children over 12 years.

Mr & Mrs Brian Talfourd-Cook   Holmwood   Shiplake Row   Binfield Heath   Henley RG9 4DP
Tel: (0118) 9478747   Fax 0118 9478637   Open: ALL YEAR (Excl. Xmas)   Map Ref No. 05

Broomhill

£30.00 to £40.00	Y	N	N

(non-smoking)

Nearest Road: A.34

Broomhill is a large comfortable family house, set in extensive grounds in a secluded lane & enjoying delightful views over the surrounding countryside. It is situated only 5 minutes between the historic town of Oxford & Abingdon-on-Thames. There are 3 double rooms & 1 single room. Each has either an en-suite or private bathroom, T.V. & tea/coffee-making facilities. Only 45 mins' from London & Heathrow Airport. An ideal base from which to explore Oxford. Children over 10.
E-mail: sara@rralden.force9.co.uk

Richard & Sara Alden   Broomhill   Lincombe Lane   Boars Hill   Oxford OX1 5DZ   Oxfordshire
Tel: (01865) 735339   Open: ALL YEAR   Map Ref No. 07

Crofters Guest House

£25.00 to £27.50	Y	N	N

(non-smoking)

Nearest Road: A.40

Situated in a lively market town, 10 miles from Oxford, on the edge of the Cotswolds, Blenheim Palace & Burford, & within easy reach of Stratford-upon-Avon. Guests are accommodated in comfortable family, double & twin rooms, all with excellent facilities. En-suite & luxury ground-floor garden rooms available. Your hosts Jean & Peter will make your stay a memorable experience. Arrive as a guest, leave as a friend.
E-mail: crofters.ghouse@virgin.net

Jean A. Crofts   Crofters Guest House   29 Oxford Hill   Witney   Oxford OX28 3JU   Oxfordshire
Tel: (01993) 778165   Fax 01993 778165   Open: ALL YEAR   Map Ref No. 08

Sandfield House

£29.00 to £37.00	Y	N	N

(non-smoking)

VISA: M'CARD: AMEX:

Nearest Road: A.40

A family-run guest house offering a high standard of comfort to guests preferring personal service & attention. Quiet & attractive accommodation which is tastefully decorated. Bedrooms are all en-suite or have a private bathroom. T.V. & hospitality tray. Guest lounge & gardens. Convenient for city-centre buses. Easy walking distance to Radcliffe Hospital Complex & Oxford Brookes University. On direct coach routes to London & Heathrow, Gatwick & Stansted Airports. Parking. Children over 6.
E-mail: stay@sandfieldguesthouse.co.uk

Dr. & Mrs B. Anderson   Sandfield House   19 London Road   Headington   Oxford OX3 7RE
Tel: (01865) 762406   Fax 01865 762406   Open: ALL YEAR (Excl. Xmas)   Map Ref No. 09

Holmwood. Binfield Heath.

Shipton Grange House. Shipton–under–Wychwood.

Oxfordshire

Highfield House

Nearest Road: A.4158

A pleasing & friendly house, with good access to the city centre & ring road. Accommodation is in 7 spacious & comfortable bedrooms, all attractively furnished & with matching decor. 5 with en-suite bathroom. All of the bedrooms have colour T.V. & tea/coffee-making facilities. A short walk brings you to the old attractive village of Iffley. Highfield House is an excellent base for exploring the historic delights of glorious Oxford.
E-mail: highfield.house@tesco.net

£25.00 to £27.50 · Y · N · N

VISA: M'CARD:

Mrs Doreen Edwards   Highfield House   91 Rose Hill   Oxford OX4 4HT   Oxfordshire
Tel: (01865) 774083   Fax 01865 774083   Open: ALL YEAR (Excl. Xmas)   Map Ref No. 09

Shipton Grange House

Nearest Road: A.361

A unique conversion of a Georgian coach house & stabling situated in the former grounds of Shipton Court. Secluded in its own walled garden, & approached by a gated archway. There are 3 elegantly furnished guest rooms, each with an en-suite/private bathroom, colour T.V. & beverage facilities. Delicious breakfasts served in the attractive dining room. The friendly hosts are animal lovers & have a number of pet dogs. Shipton Grange is a delightful house, & ideal for visiting Oxford, Blenheim, etc. Children over 12.

£28.00 to £34.00 · Y · N · N

see PHOTO over p. 253

Mrs Veronica Hill   Shipton Grange House   Shipton-under-Wychwood OX7 6DG   Oxfordshire
Tel: (01993) 831298   Fax 01993 832082   Open: ALL YEAR (Excl. Xmas)   Map Ref No. 10

The Craven

Nearest Road: A.420

Roses & clematis cover this pretty 17th-century thatched cottage where breakfast is served around the huge pine table in the farmhouse kitchen. The beamed bedrooms have lovely views. One has a 17th-century 4-poster bed with cabbage rose chintz drapes &, as with all bedrooms, hand-embroidered sheets & pillow slips. Daughter, Katie, produces excellent meals using as much local produce as possible. Glorious walks from the doorstep & a shaggy Old English sheepdog.
E-mail: carol@thecraven.co.uk

£22.50 to £38.00 · Y · Y · N

see PHOTO over p. 255

VISA: M'CARD:

Carol Wadsworth   The Craven   Fernham Road   Uffington SN7 7RD   Oxfordshire
Tel: (01367) 820449   Open: ALL YEAR   Map Ref No. 12

White House

Nearest Road: A.329

White House is an attractive, detached family home in the picturesque Thameside village of Moulsford on the edge of the Berkshire Downs, close to the Ridgeway & Thames Paths. The accommodation is at ground-floor level with its own separate front door, making access easy for disabled guests. Each room is very comfortable. There is a large garden with croquet lawn, which guests are welcome to enjoy. Delicious evening meals are available by prior arrangement. A delightful home.
E-mail: mwatsham@cwcom.net

£25.00 to £35.00 · Y · Y · N

Mrs Maria Watsham   White House   Moulsford On Thames   Wallingford OX10 9JD   Oxfordshire
Tel: (01491) 651397   Fax 01491 652560   Open: ALL YEAR (Excl. Xmas & New Year)   Map Ref No. 14

The Craven.   Uffington.

Oxfordshire

	rate £ from - to per person	children taken	evening meals	animals taken

Field View

| | £24.00 to £26.00 | N | N | N |

Nearest Road: A.40, A.4095

An attractive Cotswold stone house set in 2 acres, situated on picturesque Wood Green, mid-way between Oxford University & the Cotswolds. It is an ideal base for touring & yet is only 8 minutes walk from the centre of this lively Oxfordshire market town. A peaceful setting & a warm, friendly atmosphere await you. The accommodation offered is in 3 comfortable en-suite rooms with all modern amenities, including tea/coffee-making facilities, colour T.V., radio & hairdryer.

E-mail: jsimpson@netcomuk.co.uk

Liz & John Simpson   *Field View*   *Wood Green*   *Witney OX28 1DE*   *Oxfordshire*
Tel: (01993) 705485   *Mobile 07768 614347*   *Open: ALL YEAR*   *Map Ref No. 16*

Gorselands Hall

| | £22.50 to £25.00 | Y | N | Y |

Nearest Road: A.4095

Gorselands Hall is a lovely old Cotswold stone country house with oak beams & flagstone floors in a delightful rural setting, convenient for Oxford (8 miles), Blenheim Palace (4 miles), the Roman Villa at East End & many Cotswold villages. There are 6 attractively furnished en-suite bedrooms, a guest sitting room & a large secluded garden with a grass tennis court. This is good walking country & there is a wide choice of excellent eating places within easy reach. Animals by arrangement.

E-mail: hamilton@gorselandshall.com

VISA: M'CARD: AMEX:

Mr & Mrs N. Hamilton   *Gorselands Hall*   *Boddington Lane   North Leigh*   *Woodstock OX29 6PU*
Tel: (01993) 882292   *Fax 01993 883629*   *Open: ALL YEAR*   *Map Ref No. 17*

All the establishments mentioned in this guide are members of
The Worldwide Bed & Breakfast Association

WORLDWIDE BED & BREAKFAST ASSOCIATION

When booking your accommodation please mention
The Best Bed & Breakfast

Shropshire

Shropshire
(Heart of England)

Shropshire is a borderland with a very turbulent history. Physically it straddles highlands & lowlands with border mountains to the west, glacial plains, upland, moorlands & fertile valleys & the River Severn cutting through. It has been quarrelled & fought over by rulers & kings from earliest times. The English, the Romans & the Welsh all wanted to hold Shropshire because of its unique situation. The ruined castles & fortifications dotted across the county are all reminders of its troubled life. The most impressive of these defences is Offa's Dyke, an enormous undertaking intended to be a permanent frontier between England & Wales.

Shropshire has great natural beauty, countryside where little has changed with the years. Wenlock Edge & Clun Forest, Carding Mill Valley, the Long Mynd, Caer Caradoc, Stiperstones & the trail along Offa's Dyke itself, are lovely walking areas with magnificent scenery.

Shrewsbury was & is a virtual island, almost completely encircled by the Severn River. The castle was built at the only gap, sealing off the town. In this way all comings & goings were strictly controlled. In the 18th century two bridges, the English bridge & the Welsh bridge, were built to carry the increasing traffic to the town but Shrewsbury still remains England's finest Tudor city.

Massive Ludlow Castle was a Royal residence, home of Kings & Queens through the ages, whilst the town is also noted for its Georgian houses.

As order came out of chaos, the county settled to improving itself & became the cradle of the Industrial Revolution. Here Abraham Darby discovered how to use coke (from the locally mined coal) to smelt iron. There was more iron produced here in the 18th century than in any other county. A variety of great industries sprang up as the county's wealth & ingenuity increased. In 1781 the world's first iron bridge opened to traffic.

There are many fine gardens in the county. At Hodnet Hall near Market Drayton, the grounds cover 60 acres & the landscaping includes lakes & pools, trees, shrubs & flowers in profusion. Weston Park has 1,000 acres of parkland, woodland gardens & lakes landscaped by Capability Brown.

The house is Restoration period & has a splendid collection of pictures, furniture, china & tapestries.

Shrewsbury hosts an annual poetry festival & one of England's best flower shows whilst a Festival of Art, Music & Drama is held each year in Ludlow with Shakespeare performed against the castle ruins.

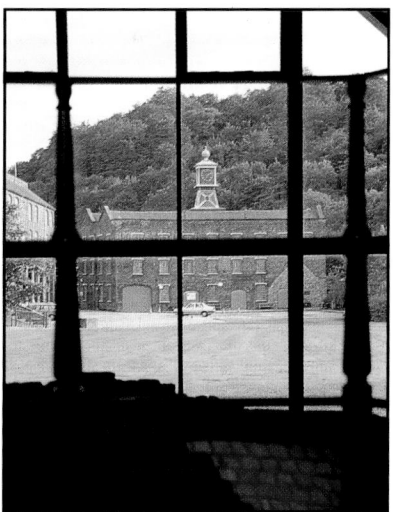

Coalbrookedale Museum.

257

Shropshire

Shropshire Gazeteer

Areas of Outstanding Natural Beauty
The Shropshire Hills.

Historic Houses & Castles

Stokesay Castle - Craven Arms
13th century fortified manor house. Still occupied - wonderful setting - extremely well preserved. Fine timbered gatehouse.
Weston Park - Nr. Shifnal
17th century - fine example of Restoration period - landscaping by Capability Brown. Superb collection of pictures.
Shrewsbury Castle - Shrewsbury
Built in Norman era - interior decorations - painted boudoir.
Benthall Hall - Much Wenlock
16th century. Stone House - mullioned windows. Fine wooden staircase - splendid plaster ceilings.
Shipton Hall - Much Wenlock
Elizabethan. Manor House - walled garden - mediaeval dovecote.
Upton Cressett Hall - Bridgnorth
Elizabethan. Manor House & Gatehouse. Excellent plaster work. . 14th century great hall.

Cathedrals & Churches

Ludlow (St. Lawrence)
14th century nave & transepts. 15th century pinnacled tower. Restored extensively in 19th century. Carved choir stalls, perpendicular chancel - original glass. Monuments.
Shrewsbury (St. Mary)
14th, 15th, 16th century glass. Norman origins.
Stottesdon (St. Mary)
12th century carvings.Norman font. Fine decorations with columns & tracery.
Lydbury North (St. Michael)
14th century transept, 15th century nave roof, 17th century box pews and altar rails. Norman font.
Longor (St. Mary the Virgin)
13th century having an outer staircase to West gallery.
Cheswardine (St. Swithun)
13th century chapel - largely early English. 19th century glass and old brasses. Fine sculpture.

Tong (St. Mary the Virgin with St. Bartholomew)
15th century. Golden chapel of 1515, stencilled walls, remains of paintings on screens, gilt fan vaulted ceiling. Effigies, fine monuments

Museums & Galleries

Clive House - Shrewsbury
Fine Georgian House - collection of Shropshire ceramics. Regimental museum of 1st Queen's Dragoon Guards.
Rowley's House Museum - Shrewsbury
Roman material from Viroconium and prehistoric collection.
Coleham Pumping Station - Old Coleham
Preserved beam engines
Acton Scott Working Farm Museum - Nr. Church Stretton
Site showing agricultural practice before the advent of mechanization.
Ironbridge Gorge Museum - Telford
Series of industrial sites in the Severn Gorge.
CoalBrookdale Museum & Furnace Site
Showing Abraham Darby's blast furnace history. Ironbridge information centre is next to the world's first iron bridge.
Mortimer Forest Museum - Nr. Ludlow
Forest industries of today and yesterday. Ecology of the forest.
Whitehouse Museum of Buildings & Country life - Aston Munslow
4 houses together in one, drawing from every century 13th to 18th, together with utensils and implements of the time.
The Buttercross Museum - Ludlow
Geology, natural & local history of area.
Reader`s House-Ludlow
Splendid example of a 16th century town house. 3 storied porch.
Much Wenlock Museum.-Much Wenlock
Geology, natural & local history.
Clun Town Museum - Clun
Pre-history earthworks, rights of way, commons & photographs.

Historic Monuments

Acton Burnell Castle - Shrewsbury
13th century fortified manor house - ruins only.

Shropshire

Boscobel House - Shifnal
17th century house.
Bear Steps - Shrewsbury
Half timbered buildings. Mediaeval.
Abbot's House - Shrewsbury
15th century half-timbered.
Buildwas Abbey - Nr. Telford
12th century - Savignac Abbey - ruins.
The church is nearly complete with 14
Norman arches.
Haughmond Abbey - Shrewsbury
12th century - remains of house of
Augustinian canons.
Wenlock Priory - Much Wenlock
13th century abbey - ruins.
Roman Town - Wroxeter
2nd century - remains of town of
Viroconium including public baths and
colonnade.
Moreton Corbet Castle - Moreton Corbet
13th century keep, Elizabethan features -
gatehouse altered 1519.
Lilleshall Abbey
12th century - completed 13th century,
West front has notable doorway.
Bridgnorth Castle - Bridgnorth
Ruins of Norman castle whose angle of
incline is greater than Pisa.
Whiteladies Priory - Boscobel
12th century cruciform church - ruins.
Old Oswestry - Oswestry
Iron age hill fort covering 68 acres; five
ramparts and having an elaborate western
portal.

Other things to see & do

Ludlow Festival of Art and Drama -
annual event
Shrewsbury Flower Show - every August
Severn Valley Railway - the longest full
guage steam railway in the country

Kings Head Inn. Shrewsbury.

SHROPSHIRE
Map reference

01 Prytz
02 Hannigan
03 Chivers
04 Ross
05 Williamson
06 Hunter
07 Harris
08 Roberts
09 Mitchell
10 Bebbington

Shropshire

rate £ from - to
per person
children taken
evening meals taken
animals taken

£25.00 to £25.00	N	Y	N

Knock Hundred Cottage

Nearest Road: A.49

Knock Hundred Cottage is believed to originate from the 16th century & enjoys an open aspect with extensive views. 1 double bedroom with a private bathroom & 1 en-suite twin-bedded room. Each room is comfortably furnished & has a T.V.. Early morning tea/coffee is served in your room & breakfast is provided in the family dining room. Evening meals by prior arrangement. Places of interest include Ludlow, the Long Mynd, Offa's Dyke, the beautiful Corve Dale & various National Trust/ English Heritage properties & gardens.

Mrs Anne Prytz   Knock Hundred Cottage   Abcott   Clungunford   Craven Arms   SY7 0PX   Shropshire
Tel: (01588) 660594   Fax 01588 660594   Open: ALL YEAR   Map Ref No. 01

£23.00 to £30.00	N	N	N

The Severn Trow

Nearest Road: A.442

The Severn Trow is a wonderful place which has seen the hand of hospitality extended by successive occupants for many centuries. It stands on the riverbank where originally travellers would berth their trows before retiring to recuperate. It has been renovated, & yet it has retained many original features which enhance its character, such as an inglenook & a Jackfield mosaic tile floor. Rooms are delightful: each is en-suite (1 ground floor) & well-appointed. A choice of eating houses nearby.
E-mail: paulineseverntrow@lineone.net

Pauline Hannigan   The Severn Trow   Church Road   Jackfield   Ironbridge TF8 7ND   Shropshire
Tel: (01952) 883551   Open: JAN - OCT   Map Ref No. 02

£37.50 to £50.00	Y	N	Y

Number Twenty Eight

Nearest Road: A.49

A warm welcome awaits you in this guest house which comprises 3 period houses & 3 Tudor cottage suites. Snug sitting rooms, book-lined walls, pictures & open fires make for a very relaxing atmosphere. All bedrooms are en-suite & individually furnished. Tea/coffee & T.V.. Many award-winning restaurants within walking distance. Castle, bookshops, antique shops to explore in this most lovely of Tudor & Georgian market towns on the Welsh Marches. (U.K. freephone 0800 0815000.)
E-mail: ross@no28.co.uk

VISA: M'CARD:

Patricia & Philip Ross   Number Twenty Eight   28 Lower Broad Street   Ludlow SY8 1PQ   Shropshire
Tel: (01584) 876996   Fax 01584 876860   Open: ALL YEAR   Map Ref No. 04

£25.00 to £32.00	Y	Y	Y

The Moor Hall

Nearest Road: A.4117

The atmosphere at The Moor Hall is relaxed & friendly; guests often comment that it's like being at a country house party with friends. The house was built by Lord Boyne in 1789 & is a lovely example of the Georgian Palladian style. The gardens extend to 5 acres & look out over miles of unspoilt countryside. There are 3 attractively furnished en-suite bedrooms. Great cooking, a licensed bar & the opportunity to fish in the small lake complete the experience.
E-mail: info@moorhall.co.uk

see PHOTO over
p. 262

Mrs B. M. Chivers   The Moor Hall   Clee Downton   Ludlow SY8 3EG   Shropshire
Tel: (01584) 823209   Fax 01584 823387   Open: ALL YEAR   Map Ref No. 03

The Moor Hall. Ludlow.

rate £ from - to per person	children taken	evening meals taken	animals taken

| £25.00 to £35.00 | N | N | N |

Nearest Road: A.41, A.53

Mickley House

When visiting Ironbridge, Shrewsbury or Chester, your hosts offer peace, quiet & comfort in their tastefully restored farmhouse, retaining many internal Victorian features. The tranquillity of the house spills out into landscaped gardens. Relax or meander through rose-scented pergolas to pools & a trickling waterfall. Excellent restaurants/pubs nearby. En-suite bedrooms of different style/decor, with all facilities. 1 bedroom with authentic Louis XV king-size bed. Also, ground-floor room.
E-mail: mickleyhouse@hotmail.com

Mrs Pauline Williamson Mickley House Faulsgreen Tern Hill Market Drayton TF9 3QW Shropshire
Tel: (01630) 638505   Fax 01630 638505   Open: ALL YEAR (Excl. Xmas)   Map Ref No. 05

| £42.00 to £50.00 | Y | Y | Y |

see PHOTO over p. 264

VISA: M'CARD: AMEX:

Nearest Road: A.5

Pen-Y-Dyffryn Country Hotel

Set almost a thousand feet up in the peaceful Shropshire/Wales border hills, this silver-stone Georgian rectory has a real 'away from it all' atmosphere. But the medieval towns of Chester & Shrewsbury are only a short drive, so civilisation is close by. High-quality local & increasingly organic food is served in the restaurant, complete with its own log fire. All bedrooms are en-suite, with colour T.V., telephone etc. & some even have their own private patios. Fully licensed.
E-mail: stay@peny.co.uk

Miles & Audrey Hunter Pen-Y-Dyffryn Country Hotel   Rhydycroesau Oswestry SY10 7JD Shropshire
Tel: (01691) 653700   Fax 01691 650066   Open: ALL YEAR   Map Ref No. 06

| £22.00 to £27.00 | N | N | N |

Nearest Road: A.49

Tudor House

This Grade II listed building is centrally situated in a quiet medieval street in picturesque & historic Shrewsbury (Brother Cadfael country). Dating from 1450, it has a wealth of oak beams, & has been tastefully redecorated & refurbished throughout. Some of the bedrooms have en-suite facilities; all have washbasins, colour T.V. & central heating & are very comfortable. Special diets available in non-smoking dining room. Drinks are served in residents' licensed lounge.

Mrs Mair Harris   Tudor House   2 Fish Street   Shrewsbury SY1 1UR   Shropshire
Tel: (01743) 351735   Open: ALL YEAR   Map Ref No. 07

| £27.50 to £32.50 | Y | Y | N |

Nearest Road: A.488, A.5

The White House

A lovely, 16th-century, black-and-white, half-timbered guest house with nearly 2 acres of gardens and river, 3 miles south-west of medieval Shrewsbury. Ironbridge, Mid-Wales and the Long Mynd within 30 mins' drive. 6 guest rooms, some en-suite, each with tea/coffee etc. 2 sitting rooms, 1 with T.V.. Car parking. The dining room offers a fresh, varied menu supplemented by vegetables and herbs from the garden, and the house hens provide your breakfast eggs! Children over 12.
E-mail: mgm@whitehousehanwood.freeserve.co.uk

Mike & Gill Mitchell   The White House   Hanwood   Shrewsbury SY5 8LP   Shropshire
Tel: (01743) 860414   Fax 01743 860414   Open: ALL YEAR   Map Ref No. 09

Pen-Y-Dyffryn Country Hotel . Rhydycroesau.

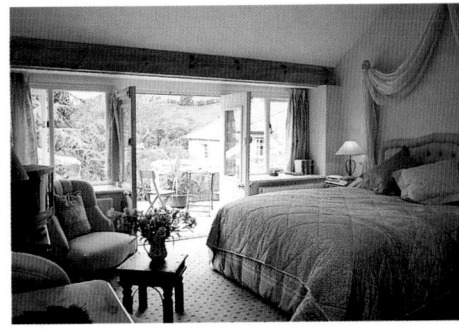

Shropshire

| rate £ from - to per person | children taken | evening meals | animals taken |

| £30.00 to £45.00 | Y | Y | N |

🚭

see PHOTO over
p. 266

VISA: M'CARD:

Nearest Road: A.458

Upper Brompton Farm is the quintessence of English country living. Croquet on the lawn, four-poster beds, a roaring open fire, roast beef & great British puddings. These things together with the personal attention of the hosts has won a prestigious award. Glorious landscapes, perfect walking country together with National Trust properties, Ironbridge (15 mins') & other places of interest are within easy reach. Only 5 mins' from Shrewsbury, it is ideally situated for exploring Shropshire.
E-mail: upper-brompton.farm@dial.pipex.com

Upper Brompton Farm

George Roberts   Upper Brompton Farm   Cross Houses   Shrewsbury SY5 6LE   Shropshire
Tel: (01743) 761629   Fax 01743 761679   Open: ALL YEAR   Map Ref No. 08

| £35.00 to £40.00 | N | N | Y |

🚭

VISA: M'CARD:

Nearest Road: A.41, A.49

In this handsome William & Mary house, Jane goes to great lengths to ensure your comfort, & you're free to come & go anytime (unusual for a B & B.) Large bedrooms are bright & sunny, with rich fabrics & deep mattresses . The Steinway in the hall encourages the most hesitant pianist. Wander through this 'conservation rich' farm to the trout lake where you can fish from bank or boat (tuition available). Molly, their flat-coat retriever will show you the way. Nationally acclaimed gardens nearby.
E-mail: dearnford_hall@yahoo.com

Dearnford Hall

Charles & Jane Bebbington   Dearnford Hall   Whitchurch SY13 3JJ   Shropshire
Tel: (01948) 662319   Fax 01948 666670   Open: ALL YEAR (Excl. Xmas)   Map Ref No. 10

All the establishments mentioned in this guide are members of
The Worldwide Bed & Breakfast Association

WORLDWIDE BED & BREAKFAST ASSOCIATION

When booking your accommodation please mention
The Best Bed & Breakfast

Upper Brompton Farm. Cross Houses.

Somerset, Bath & Bristol

Somerset
(West Country)

Fabulous legends, ancient customs, charming villages, beautiful churches, breathtaking scenery & a glorious cathedral, Somerset has them all, along with a distinctively rich local dialect. The essence of Somerset lies in its history & myth & particularly in the unfolding of the Arthurian tale.

Legend grows from the bringing of the Holy Grail to Glastonbury by Joseph of Arimathea, to King Arthur's castle at Camelot, held by many to be sited at Cadbury, to the image of the dead King's barge moving silently through the mists over the lake to the Isle of Avalon. Archaeological fact lends support to the conjecture that Glastonbury, with its famous Tor, was an island in an ancient lake. Another island story surrounds King Alfred, reputedly sheltering from the Danes on the Isle of Athelney & there burning his cakes.

Historically, Somerset saw the last battle fought on English soil, at Sedgemoor in 1685. The defeat of the Monmouth rebellion resulted in the wrath of James II falling on the West Country in the form of Judge Jeffreys & his "Bloody Assize".

To the west of the county lies part of the Exmoor National Park, with high moorland where deer roam & buzzards soar & a wonderful stretch of cliffs from Minehead to Devon. Dunster is a popular village with its octagonal Yarn market, & its old world cottages, dominated at one end by the castle & at the other by the tower on Conygar Hill.

To the east the woods & moors of the Quantocks are protected as an area of outstanding natural beauty. The Vale of Taunton is famous for its apple orchards & for the golden cider produced from them.

The south of the county is a land of rolling countryside & charming little towns, Chard, Crewkerne, Ilchester & Ilminster amongst others.

To the north the limestone hills of Mendip are honeycombed with spectacular caves & gorges, some with neolithic remains, as at Wookey Hole & Cheddar Gorge.

Wells is nearby, so named because of the multitude of natural springs. Hardly a city, Wells boasts a magnificent cathedral set amongst spacious lawns & trees. The west front is one of the glories of English architecture with its sculptured figures & soaring arches. A spectacular feature is the astronomical clock, the work of 14th century monk Peter Lightfoot. The intricate face tells the hours, minutes, days & phases of the moon. On the hour, four mounted knights charge forth & knock one another from their horses.

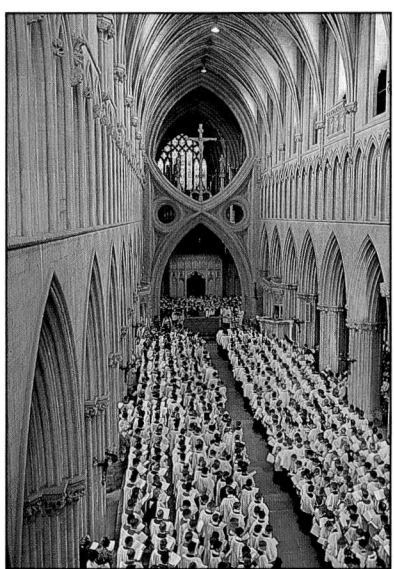

Wells Cathedral Choir.

Somerset, Bath & Bristol

Bath is one of the most loved historic cities in England. It owes its existence to the hot springs which bubble up five hundred thousand gallons of water a day at a temperature of some 120' F. According to legend, King Bladud appreciated the healing qualities of the waters & established his capital here, calling it Aquae Sulis. He built an elaborate healing & entertainment centre around the springs including reservoirs, baths & hypercaust rooms.

The Roman Baths, not uncovered until modern times, are on the lowest of three levels. Above them came the mediaeval city & on the top layer at modern street level is the elegant Georgian Pump Room.

Edward was crowned the first King of all England in 973, in the Saxon Abbey which stood on the site of the present fifteenth century abbey. This building, in the graceful perpendicular style with elegant fan vaulting, is sometimes called the "lantern of the West", on account of its vast clerestories & large areas of glass.

During the Middle Ages the town prospered through Royal patronage & the development of the wool industry. Bath became a city of weavers, the leading industrial town in the West of England.

The 18th century gave us the superb Georgian architecture which is the city's glory. John Wood, an ambitious young architect laid out Queen Anne's Square in the grand Palladian style, & went on to produce his masterpiece, the Royal Crescent. His scheme for the city was continued by his son & a number of other fine architects, using the beautiful Bath stone. Bath was a centre of fashion, with Beau Nash the leader of a glittering society.

In 1497 John & Sebastian Cabot sailed from the Bristol quayside to the land they called Ameryke, in honour of the King's agent in Bristol, Richard Ameryke. Bristol's involvement in the colonisation of the New World & the trade in sugar, tobacco & slaves that followed, made her the second city in the kingdom in the 18th century. John Cabot is commemorated by the Cabot Tower on grassy Brandon Hill - a fine vantage point from which to view the city. On the old docks below are the Bristol Industrial Museum & the SS Great Britain, Brunel's famous iron ship. Another achievement of this master engineer, the Clifton Suspension Bridge, spans Bristol's renowned beauty spot, the Clifton Gorge. For a glimpse of Bristol's elegant past, stroll through Clifton with its stately terraces & spacious Downs.

A short walk from the busy city centre & modern shopping area, the visitor in search of history will find cobbled King Street with its merchant seamen's almhouses & The Theatre Royal, the oldest theatre in continuous use in England, & also Llandoger Trow, an ancient inn associated with Treasure Island & Robinson Crusoe.

Bath Abbey.

Somerset, Bath & Bristol

Somerset, Bath & Bristol Gazeteer

Areas of Outstanding Natural Beauty
Mendip Hills. Quantock Hills. National Park - Exmoor. The Cotswolds.

Historic Houses & Castles

Abbot's Fish House - Meare
14th century house.
Barrington Court - Illminster
16th century house & gardens.
Blaise Castle House - Henbury Nr. Bristol
18th century house - now folk museum, extensive woodlands.
Brympton D'Evercy - Nr. Yeovil
Mansion with 17th century front & Tudor west front. Adjacent is 13th century priest's house & church. Formal gardens & vineyard.
Claverton Manor - Nr. Bath
Greek revival house - furnished with 17th, 18th, 19th century American originals.
Clevedon Court - Clevedon
14th century manor house, 13th century hall, 12th century tower. Lovely garden with rare trees & shrubs. This is where Thackerey wrote much of 'Vanity Fair'.
Dyrham Park - Between Bristol & Bath
17th century house - fine panelled rooms, Dutch paintings, furniture.
Dunster Castle - Dunster
13th century castle with fine 17th century staircase & ceilings.
East Lambrook Manor - South Petherton
15th century house with good panelling.
Gaulden Manor - Tolland
12th century manor. Great Hall having unique plaster ceiling & oak screen. Antique furniture.
Halsway Manor - Crowcombe
14th century house with fine panelling.
Hatch Court - Hatch Beauchamp
Georgian house in the Palladian style with China room.
King John's Hunting Lodge - Axbridge
Early Tudor merchant's house.
Lytes Carry - Somerton
14th & 15th century manor house with a chapel & formal garden.
Montacute House - Yeovil
Elizabethan house with fine examples of Heraldic Glass, tapestries, panelling & furniture. Portrait gallery of Elizabethan & Jacobean paintings.
Tintinhull House - Yeovil
17th century house with beautiful gardens.
Priory Park College - Bath
18th century Georgian mansion, now Roman Catholic school.
No. 1 Royal Crescent - Bath
An unaltered Georgian house built 1767.
Red Lodge - Bristol
16th century house - period furniture & panelling.
St. Vincent's Priory - Bristol
Gothic revival house, built over caves which were sanctuary for Christians.
St Catherine's Court - Nr. Bath
Small Tudor house - associations with Henry VIII & Elizabeth I.

Cathedrals & Churches

Axbridge (St. John)
1636 plaster ceiling & panelled roofs.
Backwell (St. Andrew)
12th to 17th century, 15th century tower, repaired 17th century. 15th century tomb & chancel, 16th century screen, 18th century brass chandelier.
Bath Abbey
Perpendicular - monastic church, 15th century foundation. Nave finished 17th century, restorations in 1674.
Bishop's Lydeard (St. Mary)
15th century. Notable tower, rood screen & glass.
Bristol Cathedral
Mediaeval. Eastern halfnave Victorian. Chapterhouse richly ornamented. Iron screen, 3 fonts, "fairest parish church in all England".
Bristol (St. Mary Radcliffe)
Bristol (St. Stephens')
Perpendicular - monuments, magnificent tower.
Bruton (St. Mary)
Fine 2 towered 15th century church. Georgian chancel, tie beam roof, Georgian reredos. Jacobean screen. 15th century embroidery.
Chewton Mendip (St. Mary Magdalene)
12th century with later additions. 12th century doorway, 15th century bench ends, magnificent 16th century tower & 17th century lecturn.

Somerset, Bath & Bristol

Crewkerne (St. Bartholomew)
Magnificent west front & roofs, 15th & 16th century. South doorway dating from 13th century, wonderful 15th century painted glass & 18th century chandeliers.
East Brent (St. Mary)
Mainly 15th century. Plaster ceiling, painted glass & carved bench ends.
Glastonbury (St. John)
One of the finest examples of perpendicular towers. Tie beam roof, late mediaeval painted glass, mediaeval vestment & early 16th century altar tomb.
High Ham (St. Andrew)
Sumptuous roofs & vaulted rood screen. Carved bench ends. Jacobean lectern, mediaeval painted glass. Norman font.
Kingsbury Episcopi (St. Martin)
14th-15th century. Good tower with fan vaulting. Late mediaeval painted glass.
Long Sutton (Holy Trinity)
15th century with noble tower & magnificent tie beam roof. 15th century pulpit & rood screen, tower vaulting.
Martock (All Saints)
13th century chancel. Nave with tie beam roof, outstanding of its kind. 17th century paintings of Apostles.
North Cadbury (St. Michael)
painted glass.
Pilton (St. John)
12th century with arcades. 15th century roofs.
Taunton (St. Mary Magdalene)
Highest towers in the county. Five nave roof, fragments of mediaeval painted glass.
Trull (All Saints)
15th century with many mediaeval art treasures & 15th century glass.
Wells Cathedral-Wells
Magnificent west front with carved figures. Splendid tower. Early English arcade of nave & transepts. 60 fine misericords c.1330. Lady chapel with glass & star vault. Chapter House & Bishop's Palace.
Weston Zoyland (St. Mary)
15th century bench ends. 16th century heraldic glass. Jacobean pulpit.
Wrington (All Souls)
15th century aisles & nave; font, stone pulpit, notable screens.

Museums & Galleries

Admiral Blake Museum - Bridgewater
Exhibits relating to Battle of Sedgemoor, archaeology.
American Museum in Britain - Claverton Nr. Bath
American decorative arts 17th to 19th century displayed in series of furnished rooms & galleries of special exhibits. Paintings, furniture, glass wood & metal work, textiles, folk sculpture, etc.
Borough Museum - Hendford Manor Hall, Yeovil
Archaeology, firearms collections & Bailward Costume Collection.
Bristol Industrial Museum - Bristol
Collections of transport items of land, sea & air. Many unique items.
Burdon Manor - Washford
14th century manor house with Saxon fireplace & cockpit.
City of Bristol Art Gallery - Bristol
Permanent & loan collections of paintings, English & Oriental ceramics.
Glastonbury Lake Village Museum - Glastonbury
Late prehistoric antiquities.
Gough's Cave Museum - Cheddar
Upper Paleolithic remains, skeleton, flints, amber & engraved stones.
Holburne of Menstrie Museum - Bath
Old Master paintings, silver, glass, porcelain, furniture & miniatures in 18th century building. Work of 20th century craftworkers.
Hinton Priory - Hinton Charterhouse
13th century - ruins of Carthusian priory.
Kings Weston Roman Villa - Lawrence Weston
3rd & 4th centuries - mosaics of villa - some walls.
Museum of Costume - Bath
Collection of fashion from 17th century to present day.
Roman Baths - Bath
Roman Museum - Bath
Material from remains of extensive Roman baths & other Roman sites.
Stoney Littleton Barrow - Nr. Bath
Neolithic burial chamber - restoration work 1858.
St. Nicholas Church & City Museum - Bristol
Mediaeval antiquities relating to local

Somerset, Bath & Bristol

history, Church plate & vestments.
Altarpiece by Hogarth.
Temple Church - Bristol
14th & 15th century ruins.
Victoria Art Gallery - Bath
Paintings, prints, drawings, glass,
ceramics, watches, coins, etc. Bygones -
permanent & temporary exhibitions.
Geology collections.
Wookey Hole Cave Museum - Wookey
Hole
Remains from Pliocene period. Relics of
Celtic & Roman civilization. Exhibition of
handmade paper-making.

Historic Monuments

Cleeve Abbey - Cleeve
Ruined 13th century house, with timber
roof & wall paintings.
Farleigh Castle - Farleigh Hungerford
14th century remains - museums in
chapel.
Glastonbury Abbey - Glastonbury
12th & 13th century ruins of St. Joseph's

chapel & Abbot's kitchen.
Muchelney Abbey - Muchelney
15th century ruins of Benedictine abbey.

Other things to see & do

Black Rock Nature Reserve - Cheddar
Circular walk through plantation woodland,
downland grazing.
Cheddar Caves
Show caves at the foot of beautiful
Cheddar Gorge.
Clifton Zoological Gardens - Bristol
Flourishing zoo with many exhibits -
beautiful gardens.
Clifton Suspension Bridge - Bristol
Designed by Isambard Kingdom Brunel,
opened in 1864. Viewpoint & picnic spot
Camera Obscura.
Cricket St. Thomas Wildlife Park - Nr.
Chard
Wildlife park, heavy horse centre,
countryside museum, etc.
The Pump Room - Bath
18th century neo-classical interior. Spa.

Clifton Suspension Bridge. Bristol.

SOMERSET, BATH & BRISTOL

Map reference

01	Dodd	05	Griffin
01	Besley	06	Riley
01	Lanz	11	Gallannaugh
01	Poole	12	Tasker
01	Ford	14	Newman-C.
01	Beckett	15	Bale
01	Addison	16	Vicary
01	Stabbins	17	Redmond
01	Huxley	18	Parsons
01	Smith	19	Cooper
01	Lanz	20	Knight
01	Metcalf	21	Brewer
01	Bryan	24	Copeland
01	Thwaites	26	Mitchem
01	Selby	29	Eyre
01	Keeling	30	Mogfod
02	Tiley	34	Frost
03	Westlake	35	Nowell
04	Graham	36	Thompson
04	Priddle	38	Durbin

Somerset

| rate £ from - to per person | children taken | evening meals | animals taken |

£30.00 to £38.00

Y | N | N

(no smoking)

VISA: M'CARD:

Nearest Road: A.4

Brocks

Brocks is a beautiful Georgian town house built in 1765 by John Wood, situated between the Circus and Royal Crescent. Very close to the Roman Baths, Assembly Rooms, etc. This really is a wonderful part of Bath. This historic house has all modern conveniences, & the comfortable bedrooms are en-suite. The aim here is to offer guests the highest standards, & personal attention. An ideal base from which to explore beautiful Bath.
E-mail: marion@brocksguesthouse.co.uk

| Marion Dodd | Brocks | 32 Brock Street | Bath BA1 2LN | Somerset |
| Tel: (01225) 338374 | Fax (01225) 334245 | | Open: ALL YEAR | Map Ref No. 01 |

£21.00 to £35.00

Y | N | Y

(no smoking)

VISA: M'CARD: AMEX:

Nearest Road: A.4

The Old Red House

This charming Victorian Gingerbread House is colourful, comfortable & warm; full of unexpected touches & intriguing little curiosities. Its leaded & stained glass windows are now double-glazed to ensure a peaceful stay. The extensive breakfast menu, a delight in itself, is served in a sunny conservatory. Parking. Special rates for 3 or more nights. Dinner available at a local riverside pub. A brochure on request. Children over 4 years. Animals by prior arrangement.
E-mail: oldredhouse@amserve.net

| Chrissie Besley | The Old Red House | 37 Newbridge Road | Bath BA1 3HE | Somerset |
| Tel: (01225) 330464 | Fax 01225 331661 | | Open: FEB - DEC | Map Ref No. 01 |

£37.50 to £65.00

Y | N | N

VISA: M'CARD: AMEX:

Nearest Road: A.431

Apsley House Hotel

An elegant Georgian country house built for the Duke of Wellington in 1830, situated just over 1 mile from the city centre with private parking. A small privately-run hotel, guests are offered a warm welcome & personal care. The interior includes many period features, the house is furnished with fine antiques & oil paintings. A sumptuous breakfast is served in the delightful dining room. Children over 5 years.
E-mail: info@apsley-house.co.uk

| David & Annie Lanz | Apsley House Hotel | 141, Newbridge Hill | Bath BA1 3PT | Somerset |
| Tel: (01225) 336966 | Fax 01225 425462 | | Open: ALL YEAR (Excl. Xmas) | Map Ref No. 01 |

£33.00 to £40.00

Y | N | N

(no smoking)

see PHOTO over p. 274

VISA: M'CARD: AMEX:

Nearest Road: A.431

Cranleigh

Situated in a quiet residential area, this comfortable Victorian house has great character, with exceptionally spacious, stylish en-suite bedrooms. Most have lovely views across the Avon Valley. You are welcome to relax in the garden. Breakfast includes such choices as fresh-fruit salad & scrambled eggs with smoked salmon. Easy access to the heart of Bath. Parking. The Pooles have a wealth of information to help you make the most of your stay in Bath. Children over 5 years.
E-mail: cranleigh@btinternet.com

| Tony & Jan Poole | Cranleigh | 159 Newbridge Hill | Bath BA1 3PX | Somerset |
| Tel: (01225) 310197 | Fax 01225 423143 | | Open: ALL YEAR | Map Ref No. 01 |

Cranleigh. Bath.

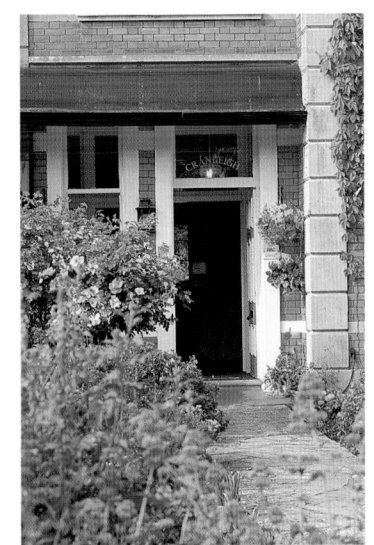

Somerset

rate £ from - to per person	children taken	evening meals	animals taken

The Gainsborough

£30.00 to £46.00 | Y | N | N

VISA: M'CARD: AMEX:

Nearest Road: A.4

The Gainsborough is a large country-house hotel, comfortably furnished & set in its own grounds near the Botanical Gardens & Victoria Park. Offering 17 attractive en-suite bedrooms, each with colour T.V., direct-dial telephone, tea/coffee-making facilities & hairdryer. The dining room & small cocktail bar overlook the lawns, where guests often relax during the summer on the sun terrace. Private parking. Special offers available.
E-mail: gainsborough_hotel@compuserve.com

Mrs Anna Ford   The Gainsborough   Weston Lane   Bath BA1 4AB   Somerset
Tel: (01225) 311380   Fax 01225 447411   Open: ALL YEAR   Map Ref No. 01

Cedar Lodge

£25.00 to £37.50 | Y | N | N

(no smoking)

Nearest Road: A.4, A.46

Within easy level walk to the historic city centre, this beautiful, detached Georgian house offers period elegance with modern amenities. 3 lovely bedrooms (1 with 4-poster, 1 half-tester, 1 twin), all with en-suite/private bathrooms. Delightful gardens & comfortable drawing room, with fire, to relax in. Ideally situated for excursions to Avebury, Stonehenge, Salisbury, Longleat, Wells, Cotswolds, Wales & many other attractions. Secure private parking. Children over 10.

Derek & Maria Beckett   Cedar Lodge   13 Lambridge   London Road   Bath BA1 6BJ   Somerset
Tel: (01225) 423468   Open: ALL YEAR   Map Ref No. 01

Dolphin House

£25.00 to £32.50 | Y | N | N

(no smoking)

Nearest Road: A.4

Dolphin House is a detached Georgian Grade II listed house with a mature terraced walled garden. Centrally heated & with period furnishings. There is a private suite consisting of a twin-bedded room, lounge & large bathroom. Also, a large double bedroom with private bathroom. T.V. & tea/coffee-making facilities in each room. All meals are served in the privacy of your own room or on the terrace. The historic city of Bath is only 2 1/2 miles. Children over 12 years welcome.

Mr & Mrs G. Riley   Dolphin House   8 Northend   Batheaston   Bath BA1 7EH   Somerset
Tel: (01225) 858915   Fax 01225 858915   Open: ALL YEAR   Map Ref No. 06

Bailbrook Lodge Hotel

£30.00 to £40.00 | Y | Y | N

see PHOTO over p. 276

VISA: M'CARD: AMEX:

Nearest Road: A.46, A.4

Bailbrook Lodge is an imposing Grade II listed Georgian house located 1 mile east of Bath. There is a choice of 12 elegantly furnished en-suite bedrooms (some 4-posters), all with T.V. & hospitality tray. Evening meals with traditional English cuisine are provided. The lounge bar & dining room overlook the garden. Bailbrook Lodge is an ideal base for exploring Bath & touring the beautiful surrounding countryside. Ample car-parking.
E-mail: hotel@bailbrooklodge.co.uk

Mr & Mrs R.N. Addison   Bailbrook Lodge Hotel   35/37 London Road West   Bath BA1 7HZ   Somerset
Tel: (01225) 859090   Fax 01225 852299   Open: ALL YEAR   Map Ref No. 01

Bailbrook Lodge. Bath.

rate £ from - to per person	children taken	evening meals	animals taken		

The Hollies

£25.00 to £32.00	Y	N	N

VISA: M'CARD:

Nearest Road: A.367

The Hollies is a lovely old Victorian, Grade II listed house situated within walking distance of the city. With just 3 pretty guest rooms, personal attention and hospitality are assured. Each room has en-suite or private facilities, colour T.V., beverage-making facilities, hairdryer & radio/alarm clock. A wide breakfast menu is served. Parking is available. Rooms overlook the secluded garden of apple trees, herbs & roses. The Hollies is a charming home, ideal for exploring Bath. Children over 5.

Mrs N. Stabbins   *The Hollies*   *Hatfield Road*   *Bath BA2 2BD*   *Somerset*
Tel: (01225) 313366   Fax 01225 313366   *Open: Mid JAN - DEC (Excl. Xmas)*   *Map Ref No. 01*

Lavender House

£32.50 to £52.00	Y	Y	N

see PHOTO over p. 278

VISA: M'CARD:

Nearest Road: A.367

Set in a quiet conservation area, within easy reach of Bath city centre. Lavender House is an Edwardian house which affords 5 lovely bedrooms. Each is individually designed & has a large, luxurious bathroom, T.V. & hospitality tray. In addition to serving a full English breakfast, using free-range & fresh local produce, there are special Vegetarian Cordon Vert options. Dinner by arrangement. Lavender House is a special place to unwind, relax & be spoiled. Parking. Children over 8.
E-mail: lavenderhouse@btinternet.com

Carol & Bill Huxley   *Lavender House*   *17 Bloomfield Park*   *Bath BA2 2BY*   *Somerset*
Tel: (01225) 314500   Fax 01225 448564   *Open: ALL YEAR*   *Map Ref No. 01*

Apartment One

£28.00 to £30.00	N	N	N

Nearest Road: A.4

An elegant, 2-storey, garden apartment within a Grade I listed Georgian house, situated in one of Bath's most desirable streets. Brian & Chan Loo Smith, who have for many years lived abroad, offer friendly hospitality in their charming home. There is 1 attractive bedroom (which can be arranged as a double, twin or family room) with an en-suite bathroom. Breakfast can be taken (weather permitting) on the pretty courtyard surrounded by potted herbs, flowers & shrubs.
E-mail: ChanlooSmith@Aptone.fsnet.co.uk

Mrs C. L. Smith   *Apartment One*   *60, Great Pulteney Street*   *Bath BA2 4DN*   *Somerset*
Tel: (01225) 464134   Fax 01225 483663   *Open: ALL YEAR*   *Map Ref No. 01*

Paradise House

£37.50 to £65.00	Y	N	N

VISA: M'CARD: AMEX:

Nearest Road: A.367

Paradise House was built in the 1720s, on the ancient Roman Fosse Way. The Fosse Way, now a cul-de-sac, is one of the quietest streets in Bath & provides easy access to the city centre. (The Roman Baths are only 7 mins' walk away.) 11 attractively furnished & well-appointed bedrooms, each with an en-suite bathroom, etc. The house enjoys fine views over the Georgian city & has over 1/2 an acre of walled gardens which compete with the golden splendour of the city below.
E-mail: info@paradise-house.co.uk

David & Annie Lanz   *Paradise House*   *86 Holloway*   *Bath BA2 4PX*   *Somerset*
Tel: (01225) 317723   Fax 01225 482005   *Open: ALL YEAR (Excl. Xmas)*   *Map Ref No. 01*

Lavender House. Bath.

Villa Magdala. Bath.

Somerset

Northwick House

Nearest Road: A.36
With outstanding views over Bath & the surrounding countryside, this comfortable & unusual Grade II listed Georgian house was built in 1821 on the upper slopes of Bathwick Hill, renowned for its Italianate villas. 5 mins' to city centre, near a regular bus route & also near the university. Wonderful walks in National Trust woodland for those weary of Bath's architectural delights! 3 attractive bedrooms, each with T.V., radio/alarm, hairdryer & tea/coffee facilities. Children over 12.
E-mail: northwickhouse@aol.com

| £28.00 to £35.00 | Y | N | Y |

Veronica Metcalfe   Northwick House   North Road   Bathwick Hill   Bath BA2 6HD   Somerset
Tel: (01225) 420963   Fax 01225 420963   Open: ALL YEAR   Map Ref No. 01

Ravenscroft

Nearest Road: A.36
Built in 1876, Ravenscroft is an elegant Victorian residence with a wealth of period features. Its elevated position provides spectacular views over the city of Bath & countryside beyond. Only a few minutes from the city centre, it is surrounded by an acre of secluded, mature gardens which offer guests peace & tranquillity. There are 4 lovely bedrooms with colour T.V., tea/coffee & hair-drying facilities. Private parking. Children over 12.
E-mail: patrickbryanr@cs.com

| £32.50 to £35.00 | Y | N | N |

Mr P. C. Bryan   Ravenscroft   North Road   Bathwick   Bath BA2 6HZ   Somerset
Tel: (01225) 461919   Fax 01225 461919   Open: ALL YEAR   Map Ref No. 01

The Villa Magdala Hotel

Nearest Road: A.36
Ideally situated, this charming Victorian town-house hotel enjoys a peaceful location overlooking Henrietta Park, only 5 mins' level walk to the city centre & the famous Roman Baths. All of the 18 spacious rooms have an en-suite bathroom, T.V., direct-dial 'phone, refreshment tray & pleasant views. (Room rates vary - please enquire.) Private parking is available for guests in the hotel grounds. Children over 7 years.
E-mail: office@villamagdala.co.uk

| £40.00 to £75.00 | Y | N | N |

see PHOTO over
p. 279

VISA: M'CARD:

Roy & Lois Thwaites   The Villa Magdala Hotel   Henrietta Road   Bath BA2 6LX   Somerset
Tel: (01225) 466329   Fax 01225 483207   Open: ALL YEAR   Map Ref No. 01

Brompton House

Nearest Road: A.36
Built as a rectory in 1777, Brompton House is an elegant Georgian residence with a car park & beautiful mature gardens. Only 5 mins' walk from many of Bath's historic sights, it is run by the Selbys who offer every comfort & service to their guests. The attractive sitting room is furnished with antiques, & the tastefully decorated en-suite bedrooms offer T.V., radio/alarm, 'phone & tea/coffee. Breakfast is a delicious choice of full English, Continental or wholefood. Children over 15.
E-mail: bromptonhouse@btinternet.com

| £30.00 to £47.50 | N | N | N |

see PHOTO over
p. 281

VISA: M'CARD: AMEX:

Mr & Mrs Selby   Brompton House   St. John's Road   Bath BA2 6PT   Somerset
Tel: (01225) 420972   Fax 01225 420505   Open: ALL YEAR (Excl. Xmas & New Year)   Map Ref No. 01

Brompton House. Bath.

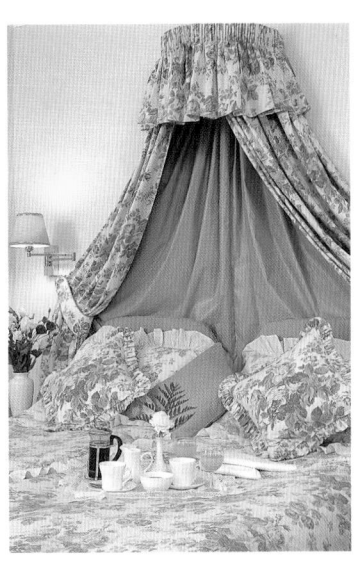

	rate £ from - to per person	children taken	evening meals	animals taken

Tasburgh House Hotel

Nearest Road: A.36

Award-winning Victorian mansion standing in 7 acres of beautiful gardens alongside the Kennet & Avon Canal with spectacular views. This lovely residence provides ideal country comfort in a city setting, convenient for Bath's city centre. All bedrooms are en-suite & tastefully furnished, having many extras to ensure a comfortable & memorable stay. Four-poster & spacious family bedrooms, elegant drawing room & stunning conservatory. Licensed. Gourmet dinners. Parking.
E-mail: hotel@bathtasburgh.co.uk

| £41.00 to £56.00 | Y | Y | N |

VISA: M'CARD: AMEX:

David & Susan Keeling   Tasburgh House Hotel   Warminster Road   Bath BA2 6SH   Somerset
Tel: (01225) 425096   Fax 01225 463842   Open: ALL YEAR   Map Ref No. 01

Lindisfarne Guest House

Nearest Road: A.36

Just 1 1/2 miles from Bath city centre, Lindisfarne is a lovely home set in attractive gardens, offering comfortable en-suite accommodation with colour T.V. & hospitality tray. A full English breakfast is served in the sunny dining room. The resident proprietors offer a warm welcome, with the local knowledge & personal attention guaranteed to make your stay enjoyable. Private car park & frequent bus service to the centre. Historic pubs & restaurants within walking distance. Children over 8.
E-mail: lindisfarne-bath@talk21.com

| £23.00 to £30.00 | Y | N | N |

VISA: M'CARD:

Ian & Carolyn Tiley   Lindisfarne Guest House   41a Warminster Road   Bathampton   Bath BA2 6XJ
Tel: (01225) 466342   Fax 01225 444062   Open: ALL YEAR   Map Ref No. 02

Monkshill Guest House

Nearest Road: A.3062

This distinguished Edwardian house is set in its own beautiful gardens, on an English-country hilltop commanding spectacular countryside views, & yet lies only 5 mins from the centre of Bath. Stroll through the small medieval village of Monkton Combe, at the valley's base, & return to tea amid the elegant antiques, fireplace & grand piano that complement the drawing room. The bedrooms are elegant, with flowing drapes, brass beds, bath/shower & views over the gardens & valley below.
E-mail: monks.hill@virgin.net

| £32.50 to £40.00 | Y | N | Y |

see PHOTO over
p. 283

VISA: M'CARD: AMEX:

Mr & Mrs M. Westlake   Monkshill Guest House   Shaft Road   Monkton Combe   Bath BA2 7HL
Tel: (01225) 833028   Fax 01225 833028   Open: ALL YEAR   Map Ref No. 03

Monmouth Lodge

Nearest Road: A.36

Set in an acre of attractive garden, looking on to the Somerset Hills surrounding this historic village. There are 3 attractively furnished ground-floor en-suite bedrooms, with T.V., tea/coffee-making facilities, king-size beds & own patio doors, which offer space & comfort. In the charming sitting room & stylish dining room, there is the same attention to detail & quality, where a good choice of excellent breakfast is served. Ideally situated for Bath, Wells, Stonehenge etc. Private parking. Famous 13th-century pub nearby. Children over 5.

| £30.00 to £35.00 | Y | N | N |

VISA: M'CARD:

Leslie & Traudle Graham   Monmouth Lodge   Norton St. Philip   Bath BA2 7LH   Somerset
Tel: (01373) 834367   Open: FEB - DEC   Map Ref No. 04

Monkshill. Monkton Combe.

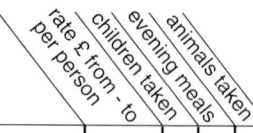

	rate £ from - to per person	evening meals children taken	animals taken

The Plaine

Nearest Road: A.366

The Plaine is a delightful listed building, dating from the 16th century & situated in the heart of an historic conservation village. There are 3 beautiful en-suite rooms, all with 4-poster beds. Opposite is the famous George Inn - one of the oldest hostelries in England. Delicious breakfasts are prepared with local produce and free-range eggs. A convenient location for Bath, Wells, Longleat and the Cotswolds. Parking. Children over 3.
E-mail: theplaine@easynet.co.uk

£29.00 to £36.00	Y	N	N

see PHOTO over p. 285

VISA: M'CARD:

Sarah Priddle & John Webster   **The Plaine**   **Bell Hill**   **Norton St. Philip**   **Bath BA2 7LT**   **Somerset**
Tel: (01373) 834723   **Fax 01373 834101**   **Open: ALL YEAR**   **Map Ref No. 04**

Winsors Farm

Nearest Road: A.39

Winsors Farm is a 16th-century Grade II listed Somerset longhouse with exposed beams, flagstone floors & inglenook fireplaces. A relaxed friendly 'home from home'. At the doorway of the Quantock Hills, enjoy gentle walks in unspoilt countryside. 2 delightful bedrooms, with views of the hills, an en-suite or private bathroom, T.V. & tea/coffee facilities. Guest sitting room. Car parking. Use of gardens & paddock. Also, a self-catering cottage. Evening meals by prior arrangement.
E-mail: info@winsors-farm.co.uk

£22.50 to £30.00	Y	Y	Y

Jackie Griffin   **Winsors Farm**   **Holford**   **Bridgwater TA5 1RY**   **Somerset**
Tel: (01278) 741435   **Open: ALL YEAR**   **Map Ref No. 05**

Spring Farm

Nearest Road: A.38

A cosy informal farmhouse set in a peaceful garden, Spring Farm has views across fields to the Mendip Hills. Offering 2 comfortable double-bedded rooms, each with an en-suite/private bathroom & tea/coffee-making facilities. The guest sitting/breakfast room has an open fire in winter. There is a good choice of pubs for an evening meal. Within easy reach by car are Chew Magna, Bristol, Bath & Wells. Spring Farm is an excellent base for exploring north Somerset & fishing on the renowned Chew & Blagdon lakes.

£22.50 to £25.00	Y	N	N

Mrs Judy Gallannaugh   **Spring Farm**   **The Street**   **Regil**   **Bristol BS40 8BB**   **Somerset**
Tel: (01275) 472735   **Fax 01275 474445**   **Open: ALL YEAR (Excl. Xmas)**   **Map Ref No. 11**

Downs Edge

Nearest Road: A.4018

Downs Edge is situated in a superb position on the very edge of Bristol's famous Downs - an open park of some 450 acres. Furnished with fine period furniture, the house is set in magnificent gardens close to the spectacular Avon Gorge & its breathtaking views. This uniquely peaceful location is ideally situated for the city centre, Clifton & the university. Downs Edge is served by an excellent public transport system with easy access to the motorway network. Children over 6 years.
E-mail: welcome@downsedge.com

£30.00 to £34.00	Y	N	N

VISA: M'CARD: AMEX:

Mrs Philippa Tasker   **Downs Edge**   **Saville Road**   **Stoke Bishop**   **Bristol BS9 1JA**   **Somerset**
Tel/Fax: (0117) 9683264   **Open: ALL YEAR (Excl. Easter, Xmas & New Year)**   **Map Ref No. 12**

The Plaine. Norton St. Philip.

Somerset

Hawthorne House

£22.50 to £30.00	Y	Y Y

Nearest Road: A.303

Hawthorne House is a cosy 19th-century stone house set in the Blackdown Hills, an Area of Outstanding Natural Beauty. It is ideally situated for an overnight stay en-route to Cornwall, & for visiting National Trust properties & the many other attractions in Somerset & Devon. Each of the 3 comfortable bedrooms has an en-suite/private bathroom & tea/coffee-making facilities. The attractive dining room has panoramic views over the extensive gardens & surrounding hills. Children over 12.
E-mail: roger-sarah@supanet.com

Roger & Sarah Newman-Coburn   Hawthorne House   Bishopswood   Chard TA20 3RS   Somerset
Tel: (01460) 234482   Fax 01460 234482   Open: ALL YEAR   Map Ref No. 14

Conygar House

£23.00 to £25.00	Y	N N

Nearest Road: A.39

Conygar House is situated in a quiet road just off the main street of medieval Dunster village. Restaurants, bars & shops are all within 1 mins' walking distance. Wonderful views of castle & moors. A delightful sunny garden & patio for guests' use. Ideal for exploring Exmoor & coast. All of the rooms are decorated & furnished to a high standard. Personal service & your comfort is guaranteed. Dunster Beach is 1 1/2 miles away, Minehead 2 1/2 miles & Porlock 8 miles.
E-mail: bale.dunster@virgin.net

Mrs B. Bale   Conygar House   2A The Ball   Dunster TA24 6SD   Somerset
Tel: (01643) 821872   Fax 01643 821872   Open: FEB - OCT   Map Ref No. 15

Larcombe Foot

£23.00 to £23.00	Y	Y Y

Nearest Road: A.358

Larcombe Foot, a comfortable old country house set in the beautiful & tranquil Upper Exe Valley, is an ideal base for walking, riding, fishing & touring Exmoor. Guests' comfort is paramount. Accommodation is in 3 bedrooms, 2 with private bathroom, & tea/coffee makers in all rooms. A comfortable sitting room with log fire & T.V., plus a pretty garden to relax in. Evening meals by prior arrangement. Winsford is considered one of the prettiest villages on the moor. Children over 8.

Mrs V. Vicary   Larcombe Foot   Winsford   Exmoor National Park TA24 7HS   Somerset
Tel: (01643) 851306   Fax 01643 851306   Open: APR - OCT   Map Ref No. 16

Number Three Hotel

£42.50 to £47.50	Y	N N

Nearest Road: M.5 Ex. 23, A.39

Number Three is a beautiful Georgian town house; once the home of Winston Churchill & his mother & also, Frederick Bligh Bond. 5 individually designed & refurbished rooms, all with en-suite bathrooms, T.V., telephone & tea/coffee-making facilities. 2 rooms are in the main house & 3 are in the Garden House, set within the large walled garden; with wonderful mature trees, floodlit at night. Car parking. Number Three stands beside Glastonbury Abbey & is a place of peace & tranquillity.
E-mail: info@numberthree.co.uk

see PHOTO over p. 287

VISA: M'CARD: AMEX:

Patricia Redmond   Number Three Hotel   3 Magdalene Street   Glastonbury BA6 9EW   Somerset
Tel: (01458) 832129   Fax 01458 834227   Open: ALL YEAR (Excl. Xmas)   Map Ref No. 17

Number Three Hotel.   Glastonbury.

	rate £ from - to per person	children taken	evening meals	animals taken

Tynings House

Nearest Road: A.39

Tynings House lies on the edge of a small village, surrounded by 8 acres of garden & meadow, with beautiful views over unspoilt countryside. 3 en-suite bedrooms with T.V. & tea/coffee-making facilities. Also, a guest lounge. The garden is a peaceful place in which to relax after a day's outing. Candlelit dinner available with prior notice. Within easy reach of Glastonbury, Bath, Wookey, Cheddar Gorge & the beautiful Mendip Hills. A peaceful retreat from the hustle & bustle of everyday life.
E-mail: b+b@tynings.co.uk

| £25.00 to £30.00 | Y | Y | N |

Mrs J. M. Parsons   Tynings House   Harters Hill Lane   Coxley   Nr. Glastonbury BA5 1RF   Somerset
Tel: (01749) 675368   Fax 01749 675368   Open: APR - OCT   Map Ref No. 18

Dollons House

Nearest Road: A.39

17th-century Dollons House nestles beneath the castle in this delightful medieval village in the Exmoor National Park. 3 attractive & very comfortable en-suite rooms, each with its own character & special decor. 100 years ago, the local pharmacist had his shop in Dollons, & in the back he made marmalade for the Houses of Parliament. A delightful home. Dunster is an ideal base for touring. Pull up outside the front door to unload & get instructions for parking.
E-mail: marilyn_mike@cornflowerblue.com

| £27.50 to £30.00 | N | N | N |

VISA: M'CARD:

Marilyn & Mike Cooper   Dollons House   10-12 Church Street   Dunster   Minehead   TA24 6SH
Tel: (01643) 821880   Fax 01643 822016   Open: ALL YEAR   Map Ref No. 19

The Lynch Country House

Nearest Road: A.303

The Lynch is a charming small hotel, standing in acres of carefully tended, wonderfully mature grounds. Beautifully refurbished & decorated to retain all its Georgian style & elegance, it now offers 5 attractively presented rooms, some with 4-posters, others with Victorian bedsteads, all with thoughtful extras including bathrobes & magazines. Each room has en-suite facilities, 'phone, radio, T.V. & tea/coffee. The elegant dining room overlooks the lawns & lake. Single supplement.
E-mail: the_lynch@talk21.com

| £24.50 to £42.50 | Y | N | Y |

see PHOTO over
p. 289

VISA: M'CARD: AMEX:

Roy Copeland   The Lynch Country House   4 Behind Berry   Somerton TA11 7PD   Somerset
Tel: (01458) 272316   Fax 01458 272590   Open: ALL YEAR (Excl. Xmas)   Map Ref No. 24

Visit our website at:
http://www.bestbandb.co.uk

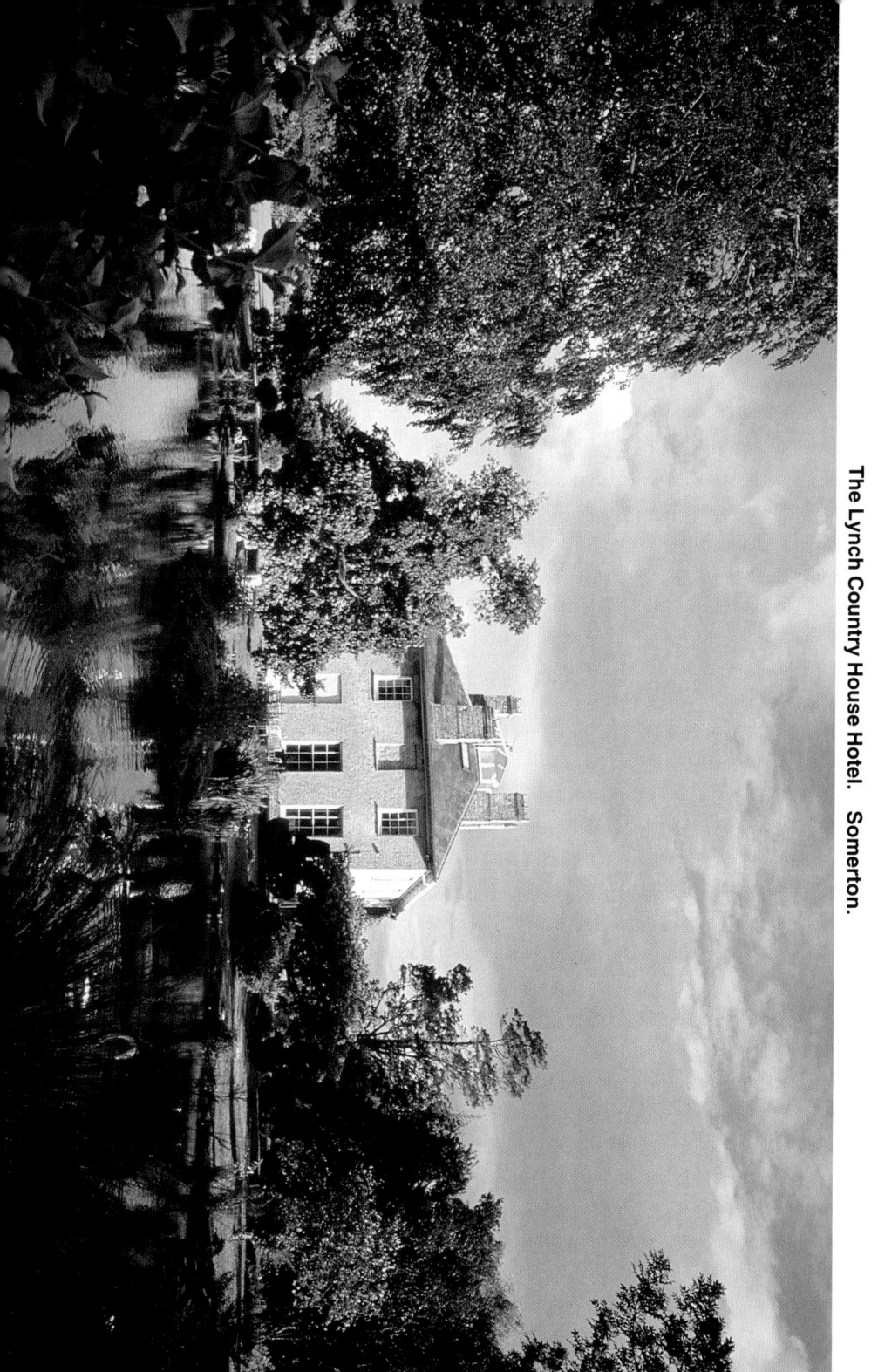

The Lynch Country House Hotel.   Somerton.

Somerset

Column headers (rotated): rate £ from - to per person | children taken | evening meals | animals taken

Mill House

Nearest Road: A.37, A.303

Ideally situated & beautifully restored, listed Georgian mill house in peaeful garden with mill stream. Close to Glastonbury & Wells & conveniently accessible from the A.303. Fish without leaving the garden, walk or cycle for miles & enjoy birdwatching on the panoramic Somerset levels. Luxury en-suite accommodation, a warm welcome & delicious breakfasts await you. Children over 8. Evening meals by arrangement.

E-mail: KnightsMillHouse@aol.com

	rate £	children	evening	animals
	£24.00 to £28.00	Y	Y	N

VISA: M'CARD:

Rita & Michael Knight   Mill House   Barton St David   Somerton TA11 6DF   Somerset
Tel: (01458) 851215   Fax 01458 851372   Open: ALL YEAR   Map Ref No. 20

Whittles Farm

Nearest Road: A.358

Guests at Whittles Farm can be sure of a high standard of accommodation & service. A superior 16th-century farmhouse set in 200 acres of pastureland, it is luxuriously carpeted & furnished in traditional style. Inglenook fireplaces & log-burners. 2 en-suite bedrooms, individually furnished, with T.V. & tea/coffee facilities. Super farmhouse food, using own meat, eggs & vegetables, & local Cheddar cheese & butter. Dinner by arrangement. Table licence. Children over 16.

E-mail: dj.CM.MITCHEM@themail.co.uk

	£24.00 to £26.00	N	Y	N

Mrs Claire Mitchem   Whittles Farm   Beercrocombe   Taunton TA3 6AH   Somerset
Tel: (01823) 480301   Fax 01823 480301   Open: FEB - NOV   Map Ref No. 26

Higher House

Nearest Road: A.358

Higher House is set 650 feet up on the southern slopes of the Quantock Hills. The views from the house & gardens are exceptional. The principal part of the house is 17th century, built around 2 courtyards, 1 with a heated pool. Each bedroom has its own bathroom, 'phone, T.V., tea/coffee facilities, books, magazines. There is a beautifully presented drawing room. An all-weather tennis court & 2 well-appointed cottages, are also available. Evening meals by prior arrangement.

E-mail: eyre@bagborough.u-net.com

	£27.00 to £27.00	Y	Y	N

see PHOTO over p. 291

Martin & Marise Eyre   Higher House   West Bagborough   Taunton TA4 3EF   Somerset
Tel: (01823) 432996   Fax 01823 433568   Open: ALL YEAR   Map Ref No. 29

The Old Stores

Nearest Road: A.371

This charming conversion of The Old Stores is between the church & the pub in the heart of this Mendip village. The en-suite bedrooms, music, open fires & a library provide a high standard of cosy comfort. You will be welcomed with home-made cakes & the use of local organic produce & home-made bread caters for all tastes. Malcolm can provide maps & books for visits & walks, including his own book on local footpaths.

E-mail: moglin980@aol.com

	£21.00 to £22.00	Y	N	Y

Malcolm & Linda Mogford   The Old Stores   Westbury-sub-Mendip   Wells BA5 1HA   Somerset
Tel: (01749) 870817   Fax 01749 870980   Open: ALL YEAR (Excl. Xmas & New Year)   Map Ref No. 30

Higher House. West Bagborough.

Somerset

Southway Farm

Nearest Road: A.39

Southway Farm is a Grade II listed Georgian farmhouse situated halfway between Glastonbury & Wells. Accommodation is in 3 comfortable & attractively furnished bedrooms, 1 en-suite & 2 with a private bathroom. A delicious full English breakfast is served, although vegetarians are also catered for. Guests may relax in the cosy lounge, with colour T.V., or in the pretty, tranquil garden. An ideal location for a restful holiday, or for touring the glorious West Country.
E-mail: southwayfarm@ukon-line.co.uk

£22.00 to £25.00	Y N N

Mrs Naomi Frost   Southway Farm   Polsham   Wells BA5 1RW   Somerset
Tel: (01749) 673396   Fax 01749 670373   Open: ALL YEAR (Excl. Xmas)   Map Ref No. 34

Beryl

Nearest Road: A.371

Beryl is a precious gem in a perfect setting, situated 1 mile from the cathedral city of Wells. This striking 19th-century Gothic mansion has beautifully furnished en-suite bedrooms, interesting views & all the accoutrements of luxury living (including a chair lift from ground to first floor.) Dinner is available by arrangement & is served in the exquisite dining room. Eddie & Holly are charming hosts, & your stay at their home is sure to be memorable.
E-mail: stay@beryl-wells.co.uk

£32.50 to £47.50	Y Y Y

see PHOTO over p. 293

VISA: M'CARD:

Eddie & Holly Nowell   Beryl   Off Hawkers Lane   Wells BA5 3JP   Somerset
Tel: (01749) 678738   Fax 01749 670508   Open: ALL YEAR (Excl. Xmas)   Map Ref No. 35

Stoneleigh House

Nearest Road: A.371

A beautiful 18th-century farmhouse (flagstone floors, beams, crooked walls) situated between Wells & Cheddar. Wonderful southerly views over unspoilt countryside to Glastonbury Tor from the bedrooms & lounge. Bedrooms are prettily furnished with country antiques & have en-suite bath/shower rooms. Round this off with a delicious breakfast, Wendy's decorative needlework, Tony's classic cars, the old forge, a cottagey garden & friendly cats. Children over 10. Good pubs nearby.
E-mail: stoneleigh@dial.pipex.com

£26.00 to £29.00	Y N N

Wendy & Tony Thompson   Stoneleigh House   Westbury-sub-Mendip   Nr. Wells BA5 1HF
Tel: (01749) 870668   Fax 01749 870668   Open: ALL YEAR (Excl. Xmas)   Map Ref No. 36

Cutthorne

Nearest Road: A.39

Tucked away in the heart of Exmoor National Park, Cutthorne offers a quiet & relaxing haven for country lovers. It is situated in an Area of Outstanding Natural Beauty, & walking & riding are unrivalled, whether by the coast or on the moors. Nearby are Lynton & Lynmouth, Tarr Steps & Dunster. The pretty bedrooms all have bathrooms & 1 has a 4-poster bed. The cuisine is traditional or vegetarian, using the finest local meat & organic vegetables. Fully licensed & non-smoking.
E-mail: durbin@cutthorne.co.uk

£25.00 to £34.00	N Y Y

Ann Durbin   Cutthorne   Luckwell Bridge   Wheddon Cross TA24 7EW   Somerset
Tel: (01643) 831255   Fax 01643 831255   Open: ALL YEAR   Map Ref No. 38

Beryl.   Wells.

Suffolk

Suffolk
(East Anglia)

In July, the lower reaches of the River Orwell hold the essence of Suffolk. Broad fields of green and gold with wooded horizons sweep down to the quiet water. Orwell Bridge spans the wide river where yachts and tan-sailed barges share the water with ocean-going container ships out of Ipswich. Downstream the saltmarshes echo to the cry of the Curlew. The small towns and villages of Suffolk are typical of an area with long seafairing traditions. This is the county of men of vision; like Constable and Gainsborough, Admiral Lord Nelson and Benjamin Britten.

The land is green and fertile and highly productive. The hedgerows shelter some of our prettiest wild flowers, & the narrow country lanes are a pure delight. Most memorable is the ever-changing sky, appearing higher and wider here than elsewhere in England. There is a great deal of heathland, probably the best known being Newmarket where horses have been trained and raced for some hundreds of years. Gorse-covered heath meets sandy cliffs on Suffolks Heritage Coast. Here are bird reserves and the remains of the great mediaeval city of Dunwich, sliding into the sea.

West Suffolk was famous for its wool trade in the Middle Ages, & the merchants gave thanks for their good fortune by building magnificent "Wool Churches". Much-photographed Lavenham has the most perfect black & white timbered houses in Britain, built by the merchants of Tudor times. Ipswich was granted the first charter by King John in 1200, but had long been a trading community of seafarers. Its history can be read from the names of the streets - Buttermarket, Friars Street, Cornhill, Dial Lane & Tavern Street. The latter holds the Great White Horse Hotel mentioned by Charles Dickens in Pickwick Papers. Sadly not many ancient buildings remain, but the mediaeval street pattern and the churches make an interesting trail to follow. The Market town of Bury St. Edmunds is charming, with much of its architectural heritage still surviving, from the Norman Cornhill to a fine Queen Anne House. The great Abbey, now in ruins, was the meeting place of the Barons of England for the creation of the Magna Carta, enshrining the principals of individual freedom, parliamentary democracy and the supremacy of the law. Suffolk has some very fine churches, notably at Mildenhall, Lakenheath, Framlingham, Lavenham & Stoke-by-Nayland, & also a large number of wonderful houses & great halls, evidence of the county's prosperity.

Lavenham.

Suffolk

Suffolk Gazeteer

Areas of Outstanding Natural Beauty

Suffolk Coast. Heathlands. Dedham Vale.

Historic Houses & Castles

Euston Hall - Thetford
18th century house with fine collection of pictures. Gardens & 17th century Parish Church nearby.

Christchurch Mansion - Ipswich
16th century mansion built on site of 12th century Augustinian Priory. Gables & dormers added in 17th century & other alteration & additions made in 17th & 18th centuries.

Gainsborough's House - Sudbury
Birthplace of Gainsborough, well furnished, collection of paintings.

The Guildhall - Hadleigh
15th century.

Glemham Hall - Nr Woodbridge
Elizabethan house of red brick - 18th century alterations. Fine stair, panelled rooms with Queen Anne furniture.

Haughley Park - Nr. Stowmarket
Jacobean manor house.

Heveningham Hall - Nr. Halesworth
Georgian mansion - English Palladian - Interior in Neo-Classical style. Garden by Capability Brown.

Ickworth - Nr. Bury St. Edmunds
Mixed architectural styles - late Regency & 18th century. French furniture, pictures & superb silver. Gardens with orangery.

Kentwell Hall - Long Melford
Elizabethan mansion in red brick, built in E plan, surrounded by moat.

Little Hall - Lavenham
15th century hall house, collection of furniture, pictures, china, etc.

Melford Hall - Nr. Sudbury
16th century - fine pictures, Chinese porcelain, furniture. Garden with gazebo.

Somerleyton Hall - Nr. Lowestoft
Dating from 16th century - additional work in 19th century. Carving by Grinling Gibbons. Tapestries, library, pictures.

Cathedrals & Churches

Bury St. Edmunds (St. Mary)
15th century. Hammer Beam roof in nave, wagon roof in chancel. Boret monument 1467.

Bramfield (St. Andrew)
Early circular tower. Fine screen & vaulting. Renaissance effigy.

Bacton (St. Mary)
15th century timbered roof. East Anglian stone & flintwork.

Dennington (St. Mary)
15th century alabaster monuments & bench ends. Aisle & Parclose screens with lofts & parapets.

Earl Stonhay (St. Mary)
14th century - rebuilt with fine hammer roof & 17th century pulpit with four hour-glasses.

Euston (St. Genevieve)
17th century. Fine panelling, reredos may be Grinling Gibbons.

Framlingham (St. Michael)
15th century nave & west tower, hammer beam roof in false vaulting. Chancel was rebuilt in 16th century for the tombs of the Howard family, monumental art treasures. Thamar organ. 1674.

Fressingfield (St. Peter & St. Paul)
15th century woodwork - very fine.

Lavenham (St. Peter & St. Paul)
15th century. Perpendicular. Fine towers. 14th century chancel screen. 17th century monument in alabaster.

Long Melford (Holy Trinity)
15th century Lady Chapel, splendid brasses. 15th century glass of note. Chantry chapel with fine roof. Like cathedral in proportions.

Stoke-by-Nayland (St. Mary)
16th-17th century library, great tower. Fine nave & arcades. Good brasses & monuments.

Ufford (St. Mary)
Mediaeval font cover - glorious.

Museums & Galleries

Christchurch Mansion - Ipswich
Country house, collection of furniture, pictures, bygones, ceramics of 18th century. Paintings by Gainsborough, Constable & modern artists.

Ipswich Museum - Ipswich
Natural History; prehistory, geology & archaeology to mediaeval period.

Suffolk

Moyse's Hall Musuem - Bury St. Edmunds
12th century dwelling house with local antiquities & natural history.

Abbot's Hall Museum of Rural Life - Stowmarket
Collections describing agriculture, crafts & domestic utensils.

Gershom-Parkington Collection - Bury St. Edmunds
Queen Anne House containing collection of watches & clocks.

Dunwich Musuem - Dunwich
Flora & fauna; local history.

Historic Monuments

The Abbey - Bury St. Edmunds
Only west end now standing.

Framlingham Castle
12th & 13th centuries - Tudor almshouses.

Bungay Castle - Bungay
12th century. Restored 13th century drawbridge & gatehouse.

Burgh Castle Roman Fort - Burgh
Coastal defences - 3rd century.

Herringfleet Priory - Herringfleet
13th century - remains of small Augustinian priory.

Leiston Abbey - Leiston
14th century - remains of cloisters, choir & trancepts.

Orford Castle - Orford
12th century - 18-sided keep - three towers.

The House in the Clouds. Thorpeness.

SUFFOLK
Map reference

01 Watchorn
02 Perrin
03 Dewsbury
04 Murphy
05 Rolfe
06 Sheppard
07 Hackett-Jones
08 Ridsdale

Suffolk

rate £ from - to per person
children taken
evening meals
animals taken

Earsham Park Farm

Nearest Road: A.143

A Victorian farmhouse set on a hill overlooking the Waveney Valley, with superb views. Park Farm offers 3 really delightful guest rooms, all furnished to a high standard. Each is en-suite, & well-equipped with T.V., radio/alarm & tea/coffee-making facilities. 1 room has a 4-poster bed. Breakfast is served in the lovely dining room. (Evening meals are available during the winter only.) Within easy reach of Norwich, Lowestoft & Southwold. A wonderful home. Dogs & horses by arrangement.
E-mail: WATCHORN_S@freenet.co.uk

£24.00 to £35.00	Y	Y	Y

VISA. M'CARD.

Mrs Bobbie Watchorn Earsham Park Farm Harleston Road Earsham Bungay NR35 2AQ Suffolk
Tel: (01986) 892180   Fax 01986 892180   Open: ALL YEAR   Map Ref No. 01

Gannocks House

Nearest Road: A.134

A Victorian country house in a delightful setting, with easy off-road parking. All 3 rooms, including a ground floor twin have fine furnishings & superb en-suite facilities. High-quality local food served at breakfast, vegetarians & special diets are catered for by prior arrangement. An elegant conservatory with views across the garden & farmland. An ideal location for exploring historical properties, medieval villages & antique shops. Wide choice of restaurants & local pubs. Children over 8.
E-mail: gannocks-house@lineone.net

£25.00 to £30.00	Y	N	N

Mr & Mrs A. Perrin Gannocks House Old Rectory Lane Shimpling Bury St. Edmunds IP29 4HG
Tel: (01284) 830499   Fax 01284 830499   Open: ALL YEAR   Map Ref No. 02

Manorhouse

Nearest Road: A.14

An award-winning 15th-century timbered house. Set in large gardens, overlooking the village green, with local inn, Manorhouse has a welcoming & relaxed atmosphere. It is attractively furnished throughout with antiques, oak beams & inglenooks. The 4 spacious en-suite bedrooms have either king-size double or twin beds, tea/coffee facilities, etc. An excellent choice of breakfasts. Ideally located 4 miles from Bury St. Edmunds & 35 mins' from Cambridge. Dinner by arrangement.
E-mail: manorhouse@beyton.com

£25.00 to £30.00	N	Y	N

Kay & Mark Dewsbury Manorhouse The Green Beyton Bury St. Edmunds IP30 9AF Suffolk
Tel: (01359) 270960   Open: ALL YEAR   Map Ref No. 03

Brook Farm

Nearest Road: A.14

Stay in a lovely old Suffolk longhouse surrounded by a moat. Relax in the beamed sitting room with log burning stove or in the pretty moated garden looking out over fields. There are 2 bedrooms, one en-suite & 1 with a private bathroom, both have T.V., radio & tea/coffee-making facilities. It is ideally situated to explore Suffolk & South Norfolk; Cambridge is only 45 mins away. Delicious breakfasts, vegetarians & vegans welcome by arrangement. Evening meals are available with notice. Children over 12. Single supplement.

£23.00 to £26.00	Y	Y	N

Isobel & Charles Murphy Brook Farm Drinkstone Road Beyton Bury St. Edmunds IP30 9AQ Suffolk
Tel: (01359) 270733   Open: ALL YEAR (Excl. Xmas)   Map Ref No. 04

Pipps Ford.   Needham Market.

Suffolk

Edge Hall

Nearest Road: A.1070

Edge Hall is a family-run Georgian house in central Hadleigh. Beautifully restored & tastefully modernised, the hotel offers the ultimate in accommodation. Particular attention is paid to friendly service & traditional home cooking with organic vegetables. Edge Hall is situated in the most picturesque part of Suffolk, & it is a good base from which to visit the surrounding towns & the many pretty villages of East Anglia.

| £25.00 to £42.50 | Y | Y | Y |

Angela & Rod Rolfe   Edge Hall   2 High Street   Hadleigh IP7 5AP   Suffolk
Tel: (01473) 822458   Fax 01473 827751   Open: ALL YEAR   Map Ref No. 05

The Old Vicarage

Nearest Road: A.1307

Set in mature grounds & woodlands, this delightful Old Vicarage has a friendly atmosphere. Complete peace & comfort are assured with wonderful views of the countryside. Guests are welcome to use the large garden. Open log fires welcome you in winter. The attractively furnished bedrooms have en-suite or private facilities & tea/coffee trays. (No smoking in bedrooms.) Evening meals with notice. Also, good pubs nearby. Perfectly situated for Newmarket, Cambridge, Long Melford, Lavenham & Constable country. Children over 7 & pets by arrangement.

| £28.00 to £28.00 | Y | Y | Y |

Jane Sheppard   The Old Vicarage   Great Thurlow   Haverhill CB9 7LE   Suffolk
Tel: (01440) 783209   Fax 01638 667270   Open: ALL YEAR   Map Ref No. 06

Pipps Ford

Nearest Road: A.14, A.140

A beautiful, Grade II listed Tudor, beamed guest house in a pretty, old-fashioned garden by the Gipping river. 7 very attractive bedrooms, with en-suite bathrooms & tea/coffee-making facilities. A very extensive breakfast menu & delicious 4-course evening meals, served in the delightful conservatory. Licensed. Colour T.V. & tennis court. Winner of The Best Bed & Breakfast award for East Anglia. A good central position for touring all of East Anglia. Children over 5. Animals by arrangement.
E-mail: b&b@pippsford.co.uk

| £27.50 to £36.00 | Y | Y | Y |

see PHOTO over
p. 299

VISA: M'CARD: AMEX:

Mrs Raewyn Hackett-Jones   Pipps Ford   Needham Market   Ipswich IP6 8LJ   Suffolk
Tel: (01449) 760208   Fax 01449 760561   Open: Mid JAN - Mid DEC   Map Ref No. 07

Cherry Tree Farm

Nearest Road: A.140

Traditional timber-framed farmhouse, standing in three quarters of an acre of garden, with orchard & duck ponds, in a peaceful Suffolk village. Accommodation is in 3 bedrooms, each with en-suite facilities. A spacious & comfortable lounge, inglenook fireplaces with log fire. Hearty English breakfast served in the oak-beamed dining room. Home-baked bread, own preserves & honey. Imaginative evening meals, with garden & local produce, good cheeses & fine English wines.

| £26.00 to £30.00 | N | Y | N |

Martin & Diana Ridsdale   Cherry Tree Farm   Mendlesham Green   Stowmarket IP14 5RQ   Suffolk
Tel: (01449) 766376   Open: ALL YEAR (Excl. Xmas & New Year)   Map Ref No. 08

Surrey

Surrey
(South East)

One of the Home Counties, Surrey includes a large area of London, south of the Thames. Communications are good in all directions so it is easy to stay in Surrey & travel either into central London or out to enjoy the lovely countryside which, despite urban development, survives thanks to the 'Green Belt' policy. The county is also very accessible from Gatwick Airport.

The land geographically, is chalk sandwiched in clay, & probably the lack of handy building material was responsible for the area remaining largely uninhabited for centuries. The North Downs were a considerable barrier to cross, but gradually settlements grew along the rivers which were the main routes through. The Romans used the gap created by the River Mole to build Stane Street between London & Chichester, this encouraged the development of small towns. The gap cut by the passage of the River Wey allows the Pilgrims Way to cross the foot of the Downs. Dorking, Reigate & Farnham are small towns along this route, all with attracitve main streets & interesting shops & buildings.

Surrey has very little mention in the Domesday Book, &, although the patronage of the church & of wealthy families established manors which developed over the years, little happened to disturb the rural tranquility of the region. As a county it made little history but rather reflected passing times, although Magna Carta was signed at Egham in 1215.

The heathlands of Surrey were a Royal playground for centuries. The Norman Kings hunted here & horses became part of the landscape & life of the people, as they are today on Epsom Downs.

Nearness to London & Royal patronage began to influence the area, & the buildings of the Tudor period reflect this. Royal palaces were built at Hampton Court & Richmond; & great houses such as Loseley near Guildford often using stone from the monasteries emptied during the Reformation. Huge deer parks were enclosed & stocked. Richmond, described as the "finest village in the British Dominions", is now beset by 20th century traffic but still has a wonderful park with deer, lakes & woodland that was enclosed by Charles I. The terraces & gardens of such buildings as Trumpeters House & Asgill House on the slopes of Richmond overlooking the Thames, have an air of spaciousness & elegance & there are lovely & interesting riverside walks at Richmond.

Polesden Lacey.

Surrey

Surrey
Gazeteer
Historic Houses & Castles
Albury Park - Albury, Nr. Guildford
A delightful country mansion designed by Pugin.
Clandon Park - Guildford
A fine house in the Palladian style by Leoni. A good collection of furniture & pictures. The house boasts some fine plasterwork.
Claremont - Esher
A superb Palladian house with interesting interior.
Detillens - Limpsfield
A fine 15th century house with inglenook fireplaces & mediaeval furniture. A large, pleasant garden.
Greathed Manor- Lingfield
An imposing Victorian manor house.
Hatchlands - East Clandon
A National Trust property of the 18th century with a fine Adam interior.
Loseley House - Guildford
A very fine Elizabethan mansion with superb panelling, furniture & paintings.
Polesden Lacy - Dorking
A Regency villa housing the Grevill collection of tapestries, pictures & furnishings. Extensive gardens.

Cathedrals & Churches
Compton (St. Nicholas)
The only surviving 2-storey sanctuary in the country. A fine 17th century pulpit.
Esher (St. George)
A fine altar-piece & marble monument.
Hascombe (St. Peter)
A rich interior with much gilding & painted reredos & roofs.
Lingfield (St. Peter & St. Paul)
15th century. Holding a chained bible.
Ockham (St. Mary & All Saints)
Early church with 13th century east window.
Stoke D'Abernon (St. Mary)
Dating back to Pre-conquest time with additions from the 12th-15th centuries. A fine 13th century painting. Early brasses.

Museums & Galleries
Charterhouse School Museum - Godalming
Peruvian pottery, Greek pottery, archaeology & natural history.
Chertsey Museum - Chertsey
18th-19th century costume & furnishing displayed & local history.
Guildford House - Guildford
The house is 17th century & of architectural interest housing monthly exhibitions.
Guildford Museum - Guildford
A fine needlework collection & plenty on local history.
Old Kiln Agricultural - Tilford
A very interesting collection of old farm implements.
Watermill Museum - Haxted
A restored 17th century mill with working water wheels & machinery.
Weybridge Museum - Weybridge
Good archaeological exhibition plus costume & local history.

The Gardens. Wisley

302

SURREY
Map reference

01 McCarthy
02 Franklin-Adams
03 Hill
04 Wallis
05 Grinsted
06 Carmichael
07 Wolf
08 Warren
09 Carey

rate £ from - to per person | evening meals | children taken | animals taken

Pineleigh

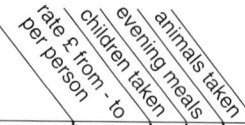

Nearest Road: A.325

Pineleigh is a spacious Edwardian house, built in 1906 & set in half an acre of mature garden in a very quiet area. Accommodation is in 4 comfortable & pleasantly decorated guest rooms, all with en-suite facilities & including telephone, T.V. & hospitality tray. Attractively furnished in Victorian style with many old prints & pictures. A full English breakfast is served, evening meals by arrangement. A charming home, Pineleigh is conveniently located for Heathrow Airport & London.

£30.00 to £35.00 — N N N

VISA: M'CARD: AMEX:

Tommy & Ann McCarthy   Pineleigh   10 Castle Road   Waverley Drive   Camberley   GU15 2DS   Surrey
Tel: (01276) 64787   Fax 01276 64787   Open: ALL YEAR   Map Ref No. 01

High Edser

Nearest Road: A.25

A large, handsome Grade II listed home, the earliest part built in the 16th century, situated in an Area of Outstanding Natural Beauty. There are three attractively furnished rooms available: two doubles and one twin. Residents' lounge and T.V.. Tennis court in grounds, and golf nearby. 35 minutes to Gatwick and London Airports. Approximately an hour's drive to London. A delightful home, ideal for a relaxing break.
E-mail: franklinadams@highedser.co.uk

£25.00 to £27.50 — Y N Y

Carol Franklin-Adams   High Edser   Shere Road   Ewhurst   Cranleigh   GU6 7PQ   Surrey
Tel: (01483) 278214   Fax 01483 278200   Open: ALL YEAR   Map Ref No. 02

Bulmer Farm

Nearest Road: A.25

Enjoy a warm welcome at this delightful 17th-century farmhouse, complete with many beams & an inglenook fireplace. Offering 3 charming rooms, all with h/c & tea/coffee-making facilities. Adjoining the house around a courtyard are 5 attractive barn-conversion en-suite bedrooms for non-smokers. Farm produce & home-made preserves are provided. Situated in a picturesque village, it is convenient for London airports. Children over 12 years. Animals by arrangement.

£23.00 to £25.00 — Y N Y

Gill Hill   Bulmer Farm   Pasturewood Road   Holmbury St. Mary   Dorking   RH5 6LG   Surrey
Tel: (01306) 730210   Open: ALL YEAR   Map Ref No. 03

Park House Farm

Nearest Road: A.25

A delightful large family home, tastefully furnished with many antiques. Accommodation is very comfortable with en-suite/private facilities, satellite T.V., tea/coffee etc.. It is set in 25 acres in an Area of Outstanding Natural Beauty within easy reach of Heathrow & Gatwick Airports, many gardens & National Trust properties. Good train service to London. Ideal walking country, with many village pubs for food. Children over 12 years.
E-mail: Peterwallis@msn.com

£25.00 to £30.00 — Y N N

VISA: M'CARD:

Ann & Peter Wallis   Park House Farm   Hollow Lane   Abinger Common   Dorking   RH5 6LW   Surrey
Tel: (01306) 730101   Fax 01306 730643   Open: ALL YEAR   Map Ref No. 04

Column headers (rotated): rate £ from - to per person | children taken | evening meals taken | animals taken

---

£25.00 to £25.00	Y	N	Y

(No smoking symbol)

VISA: M'CARD: AMEX:

The Lawn Guest House

Nearest Road: A.23

A well-appointed Victorian house only 5 mins' from Gatwick Airport & 25 miles to London or Brighton. Very useful as a base for travelling, it is close to the rail station & town centre. 12 bedrooms, all with en-suite facilities & very comfortable & well decorated, with T.V., hairdryer, 'phone & tea/coffee-making facilities, etc. A full English breakfast, or a healthy alternative including fruit, yoghurt & muesli, is served in the dining room. Also, a garden for guests' use. Single supplement. Parking.
E-mail: info@lawnguesthouse.co.uk

Adrian Grinsted   The Lawn Guest House   30 Massetts Road   Horley   Gatwick RH6 7DE   Surrey
Tel: (01293) 775751   Fax 01293 821803   Open: ALL YEAR   Map Ref No. 05

£23.00 to £28.00	Y	Y	Y

(No smoking symbol)

Deerfell

Nearest Road: A.286

A warm welcome at a spacious & comfortable stone-built home set in downland countryside, with breathtaking views to the hills & valleys of Surrey/Sussex. 3 pretty rooms with en-suite/private bathrooms & tea/coffee facilities & T.V.. Wonderful walks right on doorstep. Light suppers available on request. Close by - Haslemere station, (4 miles), London (45 mins), Guildford/Chichester (20 miles), Heathrow/Gatwick Airports 1 hour. Children over 6 years. Animals by arrangement.
E-mail: deerfell@tesco.net

Elizabeth Carmichael   Deerfell   Fernden Lane   Haslemere GU27 3BU   Surrey
Tel: (01428) 653409   Fax 01428 656106   Open: Mid JAN - Mid DEC   Map Ref No. 06

£25.00 to £30.00	Y	Y	N

The Old Farmhouse

Nearest Road: A.25

An early 15th-century medieval 4-bay hall house, which is little altered & retains many original features, including the diamond mullions for the hall window & fine panelling. It also has one of the longest unsupported crossing beams in Surrey. 2 of the attractively furnished bedrooms have brass bedsteads, & 1 has an original oak 4-poster bed. A delightful home. The Old Farmhouse is perfect for exploring the south-east of England & many places of historic interest. Children over 10.
E-mail: thecottage@dialstart.net

Philip & Judie Wolf   The Old Farmhouse   Wasp Green Lane   Outwood   Nr. Redhill RH1 5QE Surrey
Tel: (01342) 842313   Fax 01342 844744   Open: ALL YEAR (Excl. Xmas)   Map Ref No. 07

£30.00 to £30.00	Y	N	N

VISA: M'CARD:

Ashleigh House

Nearest Road: A.25

An Edwardian merchant's house situated within 600 yds of Redhill centre, with rail links to Gatwick (15 mins') & London (30 mins') & 3 miles from M.25 motorway with many historic houses within easy reach. The house is comfortably furnished & offers 8 attractive bedrooms, 6 of the rooms are en-suite. The breakfast room overlooks an English garden. Gill & Michael extend a very hospitable welcome to all their guests from around the world. Parking is available.

Michael & Gillian Warren   Ashleigh House   39 Redstone Hill   Redhill RH1 4BG   Surrey
Tel: (01737) 764763   Fax 01737 780308 Open: ALL YEAR (Excl. Xmas & New Year) Map Ref No. 08

	rate £ from - to per person	children taken	evening meals	animals taken

Swallow Barn

Nearest Road: A.3046

Situated in quiet, secluded surroundings on the edge of Chobham, attractively converted outbuildings & stables with outdoor swimming pool. 3 bedrooms with en-suite/private bathrooms, T.V. & tea/coffee. Ideal for Sunningdale, Wentworth & Foxhills golf courses. Also, Wisley & Savill Gardens are within easy reach. Convenient for M.3, M.25, Heathrow Airport, Windsor, Ascot & Hampton Court. Woking station 2 miles - London 25 mins' by train. Single supplement. Children over 8.
E-mail: swallowbarn@compuserve.com

£37.50 to £40.00 — Y — N — N

Joan & David Carey   *Swallow Barn*   *Milford Green*   *Chobham*   *Woking GU24 8AU*   *Surrey*
Tel: (01276) 856030   *Fax 01276 856030*   *Open: ALL YEAR*   *Map Ref No. 09*

All the establishments mentioned in this guide are members of
The Worldwide Bed & Breakfast Association

WORLDWIDE BED & BREAKFAST ASSOCIATION

When booking your accommodation please mention
The Best Bed & Breakfast

Sussex

Sussex
(South East)

The South Downs of Sussex stretch along the coast, reflecting the expanse of the North Downs of Kent, over the vast stretches of the Weald.

The South Downs extend from dramatic Beachy Head along the coast to Chichester & like the North Downs, they are crossed by an ancient trackway. There is much evidence of prehistoric settlement on the Downs. Mount Caburn, near Lewes, is crowned by an iron age fort, & Cissbury Ring is one of the most important archaeological sites in England. This large earthwork covers 80 acres & must have held a strategic defensive position. Hollingbury Fort carved into the hillside above Brighton, & the Trundle (meaning circle) date from 300-250 B.C., & were constructed on an existing neolithic settlement. The Long Man of Wilmington stands 226 feet high & is believed to be Nordic, possibly representing Woden, the God of War.

Only two towns are located on the Downs but both are of considerable interest. Lewes retains much of its mediaeval past & there is a folk museum in Ann of Cleves' house, which itself is partly 16th century. Arundel has a fascinating mixture of architectural styles, a castle & a superb park with a lake, magnificent beech trees & an unrivalled view of the Arun valley.

The landscape of the inland Weald ranges from bracken-covered heathlands where deer roam, to the deep woodland stretches of the Ashdown Forest, eventually giving way to soft undulating hills & valleys, patterned with hop-fields, meadows, oast houses, windmills & fruit orchards. Originally the whole Weald was dense with forest. Villages like Midhurst & Wadhurst hold the Saxon suffix "hurst" which means wood. As the forests were cleared for agriculture the names of the villages changed & we find Bosham & Stedham whose suffix "ham" means homestead or farm.

Battle, above Hastings, is the site of the famous Norman victory & 16th century Bodiam Castle, built as defence against the French in later times, has a beautiful setting encircled by a lily-covered moat.

Sussex has an extensive coastline, with cliffs near Eastbourne at Beachy Head, & at Hastings. Further east, the great flat Romney Marshes stretch out to sea, & there is considerable variety in the coastal towns.

Chichester has a magnificent cathedral & a harbour reaching deep into the coastal plain that is rich in archaeological remains. The creeks & mudflats make it an excellent place for bird watching.

Brighton is the most famous of the Sussex resorts with its Pier, the Promenade above the beaches, the oriental folly of George IV's Royal Pavilion & its Regency architecture. "The Lanes" are a maze of alleys & small squares full of fascinating shops, a thriving antique trade, & many good pubs & eating places. Hastings to the east preserves its "Old Town" where timbered houses nestle beneath the cliffs & the fishing boats are drawn up on the shingle whilst the nets are hung up to dry in curious tall, thin net stores. Winchelsea stands on a hill where it was rebuilt in the 13th century by Edward I when the original town was engulfed by the sea. It is a beautiful town with a fine Norman church, an excellent museum in the Town Hall, & many pretty houses. Across the Romney Marshes on the next hill stands Rye, its profile dominated by its church. It is a fascinating town with timbered houses & cobbled streets.

Sussex

Sussex Gazeteer

Areas of Outstanding Natural Beauty
The Sussex Downs. Chichester Harbour.

Historic Houses & Castles

Arundel Castle - Arundel
18th century rebuilding of ancient castle, fine portraits, 15th century furniture.
Cuckfield Park - Cuckfield
Elizabethan manor house, gatehouse. Very fine panelling & ceilings.
Danny - Hurstpierpoint
16th century - Elizabethan .
Goodwood House - Chichester
18th century - Jacobean house - Fine Sussex flintwork, paintings by Van Dyck, Canaletto & Stubbs, English & French furniture, tapestries & porcelain.
Newtimber Place - Newtimber
Moated house - Etruscan style wall paintings.
Purham - Pulborough
Elizabethan house containing important collection of Elizabethan, Jacobean & Georgian portraits, also fine furniture.
Petworth House - Petworth
17th century - landscaped by Capability Brown - important paintings - 14th century chapel.
St. Mary's - Bramber
15th century timber framed house - rare panelling.
Tanyard - Sharpthorne
Mediaeval tannery - 16th & 17th century additions.
The Thatched Cottage - Lindfield
Close-studded weald house - reputedly Henry VII hunting lodge.
Uppark - Petersfield
17th century - 18th century interior decorations remain unaltered.
Alfriston Clergy House - Nr. Seaford
14th century parish priest's house - pre-reformation.
Battle Abbey - Battle
Founded by William the Conqueror.
Charleston Manor - Westdean
Norman, Tudor & Georgian architectural styles - Romanesque window in the Norman wing.
Bull House - Lewes
15th century half-timbered house - was home of Tom Paine.

Bateman's - Burwash
17th century - watermill - home of Rudyard Kipling.
Bodiam Castle - Nr. Hawkshurst
14th century - noted example of mediaeval moated military architecture.
Great Dixter - Northiam
15th century half-timbered manor house - great hall - Lutyens gardens
Glynde Place - Nr. Lewes
16th century flint & brick - built around courtyard-collection of paintings by Rubens, Hoppner, Kneller, Lely, Zoffany.
Michelham Priory - Upper Dicker, Nr. Hailsham
13th century Augustinian Priory - became Tudor farmhouse - working watermill, ancient stained glass, etc., enclosed by moat.
Royal Pavilion - Brighton
Built for Prince Regent by Nash upon classical villa by Holland. Exotic Building - has superb original works of art lent by H.M. The Queen. Collections of Regency furniture also Art Nouveau & Art Deco in the Art Gallery & Museum.
Sheffield Park - Nr. Uckfield
Beautiful Tudor House - 18th century alterations - splendid staircase.

Cathedrals & Churches

Alfriston (St. Andrew)
14th century - transition from decorated style to perpendicular, Easter sepulchre.
Boxgrove (St. Mary & St. Blaise)
13th century choir with 16th century painted decoration on vaulting. Relic of Benedictine priory. 16th century chantry. Much decoration.
Chichester Cathedral
Norman & earliest Gothic. Large Romanesque relief sculptures in south choir aisle.
Etchingham (St. Mary & St. Nicholas)
14th century. Old glass, brasses, screen, carved stalls.
Hardham (St. Botolph)
11th century - 12th century wall paintings.
Rotherfield (St. Denys)
16th century font cover, 17th century canopied pulpit, glass by Burne-Jones, wall paintings, Georgian Royal Arms.

Sussex

Sompting (St. Mary)
11th century Saxon tower - Rhenish Helm Spire - quite unique.
Worth (St. Nicholas)
10th century - chancel arch is the largest Saxon arch in England. German carved pulpit c.1500 together with altar rails.
Winchelsea (St. Thomas the Apostle)
14th century - choir & aisles only. Canopied sedilia & piscina.

Museums & Galleries

Barbican House Museum - Lewes
Collection relating to pre-historic, Romano-British & , mediaeval antiquities of the area. Prints & water colours of the area.
Battle Museum-Battle
Remains from archeological sites in area. Diorama of Battle of Hastings.
Bignor Roman Villa Collection - Bignor
4th century mosaics, Samian pottery, hypocaust, etc.
Brighton Museum & Art Gallery - Brighton
Old Master Paintings, watercolours, ceramics, furniture. Surrealist paintings, Art Nouveau & Art Deco applied art, musical instruments & many other exhibits.

Marlipins Museum - Shoreham
12th century building housing collections of ship models, photographs, old maps, geological specimens, etc.
Royal National Lifeboat Institution Museum - Eastbourne
Lifeboats of all types used from earliest times to present.
Tower 73 - Eastbourne
Martello tower restored to display the history of these forts. Exhibition of equipment, uniforms & weapons of the times.
The Toy Museum - Rottingdean, Brighton
Toys & playthings from many countries - children's delight.

Other things to see & do

Bewl Water - Nr. Wadhurst
Boat trips, walks, adventure playground
Chichester Festival Theatre - Chichester
Summer season of plays from May to September.
Goodwood Racecourse

The Royal Pavilion. Brighton.

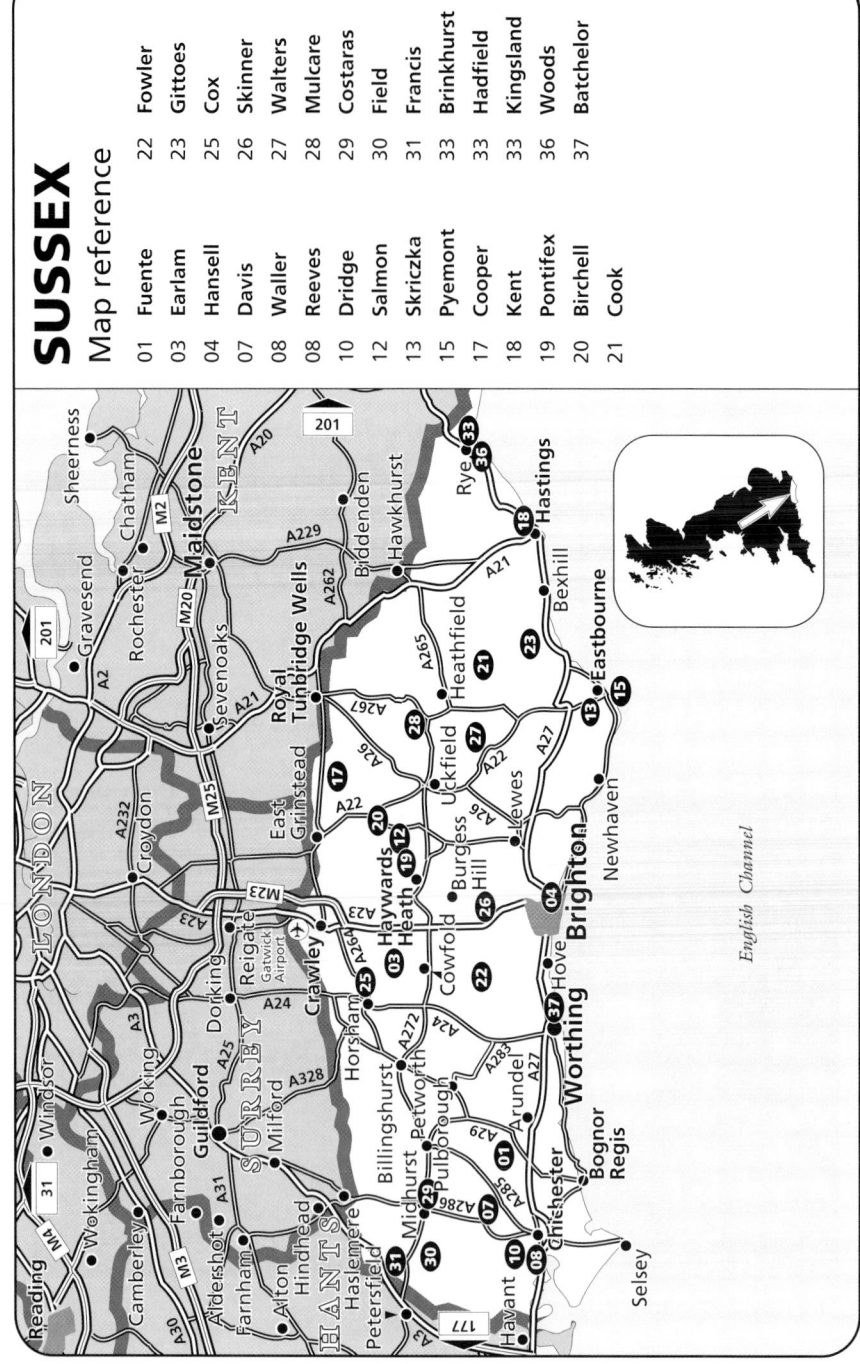

SUSSEX

Map reference

01 Fuente	22 Fowler
03 Earlam	23 Gittoes
04 Hansell	25 Cox
07 Davis	26 Skinner
08 Waller	27 Walters
08 Reeves	28 Mulcare
10 Dridge	29 Costaras
12 Salmon	30 Field
13 Skriczka	31 Francis
15 Pyemont	33 Brinkhurst
17 Cooper	33 Hadfield
18 Kent	33 Kingsland
19 Pontifex	36 Woods
20 Birchell	37 Batchelor
21 Cook	

Sussex

rate £ - from - to per person	children taken	evening meals taken	animals taken

---

£23.50 to £23.50 | Y | N | Y

Mill Lane House

Nearest Road: A.27, A.29

Mainly 17th-century house in beautiful National Trust downland village with magnificent views to the coast. 5 en-suite rooms, each with T.V.. Superb local hill walking & bird-watching from Pulborough Brooks to Pagham Harbour. Within easy reach of Arundel Castle, Fishbourne Roman Palace, Goodwood & Chichester, the cathedral & the Festival Theatre. Beaches 6 miles. Excellent pubs within easy walking distance. Evening meals available to groups by arrangement.

Peter & Sarah Fuente   Mill Lane House   Slindon   Arundel BN18 0RP   Sussex
Tel: (01243) 814440   Fax 01243 814436   Open: ALL YEAR   Map Ref No. 01

£25.00 to £35.00 | N | N | N

Timbers Edge

Nearest Road: A.272, A.23

This beautiful Sussex country house, set in spacious formal gardens & surrounded by woodlands, is extremely peaceful & quiet. Located within easy reach of Hickstead Showjumping Ground (10 mins), Nymans & Leonardslee Gardens (10 mins), South of England Showground (25 mins), Gatwick Airport (20 mins) & Brighton (30 mins). The attractive bedrooms have a colour T.V., a private bathroom & beverage-making facilities. Breakfast is served in the conservatory overlooking the pool.
E-mail: gearlam@aol.com

Mr & Mrs Earlam   Timbers Edge   Longhouse Lane   Off Spronketts Lane   Warninglid   Bolney RH17 5TE
Tel: (01444) 461456   Fax 01444 461813   Open: ALL YEAR   Map Ref No. 03

£29.50 to £32.50 | Y | N | N

VISA: M'CARD: AMEX:

Trouville Hotel

Nearest Road: A.259

The Trouville is a Regency, Grade II listed townhouse, which has been tastefully restored & furnished throughout. Accommodation is in 8 attractive bedrooms, each with colour T.V. & tea/coffee-making facilities. En-suite & 4-poster bedrooms are available. Situated in a charming seafront square, the Trouville is very convenient for shopping, the Pavilion, the Lanes, Marina & Conference Centre & the many restaurants which are all within walking distance.

John & Daphne Hansell   Trouville Hotel   11, New Steine   Brighton BN2 1PB   Sussex
Tel: (01273) 697384   Open: FEB - DEC   Map Ref No. 04

£25.00 to £35.00 | Y | N | N

VISA: M'CARD:

The Old Store Guest House

Nearest Road: A.285

A lovely 18th-century Grade II listed house offering 7 comfortable rooms with a choice of single, double or family accommodation. All rooms are en-suite & have colour T.V., tea/coffee trays, hairdryer & trouser press. A full English breakfast is served in the charming breakfast room. A guest lounge. Private car park. Good pub/restaurant close by. Adjacent to the Goodwood Estate & ideal for Chichester, Petworth & Arundel.
E-mail: alandavis@theoldstore.fsnet.co.uk

Alan & Iris Davis   The Old Store Guest House   Halnaker   Chichester PO18 0QL   Sussex
Tel: (01243) 531977   Fax 01243 531977   Open: ALL YEAR   Map Ref No. 07

Sussex

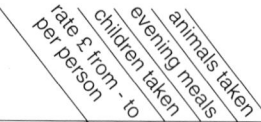
Hatpins

	rate £ from - to per person	children taken	evening meals	animals taken
	£30.00 to £50.00	N	N	N

Nearest Road: A.259

Situated in the charming, picturesque harbour village of Old Bosham, 3 miles west of Chichester, & near to Goodwood House, H.M.S. Victory & the Mary Rose, this elegant property offers luxurious & inviting interior-designed decor & antiques, including a half-tester & Victorian brass beds. Suitable, & welcoming, for honeymoon couples. All bedrooms have private/en-suite bathrooms. Hatpins is a charming home.
E-mail: mary@hatpins.co.uk

see PHOTO over
p. 313

Mrs Mary Waller   Hatpins   Bosham Lane   Old Bosham   Chichester PO18 8HG   Sussex
Tel: (01243) 572644   Fax 01243 572644   Open: ALL YEAR   Map Ref No. 08

White Barn

	£30.00 to £40.00	Y	Y	N

Nearest Road: A.259

White Barn is a unique open-plan, single-storey house on different levels in the beautiful Saxon harbour village of Bosham. 3 privately located en-suite rooms, each furnished with home-from-home comforts, including T.V. & tea/coffee facilities. Meals are served in the dining area overlooking the pretty garden. The sitting room, has a log fire in winter. White Barn is an ideal base for visiting Chichester, the South Downs, beaches & marinas, Portsmouth & Goodwood. Children over 10.
E-mail: whitebarn@compuserve.com

VISA: M'CARD:

Christine Reeves   White Barn   Crede Lane   Bosham   Chichester PO18 8NX   Sussex
Tel: (01243) 573113   Fax 01243 573113   Open: ALL YEAR   Map Ref No. 08

Chichester Lodge

	£25.00 to £35.00	N	N	N

Nearest Road: B.2178

A picturesque, Grade II listed 1840s Gothic Lodge set in very quiet country surroundings, yet only 4 mins' drive from the city centre and the Festival Theatre. Accommodation is in 2 comfortable & tastefully furnished bedrooms with 4-poster beds & en-suite bathrooms. An adjoining garden room, in which guests may choose to relax, has tea-making facilities & a cosy log-burning fire. You are assured of a warm and friendly welcome from your hosts at this charming home.

Jeannette Dridge   Chichester Lodge   Oakwood   Chichester PO18 9AL   Sussex
Tel: (01243) 786560   Fax 01243 784525   Open: ALL YEAR   Map Ref No. 10

Sliders Farm

	£27.50 to £40.00	Y	N	N

Nearest Road: A.275

A listed 16th-century farmhouse, with a wealth of oak beams & inglenook fireplaces, in a secluded setting on the Sussex Weald. All rooms are en-suite, with T.V., etc. Home-grown produce & home-cooking. Dining room & lounge with inglenooks & billiard table. An outdoor pool, tennis court & private trout fishing. Convenient for Ardingly Showground, Sheffield Park Gardens, the Bluebell Railway & N.T. properties & gardens. Coast & Gatwick 30 mins (car). London 45 mins (train).
E-mail: jean&davidsalmon@sliders.freeserve.co.uk

David & Jean Salmon   Sliders Farm   Furners Green   Danehill TN22 3RT   Sussex
Tel: (01825) 790258   Fax 01825 790258   Open: ALL YEAR   Map Ref No. 12

![Bedroom with four-poster bed and lace canopy]

Hatpins. Old Bosham.

Pinnacle Point.   Meads Village.

Sussex

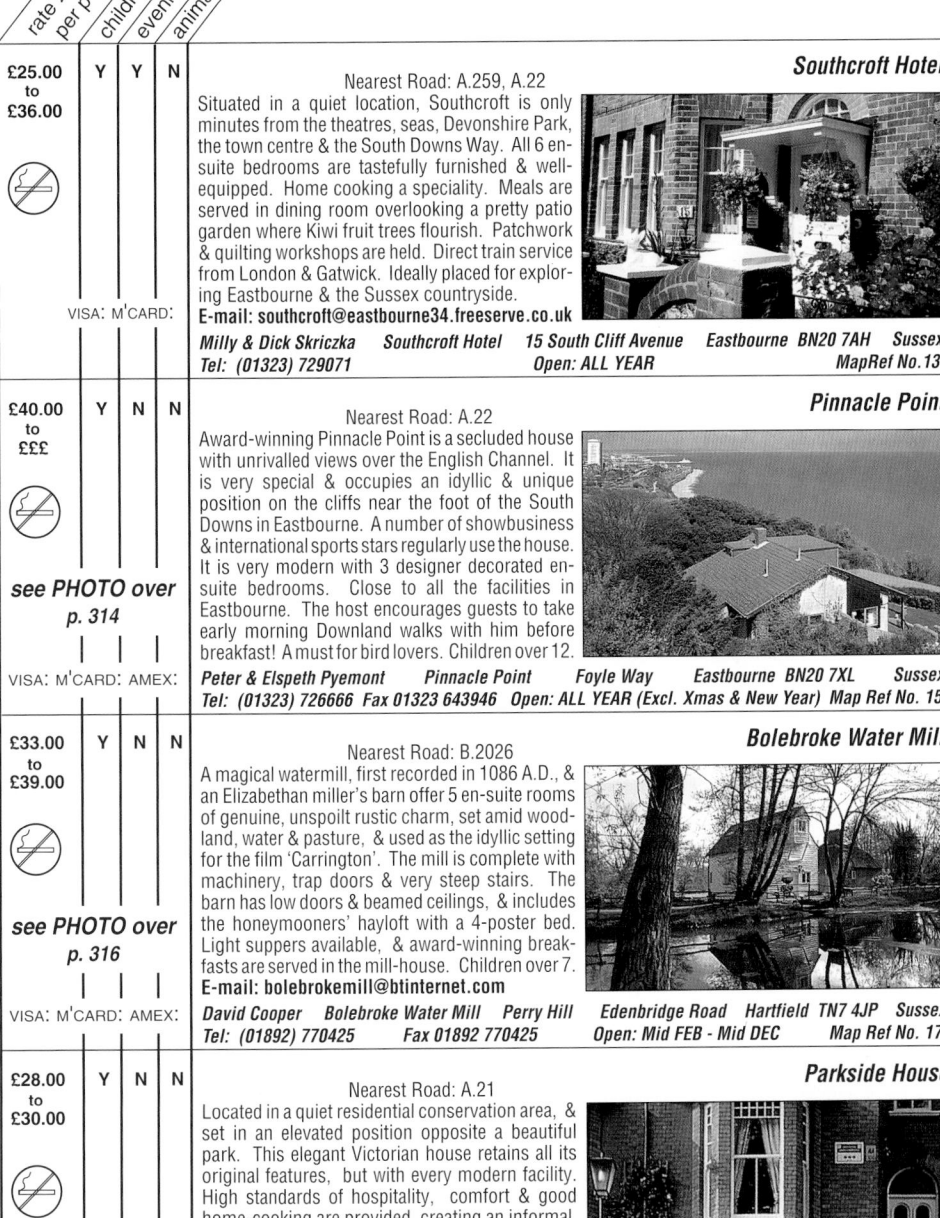

rate £ from - to per person	children taken	evening meals taken	animals taken

Southcroft Hotel

£25.00 to £36.00 — Y Y N — (non-smoking) — VISA: M'CARD:

Nearest Road: A.259, A.22

Situated in a quiet location, Southcroft is only minutes from the theatres, seas, Devonshire Park, the town centre & the South Downs Way. All 6 en-suite bedrooms are tastefully furnished & well-equipped. Home cooking a speciality. Meals are served in dining room overlooking a pretty patio garden where Kiwi fruit trees flourish. Patchwork & quilting workshops are held. Direct train service from London & Gatwick. Ideally placed for exploring Eastbourne & the Sussex countryside.
E-mail: southcroft@eastbourne34.freeserve.co.uk

Milly & Dick Skriczka   Southcroft Hotel   15 South Cliff Avenue   Eastbourne BN20 7AH   Sussex
Tel: (01323) 729071   Open: ALL YEAR   MapRef No.13

Pinnacle Point

£40.00 to £££ — Y N N — (non-smoking)

see PHOTO over p. 314

VISA: M'CARD: AMEX:

Nearest Road: A.22

Award-winning Pinnacle Point is a secluded house with unrivalled views over the English Channel. It is very special & occupies an idyllic & unique position on the cliffs near the foot of the South Downs in Eastbourne. A number of showbusiness & international sports stars regularly use the house. It is very modern with 3 designer decorated en-suite bedrooms. Close to all the facilities in Eastbourne. The host encourages guests to take early morning Downland walks with him before breakfast! A must for bird lovers. Children over 12.

Peter & Elspeth Pyemont   Pinnacle Point   Foyle Way   Eastbourne BN20 7XL   Sussex
Tel: (01323) 726666 Fax 01323 643946   Open: ALL YEAR (Excl. Xmas & New Year) Map Ref No. 15

Bolebroke Water Mill

£33.00 to £39.00 — Y N N — (non-smoking)

see PHOTO over p. 316

VISA: M'CARD: AMEX:

Nearest Road: B.2026

A magical watermill, first recorded in 1086 A.D., & an Elizabethan miller's barn offer 5 en-suite rooms of genuine, unspoilt rustic charm, set amid woodland, water & pasture, & used as the idyllic setting for the film 'Carrington'. The mill is complete with machinery, trap doors & very steep stairs. The barn has low doors & beamed ceilings, & includes the honeymooners' hayloft with a 4-poster bed. Light suppers available, & award-winning breakfasts are served in the mill-house. Children over 7.
E-mail: bolebrokemill@btinternet.com

David Cooper   Bolebroke Water Mill   Perry Hill   Edenbridge Road   Hartfield TN7 4JP   Sussex
Tel: (01892) 770425   Fax 01892 770425   Open: Mid FEB - Mid DEC   Map Ref No. 17

Parkside House

£28.00 to £30.00 — Y N N — (non-smoking) — VISA: M'CARD: AMEX:

Nearest Road: A.21

Located in a quiet residential conservation area, & set in an elevated position opposite a beautiful park. This elegant Victorian house retains all its original features, but with every modern facility. High standards of hospitality, comfort & good home-cooking are provided, creating an informal, friendly & welcoming atmosphere. Bedrooms are en-suite & offer every luxury. The 'Apricot' room has an antique French bed. A quiet location only 15 mins' walk from the town centre & sea front.

Brian W. Kent   Parkside House   59 Lower Park Road   Hastings TN34 2LD   Sussex
Tel: (01424) 433096   Fax 01424 421431   Open: ALL YEAR   Map Ref No. 18

Bolebroke Watermill.　Hartfield.

Sussex

rate £ from - to per person	children taken	evening meals	animals taken

The Pilstyes

£27.50 to £37.50	Y	N	N

Nearest Road: A.272, A.22

Romantic Elizabethan cottage in enviable location on the heart of what is reputed to be the prettiest village in Sussex, yet with easy access to Gatwick Airport, London & Brighton. Roy & Carol live in the adjoining cottage. There is a suite of 2 bedrooms, 1 has a four-poster bed with crisp linen bedding & 1 has twin beds. A comfortable sitting room with log fire. Bucks Fizz breakfast available for that special occasion! Children by arrangement.
E-mail: bnbuk@pavilion.co.uk

VISA: M'CARD: AMEX:

Carol & Roy Pontifex   The Pilstyes   106 & 108 High Street   Lindfield   Haywards Heath RH16 2HS
Tel: (01444) 484101   Open: ALL YEAR   Map Ref No. 19

Holly House

£25.00 to £27.50	Y	Y	Y

Nearest Road: A.275

Holly House, an early-Victorian forest farmhouse with character, offers a warm, friendly welcome to visitors. A 1-acre garden with long views. Situated in an Ashdown Forest village & ideal for touring Sussex, with many National Trust properties nearby. A comfortable lounge is available, & breakfast is taken in the conservatory overlooking the garden. The 5 pleasant rooms, 3 en-suite, have tea-making facilities & T.V.. A small swimming pool heated during the summer. Animals welcome.
E-mail:db@hollyhousebnb.demon.co.uk

Mrs Deirdre Birchell   Holly House   Beaconsfield Road   Chelwood Gate   Haywards Heath RH17 7LF
Tel: (01825) 740484   Fax 01825 740172   Open: ALL YEAR   Map Ref No. 20

The Cottage

£30.00 to £40.00	Y	Y	N

Nearest Road: A.265

A warm, friendly welcome & elegant, comfortable accommodation await you at The Cottage, a 16th-century family home overlooking the village green in this peaceful hamlet. Beautiful double rooms (one with four-poster) with en-suite/private facilities, T.V. & courtesy tray. Relax in the pretty drawing room, or the tranquil garden. Breakfasts include locally grown organic produce wherever possible. (Dinner by arrangement.) Only 200 yards from an award-winning village inn.
E-mail: cottageonthegreen@btinternet.com

Mrs Karen Cook   The Cottage   Rushlake Green   Heathfield TN21 9QH   Sussex
Tel: (01435) 830348   Fax 01435 830715   Open: ALL YEAR   Map Ref No. 21

Frylands

£20.00 to £22.50	Y	N	N

Nearest Road: A.272, A.23

Frylands is a timber-framed Tudor farmhouse in a quiet setting of farmland, woods & river. There are 3 lovely bedrooms, 1 with private facilities, & all with colour T.V., radio & tea/coffee tray with home-made biscuits. A traditional breakfast, cooked to order, is served with a selection of home-made preserves & local honey. Large garden with heated swimming pool. Good pubs & food nearby. Only 20 mins Gatwick & Brighton.
E-mail: b+b@frylands.co.uk

Mrs Sylvia Fowler   Frylands   Frylands Lane   Wineham   Henfield BN5 9BP   Sussex
Tel: (01403) 710214 Fax 01403 711449 Open: ALL YEAR (Excl. Xmas & New Year) Map Ref No. 22

Sussex

Column headers (rotated): rate £ from - to per person | children taken | evening meals | animals taken

Wartling Place

Nearest Road: A.271, A.27

A superb Grade II listed Georgian country house set in 2 acres of mature secluded gardens. Beautifully restored with period furnishings offering 3 luxurious, individual bedrooms & romantic 4-posters for that special occasion. Each room is en-suite with bath & shower, T.V. & courtesy tray. Ideal for visiting the many National Trust houses, castles & gardens of Sussex & Kent. Private parking. Self-catering lodge cottage available. Evening meals by prior arrangement.

E-mail: accom@wartlingplace.prestel.co.uk

	rate £ from - to per person	children taken	evening meals	animals taken
	£37.50 to £47.50	Y	Y	N

see PHOTO over
p. 319

VISA: M'CARD: AMEX:

Rowena & Barry Gittoes   Wartling Place   Wartling   Herstmonceux BN27 1RY   Sussex
Tel: (01323) 832590   Fax 01323 831558   Open: ALL YEAR   Map Ref No. 23

Glebe End

Nearest Road: A.24

Glebe End is a fascinating medieval house, with a secluded, sunny, walled garden, set in the heart of Warnham village. It retains many original features, including heavy flagstones, curving ships' timbers & an inglenook fireplace. 4 single, twin or king-sized en-suite rooms, charmingly furnished with antiques & each with T.V., etc. Mrs Cox is an excellent cook, & meals (by arrangement) include home-grown produce. Tennis & golf nearby. 20 mins Gatwick Airport. Animals by arrangement.

E-mail: CoxesWarnham@aol.com

	£25.00 to £25.00	Y	Y	Y

Liz & Chris Cox   Glebe End   Church Street   Warnham   Horsham RH12 3QW   Sussex
Tel: (01403) 261711   Fax 01403 257572   Open: ALL YEAR   Map Ref No. 25

Clayton Wickham Farmhouse

Nearest Road: A.23

A delightful, secluded 16th-century farmhouse with lovely views, set amidst the beautiful Sussex countryside. The friendly hosts have refurbished their home to a high standard, yet have retained many original features, hence there are a wealth of beams & a huge inglenook fireplace in the drawing room. A variety of tastefully furnished & well-appointed bedrooms, including a super 4-poster en-suite. 4-course candlelit dinner by arrangement. Tennis court. Animals by arrangement.

E-mail: susie@cwfbanb.fsnet.co.uk

	£35.00 to £47.50	Y	Y	Y

Mike & Susie Skinner   Clayton Wickham Farmhouse   Belmont Lane   Hurstpierpoint BN6 9EP   Sussex
Tel: (01273) 845698   Fax 01273 841970   Open: ALL YEAR   Map Ref No. 26

Shortgate Manor Farm

Nearest Road: A.22

Shortgate Manor Farm is an enchanting 18th-century farmhouse set in 8 acres approached by an avenue of poplars festooned with rambling roses. The 3 charming bedrooms all offer en-suite/private facilities, T.V.'s, courtesy trays, with bathrobes provided for your comfort. The house is surrounded by 2 acres of landscaped gardens which are open under the National Gardens Scheme every June. Glyndebourne 4 miles. A charming home from which to explore Sussex. Children over 10.

E-mail: ewalt@shortgate.co.uk

	£25.00 to £30.00	Y	N	N

David & Ethel Walters   Shortgate Manor Farm   Halland   Lewes BN8 6PJ   Sussex
Tel: (01825) 840320   Fax 01825 840320   Open: ALL YEAR   Map Ref No. 27

Wartling Place. Wartling.

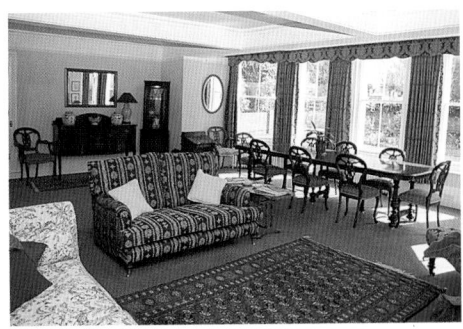

Sussex

Huggetts Furnace Farm

Nearest Road: A.272

A beautiful medieval farmhouse (Grade II listed) set well off the beaten track in tranquil countryside. 3 attractive bedrooms, all with en-suite/private facilities, radio & tea/coffee trays. The oak-beamed guests' room has an inglenook fireplace & a T.V.. Super dinners & breakfasts use home-grown & local produce. Heated outdoor swimming pool, & 120 acres of grounds. Self-catering cottage (non-smokers). Gatwick 45 mins. 30 mins coast. Nearby, many National Trust properties. Children over 7.
E-mail: huggettsfurnacefarm@freenet.co.uk

£27.50 to £32.50 — Y Y N

see PHOTO over
p. 321

Gillian & John Mulcare   Huggetts Furnace Farm   Stonehurst Lane   Five Ashes   Mayfield TN20 6LL
Tel: (01825) 830220   Fax 01825 830722   Open: ALL YEAR (Excl. Xmas)   Map Ref No. 28

Amberfold

Nearest Road: A.272

Amberfold is a charming 17th-century listed cottage, situated in quiet, idyllic countryside yet only 5 mins' drive from Midhurst. 2 self-contained annexes with access all day. 1 is situated on the ground floor. Each annex is comfortably furnished & has private facilities, T.V., clock/radio, fridge, etc. To allow you complete freedom & privacy, a large Continental breakfast is self-service & is taken in your room. An attractive garden in which to relax. Parking. An ideal base from which to explore of Goodwood, Singleton, Chichester & the coast.

£25.00 to £35.00 — N N N

Annabelle & Alexander Costaras   Amberfold   Heyshott   Midhurst GU29 0DA   Sussex
Tel: (01730) 812385   Open: ALL YEAR   Map Ref No. 29

Mill Farm

Nearest Road: A.272

A Sussex country house set in 15 acres of pasture. A large garden, with a grass tennis court. Delightful accommodation in 4 pleasant bedrooms, 1 room is en-suite, each with superb views over the South Downs. Colour T.V.s & tea-making facilities. Log fires in the hall & drawing room. Lovely walks & excellent pubs. Chichester, Goodwood & Petworth Houses, Arundel Castle, Heathrow, Gatwick & the coast within easy reach. Ideal as a holiday base. Animals by arrangement.
E-mail: johnmillfarm@aol.com

£18.00 to £27.50 — Y N Y

John & Lois Field   Mill Farm   Trotton   Petersfield GU31 5EL   Sussex
Tel: (01730) 813080   Fax 01730 815080   Open: ALL YEAR   Map Ref No. 30

Mizzards Farm

Nearest Road: A.272

This beautifully modernised farmhouse is set in gardens & farmland by the River Rother. All of the bedrooms have en-suite facilities & colour T.V.. There is an elegant drawing room, & breakfast is served in a magnificent vaulted hall dating from the 16th century. There is a covered swimming pool, for guests' use, & beautiful gardens. Situated close to the South Downs, the coast & several National Trust houses. Children over 8 years welcome. Animals by arrangement.
E-mail: julian.francis@hemscott.net

£30.00 to £34.00 — Y N Y

Mrs H. E. Francis   Mizzards Farm   Rogate   Petersfield GU31 5HS   Sussex
Tel: (01730) 821656   Fax 01730 821655   Open: ALL YEAR (Excl. Xmas)   Map Ref No. 31

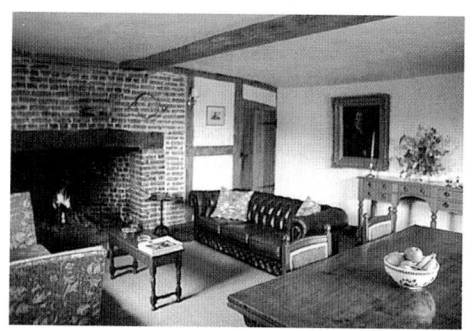

Huggetts Furnace Farm. Five Ashes.

Jeake's House.   Rye.

Column headers (rotated):
- rate £ from - to per person
- children taken
- evening meals
- animals taken

£32.00 to £45.00

Y | N | N

(No smoking)

VISA: M'CARD:

Little Orchard House

Nearest Road: A.259, A.268

This charming Georgian townhouse, with traditional walled garden & Smuggler's Watchtower, is at the heart of ancient Rye. Whilst a perfect touring base, it retains many original features. Open fires, antique furnishings & books ensure a peaceful, relaxed atmosphere. Generous country breakfasts feature organic & free-range local products. The 2 lovely en-suite bedrooms have 4-poster beds & include T.V., VCR, fridge & hot-drinks tray. Children over 12 years welcome.

Sara Brinkhurst   Little Orchard House   West Street   Rye TN31 7ES   Sussex
Tel: (01797) 223831   Fax 01797 223831   Open: ALL YEAR   Map Ref No. 33

£30.50 to £50.50

Y | N | Y

see PHOTO over p. 322

VISA: M'CARD:

Jeake's House

Nearest Road: A.259

Jeakes House is an outstanding 17th-century listed building. Retaining original features, including oak beams & wood panelling, & decorated throughout with antiques. 12 bedrooms overlook the gardens, en-suite/private facilities, T.V., etc. 4-poster available. Dine in the galleried former Baptist chapel, where full English, wholefood vegetarian or Continental breakfasts are served. Located in one of Britain's most picturesque medieval streets. Private parking. Children over 11 years.
E-mail: jeakeshouse@btinternet.com

Jenny Hadfield   Jeake's House   Mermaid Street   Rye TN31 7ET   Sussex
Tel: (01797) 222828   Fax 01797 222623   Open: ALL YEAR   Map Ref No. 33

£25.00 to £40.00

Y | Y | Y

see PHOTO over p. 324

VISA: M'CARD:

Durrant House Hotel

Nearest Road: A.259

Durrant House Hotel is a charming listed building located in the centre of ancient Rye. 7 comfortable & individually decorated bedrooms, including four-poster & triple rooms, all equipped to a high standard. There are far reaching views across the marshes from the rear garden, where breakfast may be taken during the summer. The hotel offers an informal & friendly atmosphere, wholesome food & is the perfect location for a relaxing break. Evening meals & dogs by arrangement.
E-mail: kingslands@compuserve.com

Ron & Jo Kingsland   Durrant House Hotel   Market Street   Rye TN31 7LA   Sussex
Tel: (01797) 223182   Fax 01797 226340   Open: FEB - DEC   Map Ref No. 33

£24.00 to £36.00

Y | N | N

(No smoking)

VISA: M'CARD:

The Strand House

Nearest Road: A.259

Nestling at the foot of the cliffs beneath the 13th-century Strand Gate lies The Strand House, full of atmosphere with oak beams & inglenook fireplaces. Without a level floor or wall, the bedrooms have their own individual charm. (4-poster available.) A traditional English breakfast, using local fresh produce, is served in the heavily beamed dining room. Log fires in season. Pretty gardens. Children over 5 years welcome.
E-mail: strandhouse@winchelsea98.fsnet.co.uk

Geoffrey Woods   The Strand House   Tanyard's Lane   Winchelsea TN36 4JT   Sussex
Tel: (01797) 226276   Fax 01797 224806   Open: ALL YEAR (Excl. Xmas)   Map Ref No. 36

Durrant House Hotel.   Rye.

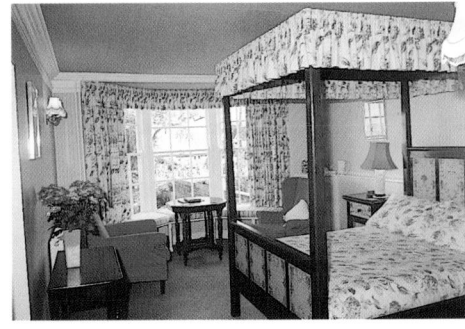

rate £ from - to per person	children taken	evening meals	animals taken		
£24.00 to £27.00	Y	N	N		**Bonchurch House**

VISA: M'CARD:

Nearest Road: A.259

Bonchurch is a home-from-home guest house where a warm welcome is extended to all guests. Accommodation is in 6 bedrooms, all well-equipped with shaver points & an en-suite/private shower/bathroom, colour T.V., easy chairs & tea/coffee-making facilities. Home cooking is a speciality. Ideally situated in a picturesque setting, yet close to the sea front, shops & entertainment. Children over 3 years welcome.

E-mail: bonchurch@enta.net

Mr & Mrs G. Batchelor   Bonchurch House   1 Winchester Road   Worthing BN11 4DJ   Sussex
Tel: (01903) 202492   Fax 01903 202492   Open: FEB - DEC   Map Ref No. 37

All the establishments mentioned in this guide are members of
The Worldwide Bed & Breakfast Association

When booking your accommodation please mention
The Best Bed & Breakfast

Warwickshire

Warwickshire
(Heart of England)

Warwickshire contains much that is thought of as traditional rural England, but it is a county of contradictions. Rural tranquillity surrounds industrial towns, working canals run along with meandering rivers, the mediaeval splendour of Warwick Castle vies with the handsome Regency grace of Leamington Spa.

Of course, Warwickshire is Shakespeare's county, with his birthplace, Stratford-upon-Avon standing at the northern edge of the Cotswolds. You can visit any of half a dozen houses with Shakespearian associations, see his tomb in the lovely Parish church or enjoy a performance by the world famous Royal Shakespeare Company in their theatre on the banks of the River Avon.

Warwickshire was created as the Kingdom of Mercia after the departure of the Romans. King Offa of Mercia left us his own particular mark - a coin which bore the imprint of his likeness known as his "pen" & this became our penny. Lady Godiva was the wife of an Earl of Mercia who pleaded with her husband to lessen the taxation burden on his people. He challenged her to ride naked through the streets of Coventry as the price of her request. She did this knowing that her long hair would cover her nakedness, & the people, who loved her, stayed indoors out of respect. Only Peeping Tom found the temptation irresistible.

The 15th, 16th, & 17th centuries were the heyday of fine building in the county, when many gracious homes were built. Exceptional Compton Wynyates has rosy pink bricks, twisted chimney stacks, battlements & moats & presents an unforgettably romantic picture of a perfect Tudor House.

Coventry has long enjoyed the reputation of a thriving city, noted for its weaving of silks and ribbons, learned from the refugee Huguenots. When progress brought industry, watches, bicycles & cars became the mainstay of the city. Coventry suffered grievously from aerial bombardment in the war & innumerable ancient & treasured buildings were lost.

A magnificent new Cathedral stands besides the shell of the old. Mystery plays enacting the life of Christ are performed in the haunting ruin.

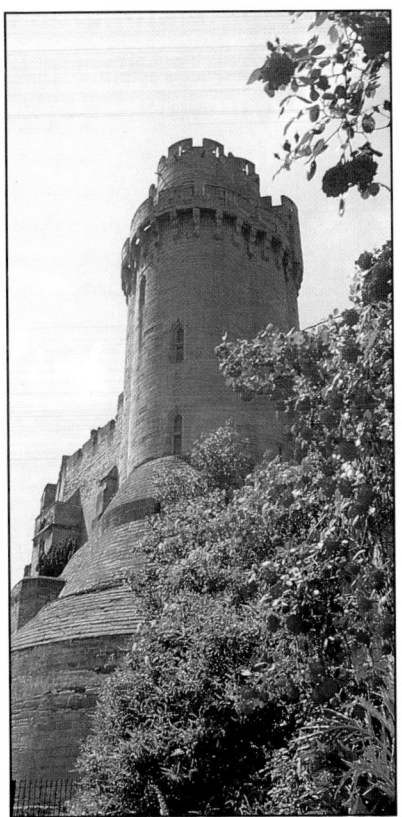

Warwick Castle.

Warwickshire

Warwickshire
Gazeteer

Areas of Outstanding Natural Beauty
The Edge Hills

Historic Houses & Castles

Arbury Hall - Nuneaton
18th century Gothic mansion - made famous by George Elliot as Cheverel Manor - paintings, period furnishings, etc.

Compton Wynyates
15th century - famous Tudor house - pink brick, twisted chimneys, battlemented walls. Interior almost untouched - period furnishing.

Coughton Court - Alcester
15th century - Elizabethan half-timbered wings. Holds Jacobite relics.

Harvard House - Stratford-upon-Avon
16th century - home of mother of John Harvard, University founder.

Homington Hall - Shipston-on-Stour
17th century with fine 18th century plasterwork.

Packwood House - Hockley Heath
Tudor timber framed house - with 17th century additions. Famous yew garden.

Ragley Hall - Alcester
17th century Palladian - magnificent house with fine collection of porcelain, paintings, furniture, etc. & a valuable library.

Shakespeare's Birthplace Trust Properties - Stratford-upon-Avon

Anne Hathaway's Cottage - Shottery
The thatched cottage home of Anne Hathaway.

Hall's Croft - Old Town
Tudor house where Shakespeare's daughter Susanna lived.

Mary Arden's House - Wilmcote
Tudor farmhouse with dovecote. Home of Shakespeare's mother.

New Place - Chapel Street
Shakespeare's last home - the foundations of his house are preserved in Elizabethan garden.

Birthplace of Shakespeare - Henley Street
Many rare Shakespeare relics exhibited in this half-timbered house.

Lord Leycester Hospital - Warwick
16th century timber framed group around courtyard - hospital for poor persons in the mediaeval guilds.

Upton House - Edge Hill
Dating from James II reign - contains Brussels tapestries, Sevres porcelain, Chelsea figurines, 18th century furniture & other works of art, including Old Masters.

Warwick Castle - Warwick
Splendid mediaeval castle - site was originally fortified more than a thousand years ago. Present castle 14th century. Armoury.

Cathedrals & Churches

Astley (St. Mary the Virgin)
17th century - has remains of 14th century collegiate church. 15th century painted stalls.

Beaudesert (St. Nicholas)
Norman with fine arches in chancel.

Brailes (St. George)
15th century - decorated nave & aisles - 14th century carved oak chest.

Crompton Wynyates
Church of Restoration period having painted ceiling.

Lapworth (St. Mary)
13th & 14th century - steeple & north aisle connected by passage.

Preston-on-Stour (The Blessed Virgin Mary)
18th century. Gilded ceiling, 17th century glass

Tredington (St. Gregory)
Saxon walls in nave - largely14th century, 17th century pulpit. Fine spire.

Warwick (St. Mary)
15th century Beauchamp Chapel, vaulted choir, some 17th century Gothic.

Wooten Wawen (St. Peter)
Saxon, with remnants of mediaeval wall painting, 15th century screens & pulpit: small 17th century chained library.

Museums & Galleries

The Royal Shakespeare Theatre Picture Gallery - Stratford-upon-Avon
Original designs & paintings, portraits of famous actors, etc.

Motor Museum - Stratford-upon-Avon
Collection of cars, racing, vintage, exotic, replica of 1930 garage. Fashions, etc. of 1920's era.

WARWICKSHIRE
Map reference

01 Lawson	05 Wootton
02 Lea	05 Andrews
03 Smith	05 P. Evans
04 Mawle	05 Tozer
05 Pettitt	05 Mander
05 Workman	06 Spencer
05 Castelli	07 Hutsby
05 Harvard	08 Waterworth
05 Machin	

8 Clarendon Crescent. Leamington Spa.

Warwickshire

8 Clarendon Crescent

Nearest Road: A.452

A Grade II listed Regency house overlooking a private dell. Situated in a quiet backwater of Leamington. Elegantly furnished with antiques, & offering accommodation in 5 tastefully furnished bedrooms, 4 en-suite. A delicious full English breakfast is served. Only 5 mins' walk from the town centre. Very convenient for Warwick, Stratford, Stoneleigh Agricultural Centre, Warwick University & the N.E.C.. Children over 4 years.
E-mail: lawson@lawson76fsnet.co.uk

| £27.50 to £30.00 | Y | N | N |

see PHOTO over p. 329

Christine & David Lawson   8 Clarendon Crescent   Leamington Spa CV32 5NR   Warwickshire
Tel: (01926) 429840   Fax 01926 424641   Open: ALL YEAR   Map Ref No. 01

Crandon House

Nearest Road: A.423

Crandon House offers an especially warm welcome & exceptionally high standard of accommodation & comfort. Set in 20 acres of beautiful countryside. There are 5 pretty bedrooms (1 ground-floor) with en-suite/private bathroom, T.V. & tea/coffee. Log fire. Extensive breakfast menu. A tranquil rural retreat, yet within easy reach of Stratford, Warwick, Oxford & the Cotswolds. Located between the M.40 Jts 11 & 12 (4 miles). Children over 8 years. Special winter breaks.
E-mail: crandonhouse@talk21.com

| £20.00 to £30.00 | Y | N | N |

VISA: M'CARD:

Deborah Lea   Crandon House   Avon Dassett   Leamington Spa CV47 2AA   Warwickshire
Tel: (01295) 770652   Fax 01295 770632   Open: ALL YEAR   Map Ref No. 02

Lower Farm

Nearest Road: A.429

On the edge of the Cotswolds, just off the Fosse Way in the pretty, unspoilt hamlet of Darlingscott stands this fine, 18th-century, listed farmhouse. The guest accommodation comprises 2 attractive double rooms & 1 twin-bedded room, each with an en-suite bathroom, colour T.V. & tea-making facilities. This is the perfect location from which to visit Chipping Campden. The magnificent gardens of Hidcote & Kiftsgate are just 5 miles away, & Stratford-upon-Avon only 9 miles. Children over 8.
E-mail: lowerfarmbb@beeb.net

| £25.00 to £30.00 | Y | N | N |

Jackie Smith   Lower Farm   Darlingscott   Shipston-on-Stour CV36 4PN   Warwickshire
Tel: (01608) 682750   Fax 01608 682750   Open: ALL YEAR   Map Ref No. 03

Lower Farm Barn

Nearest Road: A.3400, A.44

This lovely, 100-year-old, converted barn stands in the small, peaceful Warwickshire village of Great Wolford. The property retains much of its original form, including exposed beams & ancient stone work. Now tastefully modernised, it makes a very comfortable home. Accommodation is in 2 beautifully furnished double rooms, each with en-suite facilities. A delightful base from which to explore this fascinating area, & within easy reach of Stratford-upon-Avon.

| £22.00 to £24.00 | Y | N | N |

Rebecca Mawle   Lower Farm Barn   Great Wolford   Shipston-on-Stour CV36 5NQ   Warwickshire
Tel: (01608) 674435   Open: ALL YEAR   Map Ref No. 04

Twelfth Night. Stratford-upon-Avon.

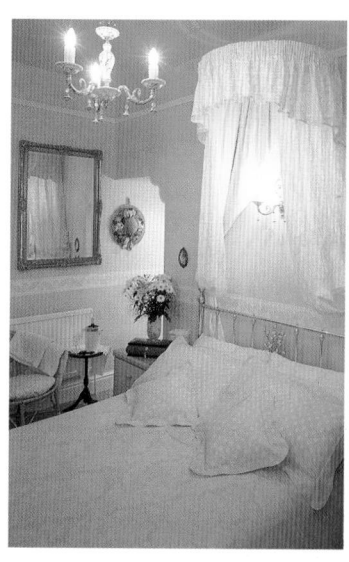

	rate £ from - to per person	children taken	evening meals	animals taken

Parkfield

Nearest Road: A.439

A delightful Victorian house, in a quiet location in Old Town just 5 mins' walk to the town centre & the Royal Shakespeare Theatre. Ideally situated for touring the Cotswolds, Warwick Castle, etc.. 7 spacious & comfortable rooms, 6 en-suite, all with colour T.V. & tea/coffee-making facilities. Excellent breakfasts. Private parking. Lots of tourist information available. Guests can be collected from the station. Children over 5 yrs.
E-mail: Parkfield@btinternet.com

| £22.50 to £22.50 | Y | N | N |

VISA: M'CARD:

Roger & Joanna Pettitt Parkfield 3 Broad Walk Stratford-upon-Avon CV37 6HS Warwickshire
Tel: (01789) 293313 Fax 01789 293313 Open: ALL YEAR Map Ref No. 05

Ravenhurst

Nearest Road: A.4390, B.439

A Victorian town house with a warm & friendly atmosphere. Ideally situated on the edge of the old town & only a few mins' walk from the Shakespeare Theatre, town centre & places of historical interest. Enjoy the comfort & quiet of this family-run guest house, where all bedrooms have colour T.V. & tea/coffee-making facilities. Special double en-suite rooms available with 4-poster beds. The Workmans are Stratfordians, therefore local knowledge is a speciality. Children over 5.
E-mail: ravaccom@waverider.co.uk

| £23.00 to £26.00 | Y | N | N |

VISA: M'CARD: AMEX:

Richard Workman Ravenhurst 2 Broad Walk Stratford-upon-Avon CV37 6HS Warwickshire
Tel: (01789) 292515 Fax 01789 292515 Open: ALL YEAR Map Ref No. 05

Twelfth Night

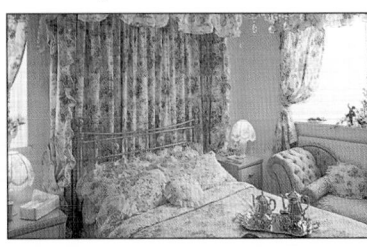

Nearest Road: B.439

Somewhere special - once owned for almost a quarter of a century by the Royal Shakespeare Company as a pied a terre for actors. Delightfully refurbished, this Victorian villa, built in 1897, has retained its character. Providing modern comforts, it includes central heating, en-suite bedrooms with pocket spring beds, brass bedsteads, canopies & half testers plus many other personal touches. Twelfth Night is centrally placed with private parking. A non-smoking establishment.

| £26.00 to £32.00 | N | N | N |

see PHOTO over p. 331

VISA: M'CARD:

Margaret Harvard Twelfth Night Evesham Place Stratford-upon-Avon CV37 6HT Warwickshire
Tel: (01789) 414595 Open: ALL YEAR Map Ref No. 05

Stretton House

Nearest Road: A.439

Stretton House is a 'home from home' where a warm & friendly welcome awaits you. Very comfortable accommodation at reasonable prices. Pretty, full en-suite bedrooms & standard rooms, all having T.V. & tea/coffee-making facilities. Excellent full English breakfast, vegetarians catered for. Limited car parking. Situated opposite lovely Fir Park, within easy reach of the country, yet only 3 mins' walk from the town centre. Children over 8.
E-mail: skyblues@strettonhouse.co.uk

| £15.00 to £28.00 | Y | N | Y |

see PHOTO over p. 333

Mr & Mrs M. Machin Stretton House 38 Grove Road Stratford-upon-Avon CV37 6PB Warwickshire
Tel: (01789) 268647 Fax 01789 268647 Open: ALL YEAR Map Ref No. 05

Stretton House. Stratford-upon-Avon.

Hardwick House. Stratford-upon-Avon.

rate £ from - to per person	children taken	evening meals taken	animals taken

---

£23.00 to £25.00 | Y | N | N

(non-smoking)

Minola House

Nearest Road: B.439

A comfortable house with a relaxed atmosphere, offering good accommodation in 5 pleasantly furnished bedrooms, 1 with private shower, 3 are en-suite; all have T.V. & tea/coffee-making facilities. Stratford offers a myriad of delights for the visitor, including the Royal Shakespeare Theatre. Set by the River Avon, this makes a lovely place for a picnic lunch or early evening meal before the performance. Children over 10 years are welcome. Italian & French spoken.

Mr & Mrs Castelli Minola House 25 Evesham Place Stratford-upon-Avon CV37 6HT Warwickshire
Tel: (01789) 293573   Fax 01789 551625   Open: ALL YEAR   Map Ref No. 05

£22.00 to £34.00 | Y | N | N

see PHOTO over
p. 334

VISA: M'CARD: AMEX:

Hardwick House

Nearest Road: A.439

Hardwick House is situated in a quiet, residential area of Stratford-upon-Avon, away from main roads yet only a 5-min. walk into the town. All 14 bedrooms are non-smoking, clean & comfortable, with tea/coffee-making facilities & T.V.. Resident proprietors ensure a warm welcome & attention to detail. There is an on-site car park. Directions from M.40: on the A.439, take the first right turn past the 30-mph sign into St. Gregory's Road, & Hardwick House is 200 yds on the right.
E-mail: hardwick@waverider.co.uk

Mr & Mrs S. Wootton Hardwick House 1 Avenue Road Stratford-upon-Avon CV37 6UY Warwickshire
Tel: (01789) 204307   Fax 01789 296760   Open: ALL YEAR   Map Ref No. 05

£24.50 to £41.00 | Y | N | Y

(non-smoking)

see PHOTO over
p. 336

VISA: M'CARD: AMEX:

Melita Private Hotel

Nearest Road: A.3400

An extremely friendly family-run hotel. Offering pleasant service, good food & accommodation in 12 excellent bedrooms, with en-suite/private facilities, T.V., tea/coffee & 'phones. A comfortable lounge/bar & pretty, award-winning garden for guests' use. Parking is available. A pleasant 5-min. walk to Shakespearian properties/theatres, shopping centre & riverside gardens. Superbly situated for Warwick Castle, Coventry & the Cotswolds.
E-mail: Melita37@email.msn.com

Patricia Andrews Melita Private Hotel   37 Shipston Road   Stratford-upon-Avon CV37 7LN   Warks.
Tel: (01789) 292432 Fax 01789 204867 Open: ALL YEAR (Excl. Xmas & New Year) Map Ref No. 05

£29.50 to £39.50 | Y | N | N

(non-smoking)

see PHOTO over
p. 337

VISA: M'CARD: AMEX:

Sequoia House

Nearest Road: A.3400

A beautifully appointed private hotel situated across the River Avon from the Royal Shakespeare Theatre. 23 bedrooms (mostly en-suite), a cocktail bar, a cottage annex & a fully air-conditioned dining room. The hotel is comfortably furnished, & decorated in a warm & restful style, with many extra thoughtful touches. The garden overlooks the town cricket ground & the old tramway. Pleasant walks along the banks of the River Avon opposite the Theatre & Holy Trinity Church. Children over 5.
E-mail: info@sequoiahotel.co.uk

Philip & Jean Evans   Sequoia House   51-53 Shipston Road   Stratford-upon-Avon CV37 7LN
Tel: (01789) 268852   Fax 01789 414559   Open: ALL YEAR (Excl. Xmas)   Map Ref No. 05

Melita Hotel. Stratford-upon-Avon.

Sequoia House. Stratford-upon-Avon.

Fulready Manor. Ettington.

Column headers (rotated): rate £ from - to per person | children taken | evening meals | animals taken

---

Fulready Manor

£55.00 to £62.50	N	N	N

(non-smoking)

see PHOTO over p. 338

Nearest Road: A.422

Michael & Maureen Spencer invite you to experience their unique home, Fulready Manor, set in 120 acres overlooking its own lake, in the beautiful south Warwickshire countryside. It is on the doorstep of the Cotswolds & is only 7 miles from historic Stratford-upon-Avon. Fulready Manor boasts sumptuously furnished, individually designed four-poster bedrooms, all with dramatic views & en-suite bathrooms. All of the rooms have been skilfully created by an interior designer.
E-mail: stay@fulreadymanor.co.uk

Mr & Mrs M. Spencer   Fulready Manor   Ettington   Stratford-upon-Avon CV37 7PE   Warwickshire
Tel: (01789) 740152   Fax 01789 740247   Open: ALL YEAR (Excl. Xmas)   Map Ref No. 06

Victoria Spa Lodge

£32.50 to £32.50	Y	N	N

(non-smoking)

see PHOTO over p. 340

VISA: M'CARD:

Nearest Road: A.3400, A.46

Large 19th-century house in country setting, overlooking Stratford canal, with ample parking. A royal coat of arms was built into the gables (with the permission of Queen Victoria) of this Grade II listed building. 7 attractive & comfortable en-suite bedrooms, each having a hostess tray, T.V., radio/alarm & hairdryer. 1 1/2 miles from the centre of town. An excellent base for visiting the Cotswolds & Shakespearian properties. Pleasant walks along the tow path to Stratford & Wilmcote.
E-mail: PTOZER@VICTORIASPALODGE.DEMON.CO.UK

Paul & Dreen Tozer   Victoria Spa Lodge   Bishopton Lane   Stratford-upon-Avon CV37 9QY   Warks.
Tel: (01789) 267985   Fax 01789 204728   Open: ALL YEAR   Map Ref No. 05

Pear Tree Cottage

£27.00 to £30.00	Y	N	N

(non-smoking)

see PHOTO over p. 341

Nearest Road: A.3400

A delightful half-timbered 16th-century house located in the Shakespeare village of Wilmcote. It retains all its original charm & character, with oak beams, flagstone floors, inglenook fireplaces, thick stone walls with deep-set windows & antiques. Offering 7 very comfortable en-suite rooms, all with tea/coffee-making facilities & colour T.V.. A delicious breakfast is served each morning in the dining room. A lovely base from which to tour the whole region. Children over 3.
E-mail: peartree3@hotmail.com

Mrs Margaret Mander   Pear Tree Cottage   7, Church Road   Wilmcote   Stratford-upon-Avon CV37 9UX
Tel: (01789) 205889 Fax 01789 262862 Open: ALL YEAR (Excl. Xmas & New Year) Map Ref No. 05

Nolands Farm & Country Restaurant

£20.00 to £26.00	Y	Y	N

see PHOTO over p. 342

VISA: M'CARD:

Nearest Road: A.422

A working farm situated in a tranquil valley 8 miles from Stratford-upon-Avon. All bedrooms are annexed, some on the ground floor, overlooking either the old stableyard or fields. A selection of 4-posters, king-size doubles, twins, family & single rooms are available. All en-suite with T.V., tea tray, hairdryers & much more. Large gardens. Your hosts also offer clay pigeon shooting, fishing, hot air balloon flights & bicycles. Horse riding nearby. Parking. Dinner by arrangement. Children over 7.
E-mail: inthecountry@nolandsfarm.co.uk

Sue Hutsby   Nolands Farm & Country Restaurant   Oxhill   Warwick CV35 0RJ   Warwickshire
Tel: (01926) 640309   Fax 01926 641662   Open: ALL YEAR (Excl. Xmas)   Map Ref No. 07

Victoria Spa Lodge. Stratford-upon-Avon.

Pear Tree Cottage. Wilmcote.

Nolands Farm. Oxhill.

Warwickshire

rate £ from - to per person	children taken	evening meals	animals taken	
£27.50 to £27.50	Y	N	N	**Merchant's House**

🚭

see PHOTO over p. 344

Nearest Road: A.439

After 11 years at Sandbarn Farm, the Waterworths have moved down the road to the tranquil conservation area of this charming village. Offering luxury accommodation in this restored, beautifully appointed beamed house, 3 miles from Stratford, Warwick & Kenilworth castles & many National Trust houses are nearby. NEC/NAC, 25 mins. All rooms are en-suite & there is a guest sitting-room with T.V.. Children over 5. Your hosts look forward to welcoming you into their new home.
E-mail: hwaterworth@hotmail.com

Helen Waterworth   *Merchant's House*   Hampton Lucy   Warwick CV35 8BE   *Warwickshire*
Tel: (01789) 842280   Open: ALL YEAR (Excl. Xmas & New Year)   Map Ref No. 08

All the establishments mentioned in this guide are members of
The Worldwide Bed & Breakfast Association

When booking your accommodation please mention
The Best Bed & Breakfast

The Merchant's House. Swaffham Bulbeck.

Wiltshire

Wiltshire
(West Country)

Wiltshire is a county of rolling chalk downs, small towns, delightful villages, fine churches & great country houses. The expanse of Salisbury Plain is divided by the beautiful valleys of Nadder, Wylye, Ebble & Avon. In a county of open landscapes, Savernake Forest, with its stately avenues of trees strikes a note of contrast. In the north west the Cotswolds spill over into Wiltshire from neighbouring Gloucestershire.

No other county is so rich in archaeological sites. Long barrows and ancient hill forts stand on the skylines as evidence of the early habitation of the chalk uplands. Many of these prehistoric sites are at once magnificent and mysterious. The massive stone arches and monoliths of Stonehenge were built over a period of 500 years with stones transported over great distances. At Avebury the small village is completely encircled by standing stones and a massive bank and ditch earthwork. Silbury Hill is a huge, enigmatic man-made mound. England's largest chambered tomb is West Kennet Long Barrow and at Bush Barrow, finds have included fine bronze and gold daggers and a stone sceptre-head similar to one found at Mycenae in Greece.

Some of England's greatest historic houses are in Wiltshire. Longleat is an Elizabethan mansion with priceless collections of paintings, books & furniture. The surrounding park was landscaped by Capability Brown and its great fame in recent years has been its Safari Park, particularly the lions which roam freely around the visiting cars. Stourhead has celebrated 18th century landscaped gardens which are exceptional in spring when rhododendrons bloom.

Two delightful villages are Castle Combe, nestling in a Cotswold valley, & Lacock where the twisting streets hold examples of buildings ranging from mediaeval half-timbered, to Tudor & Georgian. 13th century Lacock Abbey, converted to a house in the 16th century, was the home of Fox Talbot, pioneer of photography.

There are many notable churches in Wiltshire. In Bradford-on-Avon, a fascinating old town, is the church of St. Lawrence, a rare example of an almost perfect Saxon church from around 900. Farley has an unusual brick church thought to have been designed by Sir Christopher Wren, & there is stained glass by William Morris in the church at Rodbourne.

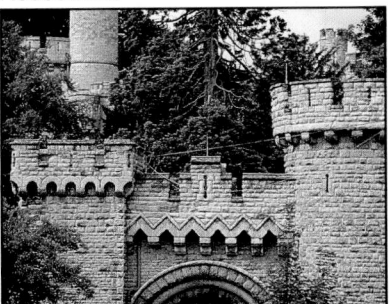

Devizes Castle

Salisbury stands where three rivers join, on a plain of luxuriant watermeadows, where the focal point of the landscape is the soaring spire of the Cathedral; at 404 feet, it is the tallest in England. The 13th century cathedral has a marvellous & rare visual unity. The body of the building was completed in just 38 years, although the spire was added in the next century. Salisbury, or "New Sarum" was founded in 1220 when the Bishop abandoned the original cathedral at Old Sarum, to start the present edifice two miles to the south. At Old Sarum you can see the foundation of the old city including the outline of the first cathedral.

Wiltshire

Wiltshire Gazeteer

Area of Outstanding Natural Beauty
The Costwolds & the North Wessex Downs.

Historic Houses & Castles

Corsham Court - Chippenham
16th & 17th centuries from Elizabethan & Georgian periods. 18th century furniture, British, Flemish & Italian Old Masters. Gardens by Capability Brown.

Great Chalfield Manor - Melksham
15th century manor house - moated.

Church House - Salisbury
15th century house.

Chalcot House - Westbury
17th century small house in Palladian manner.

Lacock Abbey - Nr. Chippenham
13th century abbey. In 1540 converted into house - 18th century alterations. Mediaeval cloisters & brewery.

Longleat House - Warminster
16th century - early Renaissance, alterations in early 1800's. Italian Renaissance decorations. Splendid state rooms, pictures, books, furniture. Victorian kitchens. Game reserve.

Littlecote - Nr. Hungerford
15th century Tudor manor. Panelled rooms, moulded plaster ceilings.

Luckington Court - Luckington
Queen Anne for the most part - fine ancient buildings.

Malmesbury House - Salisbury
Queen Anne house - part 14th century. Rococo plasterwork.

Newhouse - Redlynch
17th century brick Jacobean trinity house - two Georgian wings,

Philips House - Dinton
1816 Classical house.

Sheldon Manor - Chippenham
13th century porch & 15th century chapel in this Plantagenet manor.

Stourhead - Stourton
18th century Palladian house with framed landscape gardens.

Westwood Manor - Bradford-on-Avon
15th century manor house - alterations in 16th & 17th centuries.

Wardour Castle - Tisbury
18th century house in Palladian manner.

Wilton House - Salisbury
17th century - work of Inigo Jones & later of James Wyatt in 1810. Paintings, Kent & Chippendale furniture.

Avebury Manor - Nr Malborough
Elizabethan manor house - beautiful plasterwork, panelling & furniture. Gardens with topiary.

Bowood - Calne
18th century - work of several famous architects. Gardens by Capability Brown - famous beechwoods.

Mompesson House - Salisbury
Queen Anne town house - Georgian plasterwork.

Cathedrals & Churches

Salisbury Cathedral
13th century - decorated tower with stone spire. Part of original stone pulpitum is preserved. Beautiful large decorated cloister. Exterior mostly early English.

Salisbury (St. Thomas of Canterbury)
15th century rebuilding - 12th century font, 14th & 15th century glass, 17th century monuments. 'Doom' painting over chancel & murals in south chapel

Amesbury (St. Mary & St. Melor)
13th century - refashioned 15th & restored in 19th century. Splendid timber roofs, stone vaulting over chapel of north transept, mediaeval painted glass, 15th century screen, Norman font.

Bishops Cannings (St. Mary the Virgin)
13th-15th centuries. Fine arcading in transept - fine porch doorway. 17th century almsbox, Jacobean Holy table.

Bradford-on-Avon (St. Lawrence)
Best known of all Saxon churches in England.

Cricklade (St. Sampson)
12th -16th century. Tudor central tower vault, 15th century chapel.

Inglesham (St. John the Baptist)
Mediaeval wall paintings, high pews, clear glass, remains of painted screens.

Malmesbury (St. Mary)
Norman - 12th century arcades, refashioning in 14th century with clerestory, 15th century stone pulpitum added. Fine sculpture.

Wiltshire

Tisbury (St. John the Baptist)
14th-15th centuries. 15th-17th century roofing to nave & aisles. Two storeyed porch & chancel.
Potterne (St. Mary)
13th,14th,15th centuries. Inscribed Norman tub font. Wooden pulpit.

Museums & Galleries

Salisbury & South Wiltshire Museum - Salisbury
Collections showing history of the area in all periods. Models of Stonehenge & Old Sarum - archaeologically important collection.
Devizes Museum - Devizes
Unique archaeological & geological collections, including Sir Richard Colt-Hoare's Stourhead collection of prehistoric material.
Alexander Keiller Museum - Avebury
Collection of items from the Neolithic & Bronze ages & from excavations in district.
Athelstan Museum - Malmesbury
Collection of articles referring to the town - household, coin, etc.
Bedwyn Stone Museum - Great Bedwyn
Open-air museum showing where Stonehenge was carved.
Lydiard Park - Lydiard Tregoze
Parish church of St. Mary & a splendid Georgian mansion standing in park & also permanent & travelling exhibitions.

Borough of Thamesdown Museum & Art Gallery - Swindon
Natural History & Geology of Wiltshire, Bygones, coins, etc. 20th century British art & ceramic collection.
Great Western Railway Museum - Swindon
Historic locomotives.

Historic Monuments

Stonehenge - Nr. Amesbury
Prehistoric monument - encircling bank & ditch & Augrey holes are Neolithic. Stone circles possibly early Bronze age.
Avebury
Relics of enormous circular gathering place B.C. 2700-1700.
Old Sarum - Nr. Salisbury
Possibly first Iron Age camp, later Roman area, then Norman castle.
Silbury Hill - Nr. Avebury
Mound - conical in shape - probably a memorial c.3000-2000 B.C.
Windmill Hill - Nr. Avebury
Causewayed camp c.3000-2300 B.C.
Bratton Camp & White Horse - Bratton
Hill fort standing above White Horse. West Kennet Long Barrow
Burial place c.4000-2500 B.C.
Ludgershall Castle - Lugershall
Motte & bailey of Norman castle, earthworks, also flint walling from later castle.

Castle Combe.

WILTSHIRE
Map reference

06	Roberts	20	Brandon
07	Denning	20	Fairbrother
08	Steed	22	Patient
09	Sexton	23	Robathan
11	Stafford	24	Sykes
12	Daniel	26	Robertson
13	Eavis	28	Lanham
15	Roe	29	Hunt
16	Davies	32	Hocken
19	Gifford-Mead	34	Singer

Burghope Manor. Bradford-upon-Avon.

Wiltshire

Bradford Old Windmill

Nearest Road: A.363

A cosy, relaxed atmosphere greets you at this converted windmill high on the hill above the town. The old stone tower overflows with character, & with the many finds picked up by Peter & Priscilla on their backpacking trips around the world. All of the unusually shaped bedrooms have their own distinctive en-suite bathrooms. Imaginative healthy & unhealthy breakfasts are served beneath the massive grain weighing scales. 5 mins' walk from the town centre. Children over 6 years.

E-mail: bbbw@distinctlydifferent.co.uk

| £39.50 to £54.50 | Y | Y | N |

VISA: M'CARD: AMEX:

Priscilla & Peter Roberts   Bradford Old Windmill   4 Masons Lane   Bradford-on-Avon   Bath BA15 1QN
Tel: (01225) 866842   Fax 01225 866648   Open: MAR - DEC   Map Ref No. 06

Burghope Manor

Nearest Road: A.36

This historic 13th-century family home is set in beautiful countryside on the edge of the village of Winsley - overlooking the Avon Valley - 5 miles from Bath & 1 1/2 miles from Bradford-on-Avon. Although steeped in history, Burghope Manor is first & foremost a family home, which has been carefully modernised so that the wealth of historical features may complement the present-day comforts. A village pub & restaurant nearby. Dinner for groups only. Children over 10. Single supplement.

E-mail: burghope.manor@virgin.net

| £42.50 to £50.00 | Y | N | N |

see PHOTO over
p. 349

VISA: M'CARD: AMEX:

Elizabeth & John Denning   Burghope Manor   Winsley   Bradford-on-Avon BA15 2LA   Wiltshire
Tel: (01225) 723557   Fax 01225 723113   Open: ALL YEAR (Excl. Xmas & New Year)   Map Ref No. 07

The Cottage

Nearest Road: A.3102

This delightful cottage is reputed to have been a coaching inn, & dates back to 1450. There are 3 charming bedrooms, all with private shower, T.V. & tea/coffee makers, in a beautifully converted barn. Also, many exposed beams that were once ships' timbers. Breakfast is served in the old beamed dining room. A lovely garden & paddock for guests' use. An ideal centre for visiting Bath, Bristol, Devizes, Marlborough, Avebury, Stonehenge, Longleat, Castle Combe & Lacock.

E-mail: RJSteed@cottage16.freeserve.co.uk

| £25.00 to £25.00 | Y | N | N |

Richard & Gloria Steed   The Cottage   Westbrook   Bromham   Chippenham SN15 2EE   Wiltshire
Tel: (01380) 850255   Open: ALL YEAR   Map Ref No. 08

The Old Rectory

Nearest Road: A.350

Situated in the medieval village of Lacock, The Old Rectory, built in 1866, is a fine example of Victorian Gothic architecture, with creeper-clad walls & mullioned windows. It stands in 12 acres of its own carefully tended grounds, which include a tennis court & croquet lawn. The Old Rectory offers 3 very attractive bedrooms (1 on the ground floor), all with en-suite facilities. An excellent base from which to explore the glorious West Country.

E-mail: sexton@oldrectorylacock.co.uk

| £22.50 to £27.50 | Y | N | Y |

see PHOTO over
p. 351

Mrs R. E. Sexton   The Old Rectory   Cantax Hill   Lacock   Chippenham SN15 2JZ   Wiltshire
Tel: (01249) 730335   Fax 01249 730166   Open: ALL YEAR   Map Ref No. 09

Old Rectory. Lacock.

Wiltshire

rate £ from - to per person
children taken
evening meals
animals taken

Pickwick Lodge Farm

Nearest Road: A.4

A delightful 17th-century Cotswold stone farm-house, set in peaceful surroundings. 3 well-appointed & tastefully furnished bedrooms, each with an en-suite/private bathroom, radio, T.V. & tea/coffee-making facilities. Hearty & delicious breakfasts are served. Ideally situated for visiting many sites of historical interest, such as the Wiltshire White Horses, Avebury & Stonehenge; many stately homes & National Trust properties within easy reach. Ample parking. Children by arrangement.
E-mail: B&B@pickwickfarm.freeserve.co.uk

| | £22.50 to £25.00 | Y | N | N |

Gill Stafford   Pickwick Lodge Farm   Guyers Lane   Corsham SN13 0PS   Wiltshire
Tel: (01249) 712207   Fax 01249 701904   Open: ALL YEAR   Map Ref No. 11

Heatherly Cottage

Nearest Road: A.4

Heatherly Cottage was built in the 17th century & has a large garden with plenty of parking space & beautiful views towards the Westbury White Horse. Each of the 3 attractive bedrooms is well-equipped & has a T.V., tea/coffee-making facilities & an en-suite bathroom. In nearby Lacock & Gastard, there are traditional English pubs which serve excellent lunches & evening meals. The hosts aim to ensure that you enjoy your stay, & are happy to advise of local attractions, walks, etc. Children over 10.
E-mail: ladbrook1@aol.com

| | £23.00 to £26.00 | Y | N | N |

Mrs Jenny Daniel   Heatherly Cottage   Ladbrook Lane   Gastard Corsham SN13 9PE Wiltshire
Tel: (01249) 701402   Fax 01249 701412   Open: ALL YEAR   Map Ref No. 12

Manor Farm

Nearest Road: A.429

Relax & unwind in this charming award-winning 17th-century farmhouse, situated on a mixed working farm. There are 6 bedrooms, all with T.V. & hospitality trays. Eat your hearty breakfast in a dining room with a large inglenook fireplace. Ideal base for 1 night or longer stays for exploring the Cotswolds, Bath, Stonehenge, Lacock & many stately homes. Or, just while away the time relaxing in the walled garden. Meals are available at the local pub within walking distance. Children over 12.
E-mail: ross@manorfarmbandb.fsnet.co.uk

| | £21.00 to £24.00 | Y | N | N |

VISA: M'CARD:

Mrs Ross Eavis   Manor Farm   Corston   Malmesbury SN16 0HF   Wiltshire
Tel: (01666) 822148 Fax 01666 826565 Open: ALL YEAR (Excl. Xmas & New Year)   Map Ref No.13

Clench Farmhouse

Nearest Road: A.345, A.346

A warm & friendly atmosphere awaits guests when they arrive at this attractive 18th-century farmhouse, which is set in its own grounds & surrounded by lovely countryside. There are 2 double bedrooms & 1 twin bedroom, each with either an en-suite or private bathroom. All well decorated & furnished. Delicious dinners are also served. There is a tennis court & outdoor heated swimming pool. Well situated for Bath, Stonehenge & Salisbury. Ample parking.
E-mail: clasrissaroe@clenchfarmhouse.co.uk

| | £30.00 to £35.00 | Y | Y | Y |

Clarissa Roe   Clench Farmhouse   Clench   Nr. Marlborough SN8 4NT   Wiltshire
Tel: (01672) 810264   Fax 01672 811458   Open: ALL YEAR   Map Ref No. 15

| rate £ from - to per person | children taken | evening meals taken | animals taken |

Marridge Hill House

| £20.00 to £25.00 | Y | N | Y |

VISA: M'CARD:

Nearest Road: M.4, B.4192

The house originated in 1750 & is set in glorious countryside, only 1 hrs. drive from Heathrow Airport. You will be warmly welcomed into the relaxed, informal atmosphere of this family home, with its pleasant sitting & dining rooms, books galore & an acre of garden. 3 attractive twin bedrooms (1 en-suite). Both bathrooms have power showers. An ideal base for visiting Avebury, Salisbury, Bath, Oxford & the Cotswolds. Good pubs & restaurants nearby. Children over 5.
E-mail: judy.davies@lineone.net

Mrs Judy Davies   **Marridge Hill House**   **Ramsbury**   **Marlborough SN8 2HG**   **Wiltshire**
Tel: (01672) 520237   **Fax 01672 520053**   **Open: ALL YEAR**   **Map Ref No. 16**

The Mill House

| £25.00 to £35.00 | Y | N | N |

see PHOTO over
p. 354

Nearest Road: A.36, A.303

Stonehenge is only 3 miles away. Diana welcomes you to the Mill House set in acres of nature reserve abounding in wild flowers & infinite peace. An island paradise with the River Till running through the working mill & gardens. Diana's old fashioned roses long to see you as do the lovely walks, antiquities & houses. Built by the miller in 1785, the bedrooms all have tea/coffee facilities & T.V.. Fishing in the mill pool. Golf course & riding nearby. Attention to healthy & organic food. Sample superb cuisine at the Boot Inn. Children over 5.

Diana Gifford Mead   **The Mill House**   **Berwick St. James**   **Nr. Salisbury SP3 4TS**   **Wiltshire**
Tel: (01722) 790331   **Fax 01722 790331**   **Open: ALL YEAR**   **Map Ref No. 19**

Griffin Cottage

| £20.00 to £20.00 | N | N | N |

Nearest Road: A.36, A.30

Within 3 mins' of the market square. The house was built 300/500 years ago. Central heating & a real fire greet you in winter. Organic home-produced food where possible, including the bread. Antique furniture mixed with modern comforts to give a warm & informal welcome. The 2 guest rooms have recently been refurbished with comfortable beds, a must when staying away from home. Single supplement. (Hosts can also be contacted on Mobile 07968 225442.)
E-mail: mark@brandonasoc.demon.co.uk

Mrs Sue Brandon   **Griffin Cottage**   **10 St. Edmunds Church Street**   **Salisbury SP1 1EF**   **Wiltshire**
Tel: (01722) 328259   **Fax 01722 416928**   **Open: ALL YEAR (Excl. Xmas)**   **Map Ref No. 20**

Glen Lyn House

| £22.50 to £32.00 | Y | N | Y |

VISA: M'CARD: AMEX:

Nearest Road: A.36

Situated in a quiet tree-lined lane, 5 mins' walk from the city centre, Glen Lyn is an elegant Victorian house offering 7 individually appointed bedrooms, 4 en-suite & all with colour T.V.. Enjoy a great English breakfast & superb home-produced dinner, then relax in the lounge or listen to birdsong in the beautiful garden. The ideal tranquil base for visiting the cathedral & Stonehenge, & for exploring the New Forest. Ample parking. Children over 12. Animals prior arrangement.
E-mail: glen.lyn@btinternet.com

Patrick Fairbrother   **Glen Lyn House**   **6 Bellamy Lane**   **Milford Hill**   **Salisbury SP1 2SP**   **Wiltshire**
Tel: (01722) 327880   **Fax 01722 327880**   **Open: ALL YEAR**   **Map Ref No. 20**

The Mill House. Berwick St. James

rate £ from - to per person	children taken	evening meals taken	animals taken

---

£22.00 to £22.00   Y   N   Y   🚭

The Old Post House

Nearest Road: A.36

Built in 1650, the Grade II listed, Old Post House is situated in a beautiful & peaceful Wiltshire village which also boasts excellent pubs for evening meals. 10 mins from Stonehenge & Salisbury, it is also convenient for Bath, Stourhead, Longleat, Wilton House & Avebury. There are 3 clean & pretty en-suite bedrooms, all with T.V. & beverage trays & breakfast is cooked to order on a lovely old Aga. This is a relaxed & friendly family home in a beautiful part of the country.
E-mail: bookings@greatwishford.freeserve.co.uk

Paulene Patient   *The Old Post House*   *South Street*   *Great Wishford*   *Salisbury SP2 0NN*   *Wiltshire*
Tel: (01722) 790211   *Open: ALL YEAR (Excl. Xmas & New Year)*   *Map Ref No. 22*

£22.50 to £25.00   Y   N   N

Maddington House

Nearest Road: A.360

Maddington House is the family home of Dick & Joan Robathan. An elegant 17th-century Grade II listed house in the centre of the pretty village of Shrewton - about 2 1/2 miles from Stonehenge & 11 miles from Salisbury. 3 attractive (non-smoking) guest rooms, 2 with en-suite facilities. The village has 4 pubs, all within easy walking distance. A delightful home, & the perfect base for a relaxing break. Children over 7 years.
E-mail: rsrobathan@freenet.co.uk

Dick & Joan Robathan   *Maddington House*   *Shrewton*   *Salisbury SP3 4JD*   *Wiltshire*
Tel: (01980) 620406   *Fax 01980 620406*   *Open: ALL YEAR*   *Map Ref No. 23*

£25.00 to £26.00   Y   N   Y

Elm Tree Cottage

Nearest Road: A.36, A.303

Elm Tree Cottage is a 17th-century character cottage with inglenook & beams & a lower garden to relax in. The bedrooms, each with an en-suite/private bathroom, are light & airy, are attractively decorated & have T.V. & tea/coffee-making facilities. The atmosphere is relaxed & warm, & breakfast is served as required. Situated in a picturesque village, there are views across various valleys, & it is a good centre for Salisbury, Wilton, Longleat, Stonehenge, Avebury, etc.
E-mail: jaw.sykes@virgin.net

Christine Sykes   *Elm Tree Cottage*   *Chain Hill*   *Stapleford*   *Salisbury SP3 4LH*   *Wiltshire*
Tel: (01722) 790507   *Open: APR - OCT*   *Map Ref No. 24*

£26.00 to £30.00   N   N   N   🚭

Wyndham Cottage

Nearest Road: A.36, A.303

A charming 18th-century thatched stone cottage, lovingly restored & set in magnificent National Trust countryside on the edge of a picturesque village. Bluebells, lambs & calves in Spring, delightful walks with marvellous views of the surrounding area. The cottage garden has many interesting plants. Excellent pubs nearby. Ideally situated for several days sight-seeing: Stonehenge, Avebury, Salisbury, Bath, Wells, Wilton House, Stourhead & Longleat. 2 delightful double bedrooms with en-suite bathrooms, tea/coffee & T.V..

Ian & Rosie Robertson   *Wyndham Cottage*   *St. Mary's Road*   *Dinton*   *Salisbury SP3 5HH*   *Wiltshire*
Tel: (01722) 716343   *Mobile 0776 9911660*   *Open: APR - OCT*   *Map Ref No. 26*

Wiltshire

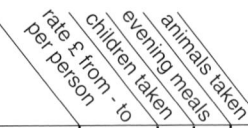
Newton Farmhouse

Nearest Road: A.36

This historic listed 16th-century farmhouse, on the borders of the New Forest, was formerly part of the Trafalgar Estate & is situated 8 miles south of Salisbury, convenient for Stonehenge, Romsey, Winchester & Portsmouth. All rooms are en-suite, 3 with genuine period 4-poster beds. The beamed dining room houses a collection of Nelson memorabilia & antiques & has an inglenook fireplace. Breakfast includes home-made breads & preserves. (Dinner by arrangement.) Swimming pool.
E-mail: enquiries@newtonfarmhouse.co.uk

| £20.00 to £30.00 | Y | Y | N |

Mrs Suzi Lanham   Newton Farmhouse   Southampton Rd   Whiteparish Salisbury SP5 2QL Wiltshire
Tel: (01794) 884416   Fax 01794 884416   Open: ALL YEAR   Map Ref No. 28

Bridge Farm B & B

Nearest Road: A.338

A warm welcome & a hearty English breakfast are assured at this charming 18th-century farmhouse on a working farm on the southern edge of Salisbury. The 2 double & 1 twin en-suite rooms are spacious & individually & tastefully furnished. Within easy walking distance of the cathedral, & has famous views of the spire along the River Avon that flows alongside the beautiful gardens. Single supplement. Children by arrangement.
E-mail: mail@bridgefarmbb.co.uk

| £24.00 to £25.00 | Y | N | N |

VISA: M'CARD:

Norma Hunt   Bridge Farm B & B   Lower Road   Britford   Salisbury SP5 4DY   Wiltshire
Tel: (01722) 332376   Fax 01722 332376   Open: ALL YEAR   Map Ref No. 29

Bugley Barton

Nearest Road: A.36

Bugley is a Grade II listed Georgian house, elegant, comfortable & traditionally furnished. Ideally placed for trips to Bath, Salisbury, Longleat, Stonehenge & Stourhead. Julie & Brian are easy-going & friendly. Homemade cake, delicious breakfasts cooked in the Aga & fresh fruit in the bedrooms. The spacious en-suite guest rooms overlook the beautiful garden & have many thoughtful added touches. Good local pubs, parking, train station nearby. Single supplement. Children over 12.
E-mail: bugleybarton@aol.com

| £30.00 to £32.50 | Y | N | N |

Brian & Julie Hocken   Bugley Barton   Victoria Road   Warminster BA12 7RB   Wiltshire
Tel: (01985) 213389 Fax 01985 300450 Open: ALL YEAR (Excl. Xmas & New Year) Map Ref No. 32

Springfield House

Nearest Road: A.350, A.36

Situated in the beautiful Wylye Valley, on the edge of the famous Longleat Estate, Springfield House is a charming village house dating from the 17th century. Rachel & Colin welcome you to their home, with its beams, open fires, fresh flowers & sunny en-suite rooms, overlooking the garden & grass tennis court. Marvellous base for touring, walking or relaxing. Bath, Salisbury, Wells, Stonehenge & Stourhead are all easily reached. Single supplement.
E-mail: springfield.house@btinternet.com

| £29.00 to £34.00 | Y | N | N |

Rachel & Colin Singer   Springfield House   Crockerton   Warminster BA12 8AU   Wiltshire
Tel: (01985) 213696   Fax 01985 213696   Open: ALL YEAR   Map Ref No. 34

Yorkshire

Yorkshire & Humberside

England's largest county is a region of beautiful landscapes, of hills, peaks, fells, dales & forests with many square miles of National Park. It is a vast area taking in big industrial cities, interesting towns & delightful villages. Yorkshire's broad rivers sweep through the countryside & are an angler's paradise. Cascading waterfalls pour down from hillside & moorland.

The North sea coast can be thrilling, with wild seas & cliff-top walks, or just fun, as at the many resorts where the waves break on long beaches & trickle into green rock-pools. Staithes & Robin Hoods Bay are fascinating old fishing villages. Whitby is an attractive port where, Abbey, the small town tumbles in red-roofed tiers down to the busy harbour from which Captain Cook sailed.

The Yorkshire Dales form one of the finest landscapes in England. From windswept moors to wide green valleys the scenery is incomparable. James Herriot tells of of the effect that the broad vista of Swaledale had on him. "I was captivated", he wrote, "completely spell-bound....". A network of dry stone walls covers the land; some are as old as the stone-built villages but those which climb the valley sides to the high moors are the product of the 18th century enclosures, when a good wall builder would cover seven meters a day.

Each of the Dales has a distinctive character; from the remote upper reaches of Swaledale & Wensleydale, where the air sings with the sound of wind, sheep, & curlew, over to Airedale & the spectacular limestone gorges of Malham Cove & Gordale Scar, & down to the soft meadows & woods of Wharfedale where the ruins of Bolton Priory stand beside the river.

To the east towards Hull with its mighty River Humber crossed by the worlds largest single-span suspension bridge, lie the Yorkshire Wolds. This is lovely countryside where villages have unusual names like Fridaythorpe & Wetwang. Beverley is a picture-postcard town with a fine 13th century Minster.

The North Yorks National Park, where the moors are ablaze with purple fire of heather in the late summer, is exhilarating country. There is moorland to the east also, on the Pennine chain; famous Ilkley Moor with its stone circle known as the twelve apostles, & the Haworth Moors around the plain Yorkshire village where the Bronte sisters lived; "the distant dreamy, dim blue chain of mountains circling every side", which Emily Bronte describes in Wuthering Heights.

The Yorkshire Pennines industrial heritage is being celebrated in fascinating museums, often based in the original Woolen Mills & warehouses, which also provide workshop space for skilled craftspeople.

Yorkshires Monastic past is revealed in the ruins of its once great Abbeys. Rievaulx, Jervaux & Fountains, retain their tranquil beauty in their pastoral settings. The wealth of the county is displayed in many historic houses with glorious gardens, from stately 18th Century Castle Howard of 'Brideshead Revisited' fame to Tudor Shibden Hall, portrayed in Wuthering Heights.

York is the finest mediaeval city in England. It is encircled by its limestone city walls with four Great Gates. Within the walls are the jumbled roof line, dog-leg streets & sudden courtyards of a mediaeval town. Half timbered buildings with over-sailing upper storeys jostle with Georgian brick houses along the network of narrow streets around The Shambles & King Edward Square.

Yorkshire

Yorkshire Gazeteer

Areas of Outstanding Natural Beauty.
The North Yorkshire Moors & The Yorkshire Dales.

Historic Houses & Castles.

Carlton Towers
17th century, remodelled in later centuries. paintings, silver, furniture, pictures. Carved woodwork, painted decorations, examples of Victorian craftmanship.

Castle Howard - Nr. York
18th century - celebrated architect, Sir John Vanbrugh - paintings, costumes, furniture by Chippendale, Sheraton, Adam. Not to be missed.

East Riddlesden Hall - Keighley
17th century manor house with fishponds & historic barns, one of which is regarded as very fine example of mediaeval tithe barn.

Newby Hall - Ripon
17th century Wren style extended by Robert Adam. Gobelins tapestry, Chippendale furniture, sculpture galleries with Roman rotunda, statuary. Award-winning gardens.

Nostell Priory - Wakefield
18th century, Georgian mansion, Chippendale furniture, paintings.

Burton Constable Hall - Hull
16th century, Elizabethan, remodelled in Georgian period. Stained glass, Hepplewhite furniture, gardens by Capability Brown.

Ripley Castle - Harrogate
14th century, parts dating during 16th & 18th centuries. Priest hole, armour & weapons, beautiful ceilings.

The Treasurer's House - York
17th & 18th centuries, splendid interiors, furniture, pictures.

Harewood House - Leeds
18th century - Robert Adam design, Chippendale furniture, Italian & English paintings. Sevres & Chinese porcelain.

Benningbrough Hall - York
18th century. Highly decorative woodwork, oak staircase, friezes etc. Splendid hall.

Markenfield Hall - Ripon
14th to 16th century - fine Manor house surrounded by moat.

Heath Hall - Wakefield

18th century, palladian. Fine woodwork & plasterwork, rococo ceilings, excellent furniture, paintings & porcelain.

Bishops House - Sheffield
16th century. Only complete timber framed yeoman farmhouse surviving. Vernacular architecture. Superb

Skipton Castle- Skipton
One of the most complete & well preserved mediaeval castles in England.

Cathedral & Churches

York Minster
13th century. Greatest Gothic Cathedral north of the Alps. Imposing grandeur - superb Chapter house, contains half of the mediaeval stained glass of England. Outstandingly beautiful.

York (All Saints, North Street)
15th century roofing in parts - 18th century pulpit wonderful mediaeval glass.

Ripon Cathedral
12th century - though in some parts Saxon in origin. Decorated choir stalls - gables buttresses. Church of 672 preserved in crypt, , Caxton Book, ecclesiastic treasures.

Bolton Percy (All Saints)
15th century.
Maintains original glass in east window. Jacobean font cover. Georgian pulpit. Interesting monuments.

Rievaulx Abbey
12th century, masterpiece of Early English architecture.
One of three great Cistercian Abbeys built in Yorkshire.
Impressive ruins.

Campsall (St. Mary Magdalene)
Fine Norman tower - 15th century rood screen, carved & painted stone altar.

Fountains Abbey - Ripon
Ruins of England's greatest mediaeval abbey - surrounded by wonderful landscaped gardens. Enormous tower, vaulted cellar 300 feet long.

Whitby (St. Mary)
12th century tower & doorway, 18th century remodelling - box pews much interior woodwork painted - galleries. High pulpit. Table tombs.

Yorkshire

Whitby Abbey - Whitby (St. Hilda)
7th century superb ruin - venue of Synod of 664. Destroyed by Vikings, restored 1078 - magnificent north transept.
Halifax (St. John the Baptist)
12th century origins, showing work from each succeeding century - heraldic ceilings. Cromwell glass.
Beverley Minster - Beverley
14th century. Fine Gothic Minster - remarkable mediaeval effigies of musicians playing instruments. Founded as monastery in 700.
Bolton Priory - Nr. Skipton
Nave of Augustinian Priory, now Bolton's Parish Church, amidst ruins of choir & transepts, in beautiful riverside setting.
Selby Abbey - Selby
11th century Benedictine abbey of which the huge church remains. Roof & furnishings are modern after a fire of 1906, but the stonework is intact.

Museums & Galleries

Aldborough Roman Museum - Boroughbridge
Remnants of Roman period of the town - coins, glass, pottery, etc.
Great Ayton
Home of Captain Cook, explorer & seaman. Exhibits of maps, etc.
Art Gallery - City of York
Modern paintings, Old Masters, watercolours, prints, ceramics.
Lotherton Hall - Nr. Leeds
Museum with furniture, paintings, silver, works of art from the Leeds collection & oriental art gallery.
National Railway Museum - York
Devoted to railway engineering & its development.
York Castle Museum
The Kirk Collection of bygones including cobbled streets, shops, costumes, toys, household & farm equipment - fascinating collection.
Cannon Hall Art Gallery - Barnsley
18th century house with fine furniture & glass, etc. Flemish & Dutch paintings. Also houses museum of the 13/18 Royal Hussars.
Mappin Art Gallery - Sheffield
Works from 18th,19th & 20th century.

Graves Art gallery-Sheffield.
British portraiture. European works, & examples of Asian & African art. Loan exhibitions are held there.
Royal Pump Room Museum - Harrogate
Original sulphur well used in the Victorian Spa. Local history costume & pottery.
Bolling Hall - Bradford
A period house with mixture of styles - collections of 17th century oak furniture, domestic utensils, toys & bygones.
Georgian Theatre - Richmond
Oldest theatre in the country - interesting theatrical memorabilia.
Jorvik Viking Centre - York
Recently excavated site in the centre of York showing hundreds of artifacts dating from the Viking period. One of the most important archaeological discoveries this century.
Abbey House Museum - Kirkstall, Leeds
Illustrated past 300 years of Yorkshire life. Shows 3 full streets from 19th century with houses, shops & workplaces.
Piece Hall - Halifax
Remarkable building - constructed around huge quadrangle - now Textile Industrial Museum, Art Gallery & has craft & antique shops.
National Museum of Photography, Film & Television - Bradford
Displays look at art & science of photography, film & T.V. Britain's only IMAX arena.
The Colour Museum - Bradford
Award-winning interactive museum,which allows visitors to explore the world of colour & discover the story of dyeing & textile printing.
Calderdale Industrial Museum - Halifax
Social & industrial Museum of the year 1987
Shibden Hall & Folk Museum of Halifax
Half-timbered house with folk museum, farmland, miniature train & boating lake.
Leeds City Art Gallery & Henry Moore Sculpture Gallery
Yorkshire Sculpture Park - Wakefield
Yorkshire Museum of Farming - Murton
Award-winning museum of farming & the countryside.

YORKSHIRE & HUMBERSIDE
Map reference

01	Gill
01	Williams
02	Knox
03	Lillie
04	Greenwood
05	Oxley
07	Watts
08	Berry
11	Kirman
12	Bendtson
12	Bateson
12	Dodds
12	Thomson
13	Stanton
14	King
15	Peters
16	Stubley
17	Marshall
18	Murray
20	Schofield
21	Hodgson
22	Chetvynd
23	Sugars
25	Johnson
26	Gordon
27	Thompson
28	Sutton
29	Steele
30	Goodrum
31	Morgan
31	Reynard
31	Hunt
31	Whitbourn-Hammond
31	Varey
31	W. Wood
31	Blanksby
31	Roe
31	Sluter-Robbins
31	Lefebve
31	J. Wood
32	Key
33	Braithwaite

360

| rate £ from - to per person | children taken | evening meals | animals taken |

£27.50 to £31.50
Y Y N
(No smoking)

Nearest Road: A.170, A.19

Daleside

Daleside is listed the oldest house in this charming stone village, with 400 year old cruck beams & oak panelling. The house has been sympathetically restored, with the 2 en-suite guests' rooms (1 twin, 1 double with half-tester bed) overlooking the garden. Dinner is available some evenings, if booked in advance. There are 2 inns in the village & other good restaurants nearby. Ampleforth is on the edge of the North York Moors National Park with excellent walks all around. Children from 12.

Paul & Pat Williams   Daleside   East End   Ampleforth YO62 4DA   Yorkshire
Tel: (01439) 788266   Open: End MAR - End OCT   Map Ref No. 01

£32.00 to £40.00
Y Y N
(No smoking)
VISA: M'CARD:

Nearest Road: A.170

Shallowdale House

This is an outstanding modern country house, with 2 acres of hillside garden, on the southern edge of the North York Moors National Park. All of the spacious rooms enjoy stunning views of unspoilt countryside & are furnished with style & attention to detail. 3 bedrooms (with bath & shower) & 2 sitting rooms. Meals are imaginatively prepared from fresh seasonal ingredients & there is a drinks licence. A perfect place to unwind when exploring Herriot country & York. Children over 12.
E-mail: stay@shallowdalehouse.demon.co.uk

Phillip Gill & Anton Van Der Horst Shallowdale House West End Ampleforth YO62 4DY Yorkshire
Tel: (01439) 788325   Fax 01439 788885   Open: ALL YEAR (Excl. Xmas & New Year) Map Ref No. 01

£20.00 to £27.50
N N Y

Nearest Road: A.684

Mill Close Farm

A 17th-century working farm surrounded by beautiful rolling countryside at the foothills of the Yorkshire Dales & Herriot country. Exceptional views yet only 3 miles from A1(M). Luxurious en-suite bedrooms with many extras - jacuzzi, super king-size bed, toiletries, hairdryers, T.V. with choice of videos. Enchanting walled garden with pond & waterfall. Sumptuous breakfasts in the conservatory dining room. Excellent local pubs. Ideal stopover for Scotland. Animals by arrangement.

Mrs Patricia Knox   Mill Close Farm   Patrick Brompton   Bedale DL8 1JY   Yorkshire
Tel: (01677) 450257   Fax 01677 450585   Open: MAR - NOV   Map Ref No. 02

£25.00 to £30.00
Y Y N
VISA: M'CARD:

Nearest Road: A.684

Elmfield Country House

Located in its own grounds in the country. Enjoy a relaxed, friendly atmosphere in spacious surroundings, with a high standard of furnishings. 9 en-suite bedrooms comprising twin-bedded, double & family rooms. 2 rooms have been adapted for disabled guests & another has a 4-poster bed. All rooms have satellite T.V., 'phone, radio/alarm & tea/coffee makers. A games room & solarium are also available. Excellent farmhouse cooking. Residential licence. A delightful home. Single supplement.
E-mail: stay@elmfieldhouse.freeserve.co.uk

Jim & Edith Lillie   Elmfield Country House   Arrathorne   Bedale DL8 1NE   Yorkshire
Tel: (01677) 450558   Fax 01677 450557   Open: ALL YEAR   Map Ref No. 03

Yorkshire

Rudstone Walk

Nearest Road: A.1034

Rudstone Walk is renowned for its hospitality & good food. Accommodation is in the very tastefully converted farm buildings, adjacent to the main farmhouse where meals are served. The attractive bedrooms have excellent en-suite facilities, T.V., 'phone, hairdryer & more. Rudstone provides a peaceful retreat after a tiring day. It is ideal for a relaxing break, & is within easy reach of York & many other attractions. Animals by arrangement.
E-mail: office@rudstone-walk.co.uk

£25.00 to £29.50   Y Y Y

VISA: M'CARD: AMEX:

Charles Greenwood   Rudstone Walk   South Cave   Brough   Nr. Beverley HU15 2AH   Yorkshire
Tel: (01430) 422230   Fax 01430 424552   Open: ALL YEAR   Map Ref No. 04

Five Rise Locks Hotel

Nearest Road: A.650

A Victorian manor house standing in mature terraced gardens overlooking the Aire Valley, minutes walk from Bingley & the Five Rise Locks. Each of the 9 en-suite bedrooms has been individually designed & furnished with antique stripped pine. The Bistro restaurant is open for lunch & dinner & offers imaginative meals complemented by a selection of wines. Five Rise Locks is the perfect spot from which to visit Haworth, Saltaire, steam trains, York, Leeds, Mill shopping, Skipton & the Dales.
E-mail: info@five-rise-locks.co.uk

£30.00 to £35.00   Y Y Y

VISA: M'CARD:

Patricia & William Oxley   Five Rise Locks Hotel   Beck Lane   Bingley BD16 4DD   Yorkshire
Tel: (01274) 565296   Fax 01274 568828   Open: ALL YEAR   Map Ref No. 05

Four Gables

Nearest Road: A.659

Visitors will love this special Art-and-Craft movement house with its wealth of original features, stripped oak & terracotta floors, fireplaces, beautiful ceilings & gardens of over 1/2 acre which contain many interesting plants & a croquet lawn. Enjoy the peaceful setting, down a private lane, yet only 3 mins' walk from the bussling Georgian stone village of Boston Spa with all its facilities, shops & restaurants, etc.. 3 en-suite bedrooms. Log fires in winter. Children over 2. Single supplement.
E-mail: info@intoto.co.uk

£26.00 to £29.00   Y Y Y

David Watts   Four Gables   Oaks Lane   Boston Spa LS23 6DS   Yorkshire
Tel: (01937) 849031/845592   Open: ALL YEAR   Map Ref No. 07

The Manor House

Nearest Road: A.165, A.166

A manor of Flamborough is recorded in the Domesday Book. The current Georgian house is a handsomely proportioned family home offering spacious & comfortable accommodation in well-appointed rooms. Historic Flamborough Head is designated a Heritage Coast, with many interesting walks & a nearby bird reserve. Ideally placed for exploration of North & East Yorkshire. Dinner, by prior arrangement, features local seafood when available. Children over 8 yrs.
E-mail: gm@flamboroughmanor.co.uk

£33.00 to £38.00   Y Y N

VISA: M'CARD: AMEX:

Lesley Berry & Geoffrey Miller   The Manor House   Flamborough Bridlington YO15 1PD   Yorkshire
Tel: (01262) 850943   Fax 01262 850943   Open: ALL YEAR (Excl. Xmas)   Map Ref No. 08

rate £ from - to per person	children taken	evening meals	animals taken

---

£27.50 to £32.50

🚭

VISA: M'CARD:

| Y | N | N |

The Old Vicarage

Nearest Road: A.19

A listed property of immense character built in the 18th century & thoughtfully brought up to modern standards, & yet still retaining many delightful features. Now offering 4 en-suite rooms with T.V. & tea/coffee makers. Standing in extensive lawned gardens, overlooking the market square, & with a croquet lawn & a walled rose garden, it is an ideal touring centre for York, the Dales, the Yorkshire Moors & 'Herriot' countryside. Parking.
E-mail: kirman@oldvic-easingwold.freeserve.co.uk

Christine & John Kirman   The Old Vicarage   Market Place   Easingwold YO61 3AL   Yorkshire
Tel: (01347) 821015   Fax 01347 823465   Open: FEB - NOV   Map Ref No. 11

£25.00 to £27.50

| Y | N | N |

Ashwood House

Nearest Road: A.61

A charming 8-bedroomed Edwardian house retaining many of its original features. Situated in a quiet, residential cul-de-sac mins' from the town centre. The attractive en-suite bedrooms are spacious, some with 4-poster beds, all with hospitality tray, T.V., hairdryer & toiletries. A delicious breakfast is served from lovely Royal Copenhagen china in the elegant dining room. A high standard of service & a warm welcome is assured. Scandinavian languages spoken. Children over 7.
E-mail: ashwoodhouse@aol.com

Gill & Kristian Bendtson   Ashwood House   7 Spring Grove   Harrogate HG1 2HS   Yorkshire
Tel: (01423) 560081 Fax 01423 527928 Open: ALL YEAR (Excl. Xmas & New Year) Map Ref No. 12

£29.00 to £34.00

🚭

| Y | N | N |

Acacia Lodge

Nearest Road: A.61

Acacia Lodge is a warm, lovingly restored & charming, small family-run hotel with pretty gardens in a select central conservation area just a short stroll from Harrogate's fashionable shops, many restaurants & attractions. It retains all its original character with fine furnishings, antiques & old paintings. Bedrooms are en-suite & well-furnished with every comfort. Award-winning breakfasts served in the oak-furnished dining room, & guests can relax in the lounge with open fire & library of books. Private floodlit car park. Children over 10 years.

Dee & Peter & Bateson   Acacia Lodge   21 Ripon Road   Harrogate HG1 2JL   Yorkshire
Tel: (01423) 560752   Fax 01423 503725   Open: ALL YEAR   Map Ref No. 12

£27.50 to £30.00

🚭

VISA: M'CARD:

| Y | N | N |

Shannon Court Hotel

Nearest Road: A.59

Charming Victorian house hotel overlooking the 'stray' in High Harrogate. Enjoy real home cooking in this family-run hotel. Accommodation is in 8 delightful bedrooms, all of which are en-suite & have every modern comfort including radio, colour T.V. & tea/coffee-making facilities. Licensed for residents & their guests. Close to town centre, railway station & conference centre, with easy parking, & direct to main routes for moors & dales. Shannon Court Hotel is an excellent touring base.
E-mail: Shannon@hotels.harrogate.com

William Dodds   Shannon Court Hotel   65 Dragon Avenue   Harrogate HG1 5DS   Yorkshire
Tel: (01423) 509858   Fax 01423 530606   Open: ALL YEAR   Map Ref No. 12

	rate £ from - to per person	children taken	evening meals	animals taken

Knox Mill House

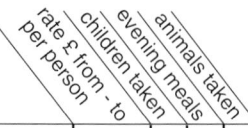

Nearest Road: A.61
Built in 1785, this lovely old millhouse stands on the banks of a stream in a quiet rural setting, & yet is only 1 1/2 miles from the centre of Harrogate. Beautifully renovated, it still retains all its original features: oak beams, an inglenook fireplace & stone arches. There are 3 delightful rooms, attractively & comfortably furnished. 2 are en-suite, & all have tea/coffee makers & views over the stream & fields. A delightful lounge with T.V., & a garden for guests' enjoyment. Single supplement. Children over 12.

£22.50 to £22.50 — Y — N — N

Peter & Marion Thomson   Knox Mill House   Knox Mill Lane   Killinghall   Harrogate HG3 2AE
Tel: (01423) 560650 Fax 01423 560650   Open: ALL YEAR (Excl. Xmas & New Year) Map Ref No. 12

Knottside Farm

Nearest Road: A.59
Knottside Farm, a beautiful 17th-century farm-house, is in Nidderdale, an Area of Outstanding Natural Beauty. It is ideal for walking, fishing, pony trekking & bird-watching or visiting the Moors, Dales, Harrogate & historic York. The guest's rooms are delightfully furnished to a very high standard & have wonderful views over this peaceful dale. Nigel creates mouth-watering Cordon Bleu dinners which include local lamb & trout. Knottside Farm is a charming home.

£28.00 to £30.00 — N — Y — N

Mr & Mrs N. Stanton   Knottside Farm   The Knott   Pateley Bridge   Harrogate HG3 5DQ Yorkshire
Tel: (01423) 712927   Fax 01423 712927   Open: ALL YEAR   Map Ref No. 13

High Winsley Cottage

Nearest Road: A.61
Traditional Dales cottage in Nidderdale, situated well off the road in peaceful countryside, with lovely views all around, & ideally placed for both town & country. Accommodation is in 2 twin & 2 double rooms, well-appointed & all with en-suite facilities. There are 2 large sitting rooms, with guide books, games, T.V., etc. Imaginative home cooking using produce from the extensive kitchen garden, complemented by wines from an interesting list. Children over 11 years.

£22.00 to £28.50 — Y — Y — N

see PHOTO over
p. 365

Clive & Gill King   High Winsley Cottage   Burnt Yates   Nr. Harrogate HG3 3EP   Yorkshire
Tel: (01423) 770662   Open: FEB - NOV   Map Ref No. 14

Redacre Mill

Nearest Road: A.646
Redacre Mill is a delightfully restored Victorian mill set in its own grounds on the banks of the Rochdale canal, providing peace & tranquillity yet within easy reach of Manchester, Leeds & Bradford. Nestling in the beautiful & unspoilt Calder Valley, Mytholmroyd is the birthplace of Ted Hughes; Bronte country & the Penine Way are nearby. The elegant en-suite bedrooms offer all amenities. Dinners, by arrangement, are served in the licensed dining room. A relaxed & welcoming atmosphere.

£29.50 to £39.00 — Y — Y — N

VISA: M'CARD:

Capt. & Mrs A. Peters   Redacre Mill   Mytholmroyd   Hebden Bridge HX7 5DQ   Yorkshire
Tel: (01442) 885563/881569   Fax 01442 885563   Open: ALL YEAR   Map Ref No. 15

High Winsley Cottage. Burnt Yates.

Yorkshire

Pinewood Hotel

Nearest Road: A.61

Pinewood Hotel is attractively furnished & decorated, with many extra touches enhancing guests comfort. Accommodation is in 10 comfortablr, very pleasant & well-equipped en-suite bedrooms. The hotel is conveniently situated for the excellent shopping facilities in Leeds, theatre, the famous Yorkshire Dales & Moors & a host of other attractions. Special weekend rates are available. A most warming welcome in a small hotel of distinction awaits all guests. (U.K. Freephone 0800 0967463.)

£24.00 to £38.00	Y	Y	N

VISA: M'CARD: AMEX:

C. M. Stubley Pinewood Hotel 78 Potternewton Lane Chapel Allerton Leeds LS7 3LW Yorkshire
Tel: (0113) 2622561 Fax 0113 2622561 Open: ALL YEAR (Excl. Xmas & New Year) Map Ref No. 16

Park Gate House

Nearest Road: A.1

A warm welcome awaits all guests at this lovely 18th-century house, situated in Lower Wensleydale, an Area of Outstanding Natural Beauty & historical interest. Park Gate House retains its charm with low oak beams, inglenook log fire & cottage gardens. Bedrooms are decorated in country-style old pine furniture, T.V. & private facilities & echo comfort & style. Breakfast is a delight & very high quality. Evening meals are available by prior arrangement. Single supplement. Children over 12.
E-mail: parkgatehouse@freenet.co.uk

£27.50 to £35.00	Y	Y	N

VISA: M'CARD:

Terry & Linda Marshall Park Gate House Constable Burton Leyburn DL8 5RG Yorkshire
Tel: (01677) 450466 Fax 01677 450466 Open: ALL YEAR Map Ref No. 17

Manor Farm

Nearest Road: A.169

A charming Georgian manor house set in spacious grounds with a hard tennis court, croquet lawn & views to the Howardian Hills. Accommodation is in 3 comfortable & attractively furnished bedrooms, with either an en-suite or a private bathroom. Excellent cooking caters for all tastes. Manor Farm is within easy reach of York, Scarborough, the Moors, Castle Howard & Flamingoland. Dogs & children over 5 are most welcome.
E-mail: cphmurray@compuserve.com

£25.00 to £30.00	Y	Y	Y

Mrs J. M. Murray Manor Farm Little Barugh Malton YO17 6UY Yorkshire
Tel: (01653) 668262 Fax 01653 668600 Open: ALL YEAR Map Ref No. 18

Elmscott

Nearest Road: A.684

Elmscott is a charming cottage-style property which is set in a delightful landscaped garden. Yet, it is situated close to the centre of Northallerton, a thriving market town. Your charming hosts offer 2 attractively furnished bedrooms, each with an en-suite bathroom, tea/coffee-making facilities & T.V.. A delicious breakfast is served. Elmscott is located mid-way between the North York Moors & the beautiful Yorkshire Dales National Parks, with their famous 'Herriott' connections. A lovely home.
E-mail: elmscott@freenet.co.uk

£25.00 to £25.00	Y	N	N

Mike & Pauline Schofield Elmscott 10 Hatfield Road Northallerton DL7 8QX Yorkshire
Tel: (01609) 760575 Open: ALL YEAR Map Ref No.20

rate £ from - to per person	children taken	evening meals	animals taken	
£22.50 to £25.00	Y	Y	N	**Little Holtby**

Nearest Road: A.1

With one foot in the past, but with present day comforts, Little Holtby is the 'somewhere special' in which to relax & unwind. Antiques, beams, polished wood floors & cosy log fires all add to the ambience of a period farmhouse. The 3 guest rooms have wonderful views over rolling countryside to the Dales. En-suite or private facilities are available. Facilities for golf, tennis, riding, fishing & walking are all close by. Children over 12. Come & spoil yourself - other guests do again & again.
E-mail: littleholtby@yahoo.co.uk

Dorothy Hodgson   Little Holtby   Leeming Bar   Northallerton DL7 9LH   Yorkshire
Tel: (01609) 748762   Fax 01609 748822   Open: ALL YEAR (Excl. Xmas)   Map Ref No. 21

rate £ from - to per person	children taken	evening meals	animals taken	
£35.00 to £42.50	Y	Y	N	**Allerston Manor House**
VISA: M'CARD:				

Nearest Road: A.170

Allerston Manor House is quietly placed on the edge of the village bordering the National Park with lovely distant views. Reconstructed around a 14th-century Knight's Templar Hall, now lovingly restored preserving old features & adding modern comforts! It is ideal for exploring the famous sights of the region & only 35 mins' to York. Meals include free-range & home-grown produce when possible. Walks & Steam Railway on the Moors. Historic castles & houses. Children over 12.
E-mail: best@allerston-manor.com

Mr & Mrs Chetwynd   Allerston Manor House   Thornton-le-Dale   Pickering YO18 7PF   Yorkshire
Tel: (01723) 850112   Fax 01723 850112   Open: ALL YEAR   Map Ref No. 22

rate £ from - to per person	children taken	evening meals	animals taken	
£22.50 to £28.50	Y	N	N	**Sevenford House**

Nearest Road: A.170

Originally a vicarage, & built from the stones of Rosedale Abbey, Sevenford House stands in 4 acres of lovely gardens in the heart of the beautiful Yorkshire Moors National Park. 3 tastefully furnished, en-suite bedrooms, with T.V., radio & tea/coffee, etc., offering wonderful views overlooking valley & moorland. A lounge/library. An excellent base for exploring the region. Riding & golf locally. Also, ruined abbeys, Roman roads, steam railways, the beautiful coastline & pretty fishing towns.
E-mail: sevenford@aol.com

Linda Sugars   Sevenford House   Rosedale Abbey   Pickering YO18 8SE   Yorkshire
Tel: (01751) 417283   Fax 01751 417505   Open: ALL YEAR   Map Ref No. 23

rate £ from - to per person	children taken	evening meals	animals taken	
£25.00 to £27.50	Y	N	N	**Mallard Grange**
VISA: M'CARD:				

Nearest Road: A.1, B.6265

Rambling 16th-century farmhouse full of character & charm in glorious countryside near Fountains Abbey. Offering superb quality & comfort, spacious rooms furnished with care & some lovely antique pieces. En-suite bedrooms have large comfortable beds, warm towels, T.V., hairdryer & refreshments tray. Delicious breakfasts with homemade preserves. Pretty walled garden tended by enthusiastic amateur. Safe parking. Excellent evening meals locally. Children over 12.
E-mail: Mallard.Grange@btinternet.com

Mrs Maggie Johnson   Mallard Grange   Aldfield   Nr. Fountains Abbey   Ripon HG4 3BE   Yorkshire
Tel: (01765) 620242   Fax 01765 620242   Open: ALL YEAR (Excl. Xmas & New Year)   Map Ref No. 25

Yorkshire

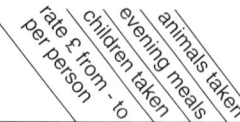
	rate £ from - to per person	evening meals	children taken	animals taken

St. George's Court

Nearest Road: A.1

St. George's Court is beautifully situated in peaceful countryside & provides comfortable ground-floor rooms in renovated farm buildings. All modern facilities whilst retaining much charm & character. Delicious breakfasts are served in the conservatory dining room, with views, in the delightful listed farmhouse. Peace & tranquillity really is the password here. St. George's Court is near Fountains Abbey & Brimham Rocks. Ripon, Harrogate & York are all within easy reach.

E-mail: stgeorgescourt@bronco.co.uk

| £25.00 to £27.50 | Y | N | Y |

VISA: M'CARD:

Mrs Sandra Gordon   St. George's Court   Old Home Farm   Grantley   Ripon HG4 3EU   Yorkshire
Tel: (01765) 620618   Fax 01765 620618   Open: ALL YEAR   Map Ref No. 26

Bank Villa

Nearest Road: A.6108, A.1

Set in half an acre of terraced garden, this welcoming Grade II listed home has recently been renovated & refurbished to a high standard. It offers guests 2 delightful lounges in which to relax & 6 double bedrooms, each with T.V. & radio, 4 with en-suite or private facilities, 2 with private shower. Bank Villa is an excellent spot for a relaxing break & it is an ideal base from which to explore the Yorkshire Dales, tour around, walk, horse-ride or fish. Children over 5. A warm welcome awaits you.

| £20.00 to £27.50 | Y | Y | N |

Bobby & Lucy Thomson   Bank Villa   The Avenue   Masham   Ripon HG4 4DB   Yorkshire
Tel: (01765) 689605   Fax 01765 689605   Open: ALL YEAR (Excl. Xmas)   Map Ref No. 27

Willerby Wold Farm

Nearest Road: A.64

Peacefully situated on an 800-acre farm on the edge of the Yorkshire Wolds, Willerby Wold Farm has been in the Sutton family for 3 generations. The elegant Victorian country house is spacious, comfortable & ideally located for exploring the east coast, the North York Moors & York. The 2 attractive double bedrooms have en-suite bathrooms, T.V. & tea & coffee-making facilities. Guests are welcome to use the garden & all-weather tennis court. Evening meals by arrangement. Children over 3 years welcome. A delightful family home.

| £22.50 to £25.00 | Y | Y | N |

Mrs Virginia Sutton   Willerby Wold Farm   Staxton   Scarborough YO12 4TF   Yorkshire
Tel: (01944) 710747   Fax 01944 710281   Open: ALL YEAR   Map Ref No. 28

Wildsmith House

Nearest Road: A.170

A former farmhouse, originating from 1720, Wildsmith House is full of character & charm. Set on the village green, at the edge of the North Yorkshire Moors. Accommodation is in 2 spacious en-suite bedrooms, decorated & furnished to a high standard, with colour T.V. & tea/coffee-making facilities. Elegant guest sitting room with log fires. Ideally situated for exploring the region with its historic houses, abbeys, unspoilt village & city of York. Children over 12.

E-mail: wildsmithhouse@talk21.com

| £25.00 to £25.00 | Y | N | N |

Chris & Malcolm Steele   Wildsmith House   Marton   Sinnington YO62 6RD   Yorkshire
Tel: (01751) 432702   Open: MAR - OCT   Map Ref No. 29

The table header (left margin, rotated):
- rate £ from - to per person
- children taken
- evening meals
- animals taken

Cliffemount Hotel

rate £ from - to per person	children taken	evening meals	animals taken
£30.00 to £40.00	Y	Y	Y

Nearest Road: A.174

As the name implies, this privately-run hotel is situated on a clifftop with panoramic views over Runswick Bay. Built in the 1920s with later additions, the hotel is tastefully decorated throughout. 12 of the 13 comfortably furnished bedrooms have en-suite facilities, & the majority have spectacular sea views. Cliffemount, with its warm & friendly atmosphere, also enjoys a good reputation for its high standard of food. Fully licensed. Log fires in winter. Animals by arrangement.

E-mail: cliffemount@runswickbay.fsnet.co.uk

VISA: M'CARD:

Mrs Ashley Goodrum   Cliffemount Hotel   Bank Top Lane   Runswick Bay   Whitby TS13 5HU
Tel: (01947) 840103   Fax 01947 841025   Open: ALL YEAR (Excl. Xmas)   Map Ref No. 30

Barbican House

rate £ from - to per person	children taken	evening meals	animals taken
£28.00 to £30.00	Y	N	N

Nearest Road: A.19

The Barbican House is a Victorian residence of individual charm & character, overlooking the medieval city walls. Leave your car in the floodlit car park & enjoy a 10 minute walk to all the citys attractions. Bedrooms have en-suite/private facilities & are attractively furnished with T.V., 'phone, tea/coffee & hairdryer etc. Enjoy a traditional English breakfast & more, in the dining room. A friendly Yorkshire welcome always assured. Arrive as guests, leave as friends. Children over 12.

E-mail: info@barbicanhouse.com

see PHOTO over
p. 370

VISA: M'CARD:

Michael & Juliet Morgan   Barbican House   20 Barbican Road   York YO10 5AA   Yorkshire
Tel: (01904) 627617 Fax 01904 647140 Open: ALL YEAR (Excl. Xmas & New Year) Map Ref No. 31

Alexander House

rate £ from - to per person	children taken	evening meals	animals taken
£24.50 to £34.50	Y	N	N

Nearest Road: A.64, A.1036

After extensive refurbishment in 2001, Dave & Gillian warmly welcome you to their lovingly restored Victorian town house, centrally situated 400 yards from the city walls. The 4 attractive bedrooms are thoughtfully equipped with every modern comfort, king-size beds, refreshingly new en-suite facilities, fluffy white bath sheets & lovely toiletries. Relax in the traditionally furnished lounge & enjoy delicious breakfasts served in the Victorian dining room. Parking. Children over 7.

E-mail: info@alexanderhouseyork.co.uk

VISA: M'CARD:

Dave & Gillian Reynard   Alexander House   94 Bishopthorpe Road   York YO23 1JS   Yorkshire
Tel: (01904) 625016   Open: ALL YEAR   Map Ref No. 31

Dairy Guest House

rate £ from - to per person	children taken	evening meals	animals taken
£20.00 to £25.00	Y	N	Y

Nearest Road: A.64

The Dairy is a tastefully renovated Victorian house within walking distance of the city centre & just 200 yards from the medieval city walls. Decorated & furnished in the styles of Habitat, Sanderson's & Laura Ashley, with the emphasis on pine & plants. 5 bedrooms, some en-suite (& 4-poster available), each with modern amenities, T.V., hot-drink facilities & information on Yorkshire. A lovely enclosed courtyard. Breakfast choices range from English to wholefood vegetarian. Animals by arrangement.

E-mail: filcis@globalnet.co.uk

Phillip Hunt & Chris Andrade   Dairy Guest House   3 Scarcroft Road   York YO23 1ND   Yorkshire
Tel: (01904) 639367   Open: FEB - DEC   Map Ref No. 31

Barbican House.   York.

rate £ from - to per person	children taken	evening meals	animals taken		

£26.50 to £32.50 | Y | N | N

🚭

Nunmill House

Nearest Road: A.64, A.59

A warm friendly welcome awaits you at Nunmill House, a delightful late-Victorian house, tastefully restored throughout with Laura Ashley furnishings to enhance the original architectural features. Offering a choice of 8 delightful bedrooms, each with en-suite or private facilities. Ideally situated just outside the medieval walls, & a 10-minute walk to all the historic attractions of the city. Complimentary tea & coffee are available, & special diets can be catered for by arrangement.
E-mail: info@nunmill.co.uk

Russell & Cherry Whitbourn-Hammond   Nunmill House   85 Bishopthorpe Road   York YO23 1NX
Tel: (01904) 634047   Fax 01904 655879   Open: FEB - NOV   Map Ref No. 31

£37.50 to £40.00 | Y | N | N

VISA: M'CARD:

Arndale Hotel

Nearest Road: A.64

A delightful Victorian house, directly overlooking York's famous race course, with beautiful enclosed walled gardens giving a country-house atmosphere within the city. There is a spacious, elegant lounge, complete with antiques, fresh flowers, paintings & a small bar. The 12 outstanding & thoughtfully equipped bedrooms are all en-suite. Many bathrooms are Victorian in style, with modern whirlpool baths. Antique half-tester/4-poster beds. Delicious quality breakfasts. Friendly, attentive service. Large enclosed gated car park.

Mrs M. Varey   Arndale Hotel   290 Tadcaster Road   York YO24 1ET   Yorkshire
Tel: (01904) 702424   Fax 01904 709800   Open: ALL YEAR   Map Ref No. 31

£27.50 to £35.00 | Y | N | N

🚭

VISA: M'CARD:

Curzon Lodge & Stable Cottages

Nearest Road: A.1036

A charming 17th-century Grade II listed house & oak-beamed stables within city conservation area overlooking York racecourse. Once a home of the Terry 'chocolate' family, guests are now invited to share the unique atmosphere in 10 delightful & fully-equipped en-suite rooms, some with 4-poster & brass beds. Country antiques, prints, books, fresh flowers & complimemtary sherry in the cosy sitting room lend traditional ambience. Delicious English breakfasts. Restaurants just 1-min walk. Parking in grounds. Warm & relaxed hospitality.

Mrs W. Wood   Curzon Lodge & Stable Cottages   23 Tadcaster Road Dringhouses   York YO24 1QG
Tel: (01904) 703157   Fax 01904 703157   Open: ALL YEAR (Excl. Xmas)   Map Ref No. 31

£35.00 to £55.00 | Y | N | N

🚭

see PHOTO over p. 372

VISA: M'CARD:

Holmwood House Hotel

Nearest Road: A.59

The conversion of 2 listed, early-Victorian town houses has created an elegant hotel that offers guests a feeling of home with a touch of luxury. All rooms, of course, have en-suite facilities but are very different in both size & decoration. There are 3 honeymoon rooms (2 with 4-poster beds) & 1 with a spa bath. 3 family suites are available. The guest sitting room, with an open fire, is on the ground floor. Children over 8 welcome.
E-mail: holmwood.house@dial.pipex.com

Rosie Blanksby & Bill Pitts Holmwood House Hotel   114 Holgate Road   York YO24 4BB   Yorkshire
Tel: (01904) 626183   Fax 01904 670899   Open: ALL YEAR   Map Ref No. 31

Holmwood House Hotel.   York.

Arnot House.   Bootham.

Yorkshire

Four Seasons Hotel

Nearest Road: A.19

An elegant Victorian residence. Ideally situated in a peaceful cul-de-sac only 7 mins' stroll from the Minster & York's many other historic attractions. There are 5 beautifully appointed & tastefully furnished en-suite bedrooms, all fully equipped. Four-course English breakfast, residential licence & private car parking. The Four Seasons Hotel is an ideal base to explore York, & is within easy reach of Harrogate & the beautiful Yorkshire Dales.
E-mail: roe@fourseasons.supanet.com

£28.00 to £32.00   Y   N   N

VISA: M'CARD:

Mr & Mrs S. J. Roe   Four Seasons Hotel   7 St. Peters Grove   Bootham   York   YO30 6AQ   Yorkshire
Tel: (01904) 622621   Fax 01904 620976   Open: FEB - DEC   Map Ref No. 31

Arnot House

Nearest Road: A.19

Overlooking Bootham Park, only 5 mins' walk from the York Minster & city centre. Arnot House is a Victorian town house built for a wealthy merchant in 1865. The house is beautifully decorated, & there are fine antiques & paintings. Many of its original features have been retained including marble fireplaces & ornate coving. The 4 attractive bedrooms have either Victorian brass or wooden beds & every facility. An excellent location.
E-mail: kim.robbins@virgin.net

£25.00 to £29.00   N   N   N

see PHOTO over
p. 373

VISA: M'CARD:

Mrs Ann & Miss Kim Sluter-Robbins   Arnot House   17 Grosvenor Terrace   York   YO30 7AG   Yorkshire
Tel: (01904) 641966   Fax 01904 641966   Open: ALL YEAR   Map Ref No. 31

The Bentley

Nearest Road: A.19

The Bentley really is the place to stay if you're looking for the following: An elegant Victorian town house offering en-suite accommodation in rooms furnished with quality, care & comfort in mind; views of York Minster across parkland; delicious breakfasts; guaranteed friendliness, help & courtesy; 8-10 mins walk into the city centre; parking permits; & above all, the ultimate resting place for horse racing enthusiasts. Children over 10.
E-mail: p.a.lefebve@tesco.net

£21.00 to £27.50   Y   N   N

see PHOTO over
p. 375

Will & Penny Lefebve   The Bentley   25 Grosvenor Terrace   Bootham   York   YO30 7AG   Yorkshire
Tel/Fax: (01904) 644313   Mobile 07860 199440   Open: FEB - DEC   Map Ref No. 31

Ascot House

Nearest Road: A.1036

Ascot House is a family-run Victorian villa built in 1869. 15 en-suite rooms of character, many having four-poster or canopy beds. Each is well-equipped with T.V., tea/coffee-making facilities, etc. Delicious traditional English or vegetarian breakfasts are served in the dining room. Ascot House is only 15 mins' walk to the city centre with its ancient narrow streets, medieval churches, Roman, Viking & National Railway Museums & the York Minster. Licensed. Sauna available. Car park.
E-mail: J+K@ascot-house-york.demon.co.uk

£20.00 to £26.00   Y   N   Y

VISA: M'CARD:

June & Keith Wood   Ascot House   80 East Parade   York   YO31 7YH   Yorkshire
Tel: (01904) 426826   Fax 01904 431077   Open: ALL YEAR (Excl. Xmas)   Map Ref No. 31

The Bentley. York.

Yorkshire

	rate £ from - to per person	children taken	evening meals	animals taken

Laurel Manor Farm

Nearest Road: A.1, A.19

Hidden up a lane, beside the village church, is Laurel Manor Farm, its 28 acres running down to the River Swale. The recently refurbished bedrooms have en-suite/private bathrooms & are furnished with antiques, a 4-poster, family portraits & open fireplaces. Dine with your hosts (by arrangement) or at one of 4 local inns. The Keys have a tennis court, croquet lawn & river walks, & are licensed. Situated only 4 miles from the A.1M. 12 miles York/Harrogate. Animals by arrangement.
E-mail: laurelmf@aol.com

£30.00 to £40.00 — Y Y Y

see PHOTO over p. 377

Sam & Annie Key   *Laurel Manor Farm*   *Brafferton*   *York YO61 2NZ*   *Yorkshire*
Tel: (01423) 360436   Fax 01423 360437   *Open: ALL YEAR*   *Map Ref No. 32*

Plumpton Court

Nearest Road: A.170

Plumpton Court is a family-run 17th-century guest house set in the foothills of the North Yorkshire Moors, & is ideally situated for York & exploring the east coast. Offering 7 en-suite, comfortable & well-appointed bedrooms, many with bath & shower, all with clock/radio, tea/coffee-making facilities & T.V.. There is a comfortable lounge in which guests may relax, with real fire, small bar & T.V.. Delicious evening meals served using fresh local produce. Secure, gated car park & garden. Children over 12.
E-mail: chrisandsarah@plumptoncourt.com

£21.00 to £26.00 — Y Y N

Chris & Sarah Braithwaite   *Plumpton Court*   *High Street*   *Nawton*   *York YO62 7TT*   *Yorkshire*
Tel: (01439) 771223   Fax 01439 771223   *Open: ALL YEAR*   *Map Ref No. 33*

All the establishments mentioned in this guide are members of
The Worldwide Bed & Breakfast Association

When booking your accommodation please mention
The Best Bed & Breakfast

Laurel Farm. Brafferton.

Scotland

Scotland

Scotland's culture & traditions, history & literature, languages & accents, its landscape & architecture, even its wildlife set it apart from the rest of Britain. Much of Scotland's history is concerned with the struggle to retain independence from England.

The Romans never conquered the Scottish tribes, but preferred to keep them at bay with Hadrian's Wall, stretching across the Border country from Tynemouth to the Solway Firth.

Time lends glamour to events, but from the massacre of Glencoe to the Highland Clearances, much of Scotland's fate has been a harsh one. Robert the Bruce did rout the English enemy at Bannockburn after scaling the heights of Edinburgh Castle to take the city, but in later years Mary, Queen of Scots was to spend much of her life imprisoned by her sister Elizabeth I of England. Bonnie Prince Charlie (Charles Edward Stuart) led the Jacobite rebellion which ended in defeat at Culloden.

These events are recorded in the folklore & songs of Scotland. The Border & Highland Gatherings & the Common Ridings are more than a chance to wear the Tartan, they are reminders of national pride.

Highland Games are held throughout the country where local & national champions compete in events like tossing the caber & in piping contests. There are sword dances & Highland flings, the speciality of young men & boys wearing the full dress tartan of their clan.

Scotland's landscape is rich in variety from the lush green lowlands to the handsome splendour of the mountainous Highlands, from the rounded hills of the Borders to the far-flung islands of the Hebrides, Orkney & Shetland where the sea is ever-present.

There are glens & beautiful lochs deep in the mountains, a spectacular coastline of high cliffs & white sandy beaches, expanses of purple heather moorland where the sparkling water in the burns runs brown with peat, & huge skies bright with cloud & gorgeous sunsets.

Argyll & The Islands

This area has ocean & sea lochs, forests & mountains, 3000 miles of coastline, about 30 inhabited islands, the warming influence of the Gulf Stream & the tallest tree in Britain (in Strone Gardens, near Loch Fyne).

Sites both historic & prehistoric are to be found in plenty. There is a hilltop fort at Dunadd, near Crinan with curious cup-&-ring carvings, & numerous ancient sites surround Kilmartin, from burial cairns to grave slabs.

Kilchurn Castle is a magnificent ruin in contrast to the opulence of Inveraray. Both are associated with the once-powerful Clan Campbell. There are remains of fortresses built by the Lords of the Isles, the proud chieftains who ruled the west after driving out the Norse invaders in the 12th century.

Oban is a small harbour town accessible by road & rail & the point of departure for many of the islands including Mull.

Tobermory. Isle of Mull.

378

Scotland

Mull is a peaceful island with rugged seascapes, lovely walks & villages, a miniature railway & the famous Mull Little Theatre. It is a short hop from here to the tiny island of Iona & St. Columba's Abbey, cradle of Christianity in Scotland.

Coll & Tiree have lovely beaches & fields of waving barley. The grain grown here was once supplied to the Lords of the Isles but today most goes to Islay & into the whisky. Tiree has superb windsurfing.

Jura is a wilder island famous for its red deer. The Isles of Colonsay & Oronsay are joined at low water.

Gigha, 'God's Isle', is a fertile area of gardens with rare & semitropical plants.The Island of Staffa has Fingal's Cave.

The Borders, Dumfries & Galloway

The borderland with England is a landscape of subtle colours & contours from the round foothills of the Cheviots, purple with heather, to the dark green valley of the Tweed.

The Lammermuir Hills sweep eastwards to a coastline of small harbours & the spectacular cliffs at St. Abbs Head where colonies of seabirds thrive.

The Border towns, set in fine countryside, have distinctive personalities. Hawick, Galashiels, Selkirk & Melrose all played their parts in the various Border skirmishes of this historically turbulent region & then prospered with a textile industry which survives today. They celebrate their traditions in the Common Riding ceremonies.

The years of destructive border warfare have left towers & castles throughout the country. Roxburgh was once a Royal castle & James II was killed here during a seige. Now there are only the shattered remains of the massive stone walls. Hermitage Castle is set amid wild scenery near Hawick & impressive Floors Castle stands above Kelso.

At Jedburgh the Augustine abbey is remarkably complete, & a visitors centre here tells the story of the four great Border Abbeys; Jedburgh itself, Kelso, Dryburgh & Melrose.

The lovely estate of Abbotsford where Sir Walter Scott lived & worked is near Melrose. A prolific poet & novelist, his most famous works are the Waverley novels written around 1800. His house holds many of his possessions, including a collection of armour. Scott's View is one of the best vantage points in the borderlands with a prospect of the silvery Tweed & the three distinctive summits of the Eildon Hills.

Eildon Hills.

There are many gracious stately homes. Manderston is a classical house of great luxury, & Mellerstain is the work of the Adam family. Traquair was originally a Royal hunting lodge. Its main gates were locked in 1745 after a visit from Bonnie Prince Charlie, never to be opened until a Stuart King takes the throne.

Dumfries & Galloway to the southwest is an area of rolling hills with a fine coastline.

Plants flourish in the mild air here & there are palm trees at Ardwell House & the Logan Botanic Garden.

Scotland

The gardens at Castle Kennedy have rhododendrons, azaleas & magnolias & Threave Gardens near Castle Douglas are the National Trust for Scotland's School of gardening.

The Galloway Forest Park covers a vast area of lochs & hills & has views across to offshore Ailsa Craig. At Caerlaveroch Castle, an early Renaissance building near the coast of Dumfries, there is a national nature reserve.

The first church in Scotland was built by St. Ninian at Whithorn in 400 on a site now occupied by the 13th century priory. The spread of Christianity is marked by early memorial stones like the Latinus stone at Whithorn, & the abbeys of Dundrennan, Crossraguel, Glenluce & Sweetheart, named after its founder who carried her husband's heart in a casket & is buried with it in the abbey.

At Dumfries is the poet Burns' house, his mausoleum & the Burns Heritage Centre overlooking the River Nith.

In Upper Nithsdale the Mennock Pass leads to Wanlockhead & Leadhills, once centres of the lead-mining industry. There is a fascinating museum here & the opportunity of an underground trip.

Lowland

The Frith of Clyde & Glascow in the west, & the Firth of Forth with Edinburgh in the east are both areas of rich history, tradition & culture.

Edinburgh is the capital of Scotland & amongst the most visually exciting cities in the world. The New Town is a treasure trove of inspired neo-classical architecture, & below Edinburgh Castle high on the Rock, is the Old Town, a network of courts, closes, wynds & gaunt tenements around the Royal Mile.

The Palace of Holyrood House, home of Mary, Queen of Scots for several years overlooks Holyrood Park & nearby Arthur's Seat, is a popular landmark.

The City's varied art galleries include The Royal Scottish Academy, The National Gallery, Portrait Gallery, Gallery of Modern Art & many other civic & private collections.

The Royal Museum of Scotland displays superb historical & scientific material. The Royal Botanic Gardens are world famous.

Cultural life in Edinburgh peaks at Festival time in August. The official Festival, the Fringe, the Book Festival, Jazz Festival & Film Festival bring together artistes of international reputation.

The gentle hills around the city offer many opportunities for walking. The Pentland Hills are easily reached,

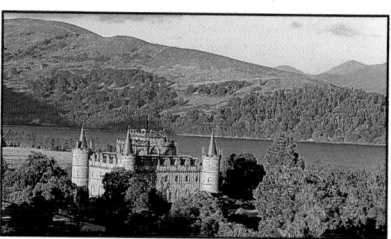

Inverary Castle.

with the Lammermuir Hills a little further south. There are fine beaches at Gullane, Yellowcraigs, North Berwick & at Dunbar.

Tantallon Castle, a 14th century stronghold, stands on the rocky Firth of Forth, & 17th century Hopetoun House, on the outskirts of the city is only one of a number of great houses in the area.

North of Edinburgh across the Firth of Forth lies the ancient Kingdom of Fife. Here is St. Andrews, a pleasant town on the seafront, an old university

Scotland

town & Scotland's ecclesiastical capital, but famous primarily for golf.

Glasgow is the industrial & business capital of Scotland. John Betjeman called it the 'finest Victorian city in Britain' & many buildings are remarkable examples of Victorian splendour, notably the City Chambers.

Many buildings are associated with the architect Charles Rennie MacKintosh; the Glasgow School of Art is one of them. Glasgow Cathedral is a perfect example of pre-Reformation Gothic architecture.

Glasgow is Scotland's largest city with the greatest number of parks & fine Botanic Garden. It is home to both the Scottish Opera & the Scottish Ballet, & has a strong & diverse cultural tradition from theatre to jazz. Its museums include the matchless Burrell Collection, & the Kelvingrove Museum & Art Gallery, which houses one of the best civic collections of paintings in Britain, as well as reflecting the city's engineering & shipbuilding heritage.

The coastal waters of the Clyde are world famous for cruising & sailing, with many harbours & marinas. The long coastline offers many opportunities for sea-angling from Largs to Troon & Prestwick, & right around to Luce Bay on the Solway.

There are many places for birdwatching on the Estuary, whilst the Clyde Valley is famous for its garden centres & nurseries.

Paisley has a mediaeval abbey, an observatory & a museum with a fine display of the famous 'Paisley' pattern shawls.

Further south, Ayr is a large seaside resort with sandy beach, safe bathing & a racecourse. In the Ayrshire valleys there is traditional weaving & lace & bonnet making, & Sorn, in the rolling countryside boasts its 'Best Kept Village' award.

Culzean Castle is one of the finest Adam houses in Scotland & stands in spacious grounds on the Ayrshire cliffs.

Robert Burns is Scotland's best loved poet, & 'Burns night' is widely celebrated. The region of Strathclyde shares with Dumfries & Galloway the title of 'Burns Country'. The son of a peasant farmer, Burns lived in poverty for much of his life. The simple house where he was born is in the village of Alloway. In the town of Ayr is the Auld Kirk where he was baptised & the footbridge of 'The Brigs of Ayr' is still in use. The Tam O'Shanter Inn is now a Burns museum & retains its thatched roof & simple fittings. The Burns Trail leads on to Mauchline where Possie Nansie's Inn remains. At Tarbolton the National Trust now care for the old house where Burns founded the 'Batchelors Club' debating society.

Perthshire, Loch Lomond & The Trossachs

By a happy accident of geology, the Highland Boundary fault which separates the Highlands from the Lowlands runs through Loch Lomond, close to the Trossachs & on through Perthshire, giving rise to marvellous scenery.

In former times Highlanders & Lowlanders raided & fought here. Great castles like Stirling, Huntingtower & Doune were built to protect the routes between the two different cultures.

Stirling was once the seat of Scotland's monarchs & the great Royal castle is set high on a basalt rock. The Guildhall & the Kirk of the Holy Rude are also interesting buildings in the town, with Cambuskenneth Abbey & the Bannockburn Heritage Centre close by.

Perth 'fair city' on the River Tay,

Scotland

has excellent shops & its own repertory theatre. Close by are the Black Watch Museum at Balhousie Castle, & the Branklyn Gardens, which are superb in May & June.

Scone Palace, to the north of Perth was home to the Stone or Scone of Destiny for nearly 500 years until its removal to Westminster. 40 kings of Scotland were crowned here.

Pitlochry sits amid beautiful Highland scenery with forest & hill walks, two nearby distilleries, the famous Festival theatre, Loch Faskally & the Dam Visitor Centre & Fish Ladder.

In the Pass of Killiecrankie, a short drive away, a simple stone marks the spot where the Highlanders charged barefoot to overwhelm the redcoat soldiers of General MacKay.

Queens View.

Famous Queen's View overlooks Loch Tummel beyond Pitlochry with the graceful peak of Schiehallion completing a perfect picture.

Other lochs are picturesque too; Loch Earn, Loch Katrine & bonnie Loch Lomond itself, & they can be enjoyed from a boat on the water. Ospreys nest at the Loch of the Lowes near Dunkeld.

Mountain trails lead through Ben Lawers & the 'Arrocher Alps' beyond Loch Lomond. The Ochils & the Campsie Fells have grassy slopes for walking. Near Callander are the Bracklinn Falls, the Callander Crags & the Falls of Leny.

Wooded areas include the Queen Elizabeth Forest Park & the Black Wood of Rannoch which is a fragment of an ancient Caledonian forest. There are some very tall old trees around Killiecrankie, & the world's tallest beech hedge - 26 metres high - grows at Meikleour near Blairgowrie.

Creiff & Blairgowrie have excellent golf courses set in magnificent scenery.

The Grampians, Highlands & Islands

This is spacious countryside with glacier-scarred mountains & deep glens cut through by tumbling rivers. The Grampian Highlands make for fine mountaineering & walking.

There is excellent skiing at Glenshee, & a centre at the Lecht for the less experienced, whilst the broad tops of the giant mountains are ideal for cross-country skiing. The chair-lift at Glenshee is worth a visit at any season.

The Dee, The Spey & The Don flow down to the coastal plain from the heights. Some of the world's finest trout & salmon beats are on these rivers.

Speyside is dotted with famous distilleries from Grantown-on-Spey to Aberdeen, & the unique Malt Whisky Trail can be followed.

Royal Deeside & Donside hold a number of notable castles. Balmoral is the present Royal family's holiday home, & Kildrummy is a romantic ruin in a lovely garden. Fyvie Castle has five dramatic towers & stands in peaceful parkland. Nearby Haddo House, by contrast, is an elegant Georgian home.

There is a 17th century castle at Braemar, but more famous here is the Royal Highland Gathering. There are wonderful walks in the vicinity -

Scotland

Morrone Hill, Glen Quoich & the Linn O'Dee are just a few.

The city of Aberdeen is famed for its sparkling granite buildings, its university, its harbour & fish market & for North Sea Oil. It also has long sandy beaches & lovely year-round flower displays, of roses in particular.

Around the coast are fishing towns & villages. Crovie & Pennan sit below impressive cliffs. Buckie is a typical small port along the picturesque coastline of the Moray Firth.

The Auld Kirk at Cullen has fine architectural features & elegant Elgin has beautiful cathedral ruins. Pluscarden Abbey, Spynie Palace & Duffus Castle are all nearby.

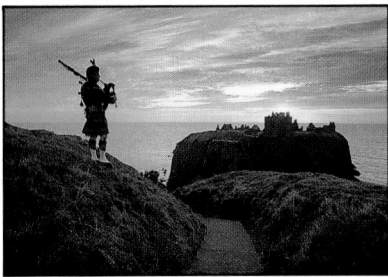

Dunnottar Castle.

Nairn has a long stretch of sandy beach & a golf course with an international reputation. Inland are Cawdor Castle & Culloden Battlefield.

The Northern Highlands are divided from the rest of Scotland by the dramatic valley of the Great Glen. From Fort William to Inverness, sea lochs, canals & the depths of Loch Ness form a chain of waterways linking both coasts.

Here are some of the wildest & most beautiful landscapes in Britain. Far Western Knoydart, the Glens of Cannich & Affric, the mysterious lochs, including Loch Morar, deeper than the North Sea, & the marvellous coastline; all are exceptional.

The glens were once the home of crofting communities, & of the clansmen who supported the Jacobite cause. The wild scenery of Glencoe is a favourite with walkers & climbers, but it has a tragic history. Its name means 'the glen of weeping' & refers to the massacre of the MacDonald clan in 1692, when the Royal troops who had been received as guests treacherously attacked their hosts at dawn.

The valleys are empty today largely as a result of the infamous Highland Clearances in the 19th century when the landowners turned the tenant crofters off the land in order to introduce the more profitable Cheviot sheep. The emigration of many Scots to the U.S.A. & the British Colonies resulted from these events.

South of Inverness lie the majestic Cairngorms. The Aviemore centre provides both summer & winter sports facilities here.

To the north of Loch Ness are the remains of the ancient Caledonian forest where red deer & stags are a common sight on the hills. Rarer are sightings of the Peregrine Falcon, the osprey, the Golden Eagle & the Scottish wildcat. Kincraig has excellent wildlife parks.

Inverness is the last large town in the north, & a natural gateway to the Highlands & to Moray, the Black Isle & the north-east.

The east coast is characterised by the Firths of Moray, Cromarty & Dornoch & by its changing scenery from gentle pastureland, wooded hillsides to sweeping coastal cliffs.

On the Black Isle, which is not a true island but has a causeway & bridge links with the mainland, Fortrose & Rosemarkie in particular have lovely beaches, caves & coastal walks. There is golf on the headland at Rosemarkie & a 13th century cathedral of rosy pink sandstone stands in Fortrose.

Scotland

Scotland Gazeteer

Areas of outstanding natural beauty

It would be invidious, not to say almost impossible, to choose any particular area of Scotland as having a more beautiful aspect than another - the entire country is a joy to the traveller. The rugged Highlands, the great glens, tumbling waters, tranquil lochs - the deep countryside or the wild coastline - simply come & choose your own piece of paradise.

Historic Houses & Castles

Bowhill - Nr. Selkirk
18th-19th century - home of the Duke of Bucceleugh & Queensberry. Has an outstanding collection of pictures by Canaletto, Claude, Gainsborough, Reynolds & Leonardo da Vinci. Superb silver, porcelain & furniture. 16th & 17th century miniatures.

Traquair House - Innerleithen
A unique & ancient house being the oldest inhabited home in Scotland. It is rich in associations with every form of political history & after Bonnie Prince Charlie passed through its main gates in 1745 no other visitor has been allowed to use them. There are treasures in the house dating from 12th century, & it has an 18th century library & a priest's room with secret stairs.

Linlithgow Palace - Linlithgow
The birthplace of Mary, Queen of Scots.

Stirling Castle - Stirling
Royal Castle.

Drumlanrigg Castle - Nr. Thornhill
17th century castle of pale pink stone - romantic & historic - wonderful art treasures including a magnificent Rembrandt & a huge silver chandelier. Beautiful garden setting.

Braemar Castle - Braemar
17th century castle of great historic interest. Has round central tower with spiral staircase giving it a fairy-tale appearance.

Drum Castle - Nr. Aberdeen
Dating in part from 13th century, it has a great square tower.

Cawdor Castle - Nairn
14th century fortress - like castle - has always been the home of the Thanes of Cawdor - background to Shakespeare's Macbeth.

Dunvegan Castle - Isle of Skye
13th century - has always been the home of the Chiefs of McLeod.

Hopetoun House - South Queensferry
Very fine example of Adam architecture & has a fine collection of pictures & furniture. Splendid landscaped grounds.

Inverary Castle - Argyll
Home of the Dukes of Argyll. 18th century - Headquarters of Clan Campbell.

Burn's Cottage - Alloway
Birthplace of Robert Burns - 1659 - thatched cottage - museum of Burns' relics.

Bachelors' Club - Tarbolton
17th century house - thatched - where Burns & friends formed their club - 1780.

Blair Castle - Blair Atholl
Home of the Duke of Atholl, 13th century Baronial mansion - collection of Jacobite relics, armour, paintings, china & many other items.

Glamis Castle - Angus
17th century remodelling in Chateau style - home of the Earl of Strathmore & Kinghorne. Very attractive castle - lovely grounds by Capability Brown.

Scone Palace - Perth
has always been associated with seat of Government of Scotland from earliest times. The Stone of Destiny was removed from the Palace in 1296 & taken to Westminster Abbey. Present palace rebuilt in early 1800's still incorporating parts of the old. Lovely gardens.

Edinburgh Castle
Fortress standing high over the town - famous for military tattoo.

Culzean Castle & Country Park - Maybole
Fine Adam house & spacious gardens perched on Ayrshire cliff.

Dunrobin Castle - Golspie
Ancient seat of the Earls & Dukes of Sutherland.

Eilean Donan Castle - Wester Ross
13th century castle, Jacobite relics.

Manderston - Duns
Great classical house with only silver staircase in the world. Stables, marble dairy, formal gardens.

Scotland

Cathedrals & Churches

Dunfermline Abbey - Dunfermline
Norman remains of beautiful church. Modern east end & tower.

Edinburgh (Church of the Holy Rood)
15th century - was divided into two in 17th century & re-united 1938. Here Mary, Queen of Scots was crowned.

Glasgow (St. Mungo)
12th-15th century cathedral - 19th century interior. Central tower with spire.

Kirkwall (St. Magnus)
12th century cathedral with very fine nave.

Falkirk Old Parish Church - Falkirk
The spotted appearance (faw) of the church (kirk) gave the town its name. The site of the church has been used since 7th century, with succesive churches built upon it. The present church was much rebuilt in 19th century. Interesting historically.

St Columba's Abbey - Iona

Museums & Galleries

Agnus Folk Museum - Glamis
17th century cottages with stone slab roofs, restored by the National Trust for Scotland & houses a fine folk collection.

Mary, Queen of Scots' House - Jedburgh
Life & times of the Queen along with paintings, etc.

Andrew Carnegie Birthplace - Dunfermline
The cottage where he was born is now part of a museum showing his life's work.

Aberdeen Art Gallery & Museum - Aberdeen
Sculpture, paintings, watercolours, prints & drawings. Applied arts. Maritime museum exhibits.

Provost Skene's House - Aberdeen
17th century house now exhibiting local domestic life, etc.

Highland Folk Museum - Kingussie
Examples of craft work & tools - furnished cottage with mill.

West Highland Museum - Fort William
Natural & local hsitory. Relics of Jacobites & exhibition of the '45 Rising.

Clan Macpherson House - Newtonmore
Relics of the Clan.

Glasgow Art Gallery & Museum - Glasgow
Archaeology, technology, local & natural history. Old Masters, tapestries, porcelain, glass & silver, etc. Sculpture.

Scottish National Gallery - Edinburgh
20th century collection - paintings & sculpture - Arp, Leger, Giacometti, Matisse, Picasso. Modern Scottish painting.

National Museum of Antiquities in Scotland - Edinburgh
Collection from Stone Age to modern times - Relics of Celtic Church, Stuart relics, Highland weapons, etc.

Gladstone Court - Biggar
Small indoor street of shops, a bank, schoolroom, library, etc.

Burns' Cottage & Museum - Alloway
Relics of Robert Burns - National Poet.

Inverness Museum & Art Gallery - Inverness
Social history, archaeology & cultural life of the Highlands. Display of the Life of the Clans - good Highland silver - crafts, etc.

Kirkintilloch - Nr. Glasgow
Auld Kirk Museum. Local history, including archaeological specimens from the Antonine Wall (Roman). Local industries, exhibitions, etc

Pollock House & Park - Glasgow
18th century house with collection of paintings, etc. The park is the home of the award-winning Burrell Collection
The foregoing are but a few of the many museums & galleries in Scotland - further information is always freely available from the Tourist Information.

Historic Monuments

Aberdour Castle - Aberdour
14th century fortification - part still roofed.

Balvenie Castle - Duffton
15th century castle ruins.

Cambuskenneth Abbey - Nr. Stirling
12th century abbey - seat of Bruce's Parliament in 1326. Ruins.

Dryburgh Abbey - Dryburgh
Remains of monastery.

Loch Leven Castle - Port Glasgow
15th century ruined stronghold - once lived in by Mary, Queen of Scots.

SCOTLAND

SCOTLAND
Map references

00	D. White	19	Maguire	33	Pottie
01	Broadbent	19	C.Hamilton	34	Wilcken
02	McKay	19	Fraser	35	Ridsdill-S.
03	Dick	19	Drummond	36	Booth
04	MacArther	19	A.Vidler	37	Lindsay
04	Rice-Garwood	20	MacDonald	40	Meicklejohn
04	Sutherland	21	D.Scott	41	G. Stewart
05	Rozga	22	Lawson	41	Bouchard
06	Wagstaff	23	Steven	43	Roebuck
08	C.McDonald	24	Black	44	Gunn
09	Martin	25	Erskine	45	Gaughan
10	Gemmell	26	Gilbert	47	Graham
11	Crosthwaite	27	Allison	49	Stiell
12	Deeney	28	Anderson	50	Maxwell
13	Thomson	29	Gardner	50	Sanderson
14	Taylor	30	Cairns	50	Mathieson
15	O'Dell	31	Campbell	53	Irvine
16	Dickson	31	Henderson	54	B.Smith
17	Fordyce	32	Ozmus	55	Willis
18	White	32	Parsons	56	Haslam
19	Sandeman			57	Beatts
19	Martin			58	Chapman
19	Rowan				
19	D.Vidler				
19	Urquhart				
19	Redmayne				
19	J.Hamilton				
19	Alexander				
19	Walton				
19	Hill				
19	Della-Porta				
19	S.Hamilton				
19	Leishman				
19	G. Stuart				
19	Virtue				
19	Welch				
19	Stark				

OUTER HEBRIDES
LEWIS
WESTERN ISLES
SKYE
HIGHLANDS
MORAY
ABERDEENSHIRE
ABERDEEN
INNER HEBRIDES
MULL
PERTHSHIRE & KINROSS
ANGUS
DUNDEE
ARGYLL & BUTE
STIRLING
FIFE
EAST LOTHIAN
JURA
ISLAY
NORTH AYRSHIRE
SOUTH LANARK-SHIRE
EAST AYRSHIRE
ARRAN
BORDERS
SOUTH AYRSHIRE
DUMFRIES & GALLOWAY

1 INVERCLYDE
2 DUNBARTON & CLYDEBANK
3 RENFREWSHIRE
4 EAST RENFREWSHIRE
5 GLASGOW
6 EAST DUNBARTONSHIRE
7 NORTH LANARKSHIRE
8 FALKIRK
9 CLACKMANNAN
10 WEST LOTHIAN
11 EDINBURGH
12 MID LOTHAIN

Scotland
Aberdeenshire & Argyll

Lys-Na-Greyne House

Nearest Road: A.93

Lys-Na-Greyne is a beautiful Edwardian mansion situated in idyllic surroundings on the banks of the River Dee on the outskirts of Aboyne in Royal Deeside, in grounds of 3 acres. This is a perfect place for exploring the surrounding countryside where there are many castles & places of historic interest. Golf, riding, fishing, hillwalking & tennis available locally. Shooting, stalking available by arrangement. All rooms with en-suite/private bathroom & breathtaking views over the garden or river.
E-mail: dwhite7301@aol.com

| | £27.00 to £40.00 | Y | Y | N |

Mr & Mrs D. White   Lys-Na-Greyne House   Rhu-Na-Haven Road   Aboyne AB34 5JD   Aberdeenshire
Tel: (013398) 87397   Fax 013398 86441   Open: ALL YEAR   Map Ref No. 00

Lochside Cottage

Nearest Road: A.828

Total peace on the shore of Loch Baile Mhic Chailen, in an idyllic glen of outstanding beauty. There are many walks from the cottage garden; or, visit Fort William, Glencoe & Oban, from where you can board a steamer to explore the Western Isles. At the end of the day, a warm welcome awaits you: delicious home-cooked dinner, a log fire & the certainty of a perfect night's sleep in one of 3 attractive en-suite bedrooms. Children & animals by prior arrangement.
E-mail: broadbent@lochsidecottage.fsnet.co.uk

| | £24.00 to £32.00 | Y | Y | Y |

Earle & Stella Broadbent   Lochside Cottage   Fasnacloich   Appin PA38 4BJ   Argyll
Tel: (01631) 730216   Fax 01631 730216   Open: ALL YEAR   Map Ref No. 01

Allt-na-Craig

Nearest Road: A.83

The McKays warmly welcome all their guests to Allt-na-Craig, a lovely old Victorian mansion set in picturesque grounds overlooking Loch Fyne. Accommodation is in 6 comfortable en-suite bedrooms with tea/coffee makers. A guests' lounge with open fire & dining room is also available. This is a perfect base for outdoor activities, like hillwalking, fishing, golf, riding & windsurfing, or for visiting the islands. Delicious evening meals by arrangement. A charming home.

| | £32.00 to £35.00 | Y | Y | Y |

Margaret McKay   Allt-na-Craig   Tarbert Road   Ardrishaig PA30 8EP   Argyll
Tel: (01546) 603245   Open: ALL YEAR (Excl. Xmas & New Year)   Map Ref No. 02

Abbot's Brae Hotel

Nearest Road: A.815

Abbot's Brae is an award-winning family-run country house hotel, set in its own secluded woodland garden with breathtaking views of the sea & hills. 7 spacious en-suite bedrooms including four-poster, king-size double & twin rooms. All are well-equipped & attractively furnished throughout. The welcoming, homely atmosphere & appetising menus ensure a memorable stay. Abbot's Brae is an ideal base from which to explore Argyll & the Western Highlands. Only 1 hour from Glasgow Airport.
E-mail: enquiry@abbotsbrae.co.uk

| | £30.00 to £40.00 | Y | Y | Y |

VISA: M'CARD:

Gavin & Helen Dick   Abbot's Brae Hotel   West Bay   Dunoon PA23 7QJ   Argyll
Tel: (01369) 705021   Fax 01369 701191   Open: ALL YEAR   Map Ref No. 03

rate £ from - to per person	children taken	evening meals	animals taken

Ardsheal Home Farm

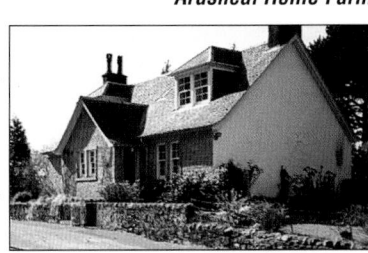

£18.00 to £19.00 — Y Y N

🚭

Nearest Road: A.828

A charming Scottish hill farm of 1,000 acres, surrounded by breathtaking scenery on the shores of Loch Linnhe, overlooking the Morvern Hills. A warm welcome is assured from the friendly hosts. 3 attractive bedrooms, comfortable & well-furnished, with tea/coffee-making facilities, electric blankets, etc. Seafood & other eating places nearby. Convenient for touring & sailing to the inner Isles. An idyllic holiday retreat, there is even 1 mile of private beach. Riding nearby. Single supplement.

Flavia J. MacArthur   **Ardsheal Home Farm**   Kentallen   Duror in Appin PA38 4BZ   *Argyll*
Tel: (01631) 740229   Fax 01631 740229   *Open: APR - OCT*   Map Ref No. 04

The House of Keil

£27.00 to £27.00 — Y Y N

🚭

VISA: M'CARD:

Nearest Road: A.828

A family home set on the shores of Loch Linnhie, with 1 mile of private foreshore. 2 bedrooms overlook the loch & have stunning views to the Morven hills. Pony trekking, boat hire/fishing & the historic & picturesque Castle Stalker are within 5 miles; Glencoe within 10 miles. An old Stewart house with many unusual features, it is situated close to the burial ground, where James Stewart is reputed to be buried. An ideal base from which to explore the west coast. Dinner by arrangement.
E-mail: thehouseofkeil@hotmail.com

Ronald W. Rice-Garwood   **The House of Keil**   Duror PA38 4BW   *Argyll*
Tel: (01631) 740255   Fax 01631 740365   *Open: MAR - OCT*   Map Ref No. 04

Kilmeny Country Guest House

£36.00 to £36.00 — Y Y Y

🚭

Nearest Road: A.846

Islay is well-known for its abundant & wonderful wildlife & its many malt-whisky distilleries. Kilmeny Country Guest House, in the heart of a 300-acre beef farm, commands magnificent views of the surrounding hills & glen. This family-run business places emphasis on quality & personal service. The exquisite en-suite bedrooms, with country views, are elegantly furnished. The public rooms are charming, with a country-house influence. A 4-course dinner menu is available. Children over 5.
E-mail: info@kilmeny.co.uk

Mrs Margaret Rozga   **Kilmeny Country Guest House**   Ballygrant   Isle of Islay PA45 7QW   *Argyll*
Tel: (01496) 840668   Fax 01496 840668   *Open: ALL YEAR*   Map Ref No. 05

Red Bay Cottage

£16.50 to £16.50 — Y Y Y

Nearest Road: A.849

A really warm welcome awaits the visitor to this charming modern house, offering 3 very comfortable rooms with modern facilities. Situated only 20 metres from the sea, & overlooking Iona Sound & the white sandy beaches on the Isle of Iona, this surely must be the ideal base for a relaxing & peaceful holiday. Mr Wagstaff offers superb food. Eleanor is a qualified, practising silversmith, so why not enjoy a winter break on their residential silversmithing course?

John & Eleanor Wagstaff   **Red Bay Cottage**   Deargphort   Fionnphort   Isle of Mull PA66 6BP   *Argyll*
Tel: (01681) 700396   *Open: ALL YEAR*   Map Ref No. 06

Column headers (rotated): rate £ from - to per person | children taken | evening meals | animals taken

Ardsheal House

Nearest Road: A.828

Ardsheal House is spectacularly situated on the shores of Loch Linnhe, in 800 acres of woodlands, fields & gardens. It is a wonderful place for a relaxing holiday. This historic mansion is elegantly furnished throughout with family antiques & pictures, & offers 8 en-suite bedrooms which are attractive & well-appointed. The food at Ardsheal is excellent. It delights the eye & pleases the palate, & includes local fresh produce & home-made bread & preserves. (Evening meals by arrangement.)
E-mail: info@ardsheal.co.uk

£45.00 to £50.00 — Y Y Y

see PHOTO over
p. 391

VISA: M'CARD: AMEX:

Neil & Philippa Sutherland	Ardsheal House	Kentallen of Appin PA38 4BX	Argyll
Tel: (01631) 740227	Fax 01631 740342	Open: FEB - NOV	Map Ref No. 04

The Crescent

Nearest Road: A.70

Elegant Victorian terraced house set in the heart of Ayr. All rooms are comfortably furnished & individually styled including 1 with a 4-poster bed. Each of the bedrooms has a private bathroom. Within 5 minutes walk, guests can enjoy a leisurely stroll along the promenade or a relaxing drink in one of Ayr's cosy pubs. The Crescent is in an ideal location for golf, Burns Heritage, Culzean Castle & the Galloway Forest.
E-mail: carrie@26crescent.freeserve.co.uk

£25.00 to £32.00 — Y N N

VISA: M'CARD:

Caroline McDonald	The Crescent	26 Bellevue Crescent	Ayr KA7 2DR	Ayrshire
Tel: (01292) 287329	Fax 01292 286779	Open: ALL YEAR		Map Ref No. 08

Greenan Lodge

Nearest Road: A.719

A warm welcome is assured at Greenan Lodge. Located on the coastal route yet only 2 miles from Ayr town centre & 1 1/2 miles from the A.77. Set in the heart of Burns country, a perfect base for Turnberry, Troon & Prestwick golf courses & nearby Culzean Castle. All rooms are en-suite with T.V. & tea/coffee makers. After a day touring, relax & unwind in the comfort of the spacious lounge & enjoy breakfast in the conservatory style dining room. An excellent location for a relaxing break.
E-mail: helen@greenanlodge.com

£30.00 to £30.00 — N N Y

Helen Martin	Greenan Lodge	39 Dunure Road	Doonfoot	Ayr KA7 4HR	Ayrshire
Tel: (01292) 443939		Open: ALL YEAR			Map Ref No. 09

Dunduff House

Nearest Road: A.719

A warm friendly welcome awaits you at Dunduff House. Situated just south of Ayr at the coastal village of Dunure, this family-run beef & sheep unit of some 600 acres, is only 15 mins from the shore. Excellent accommodation, yet homely & comfortable. Bedrooms have panoramic coastal views over Arran, the Holy Isle, Mull of Kintyre & Ailsa Craig. Each room has an en-suite or private bathroom. Ideal for south-west Scotland, Culzean Castle, Robert Burns' Cottage & the Heritage Trail.
E-mail: gemmelldunduff@aol.com

£23.00 to £26.00 — N N N

VISA: M'CARD:

Agnes Gemmell	Dunduff House	Dunure	Ayr KA7 4LH	Ayrshire
Tel: (01292) 500225	Fax 01292 500222	Open: FEB - NOV		Map Ref No. 10

Ardsheal House. Kentallen of Appin.

Scotland
Ayrshire

Cosses Country House

Nearest Road: A.77

A former shooting lodge (1800s) & home farm (1900s), set in a secluded valley of garden & woodland. Superb accommodation, en-suite facilities, T.V., a hospitality tray & a roaring log fire on chilly evenings. The kitchen & herb garden supplement local produce for you to enjoy the 'Taste of Scotland' dinners. Castles (incl. Culzean), gardens, Burns' birthplace, golf, fishing, walks & cycling within easy reach. Irish ferry terminals 30 mins' drive. Children over 6.
E-mail: cosses@compuserve.com

£32.00 to £38.00 | Y | Y | Y

VISA: M'CARD:

Susan & Robin Crosthwaite   Cosses Country House   Ballantrae KA26 0LR   Ayrshire
Tel: (01465) 831363   Fax 01465 831598   Open: MAR - OCT   Map Ref No. 11

Fairways

Nearest Road: A.77

Nestling in the heart of Turnberry & only a '9-iron' from the famous golf course, Fairways promises comfortable accommodation in an ideal location. 2 spacious bedrooms, 1 with an en-suite shower & super king-size bed & the other with a private bathroom. Both rooms have T.V. & tea/coffee-making facilities etc. Fairways is also ideally placed for many other attractions including Culzean Castle (5 mins' drive), Robert Burns Country & Galloway Forest Park (walking & cycling.) Children over 12.
E-mail: sands.deen@virgin.net

£20.00 to £30.00 | Y | N | N

Mrs Sandra Deeney   Fairways   Lodge Road   Turnberry   Girvan KA26 9LX   Ayrshire
Tel: (01655) 331522   Open: ALL YEAR   Map Ref No. 12

Nether Underwood Country House

Nearest Road: A.77

Nether Underwood is a delightful country house set in 15 acres of garden, fields & woodland. Tucked into Ayrshire's rolling farmland, it promises superb accommodation & wonderful food. All bedrooms have en-suite or private bathrooms, T.V. & early morning tea. A log fire in the drawing room, where afternoon tea & pre-dinner drinks can be enjoyed. Evening meals by arrangement. The house is very well placed for major golf courses, Burn's birthplace & Glasgow's museums & galleries.
E-mail: netherund@aol.com

£40.00 to £40.00 | N | Y | N

VISA: M'CARD:

Felicity Thomson   Nether Underwood Country House   Symington   Kilmarnock KA1 5NG   Ayrshire
Tel: (01563) 830666   Fax 01563 830777   Open: ALL YEAR   Map Ref No. 13

Visit our website at:
http://www.bestbandb.co.uk

rate £ from - to per person | *children taken* | *evening meals* | *animals taken*

| £25.00 to £28.00 | Y | Y | N |

🚭

Kirkside House

Nearest Road: A.1

Kirkside House is an early-Victorian former manse, situated in a peaceful rural location. The spacious & attractively decorate bedrooms have lovely views to the hills & are well-equipped. Guests are welcome to relax in the charming walled garden with its herbaceous borders, old roses & ornamental pond. Kirkside House is ideally located for exploring the Borders area, & wonderful hill & coastal walks. Edinburgh is approx. 1 hr. Children over 12 years welcome. A charming home.

Martin & Libby Taylor   Kirkside House   Bonkyl   Duns TD11 3RJ   Berwickshire
Tel: (01361) 884340   Fax 01361 882273 Open: ALL YEAR (Excl. Xmas & New Year) Map Ref No. 14

| £22.00 to £24.00 | Y | N | Y |

🚭

VISA: M'CARD:

Westbourne House

Nearest Road: A.91

A Victorian mill-owner's mansion set in wooded grounds beneath Ochil Hills, in excellent walking country with numerous golf courses. Warm, friendly atmosphere, delicious home-cooking including vegetarian dishes. Log fires, croquet lawn, T.V., radio & tea/coffee-making facilities in all rooms (en-suite is on the ground floor). Centrally situated for Edinburgh, Glasgow, Perth & Stirling, home of 'Braveheart'. Secure off-street parking.
E-mail: odellwestbourne@compuserve.com

Mrs J.O'Dell   Westbourne House   10 Dollar Road Tillicoultry Stirling FK13 6PA Clackmannanshire
Tel: (01259) 750314   Fax 01259 750642   Open: ALL YEAR   Map Ref No. 15

| £36.00 to £36.00 | Y | Y | N |

Chipperkyle

Nearest Road: A.75

Chipperkyle is a beautiful 18th-century Georgian house, without a hint of formality. The Dicksons are both engaging & sociable & will endeavour to make you feel at ease in their elegant home. Bedrooms are light & charming decorated with cast iron beds, excellent furniture & masses of books. An attractive sitting room with feng shui cabinet. 200 acres of grazing land with a dog, cat, donkey & free-ranging hens. Threave & Logan gardens, Drumlanrig & Culzean are within an easy drive.
E-mail: dickson@chipperkyle.freeserve.co.uk

Willie & Catriona Dickson Chipperkyle Kirkpatrick Durham Castle Douglas DG7 3EY Dumfriesshire
Tel: (01556) 650223   Fax 01556 650223   Open: ALL YEAR (Excl. Xmas)   Map Ref No. 16

| £35.00 to £35.00 | Y | Y | Y |

see PHOTO over p. 394

VISA: M'CARD:

Cavens

Nearest Road: A.710

Formerly an old mansion with a strong American historical connection, Cavens, now a charming small country house hotel, offers 8 comfortable en-suite bedrooms. 2 lounges with open fires add to the ambience of the house. Standing in 11 acres of gardens & woodland, it is ideal for those wishing to explore the joys of the Solway Coast, with its beautiful scenery & beaches. Sailing, walking, golfing, shooting, fishing & riding by arrangement. Animals by arrangement. Excellent cuisine.
E-mail: enquiries@cavens-hotel.co.uk

A. Fordyce   Cavens   Kirkbean by Dumfries DG2 8AA   Dumfriesshire
Tel: (01387) 880234   Fax 01387 880467   Open: ALL YEAR   Map Ref No. 17

Cavens House.   Kirkbean-by-Dumfries.

rate £ from - to per person / children taken / evening meals / animals taken

£24.00 to £24.00	Y	Y	Y	

Hartfell House

Nearest Road: A.701

Hartfell House is a splendid Victorian manor house located in a rural setting overlooking the hills, yet only a few mins' walk from the town. A listed building known locally for its fine interior wood-work. Accommodation is in 8 attractive, spacious & tastefully furnished bedrooms, 7 with en-suite facilities. Standing in gardens of lawns & trees, & providing an atmosphere of peaceful relaxation. Hartfell House is an elegant home.
E-mail: robert.white@virgin.net

Margaret White   Hartfell House   Hartfell Crescent   Moffat DG10 9AL   Dumfriesshire
Tel: (01683) 220153   Open: ALL YEAR (Excl. Xmas & New Year)   Map Ref No. 18

£28.50 to £35.00	Y	Y	Y	

see PHOTO over p. 396

VISA: M'CARD: AMEX:

Kirkton House

Nearest Road: A.814

Experience a blend of "olde worlde" charm, mod-ern amenities & superb views at this converted 18/19th-century farmhouse, set in a tranquil location & yet handy for Glasgow Airport (20/25 mins'), Loch Lomond, The Trossachs & most West High-land routes. En-suite bedrooms. A roaring fire on chilly evenings. Enjoy home-cooked food & good wine at dinner by oil lamplight. The dining room has the original stone walls & a fireplace, with the old swee from which the cooking pots were hung.
E-mail: bbiw@kirktonhouse.co.uk

Mr & Mrs Macdonald Kirkton House Darleith Road Cardross Dumbarton G82 5EZ Dunbartonshire
Tel: (01389) 841951   Fax (01389) 841868   Open: FEB - NOV   Map Ref No. 20

£30.00 to £36.00	N	N	N	

(no smoking)

Sandeman House

Nearest Road: A.702

Built in 1860, Sandeman House is a charming family home which has been sympathetically re-stored by Neil & Joyce Sandeman. The 3 bed-rooms are individually furnished & are bright & tastefully decorated to a very high standard. Each has an en-suite/private bathroom, T.V., tea/coffee-making facilities, hairdryer etc. A full traditional Scottish breakfast is served including home-made preserves. Shops, bars & restaurants close by. Within easy reach of most of the city's attractions.
E-mail: joycesandeman@freezone.co.uk

Joyce Sandeman   Sandeman House   33 Colinton Road   Edinburgh EH10 5DR   Edinburgh
Tel: (0131) 4478080   Fax 0131 4478080   Open: ALL YEAR   Map Ref No. 19

£25.00 to £35.00	Y	Y	N	

(no smoking)

VISA: M'CARD:

Spylaw Bank House

Nearest Road: A.70

Built in 1790, this elegant family home is situated in its own secluded grounds, only 3 miles from Edinburgh. The luxuriously appointed en-suite rooms offer T.V., tea/coffee facilities & many ex-tras. The original drawing rooms & dining rooms have open fires, period furnishings & views of the beautiful gardens where the guests may relax. A frequent bus service, 15 mins' to the centre & ample parking makes this an ideal base for sightseeing. Children over 8. Dinner by arrangment.
E-mail: angela@spylawbank.freeserve.co.uk

Mr & Mrs Martin Spylaw Bank House 2, Spylaw Avenue Colinton Edinburgh EH13 0LR Edinburgh
Tel: (0131) 4415022   Open: ALL YEAR   Map Ref No. 19

Kirkton House. Cardross.

rate £ from - to per person	children taken	evening meals	animals taken

Camus Guest House

£20.00 to £30.00 | Y | N | Y

VISA: M'CARD: AMEX:

Nearest Road: A.1

A Victorian, terraced villa overlooking the Firth of Forth, Camus House enjoys the peace of the seaside, along with an excellent bus service to the city centre, with its cultural, historical and leisure interests. The 5 guest rooms are attractive & comfortably furnished, and have wash basins, colour T.V., radio alarms & tea/coffee-making facilities. 4 of the rooms are en-suite. A genuine and friendly welcome is assured at Camus House.
E-mail: rowan@camus.ndo.co.uk

Debbie Rowan   Camus Guest House   4 Seaview Terrace   Joppa   Edinburgh EH15 2HD   Edinburgh
Tel: (0131) 6572003   Fax 0131 6572003   Open: ALL YEAR   Map Ref No. 19

Kenvie Guest House

£26.00 to £30.00 | Y | N | N

VISA: M'CARD:

Nearest Road: A.7, A.68, A.1

Kenvie Guest House is charming, comfortable, warm, friendly & inviting. This small Victorian town house is situated in a quiet residential street, 1 small block from the main road, leading to the city centre (an excellent bus service) & the bypass to all routes. Offering, for your comfort, lots of caring touches, including complimentary tea/coffee, colour T.V. & no-smoking rooms. Private facilities available. A warm welcome awaits you.
E-mail: dorothy@kenvie.co.uk

Mrs Dorothy Vidler   Kenvie Guest House   16 Kilmaurs Road   Edinburgh EH16 5DA   Edinburgh
Tel: (0131) 6681964   Fax 0131 6681926   Open: ALL YEAR   Map Ref No. 19

Kildonan Lodge Hotel

£35.00 to £59.00 | Y | Y | N

see PHOTO over p. 398

VISA: M'CARD: AMEX:

Nearest Road: A.701

Ideally situated in central Edinburgh, Kildonan Lodge is an outstanding example of Victorian elegance providing the perfect setting for your visit to Scotland's capital. Relax & enjoy a 'dram' at the Honesty bar. Each of the well-appointed non-smoking en-suite bedrooms have T.V., 'phone, radio/alarm & welcome trays. Spa bath & 4-poster beds available in selected rooms. Car park. Delicious wholesome Scottish breakfasts are served. A warm friendly welcome awaits you.
E-mail: kildonanlodge@compuserve.com

Mrs Maggie Urquhart   Kildonan Lodge Hotel   27 Craigmillar Park   Edinburgh EH16 5PE   Edinburgh
Tel: (0131) 6672793   Fax 0131 6679777   Open: ALL YEAR   Map Ref No. 19

Kingsley Guest House

£20.00 to £35.00 | Y | N | N

Nearest Road: A.701

A warm, friendly welcome awaits you at this Victorian terraced villa. Offering 5 comfortably furnished bedrooms, each with either en-suite or private facilities, T.V. & tea/coffee-making facilities. A full English or Continental breakfast is served. Kingsley Guest House is conveniently situated in the south of the city with an excellent bus service at the door to & from the city centre with its many tourist attractions. Private parking.
E-mail: accom.kingsley@virgin.net

Lyn Redmayne   Kingsley Guest House   30 Craigmillar Park   Newington   Edinburgh EH16 5PS
Tel: (0131) 6673177   Tel/Fax 0131 6678439   Open: ALL YEAR   Map Ref No. 19

Kildonan Lodge Hotel. Edinburgh.

rate £ from - to per person	children taken	evening meals taken	animals taken		

Southdown Guest House

£18.00 to £40.00	Y	N	Y

see PHOTO over p. 400

VISA: M'CARD:

Nearest Road: A.701

Good value accommodation is offered at this friendly guest house which is situated on the south side of Edinburgh. John & Muriel are welcoming hosts who enjoy caring for their guests. There is a comfortable lounge with books & board games in which guests may choose to relax after a day's sight-seeing. A hearty Scottish breakfast is served. 6 comfortable bedrooms (non-smoking), each with T.V. & tea/coffee facilities. Parking. An ideal spot from which to explore historic Edinburgh.
E-mail: muriel@southdownguesthouse.fsnet.co.uk

John & Muriel Hamilton	Southdown Guest House	20 Craigmillar Park	Edinburgh EH16 5PS
Tel: (0131) 6672410	Fax 0131 6676056	Open: ALL YEAR	Map Ref No. 19

Tiree Guest House

£22.50 to £30.00	Y	N	N

Nearest Road: A.701

Situated on the south side of Edinburgh, about 1 1/2 miles from the city centre. Offering accommodation in 6 comfortable rooms, all with en-suite facilities. All rooms have colour T.V. & tea/coffee makers. Conveniently located for Edinburgh University, Holyrood Palace & the shopping centre. Children are very welcome here, & are given reduced rates. (Min. age 6 years.) A full Scottish breakfast is served.
E-mail: resrvations@tireeguesthouse.com

Norah Alexander	Tiree Guest House	26 Craigmillar Park	Edinburgh EH16 5PS	Edinburgh
Tel: (0131) 667 7477	Fax 0131 662 1608	Open: ALL YEAR		Map Ref No. 19

Frederick House Hotel

£25.00 to £45.00	Y	Y	N

VISA: M'CARD: AMEX:

Nearest Road: A.1

Frederick House Hotel is perfectly situated in the very heart of Edinburgh's city centre, a stones' throw from Princes Street. All of the 44 newly refurbished & tastefully decorated bedrooms feature en-suite bathrooms (with bath & shower); breakfast is served in your room. Your hosts' aim is to make your stay as comfortable & relaxing as possible, with all modern conveniences combined together with an 'olde worlde' atmosphere.
E-mail: frederickhouse@ednet.co.uk

Emily Walton	Frederick House Hotel	42 Frederick Street	Edinburgh EH2 1EX	Edinburgh
Tel: (0131) 2261999	Fax 0131 6247064	Open: ALL YEAR		Map Ref No. 19

Elmview

£37.50 to £47.50	N	N	N

VISA: M'CARD:

Nearest Road: A.702

Marny Hill's luxurious bed & breakfast is situated in the heart of Edinburgh within easy walking distance of Edinburgh Castle & Princes Street (1 km). Elmview is a wonderful base from which to enjoy your stay in Edinburgh. Each bedroom has been elegantly furnished throughout & all have en-suite facilities. Direct-dial 'phones, fridges, fresh flowers are but a few of the thoughtful extras in each bedroom. A delightful home.
E-mail: marny@elmview.co.uk.

Marny Hill	Elmview	15 Glengyle Terrace	Edinburgh EH2 9LN	Edinburgh
Tel: (0131) 228 1973	Fax 0131 229 7296	Open: ALL YEAR		Map Ref No. 19

Southdown Guest House.   Edinburgh.

Gerald's Place. Edinburgh.

	rate £ from - to per person	children taken	evening meals	animals taken

Geralds Place

Nearest Road: A.1

Your host Gerald, welcomes you to his delightful home full of character, colour & comforts. The accommodation includes 2 double bedrooms (each with one king-size bed or 2 3ft beds of supreme comfort & quality) with 2 private bathrooms (each with power shower & bath tub). It is the ideal place for 2 couples travelling together. The full Scottish breakfast is a feast. Abercromby Place is at the very centre of the city, only 6 mins' walk from Waverley station. One of the finest streets in Edinburgh.
E-mail: bbb@geraldsplace.com

£29.50 to £39.50	N	N	N

see PHOTO over
p. 401

Gerald Della-Porta   Geralds Place   21B Abercromby Place   Edinburgh EH3 6QE   Edinburgh
Tel: (0131) 5587017   Fax 0131 5587014   Open: ALL YEAR   Map Ref No. 19

16 Lynedoch Place

Nearest Road: A.1

A beautiful, listed Georgian terraced house, built in 1821 & situated in the heart of Georgian New Town. This elegantly furnished house, though modernised to the highest of standards, still retains all its original features including sash windows, cornices & marble fireplaces. There are 3 attractive & well-appointed en-suite bedrooms. Situated within 2 mins' walk of Princes Street, this is the perfect spot for exploring this vibrant city with shops, restaurants & places of historic interest.
E-mail: susie.lynedoch@btinternet.com

£35.00 to £50.00	Y	N	Y

VISA: M'CARD:

Susie Hamilton   16 Lynedoch Place   Edinburgh EH3 7PY   Edinburgh
Tel: (0131) 2255507   Fax 0131 2264185   Open: ALL YEAR   Map Ref No.19

Ellesmere Guest House

Nearest Road: A.702

Guests are made welcome at this very elegant tastefully restored Victorian town house, quietly situated overlooking golf links in the centre of Edinburgh. Rooms are all en-suite & decorated to a very high standard & well-equipped with every comfort in mind. Delicious breakfasts are served. 'A home away from home.' Convenient for castle, Princes Street, Royal Mile, International Conference Centre, theatres & restaurants.
E-mail: celia@edinburghbandb.co.uk

£28.00 to £38.00	N	N	N

see PHOTO over
p. 403

Mrs C. Leishman   Ellesmere Guest House   11 Glengyle Terrace   Edinburgh EH3 9LN   Edinburgh
Tel: (0131) 229 4823   Fax 0131 229 5285   Open: ALL YEAR   Map Ref No. 19

Visit our website at:
http://www.bestbandb.co.uk

Ellesmere Guest House. Edinburgh.

Scotland
Edinburgh

The Stuarts

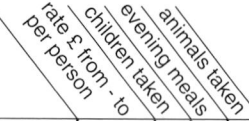

Nearest Road: A.702

Quietly situated overlooking a park, Stuarts is warm, comfortable & spacious, with a friendly atmosphere. There are 3 attractive rooms, all with colour T.V. & tea/coffee-making facilities & an en-suite bathroom. Jon & Gloria will welcome you, & help you with where to go, what to do & where to eat. Bookings of 3 nights or more taken in advance. Centrally located & within easy reach of the Castle, Princes St., shops, theatres & restaurants.
E-mail: best@the-stuarts.com

£40.00 to £50.00   Y   N   N

VISA: M'CARD: AMEX:

Jon & Gloria Stuart   The Stuarts   17 Glengyle Terrace   Edinburgh EH3 9LN   Edinburgh
Tel: (0131) 2299559   Fax 0131 2292226   Open: ALL YEAR   Map Ref No. 19

The Town House

Nearest Road: A.702

Attractive Victorian town house, located in the city centre. Theatres & restaurants are only minutes walk away. The Town House has been fully restored & tastefully decorated, retaining many original architectural features. The bedrooms are tastefully furnished & individually decorated, all have en-suite bath or shower & w.c., radio/alarm, colour T.V., hairdryer & tea/coffee tray. Parking is situated at the rear of the house. Self-catering apartment also available. Children over 10.
E-mail: susan@thetownhouse.com

£28.00 to £38.00   Y   N   N

Susan Virtue   The Town House   65 Gilmore Place   Edinburgh EH3 9NU   Edinburgh
Tel: (0131) 2291985   Open: ALL YEAR   Map Ref No. 19

Ravensdown Guest House

Nearest Road: A.1, A.199

Built at the beginning of the 1900s, Ravensdown offers unsurpassed panoramic views of the Edinburgh skyline. 6 individually decorated rooms with T.V. & coffee/tea facilities & an en-suite or private bathroom. Guests may socialise in the lounge. Your friendly hosts are on hand to give advice about local attractions & tours. A delicious breakfast sets you up for a busy day of sightseeing. Excellent bus service means you can leave the car in the car park & commute the 2 miles to the centre.
E-mail: len@ravensdown.freeserve.co.uk

£23.00 to £35.00   Y   N   N

Leonard Welch   Ravensdown Guest House   248 Ferry Road   Edinburgh EH5 3AN   Edinburgh
Tel: (0131) 5525438   Fax 0131 5527559   Open: ALL YEAR   Map Ref No. 19

Ben Cruachan

Nearest Road: A.1

Guests are assured of a warm welcome & a friendly atmosphere at this attractive house, situated 1 km from Princes Street. Offering comfortable en-suite bedrooms, well-equipped with every comfort in mind & serving an excellent breakfast. Centrally situated within easy reach of the castle, Royal Mile, Holyrood Palace, shops, theatres & restaurants. Unrestricted parking & on all main bus routes. Children over 10 years welcome.
E-mail: bencruachan@blueyonder.co.uk

£25.00 to £35.00   Y   N   N

N. Stark   Ben Cruachan   17 McDonald Road   Edinburgh EH7 4LX   Edinburgh
Tel: (0131) 5563709   Open: APR - OCT   Map Ref No. 19

rate £ from - to per person	children taken	evening meals taken	animals taken		

Greenside Hotel

£22.50 to £45.00 | Y | Y | N

Nearest Road: A.1

Built in 1820, the Greenside Hotel is an elegant Georgian town-house hotel situated in the city centre & surrounded by peaceful garden settings in one of Edinburgh's most prestigious terraces. A few mins' walk from Waverly Station, Princes St., tourist attractions, local restaurants & theatre. There are 16 tastefully decorated rooms with all facilities. Large family rooms also available. A full Scottish Breakfast is served each morning.

VISA: M'CARD: AMEX:

E-mail: greensidehotel@ednet.co.uk

Alan Maguire   Greenside Hotel   9 Royal Terrace   Edinburgh EH7 5AB   Edinburgh
Tel: (0131) 5570022/5570121   Fax 0131 5570022   Open: ALL YEAR   Map Ref No. 19

Ailsa Craig Hotel

£22.50 to £45.00 | Y | Y | N

Nearest Road: A.1

Ailsa Craig Hotel is situated in the heart of Edinburgh near the city centre in one of the most prestigious terraces. This elegant Georgian town house hotel is situated only 10 mins' walk from Princes Street, Waverly Station & many attractions. 18 tastefully furnished & decorated bedrooms, 16 with en-suite facilities, & all with 'phone, hairdryer, colour T.V. & tea/coffee-making facilities. A delicious breakfast & good evening meals are served. A perfect base for exploring Edinburgh.

VISA: M'CARD: AMEX:

E-mail: ailsacraighotel@ednet.co.uk

Cathy Hamilton   Ailsa Craig Hotel   24 Royal Terrace   Edinburgh EH7 5AH   Edinburgh
Tel: (0131) 5566055/5561022   Fax 0131 5566055   Open: ALL YEAR   Map Ref No. 19

Glenalmond Guest House

£25.00 to £40.00 | Y | N | N

Nearest Road: A.701

Glenalmond is an attractive family-run guest house, situated only 5 mins' from the city centre. The house is beautifully furnished throughout & offers 10 delightful bedrooms, many with either 4-poster or canopy beds. (5 ground floor rooms.) Each bedroom is spacious & has quality furnishings, T.V. & a tea/coffee tray. A full Scottish breakfast is served & includes porridge & home-baked scones. This is an elegant base from which to explore Edinburgh. Parking. Children over 3.

E-mail: glen@almond25.freeserve.co.uk

Deb & Dave Fraser Glenalmond Guest House 25 Mayfield Gardens Edinburgh EH9 2BX Edinburgh
Tel: (0131) 6682392   Fax 0131 6682392   Open: ALL YEAR   Map Ref No. 19

Parklands Guest House

£20.00 to £35.00 | Y | N | N

Nearest Road: A.701

Parklands is an attractive Victorian terraced house conveniently located 1 1/2 miles from Princes Street & all the main tourist attractions. Accommodation in 6 bedrooms, each is furnished to a high standard & is fully equipped with en-suite/private facilities, colour T.V. & tea/coffee makers. A full Scottish breakfast is served. Nearby are many excellent restaurants. Parklands is family-run with a friendly atmosphere. You are assured of a warm welcome.

E-mail: parklands_guesthouse@yahoo.com

Alan Drummond   Parklands Guest House   20 Mayfield Gardens   Edinburgh EH9 2BZ   Edinburgh
Tel: (0131) 6677184   Fax 0131 6672011   Open: ALL YEAR   Map Ref No. 19

Scotland
Edinburgh & Fifeshire

| | rate £ from - to per person | evening meals | children taken | animals taken |

Rowan Guest House

Nearest Road: A.701

Elegant Victorian home in one of the city's loveliest areas with free parking & only a 10-min. bus ride to the centre. The castle, Royal Mile, restaurants & other amenities easily reached. The charmingly decorated bedrooms are comfortably & tastefully furnished with complimentary tea/coffee & biscuits. Breakfast, including traditional porridge & freshly baked scones, will keep you going until dinner! Attentive, welcoming & friendly hosts. Partially non-smoking.
E-mail: angela@rowan-house.co.uk

£25.00 to £34.00 — Y N N

VISA: M'CARD:

Alan & Angela Vidler   Rowan Guest House   13 Glenorchy Terrace   Edinburgh EH9 2DQ   Edinburgh
Tel: (0131) 6672463   Fax 0131 6672463   Open: ALL YEAR   Map Ref No. 19

Ashcroft Farm Guest House

Nearest Road: A.71

New farmhouse set in beautifully landscaped gardens, enjoying lovely views of the surrounding farmland. 10 miles from Edinburgh, 5 miles from the airport, city bypass, M.8/M.9, Ingliston & Livingston. Parking. Bedrooms, including a 4-poster, are attractively furnished in pine with co-ordinating fabrics. Good bus/train service to city centre (20 mins). Choice of breakfasts with home-made sausage, smoked salmon, kippers, local produce & even whisky marmalade. Children over 5.
E-mail: scott5diamonds@aol.com

£28.00 to £30.00 — Y N N

VISA: M'CARD: AMEX:

Derek & Elizabeth Scott   Ashcroft Farm Guest House   East Calder Nr. Edinburgh EH53 0ET   Edinburgh
Tel: (01506) 884327   Fax 01506 881810   Open: ALL YEAR   Map Ref No. 21

The Spindrift

Nearest Road: A.917

Set in the picturesque fishing village of Anstruther, The Spindrift is an imposing, stone-built Victorian home with many original features carefully restored. 8 individually & tastefully furnished bedrooms with en-suite/private bathrooms, T.V., hospitality tray & more. Delicious evening meals served. Only 10 mins' from St. Andrews with its famous golf courses & excellent beaches. An ideal base for exploring the splendours of central Scotland. Children over 10. Animals by arrangement.
E-mail: info@thespindrift.co.uk

£26.50 to £32.50 — Y Y Y

VISA: M'CARD:

Kenneth & Christine Lawson   The Spindrift   Pittenweem Road   Anstruther KY10 3DT   Fifeshire
Tel: (01333) 310573   Fax 01333 310573   Open: ALL YEAR   Map Ref No. 22

Ardchoille Farmhouse

Nearest Road: A.91, B.936

Relax & enjoy the warm comfort, delicious Taste of Scotland food & the excellent hospitality at Ardchoille Farmhouse. 3 tastefully furnished twin-bedded rooms, each with an en-suite/private bathroom, colour T.V. & tea/coffee trays offering home-made butter shortbread. Large comfortable lounge, & elegant dining room with fine china & crystal. Dinner by arrangement. Close by the Royal Palace of Falkland, home of Mary Queen of Scots. 20 mins from St. Andrews, & 1 hr Edinburgh. Ideal base for golfing & touring. Children over 12.

£25.00 to £35.00 — Y Y N

VISA: M'CARD:

Donald & Isobel Steven   Ardchoille Farmhouse   Dunshalt   Auchtermuchty KY14 7EY   Fifeshire
Tel: (01337) 828414   Fax 01337 828414   Open: ALL YEAR   Map Ref No. 23

rate £ from - to per person	children taken	evening meals	animals taken		

Pitlethie Farm B & B

£25.00 to £30.00 | Y | Y | N

VISA: M'CARD:

Nearest Road: A.919

Pitlethie, a comfortable family farmhouse is situated in quiet countryside with views over prime farmland to Tentsmuir Forest which skirts miles of unspoilt sandy beach. The accommodation (2 bedrooms) is ideal for up to 4 people travelling together. Private facilities. The house is artistically decorated, chintz, tapestries & patchwork prevail to make this a comfortable & convenient place to stay whilst enjoying historic St. Andrews & the surrounding area. Dinner by arrangement (local & home produce). Children over 8.

Mrs Gillian Black   Pitlethie Farm B & B   Leuchars   St. Andrews KY16 0DP   Fifeshire
Tel: (01334) 838649   Fax 01334 839281   Open: ALL YEAR   Map Ref No. 24

Cambo House

£42.00 to £48.00 | Y | Y | N

VISA: M'CARD:

Nearest Road: A. 917

The Erskine family home since 1688, this impressive Victorian mansion house, built in 1881, lies at the heart of a 1200 acre estate in one of the most unspoilt areas of Scotland yet is only 1 1/2 hours from Edinburgh & the Highlands. 3 elegantly furnished bedrooms (1 with 4-poster) with en-suite/private facilities. The family welcome you to share the comfort of their home, absorb the beauty of the gardens & woodland walks & unwind in the restful atmosphere. Dinner by arrangement.
E-mail: cambohouse@cs.com

Peter & Catherine Erskine   Cambo House   Kingsbarns   St. Andrews KY16 8QD   Fifeshire
Tel: (01333) 450054   Fax 01333 450987   Open: ALL YEAR (Excl. Xmas & New Year)   Map Ref No. 25

Theatre Hotel

£22.50 to £35.00 | Y | N | N

VISA: M'CARD: AMEX:

Nearest Road: M.8

Peacefully located in the heart of Glasgow, this 52 bedroom hotel is a stylish listed Victorian building, combining elegant accommodation with the warmth of traditional Scottish hospitality. Only 2 mins drive from the M.8, it is also within walking distance of Glasgow's mainline stations & only 15 mins from Glasgow International Airport. Closeby are many museums, galleries, theatres & shops. (Please note only a Continental breakfast is provided here & it is taken in your room.)
E-mail: theatrehotel@clara.net

Michael Gilbert   Theatre Hotel   27 Elmbank Street   Glasgow G2 4PB   Glasgow
Tel: (0141) 227 2772   Fax 0141 227 2774   Open: ALL YEAR   Map Ref No. 26

New Borland

£24.00 to £25.00 | Y | N | N

Nearest Road: A.77, A.726

Near the picturesque village of Eaglesham, yet only 9 miles from Glasgow, a warm Scottish welcome is assured at this converted barn. 2 twin rooms (ensuite) & 2 single rooms sharing a bathroom. All rooms have T.V., radio/alarm & hostess tray, & are furnished to a high standard. Lounge (log fire) & games room. Hearty Scottish breakfasts are served. Convenient for Glasgow, M.74, Loch Lomond, The Trossachs, Burns Country & the Burrell. Golf & fishing nearby. Parking. Children over 12.
E-mail: newborland@dial.pipex.com

Mrs Fiona Allison   New Borland   Glasgow Road   Eaglesham   Glasgow G76 0DN   Glasgow
Tel: (01355) 302051   Fax 01355 302051   Open: ALL YEAR   Map Ref No. 27

The Grange. Fort William.

Column headers (rotated): rate £ from - to per person | children taken | evening meals | animals taken

East Lochhead Country House

rate £ from-to per person	children taken	evening meals	animals taken
£32.50 to £32.50	Y	Y	Y

(No smoking symbol)

Nearest Road: A.760

East Lochhead is a large 100-year-old Scottish farmhouse commanding beautiful views to the south east over Barr Loch & the Renfrewshire hills. 3 beautifully furnished bedrooms with panoramic views, an en-suite/private bathroom, T.V. & tea/coffee facilities. Janet is an enthusiastic cook & the breakfast & dinner are delicious. (Vegetarian & special diets catered for.) An ideal base for visiting Glasgow & touring Ayrshire, the Clyde coast, the Trossachs (Rob Roy country) & Loch Lomond.
E-mail: eastlochhead@aol.com

VISA: M'CARD: AMEX:

Janet Anderson   East Lochhead Country House   Largs Road   Lochwinnoch PA12 4DX   Glasgow
Tel: (01505) 842610   Fax 01505 842610   Open: ALL YEAR   Map Ref No. 28

Feith Mhor Lodge

£25.00 to £28.00	Y	N	Y

Nearest Road: A.9

Situated in a peaceful but accessible valley, 25 miles south of Inverness, Feith Mhor Lodge ('Fay Moor') offers bed & breakfast accommodation in an elegant Victorian country home with 6 tastefully furnished en-suite bedrooms. Your hosts specialise in party bookings for groups enjoying the many sporting activities of the area. Shooting, fishing, falconry & golf parties can be exclusively booked on a full board basis.
E-mail: feith.mhor@btinternet.com

VISA: M'CARD:

John Gardner   Feith Mhor Lodge   Station Road   Carrbridge PH23 3AP   Inverness-shire
Tel: (01479) 841621   Fax 01479 841621   Open: ALL YEAR   Map Ref No. 29

Invergloy House

£23.00 to £25.00	Y	N	N

(No smoking symbol)

Nearest Road: A.82

A really interesting Scottish coach house, dating back 120 years, offering 3 charming, comfortable twin-bedded rooms, with modern facilities, 2 with en-suite shower rooms & 1 with an en-suite bathroom. 5 miles north of the village of Spean Bridge towards Inverness, it is signposted on the left, along a wooded drive. Guests have use of own sitting room, overlooking Loch Lochy in 50 acres of superb woodland of rhododendron & azaleas. Fishing from the private beach. Children over 8 .
E-mail: cairns@invergloy-house.co.uk

Mrs Margaret Cairns   Invergloy House   Spean Bridge   Nr. Fort William PH34 4DY   Inverness-shire
Tel: (01397) 712681   Fax 01397 712681   Open: ALL YEAR   Map Ref No. 30

The Grange

£40.00 to £48.00	N	N	N

(No smoking symbol)

see PHOTO over p. 408

Nearest Road: A.82

Set in quiet gardens overlooking Loch Linnhe, yet only 10 mins from the town centre. The Grange offers superb accommodation in 4 en-suite rooms, each well-equipped & enhanced by a very relaxed atmosphere. The area is charming & the house is well-situated, only 1 1/2 hrs from Oban, Inverness & the Isles. An ideal base for touring the Highlands, & returning to a comfortable lounge log fire for chilly evenings. Vegetarians catered for.
E-mail: jcampbell@grangefortwilliam.com

VISA: M'CARD:

John & Joan Campbell   The Grange   Grange Road   Fort William PH33 6JF   Inverness-shire
Tel: (01397) 705516   Fax 01397 701595   Open: MAR - NOV   Map Ref No. 31

Ashburn House. Fort William.

Column headers (rotated):
- rate £ from - to per person
- children taken
- evening meals
- animals taken

Ashburn House

rate £ from-to per person	children taken	evening meals	animals taken
£30.00 to £45.00	Y	N	N

(non-smoking symbol)

see PHOTO over p. 410

VISA: M'CARD: AMEX:

Nearest Road: A.82

Ashburn is a splendid Victorian house personally run by Highland hosts. Quietly situated by the shores of Loch Linnhe only 600 yards from the town centre & among others the renowned Crannog Seafood Restaurant. An excellent base for touring the Highlands. Sample an imaginative Highland breakfast, served at your own individual table, complemented with freshly baked scones from the aga. 7 en-suite bedrooms, 4 with super-king-size beds. Parking. Brochure & weekly rates available.
E-mail: ashburn.house@tinyworld.co.uk

B. B. Henderson   Ashburn House   Achintore Road   Fort William PH33 6RQ   Inverness-shire
Tel: (01397) 706000   Fax 01397 702024   Open: MAR - NOV   Map Ref No. 31

The Old Royal Guest House

rate £ from-to per person	children taken	evening meals	animals taken
£20.00 to £30.00	Y	N	N

VISA: M'CARD:

Nearest Road: A.9

Personally managed by the resident proprietor Jane Ozmus, The Old Royal is conveniently situated in the centre of town, opposite the railway station. Accommodation is in 12 comfortable guest bedrooms, 5 with en-suite facilities. All have colour T.V. & tea/coffee makers. The Old Royal has a home-from-home atmosphere, & provides visitors with a comfortable holiday base from which to tour the locality. Children over 3 yrs.
E-mail: info@old-royal.co.uk

Jane Ozmus   The Old Royal Guest House   10 Union Street   Inverness IV1 1PL   Inverness-shire
Tel: (01463) 230551   Fax 01463 711916   Open: ALL YEAR   Map Ref No. 32

Ballindarroch House

rate £ from-to per person	children taken	evening meals	animals taken
£20.00 to £30.00	Y	N	Y

Nearest Road: A.9, B.862

Ballindarroch was originally built as a shooting lodge around 1870, & stands in 10 acres of woodland gardens above the Caledonian Canal. Decorated with hand-painted wallpaper & furnished with antiques & an eclectic selection of family pieces, the house offers a totally relaxing & peaceful environment only 10 mins' from Inverness. The generous breakfast includes local specialities & home-made bread. Lovely river & woodland walks. French, Italian, Spanish & German spoken.
E-mail: BandB@ballindarroch.fsnet.co.uk

Alison Parsons & Philip Alvy   Ballindarroch House   Aldourie   Inverness IV2 6EL   Inverness-shire
Tel: (01463) 751348   Fax 01463 751372   Open: ALL YEAR   Map Ref No. 32

Easter Dalziel Farmhouse

rate £ from-to per person	children taken	evening meals	animals taken
£20.00 to £23.00	Y	Y	Y

VISA: M'CARD:

Nearest Road: A.96, B.9039

This Scottish farming family offer the visitor a friendly Highland welcome on their 200-acre stock/arable farm. 3 charming bedrooms are available in the delightful early-Victorian farmhouse. The lounge has log fire & T.V. Delicious home cooking & baking served, including a choice of breakfasts. Evening meals available summer only. Ideal base for exploring the scenic Highlands. Local attractions are Cawdor Castle, Culloden, Fort George, Loch Ness & nearby Castle Stuart.
E-mail: BBB@easterdalzielfarm.co.uk

Bob & Margaret Pottie   Easter Dalziel Farmhouse   Dalcross   Inverness IV2 7JL   Inverness-shire
Tel: (01667) 462213 Fax 01667 462213 Open: ALL YEAR (Excl. Xmas & New Year)   Map Ref No. 33

Scotland
Isle of Skye & Kinross

Corry Lodge

Nearest Road: A.87

Corry Lodge, on the Isle of Skye, is a most attractive period house dating from the late 18th century. It has a fine open outlook over Broadford Bay, but with a sheltered location, & approximately 1,150 metres of unspoilt sea frontage. There are 4 comfortable & tastefully furnished bedrooms, each with en-suite bathroom, radio, colour T.V. & tea/coffee-making facilities. Corry Lodge forms an ideal base from which to tour the island either by car or bicycle, or on foot. Animals by arrangement.

E-mail: jane@corrylodge.co.uk

| | £25.00 to £30.00 | Y | Y | Y |

VISA: M'CARD:

Anthony & Jane Wilcken
Tel: (01471) 822235
Corry Lodge Liveras
Fax 01471 822318
Broadford IV49 9AA Isle of Skye
Open: APR - OCT Map Ref No. 34

Lyndale House

Nearest Road: A.850

Lyndale is an elegant house in a wonderfully secluded position overlooking the sea. The spacious rooms are tastefully & comfortably furnished to the highest standard. Hidden at the end of a long wooded driveway, Lyndale House has been painstakingly restored to its original 18th-century style. It is now a beautiful family home & offers tranquility & seclusion with magnificent views & stunning sunsets. Ideally situated for exploring the rest of the island. A non-smoking house.

E-mail: linda@lyndale.free-online.co.uk

| | £40.00 to £40.00 | Y | N | N |

Marcus & Linda Ridsdill Smith
Tel: (01470) 582329
Lyndale House Edinbane IV51 9PX Isle of Skye
Open: ALL YEAR (Excl. Xmas & New Year) Map Ref No. 35

Glenview Inn & Restaurant

Nearest Road: A.855

A traditional island house lying between Trotternish Ridge & the sea & ideally situated for exploring North Skye. All the bedrooms have private facilities & are individually decorated, warm & comfortable, with tea/coffee-making facilities. Glenview offers a relaxed & friendly atmosphere & the best of Scotland's varied larder. Only fresh food is used to create a menu including traditional, ethnic & vegetarian specialities. Glenview is an excellent base for a relaxing break.

E-mail: valtos@lineone.net

| | £20.00 to £30.00 | Y | Y | Y |

VISA: M'CARD:

Paul & Cathie Booth
Tel: (01470) 562248
Glenview Inn & Restaurant Culnacnoc Staffin IV51 9JH Isle of Skye
Fax 01470 562211
Open: MAR - OCT Map Ref No. 36

Caplawhead

Nearest Road: A.823, A.91

In the beautiful 'Heart of Scotland' lies Caplawhead, a lovingly restored country house & haven to the traveller. On arrival you are given tea in the drawing room with its tower which opens to the garden beyond. Upstairs, the comfortable & attractive bedrooms, 1 double & 1 twin, have lovely views & en-suite facilities. Breakfast is a feast with local produce & homemade preserves & a wonderful village pub provides evening meals. Children & animals by arrangement.

E-mail: hamish-frances@caplawhead.freeserve.co.uk

| | £22.50 to £25.00 | Y | N | Y |

Hamish & Frances Lindsay
Tel: (01259) 781556
Caplawhead Yett's O'Muckhart Rumbling Bridge KY13 0QD Kinross
Open: ALL YEAR (Excl. Xmas) Map Ref No. 37

rate £ from - to per person	children taken	evening meals taken	animals taken

---

Blervie

£30.00 to £30.00 — Y Y Y

VISA: M'CARD:

Nearest Road: A.96

Don't come here if you like colour T.V. in bedrooms, wall-mounted hairdryers, or fixed, insincere smiles. However, if you would like to stay with "country gentlefolk marooned in the 21st-century", in what is primarily a family home, then come to Blervie. Enjoy well-appointed furniture & furnishings, family memorabilia, pictures, 4-poster beds & private bathrooms; while experiencing genuine old-fashioned hospitality in a charming A-listed, 18th-century country house. Children over 10.
E-mail: meiklejohn@btinternet.com

Lt. Cdr. & Mrs I. P. F. Meiklejohn   Blervie   By Forres IV36 2RH   Morayshire
Tel: (01309) 672358   Fax 01309 672358   Open: ALL YEAR   Map Ref No. 40

The Pines

£30.00 to £45.00 — Y Y Y

(non-smoking)

VISA: M'CARD:

Nearest Road: A.9, A.95

The Pines has a timeless atmosphere of peaceful tranquillity & backs directly onto beautiful woodlands. Antiques, water colours & oil paintings increase the sense of heritage in this fine 19th-century Scottish country house. Bedrooms have en-suite or private facilities & their own distinctive style & furnishings. The dining room creates a warm ambience for the candlelit dinners which are a blend of traditional & modern Scottish cooking. Children over 12. Animals by arrangement.
E-mail: info@thepinesgrantown.co.uk

Gwen & Michael Stewart   The Pines   Woodside Avenue   Grantown-on-Spey PH26 3JR   Morayshire
Tel: (01479) 872092   Fax 01479 872092   Open: APR - OCT (& by arrangement)   Map Ref No. 41

Ardconnel House

£28.00 to £35.00 — Y Y N

(non-smoking)

*see PHOTO over
p. 414*

VISA: M'CARD:

Nearest Road: A.95

Built in 1890, during the Victorian era of elegance, the award-winning Ardconnel House stands in its own spacious grounds overlooking a glorious pine forest, Lochan & Cromdale Hills. 6 bedrooms are en-suite, with quality beds, colour T.V., hairdryer & welcome tray, & are charmingly decorated. A superb 4-poster bedroom. Excellent home cooking is complemented by a well-selected, modestly priced wine list. Taste of Scotland selected member. Children over 8 yrs.
E-mail: enquiry@ardconnel.com

Mr & Mrs Bouchard   Ardconnel House   Woodlands Terrace   Grantown-on-Spey PH26 3JU   Morayshire
Tel: (01479) 872104   Fax 01479 872104   Open: APR - OCT   Map Ref No. 41

Creagan House

£42.50 to £52.50 — Y Y Y

VISA: M'CARD: AMEX:

Nearest Road: A.84

A peaceful little gem of comfort surrounded by beautiful scenery. Accommodation is in 5 charming bedrooms with many thoughtful extras & a growing collection of antiques. Friendly perfection is your hosts' aim. The baronial dining hall helps make each evening a special occasion, using meat from Perthshire, fruits & vegetables grown locally, herbs from the garden, all complemented by a good selection of fine wines.
E-mail: eatandstay@creaganhouse.co.uk

Cherry & Gordon Gunn   Creagan House   Strathyre   Callander FK18 8ND   Perthshire
Tel: (01877) 384638   Fax 01877 384319   Open: MAR - JAN   Map Ref No. 44

Ardconnel House. Grantown-on-Spey.

rate £ from - to per person	children taken	evening meals	animals taken

---

Leny House

| £45.00 to £55.00 | Y | Y | N |

Nearest Road: A.84

Award-winning Leny House is a spacious country mansion, set in acres of farmland in the Leny Hills. This outstanding house was originally built as a fortalice in 1513 & featured heavily in much of the local history, particularly during the Jacobite rebellion. Now, it has been sympathetically restored & is elegantly furnished throughout. The attractive guest bedrooms offer every modern-day comfort. Dinner is available at the inn on the estate. A perfect location for a relaxing break. Children over 12.

E-mail: res@lenyestate.com

see PHOTO over
p. 416

VISA: M'CARD:

| *Frances Roebuck* | *Leny House* | *Callander FK17 8HA* | *Perthshire* |
| *Tel: (01877) 331078* | *Fax 01877 331335* | *Open: APR - OCT* | *Map Ref No. 43* |

The Lodge House

| £25.00 to £25.00 | Y | Y | Y |

Nearest Road: A.82

Although just by the roadside, The Lodge is secluded & all rooms enjoy an excellent view of the surrounding hills & glens. With only 6 rooms (all of which are very comfortable), your hosts aim to provide a personal service & compliment this with good Scottish home-cooking. In the small, informal bar, there is an extensive selection of malts for guests to enjoy both before & after dinner. The Lodge House is ideal for a relaxing break.

E-mail: stay@lodgehouse.co.uk

VISA: M'CARD:

| *Gordon Gaughan* | *The Lodge House* | *Crianlarich FK20 8RU* | *Perthshire* |
| *Tel: (01838) 300276* | *Fax 01838 300276* | *Open: ALL YEAR* | *Map Ref No. 45* |

Mackeanston House

| £36.00 to £38.00 | Y | Y | Y |

Nearest Road: A.84

Here you will find a touch of luxury in a peaceful rural setting. A 17th-century family home with stylish en-suite bedrooms set in a mature garden looking south to Stirling Castle & the Wallace monument, within sight of Rob Roy country & the Trossachs. 1 hr's drive from Glasgow, Perth & Edinburgh & easy reach of airports. Home-baked bread, fresh fruit & vegetables from the garden feature in gourmet menus. A pretty traditional cottage is available as an annexe.

E-mail: mackean.house@cwcom.net

VISA: M'CARD:

| *Colin & Fiona Graham* | *Mackeanston House* | *Doune FK16 6AX* | *Perthshire* |
| *Tel: (01786) 850213* | *Fax 01786 850414* | *Open: ALL YEAR* | *Map Ref No. 47* |

Kinnaird Guest House

| £22.50 to £25.00 | N | N | N |

Nearest Road: A.85

Would you like to relax in comfort? Then the warm, friendly atmosphere at Kinnaird is just the place. John & Tricia aim for high standards & traditional home comforts & cater for individual needs. Beautifully situated overlooking a leafy park to the south, & the charming town centre is within easy walking distance. Buses & trains are also within easy reach. An ideal base for exploring this beautiful region & many historical attractions. Children over 12 years welcome.

E-mail: tricia@kinnaird-gh.demon.co.uk

VISA: M'CARD:

| *John & Tricia Stiell* | *Kinnaird Guest House* | *5 Marshall Place* | *Perth PH2 8AH* | *Perthshire* |
| *Tel: (01738) 628021* | *Fax 01738 444056* | *Open: ALL YEAR* | | *Map Ref No. 49* |

Leny House.   Callander.

rate £ from - to per person	children taken	evening meals	animals taken		

£20.00 to £28.00 — Y N N — Non-smoking

Craigroyston House

Nearest Road: A.9

Quietly situated in its own grounds, this fine Victorian villa has direct access from the grounds to the town centre. The spacious en-suite bedrooms, some with Four-poster beds & original antique pieces are beautifully decorated in keeping with the period. Also, as are the comfortable lounge with seasonal log fire & the dining room with views to the south, where guests can enjoy a traditional Scottish breakfast. Safe off-street parking.
E-mail: reservations@craigroyston.co.uk

| Douglas & Gretta Maxwell | Craigroyston House | 2 Lower Oakfield | Pitlochry | PH16 5HQ | Perthshire |
| Tel: (01796) 472053 | Fax 01796 472053 | Open: ALL YEAR | | | Map Ref No. 50 |

£22.00 to £25.00 — Y N N — Non-smoking

Tigh Dornie

Nearest Road: A.9

Tigh Dornie is situated amid beautiful Perthshire scenery, approx. 5 miles north of Pitlochry. Offering attractive accommodation in 2 very comfortable & tastefully furnished guest bedrooms, each with an en-suite bathroom, T.V. & tea/coffee-making facilities. A warm & friendly welcome is assured from your hosts, who will ensure that your stay is a memorable one. An ideal spot for touring Scotland. Ample car parking. Children over 10.
E-mail: tigh_dornie@btinternet.com

| Elizabeth Sanderson | Tigh Dornie | Aldclune | Killiecrankie | Pitlochry PH16 5LR | Perthshire |
| Tel: (01796) 473276 | Fax 01796 473276 | Open: ALL YEAR | | | Map Ref No. 50 |

£28.00 to £28.00 — N N N — Non-smoking

see PHOTO over p. 418

VISA: M'CARD:

Easter Dunfallandy Country House

Nearest Road: A.9

A delightful Victorian country house quietly situated 2 miles south of Pitlochry, off the road to Logierait with wonderful views. 3 twin/double rooms with en-suite bath/shower, T.V. & complimentary toiletries. Each room is individually decorated & furnished. Breakfast includes porridge made from local stoneground oats, fresh cream & heather honey & scrambled free-range eggs with cream & smoked salmon - delicious! An elegant home, perfectly situated for a relaxing break.
E-mail: sue@dunfallandy.co.uk

| Sue Mathieson | Easter Dunfallandy Country House | Pitlochry PH16 5NA | Perthshire |
| Tel: (01796) 474128 | Fax 01796 474128 | Open: MAR - NOV | Map Ref No. 50 |

£18.00 to £20.00 — Y N N

Froylehurst

Nearest Road: A.68

An attractive Grade 'B' listed late-Victorian sandstone townhouse retaining most original features, offering 4 comfortable guest bedrooms & residents lounge. All rooms have washbasins with h & c, tea/coffee-making facilities, colour T.V. & radio/alarms. Two shared bathrooms & toilets. Situated in a large garden overlooking the town in a quiet residential area but within 2 mins' walking distance of many good pubs & restaurants. Ample parking. Children over 5 welcome. An ideal base from which to explore this region.

| H. H. Irvine | Froylehurst | Friars | Jedburgh TD8 6BN | Roxburghshire |
| Tel: (01835) 862477 | Fax 01835 862477 | Open: MAR - NOV | Map Ref No. 53 |

Easter Dunfallandy Country House. Pitlochry.

Column headers (rotated): rate £ from - to per person | children taken | evening meals taken | animals taken

Whitehill Farm

£23.00 to £23.00	Y	Y	Y

Nearest Road: A.6089

A comfortable & peaceful farmhouse with a large garden standing on a 455-acre, mixed farm 4 miles from Kelso. 4 attractive bedrooms - 2 single & 2 twin, 1 with en-suite shower room - have superb views over rolling countryside. All have central heating & washbasins. A pleasant sitting room with log fire is available to guests. An ideal base for touring this glorious region; maps available. Good home cooking. Dinner by prior arrangement. (Smoking restricted.)
E-mail: besmith@whitehillfarm.freeserve.co.uk

Mrs Betty Smith   Whitehill Farm   Nenthorn   Kelso TD5 7RZ   Roxburghshire
Tel: (01573) 470203 Fax 01573 470203 Open: ALL YEAR (Excl. Xmas & New Year) Map Ref No. 54

The Barns of Shannochill

£30.00 to £35.00	Y	Y	Y

VISA

Nearest Road: A.81

In a setting to dream of - 170 tranquil acres, set in the glorious Trossachs - Scotland's first National Park. A superb base to explore Stirling, Loch Lomond, the Trossachs, Edinburgh, Glasgow or Perth. Self-contained en-suite guest wing, sleeping 4, features its own entrance & sitting area with stunning panoramic views over the lake of Montieth to the Campsie Fells & Beyond. Enjoy aga-cooked breakfasts & dinners. Many outdoor pursuits on the doorstep. (Reductions for longer stays.)
E-mail: shannochill@aol.com

Val Willis   The Barns of Shannochill   Aberfoyle FK8 3UZ   Stirlingshire
Tel: (01877) 382878   Fax 01877 382964   Open: ALL YEAR   Map Ref No. 55

Culreuch Castle Hotel & Country Park

£38.00 to £80.00	Y	Y	Y

see PHOTO over
p. 420

VISA: M'CARD: AMEX

Nearest Road: A.811

Retreat to 700 years of history at magical Culcreuch, the ancestral fortalice & clan castle of the Galbraiths, home of the Barons of Culcreuch, & now a country house hotel where the Laird and his family extend an hospitable welcome. Set in 1,600 spectacular acres, yet only 19 miles from central Glasgow & 17 miles from Stirling. 13 well-appointed bedrooms with en-suite or private facilities, 4-poster bedroom supplement. Elegant period-style decor, antiques & log fires. Animals by arrangement.
E-mail: info@culcreuch.com

Laird Andrew Haslam   Culcreuch Castle Hotel   Fintry   Loch Lomond G63 0LW   Stirlingshire
Tel: (01360) 860555   Fax 01360 860556   Open: ALL YEAR   Map Ref No. 56

Rokeby House

£45.00 to £55.00	Y	Y	N

VISA: M'CARD

Nearest Road: A.820

Fine period Scottish country house on the outskirts of the village, within walking distance of the Allan Water, the medieval cathedral & the old town. Personal, warm & friendly service. Very comfortable rooms with luxurious en-suite bathrooms & delightful garden views. Home cooking & old fashioned hospitality. (Wine list available.) Quiet, peaceful location, ideal for touring Stirling & the Trossachs. Parking. Edinburgh & Glasgow are less than 1 hour by train or car. Children over 14.
E-mail: rokeby.house@btconnect.com

Richard Beatts   Rokeby House   Doune Road   Dunblane   Stirling FK15 9AT   Stirlingshire
Tel: (01786) 824447   Fax 01786 821399   Open: ALL YEAR   Map Ref No. 57

Culcreuch Castle.   Fintry.

rate £ from - to	per person	children taken	evening meals	animals taken		
£21.00 to £25.00	N	N	Y			*Veyatie - Lochinver*

VISA: M'CARD:

Nearest Road: A.837

Veyatie is a modern bungalow with unique character, situated in a beautiful, peaceful setting. All bedrooms are well-appointed with many refinements for your comfort. The conservatory offers panoramic views over Lochinver Bay to magnificent mountains beyond. An Area of Outstanding Natural Beauty & home to many varieties of wildlife. Woodland, coastal & hill walks, white beaches, specatacular scenery, great breakfasts, comfortable rooms - all ingredients for a great vacation.

E-mail: veyatie@baddid.freeserve.co.uk

Mrs D. Chapman   Veyatie - Lochinver   66 Baddidarroch   Lochinver IV27 4LP   Sutherland
Tel: (01571) 844424   Fax 01571 844424   Open: JAN - OCT   Map Ref No. 58

All the establishments mentioned in this guide
are members of
The Worldwide Bed & Breakfast Association

When booking your accommodation please
mention
The Best Bed & Breakfast

Wales

Wales

Wales is a small country with landscapes of intense beauty. In the north are the massive mountains of the Snowdonia National Park, split by chasms & narrow passes, & bounded by quiet vales & moorland. The Lleyn peninsula & the Isle of Anglesey have lovely remote coastlines.

Forests, hills & lakeland form the scenery of Mid Wales, with the great arc of Cardigan Bay in the west.

To the south there is fertile farming land in the Vale of Glamorgan, mountains & high plateaux in the Brecon Beacons, & also the industrial valleys. The coastline forms two peninsulas, around Pembroke & the Gower.

Welsh, the oldest living language of Europe is spoken & used, most obviously in the north, & is enjoying a resurgence in the number of its speakers.

From Taliesin, the 6th century Celtic poet, to Dylan Thomas, Wales has inspired poetry & song. Every August, at the Royal National Eisteddfod, thousands gather to compete as singers, musicians & poets, or to listen & learn. In the small town of Llangollen, there is an International Music Eisteddfod for a week every July

North Wales.

North Wales is chiefly renowned for the 850 miles of the Snowdonia National Park. It is a land of mountains & lakes, rivers & waterfalls & deep

The Snowdon Mountain Railway.

glacier valleys. The scenery is justly popular with walkers & pony-trekkers, but the Snowdon Mountain Railway provides easy access to the summit of the highest mountain in the range with views over the "roof of Wales".

Within miles of this wild highland landscape is a coastline of smooth beaches & little fishing villages.

Barmouth has mountain scenery on its doorstep & miles of golden sands & estuary walks. Bangor & Llandudno are popular resort towns.

The Lleyn peninsula reaches west & is an area of great charm. Abersoch is a dinghy & windsurfing centre with safe sandy beaches. In the Middle Ages pilgrims would come to visit Bardsey, the Isle of 20,000 saints, just off Aberdaron, at the tip of the peninsula.

The Isle of Anglesey is linked to the mainland by the handsome Menai Straits Suspension Bridge. Beaumaris has a 13th century castle & many other fine buildings in its historic town centre.

Historically North Wales is a fiercely independent land where powerful local lords resisted first the Romans & later the armies of the English Kings.

The coastline is studded with 13th century castles. Dramatically sited Harlech Castle, famed in fable & song, commands the town, & wide sweep of the coastline.

The great citadel of Edward I at Caernarfon comprises the castle & the encircling town walls. In 1969 it was the scene of the investiture of His Royal Highness Prince Charles as Prince of Wales.

There are elegant stately homes like Plas Newydd in Anglesey & Eriddig House near Wrexham, but it is the variety of domestic architecture that is most charming. The timber-frame buildings of the Border country are seen at their best in historic Ruthin set in the

Wales

beautiful Vale of Clwyd. Further west, the stone cottages of Snowdonia are built of large stones & roofed with the distinctive blue & green local slate. The low, snow-white cottages of Anglesey & the Lleyn Peninsula are typical of the "Atlantic Coast" architecture that can be found on all the western coasts of Europe. The houses are constructed of huge boulders with tiny windows & doors.

By contrast there is the marvellous fantasy of Portmeirion village. On a wooded peninsula between Harlech & Porthmadog, Sir Clough Williams Ellis created a perfect Italianate village with pastel coloured buildings, a town hall & luxury hotel.

Mid Wales

Mid Wales is farming country where people are outnumbered three to one by sheep. A flock of ewes, a lone shepherd & a Border Collie are a common sight on these green hills. Country towns like Old Radnor, Knighton & Montgomery with its castle ruin, have a timeless quality. The market towns of Rhyader, Lampeter & Dolgellau have their weekly livestock sales & annual agricultural festivals, the largest of which is the Royal Welsh Show at Builth Wells in July.

This is the background to the craft of weaving practised here for centuries. In the valley of the River Tefi & on an upper tributary of the Wye & the Irfon, there are tiny riverbank mills which produce the colourful Welsh plaid cloth.

Towards the Snowdonia National Park in the North, the land rises to the scale of true mountains. Mighty Cader Idris & the expanses of Plynlimon, once inaccessible to all but the shepherd & the mountaineer, are now popular centres for walking & pony trekking with well-signposted trails.

The line of the border with England is followed by a huge earth work of bank & ditch. This is Offa's Dyke, built by the King of Mercia around 750 A.D. to deter the Welsh from their incessant raids into his kingdom. Later the border was guarded by the castles at Hay-on-Wye, Builth Wells, Welshpool, & Chirk which date from mediaeval times.

North from Rhayader, lies the Dovey estuary & the historic town of Machynlleth. This is where Owain Glyndwr's parliament is thought to have met in 1404, & there is an exhibition about the Welsh leader in the building, believed to have been Parliament House.

Wales lost many fine religious houses during the Dissolution of the Monasteries under Henry VIII. The ruins at Cymer near Dolgellau & at Strata Florida were abbeys of the Cistercian order. However, many remote Parish Churches show evidence of the skills of mediaeval craftsmen with soaring columns & fine rood screens.

The Cambrian Coast (Cardigan Bay) has sand dunes to the north & cliffs to the south with sandy coves & miles of cliff walks.

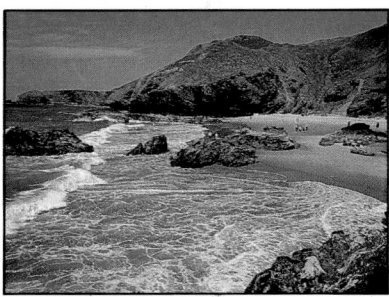
Llangrannog Headland.

Aberystwyth is the main town of the region with two beaches & a yachting harbour, a Camera Obscura on the cliff top & some fine walks in the area.

Water-skiing, windsurfing &

Wales

sailing are popular at Aberdovey, Aberaeron, New Quay, Tywyn & Barmouth & there are delightful little beaches further south at Aberporth, Tresaith or Llangrannog.

South Wales

South Wales is a region of scenic variety. The Pembrokeshire coastline has sheer cliffs, little coves & lovely beaches. Most of the area is National Park with an 80 mile foot path running along its length, passing pretty harbour villages like Solva & Broad Haven.

A great circle of Norman Castles stands guard over South Pembrokeshire, Roch, Haverfordwest, Tenby, Carew, Pembroke & Manorbier.

The northern headland of Saint

Tenby.

Brides Bay is the most westerly point in the country & at the centre of a tiny village stands the Cathedral of Saint David, the Patron Saint of Wales. At Bosherton near Saint Govans Head, there is a tiny chapel hidden in a cleft in the massive limestone cliffs.

The Preseli Hills hold the vast prehistoric burial chambers of Pentre Ifan, & the same mountains provided the great blue stones used at faraway Stonehenge.

Laugharne is the village where Dylan Thomas lived & worked in what was a boat-house & is now a museum.

In the valleys, towns like Merthyr Tydfil, Ebbw Vale & Treorchy were in the forefront of the boom years of the Industrial Revolution. Now the heavy industries are fast declining & the ravages of the indiscriminate mining & belching smoke of the blast furnaces are disappearing. The famous Male Voice Choirs & the love of rugby football survives.

The Vale of Glamorgan is a rural area with pretty villages. Beyond here the land rises steeply to the high wild moorlands & hill farms of the Brecon Beacons National Park & the Black Mountains, lovely areas for walking & pony trekking.

The Wye Valley leads down to Chepstow & here set amidst the beautiful woodlands is the ruin of the Great Abbey of Tintern, founded in 1131 by the Cistercian Order.

Swansea has a strong sea-faring tradition maintained by its new Marine Quarter - marina, waterfront village, restaurants, art gallery & theatre.

Cardiff, the capital of Wales, is a pleasant city with acres of parkland, the lovely River Taff, & a great castle, as well as a new civic centre, two theatres & the ultra-modern St. David's Concert Hall. It is the home of the Welsh National Opera & here also is the National Stadium where the singing of the rugby crowd on a Saturday afternoon is a treat.

Pony Trekking

Wales

Wales
Gazeteer

Areas of Outstanding Natural Beauty
The Pembrokeshire Coast. The Brecon
Beacons. Snowdonia. Gower.'

Historic Houses & Castles

Cardiff Castle - Cardiff
Built on a Roman site in the 11th century.
Caerphilly Castle - Caerphilly
13th century fortress.
Chirk Castle - Nr. Wrexham
14th century Border Castle. Lovely
gardens.
Coity Castle - Coity
Mediaeval stronghold - three storied round
tower.
Gwydir Castle - Nr. Lanrwst
Royal residence in past days - wonderful
Tudor furnishings. Gardens with
peacocks.
Penrhyn Castle - Bangor
Neo-Norman architecture 19th century -
large grounds with museum & exhibitions.
Victorian garden.
Picton Castle - Haverfordwest
12th century - lived in by the same family
continuously. Fine gardens.
Caernarfon Castle - Caernarfon
13th century - castle of great importance
to Edward I.
Conway Castle - Conwy
13th century - one of Edward I's chain of
castles.
Powis Castle - Welshpool
14th century - reconstruction work in 17th
century.
Murals, furnishings, tapestries & paintings,
terraced gardens.
Pembroke Castle - Pembroke
12th century Norman castle with huge
keep & immense walls.
Birthplace of Henry VII.
Plas Newydd - Isle of Anglesey
18th century Gothic style house.
Home of the Marquis of Anglesey.
Stands on the edge of the Menai Strait
looking across to the Snowdonia Range.
Famous for the Rex Whistler murals.
The Tudor Merchant's House - Tenby
Built in 15th century.
Tretower Court & Castle - Crickhowell
Mediaeval - finest example in Wales.

Cathedrals & Churches

St. Asaph Cathedral
13th century - 19th century restoration.
Smallest of Cathedrals in England &
Wales.
Holywell (St. Winifred)
15th century well chapel & chamber - fine
example.
St. Davids (St. David)
12th century Cathedral - splendid tower -
oak roof to nave.
Gwent (St. Woolos)
Norman Cathedral - Gothic additions -
19th century restoration.
Abergavenny (St. Mary)
14th century church of 12th century
Benedictine priory.
Llanengan (St. Engan)
Mediaeval church - very large with original
roof & stalls 16th century tower.
Esyronen
17th century chapel, much original interior
remaining.
Llangdegley (St. Tegla)
18th century Quaker meeting house -
thatched roof - simple structure divided
into schoolroom & meeting room.
Llandaff Cathedral (St. Peter & St. Paul)
Founded in 6th century - present building
began in 12th century. Great damage
suffered in bombing during war, restored
with Epstein's famous figure of Christ.

Museums & Galleries

National Museum of Wales - Cardiff (also
Turner House)
Geology, archaeology, zoology, botany,
industry, & art exhibitions.
Welsh Folk Museum - St. Fagans Castle
- Cardiff
13th century walls curtaining a 16th
century house - now a most interesting &
comprehensive folk museum.
County Museum - Carmarthen
Roman jewellery, gold, etc. Romano-
British & Stone Age relics.
National Library of Wales - Aberystwyth
Records of Wales & Celtic areas. Great
historical interest.
University College of Wales Gallery -
AberystwythTravelling exhibitions of
painting & sculpture.

Wales

Museum & Art Gallery - Newport
Specialist collection of English
watercolours - natural history, Roman
remains, etc.
Legionary Museum - Caerleon
Roman relics found on the site of
legionary fortress at Risca.
Nelson Museum - Monmouth
Interesting relics of Admiral Lord Nelson &
Lady Hamilton.
Bangor Art Gallery - Bangor
Exhibitions of contemporary paintings &
sculpture.
Bangor Museum of Welsh Antiquities -
Bangor
History of North Wales is shown. Splendid
exhibits of furniture, clothing, domestic
objects, etc. Also Roman antiquities.
Narrow Gauge Railway Museum - Tywyn
Rolling stock & exhibitions of narrow
gauge railways of U.K.
Museum of Childhood - Menai Bridge
Charming museum of dolls & toys &
children's things.

Brecknock Museum - Brecon
Natural history, archaeology, agriculture,
local history, etc.
Glynn Vivian Art Gallery & Museum -
Swansea
Ceramics, old & contemporary, British
paintings & drawings, sculpture, loan
exhibitions.
Stone Museum - Margam
Carved stones & crosses from pre-
historic times.
Plas Mawr - Conwy
A beautiful Elizabethan town mansion
house in its original condition. Now holds
the Royal Cambrain Academy of Art.

Historic Monuments

Rhuddlan Castle - Rhuddlan
13th century castle - interesting diamond
plan.
Valle Crucis Abbey - Llangollen
13th century Cistercian Abbey Church.

Cader Idris.

WALES

02 Amlwch
ISLE of ANGLESEY
04
Holyhead
A5
03
Llangefni
01 Bangor
Caernarfon 27 28

Liverpool
Birkenhead
12 Llandudno
Conwy 21
A55 Abergele
13 20
19 22 Chester
Denbigh
A525
14 11
09
07 Betws-y-Coed
15 Corwen
Ruthin 17 18
A5
A483 Wrexham

Caernarfon Bay

Nefyn 29
Porthmadog Ffestiniog
Pwllheli 32
Harlech
Barmouth

Llangollen
60
A4212 26 Bala
A494
A5

Dolgellau
A458 Shrewsbury
Mallwyd
63
33 Welsh-pool
34
Machynlleth A470
61 A489
Newtown
Aberystwyth A44 Llanidloes SHROPSHIRE
Llangurig

Cardigan Bay

Aberaeron
Tregaron A485
Cardigan 42 A487 Lampeter
Fishguard A478
A40
St Davids Haver-fordwest
45
47
46
49 Tenby Llanelli
Carmarthen Bay

Builth Wells
A488 Ludlow
59 Leominster
A44 HEREFORD and WORCESTER
53 Hay-on-Wye 55
Llanwrtyd-Wells 58
Brecon Hereford
05 Llandeilo 50
A40 51 52
A4067 54 Monmouth
A48 36 Abergavenny
Merthyr 37
Tydfil 24 Ebbw Vale
A465 Neath A472 25 Chepstow 41
Swansea 64 Cwmbran
Pontypridd 38 40 Newport
Bridgend M4
A48 Cardiff
23 Clevedon Bristol
Bristol Channel Weston-Super-Mare

427

WALES
Map references

01	Roberts	36	Harris
02	Hirst	37	Weatherill
03	Bown	38	Price
04	Hughes	41	Stubbs
05	Dent	42	Phillips
07	Baxter	45	Webber
07	Betteney	46	Moonie
09	Howard	47	Lort-Phillips
09	K. Jones	49	McHugh
11	Pitman		
12	Saunders		
13	Marrow		
14	Nichols		
15	Hart		
17	J. Spencer		
18	Parry		
19	A. Roberts		
20	M. Jones		
21	Steele-Mortimer		
22	T. Spencer		
23	Farthing		
24	Hurley		
25	Watkins		
26	Hind		
27	Bayles		
28	Kettle		
29	Murray		
32	Williams		
33	Sylvester		

50	Cole
51	P. Jackson
52	Gray
53	N. Jones
54	C. Jackson
55	Newall
58	P. Roberts
59	Millan
60	Raines
61	Bright
63	S. Jones
64	Maybery

ANGLESEY
CONWY
FLINTSHIRE
DENBIGHSHIRE
WREXHAM
GWYNEDD
CEREDIGION
POWYS
PEMBROKESHIRE
CARMARTHENSHIRE
MONMOUTH-SHIRE
SWANSEA
NEATH & PORT TALBOT
VALE OF GLAMORGAN
CARDIFF
NEWPORT

1 BRIDGEND
2 RHONDA CYNON TAFF
3 MERTHYR TYDFIL
4 CAERPHILLY
5 BLAENAU GWENT
6 TORFAEN

Llwydiarth Fawr Farm. Anglesey.

Wales
Isle of Anglesey

Bodlawen

Nearest Road: A.4080

A beautiful large house in a glorious location looking onto Snowdonia & Carenarfon Castle, a short walk to the shore of the tranquil Menai Strait. Ideally based for touring Anglesey & the mainland, its sights & beaches. Close to Plas Newydd (National Trust), the Sea Zoo & the Foel open farm. All bedrooms have en-suite facilities, T.V. & beverage tray. The lounge & dining room are exquisitely furnished & there is a grand piano. Your host, Marian, a well-known soprano soloist, is Welsh speaking & very welcoming. Children over 4.

£22.50 to £22.50 | Y | N | N

VISA: M'CARD:

Marian Roberts   Bodlawen   Brynsiencyn   Isle of Anglesey LL61 6TQ   Anglesey
Tel: (01248) 430379/430430   Open: ALL YEAR (Excl. Xmas)   Map Ref No. 01

Hafod Country House

Nearest Road: A.5025

A spacious Edwardian house set in an acre of beautiful gardens with wildlife pond, superb sea & mountain views. Peacefully situated on the outskirts of Cemaes with its picturesque harbour & sandy beach. 3 fully equipped en-suite bedrooms. A drawing room with antiques & a dining room where a superb breakfast is served & includes homemade preserves & fresh apple/pear juice when in season. Good local pubs. Nearby bird sanctuary, lake/sea fishing, golf & superb headland walks.
E-mail: gina@hirst-hafod.co.uk

£22.00 to £24.00 | Y | N | N

VISA: M'CARD:

Gina Hirst   Hafod Country House   Cemaes Bay   Isle of Anglesey LL67 0DS   Anglesey
Tel: (01407) 710500   Fax 01407 710055   Open: Easter - SEPT   Map Ref No. 02

Drws-Y-Coed

Nearest Road: A.5025, A.55

Enjoy wonderful panoramic views of Snowdonia & countryside at this beautifully appointed farmhouse on a 550-acre working beef, sheep & arable farm. It is situated in peaceful, wooded countryside in the centre of Anglesey. An ideal base from which to explore the island. Tastefully decorated & furnished, superb en-suite bedrooms with all facilities. An inviting spacious lounge with antiques & log fire. Excellent breakfasts. Historic farmstead. Lovely private walks. 25 mins' to Holyhead Port. A warm Welsh welcome is assured.

£23.00 to £25.00 | Y | N | N

VISA: M'CARD:

Mrs Jane Bown   Drws-Y-Coed   Llannerch-Y-Medd   Isle of Anglesey LL71 8AD   Anglesey
Tel: (01248) 470473   Fax 01248 470473   Open: ALL YEAR   Map Ref No. 03

Llwydiarth Fawr Farm

Nearest Road: A.55

Secluded Georgian mansion set in 800 acres of woodland & farmland, with lovely open views. Ideal touring base for the island's coastline, Snowdonia & North Wales coast. 5 delightfully furnished bedrooms with en-suite facilities & T.V., & 1 cottage suite. Full central heating, log fires. Enjoy a taste of Wales with delicious country cooking using farm & local produce. Personal attention & a warm Welsh welcome to guests, who will enjoy the scenic walks & private fishing. Convenient for Holyhead-to-Ireland crossings.

£25.00 to £25.00 | Y | Y | N

see PHOTO over p. 429

VISA: M'CARD:

Margaret Hughes   Llwydiarth Fawr Farm   Llanerchymedd   Isle of Anglesey LL71 8DF   Anglesey
Tel: (01248) 470321/470540   Open: ALL YEAR (Excl. Xmas)   Map Ref No. 04

rate £ from - to per person	children taken	evening meals	animals taken

---

| £25.00 to £25.00 | Y | N | Y |

Plas Alltyferin

Nearest Road: A.40

A classic Georgian country house lying in the hills above the beautiful Towy Valley, overlooking a Norman hillfort & the River Cothi - famous for salmon & sea trout. 2 spacious en-suite twin bedrooms, each with stunning views, for guests who are welcomed as friends of the family. Antique furniture & log fires. Good local pubs & restaurants. Totally peaceful. Ideal touring country for castles, beaches & rural Wales. National Botanic Garden of Wales (5 miles). Children over 10.
E-mail: dent@alltyferin.fsnet.co.uk

Mr & Mrs G. Dent Plas Alltyferin Pontargothi Nantgaredig Carmarthen SA32 7PF Carmarthenshire
Tel: (01267) 290662   Fax 01267 290919   Open: ALL YEAR (Excl. Xmas)   Map Ref No. 05

| £20.00 to £24.00 | Y | N | N |

VISA: M'CARD:

The Ferns Guest House

Nearest Road: A.5

A Victorian house, conveniently situated in the village of Betws-y-Coed in the beautiful Snowdonia National Park. 9 attractively furnished bedrooms, all en-suite with T.V. & tea/coffee-making facilities. Ideal base for many local walks, Bodnant Gardens, Conway Castle, Snowdon mountain railway, Portmerion & Carnarfon Castle. Cosy guests' lounge. Hearty British breakfasts. Small garden. Private car parking. Restaurants within easy walking distance. Children over 7.
E-mail: ferns@betws-y-coed.co.uk

Ian & Deborah Baxter   The Ferns Guest House   Holyhead Road   Betws-y-Coed LI24 0AN   Conwy
Tel: (01690) 710587   Fax 01690 710587   Open: ALL YEAR   Map Ref No. 07

| £20.00 to £25.00 | Y | N | N |

Bryn Afon

Nearest Road: A.5

A Victorian stone-built house situated on the banks of the River Llugwy overlooking the Pont-Y-Pair Bridge & waterfall. The well-appointed bedrooms with comfortable beds ensure a good night's sleep. Central for all tourist attractions & many local walks through the forests. Drying facilities are available. There is parking for all guests on the premises & a good selection of restaurants within 5-10 mins' walking distance.
E-mail: WBETTENEY@aol.com

Marion & William Betteney   Bryn Afon   Pentre Felin   Betws-Y-Coed LL24 0BB   Conwy
Tel: (01690) 710403   Fax 01690 710989   Open: ALL YEAR   Map Ref No. 07

| £22.00 to £25.00 | Y | Y | N |

see PHOTO over p. 432

Tan Dinas Country House

Nearest Road: A.5

A Victorian country house, offering peace, seclusion & a wonderful view. Surrounded by woodland yet only 500 yds from the village. Start with a delicious breakfast & finish your day with a candlelit dinner in the elegant dining room. Relax in the comfortable lounge or retire with a video or book to an attractive, individually furnished bedroom which is appointed for your comfort. There are forest walks from house. An ideal touring centre. Ample parking. A delightful home.

Ann Howard   Tan Dinas Country House   Coed Cyn Helier   Betws-Y-Coed LL24 0BL   Conwy
Tel: (01690) 710635   Fax 01690 710815   Open: ALL YEAR   Map Ref No. 09

Tan Dinas. Betws-Y-Coed

Column headers (rotated): rate £ from - to per person | children taken | evening meals | animals taken

---

£22.00 to £25.00 | Y | N | N

(non-smoking symbol)

see PHOTO over p. 434

VISA: M'CARD:

Aberconwy House

Nearest Road: A.470

A high standard of comfort & friendly, helpful hosts await you at Aberconwy. This large Victorian home, located in a lovely position above the picturesque village of Betws-Y-Coed, has panoramic views of the Llugney Valley, mountains & the River Conway. There are 8 very comfortable en-suite bedrooms, with T.V. & tea/coffee makers. Most also have wonderful views. A residents' T.V. lounge & garden are available. This is an ideal centre for touring, walking, fishing & golf. Children over 8.
E-mail: welcome@aberconwy-house.co.uk

Kevin & Dianne Jones   Aberconwy House   Lon Muriau   Betws-Y-Coed LL24 0HD   Conwy
Tel: (01690) 710202   Fax 01690 710800   Open: ALL YEAR   Map Ref No. 09

£49.50 to £75.00 | Y | Y | N

(non-smoking symbol)

VISA: M'CARD: AMEX:

Tan-Y-Foel Country House

Nearest Road: A.470, A.5

Part 16th-century Welsh stone country house, set within the peaceful woodland & green pastures of Snowdonia National Park, just outside Betws-y-Coed. 6 award-winning en-suite bedrooms, 4 of which enjoy panoramic mountain & garden views, all appointed with T.V., ironing facilities, hairdryer & telephones. Top honours have been received for the restaurant's culinary skills, which uses organic produce where possible. Ideal base for touring, walking & sightseeing. Parking. Children over 7.
E-mail: enquiries@tyfhotel.co.uk

Mr & Mrs Pitman   Tan-Y-Foel Country House   Capel Garmon   Betws-Y-Coed LL26 0RE   Conwy
Tel: (01690) 710507   Fax 01690 710681   Open: ALL YEAR   Map Ref No. 11

£23.00 to £37.00 | Y | Y | Y

VISA: M'CARD:

Tan Lan Hotel

Nearest Road: A.55

Tan Lan is a warm, welcoming hotel on the edge of town, close to the sea. Service is attentive & is combined with a friendly atmosphere in which you can feel genuinely at home. The hotel is renowned for its excellent food. There are 17 comfortably furnished & well-equipped en-suite rooms, 3 non-smoking, together with a restaurant & cosy lounge bar. Ideal base to explore castles, Snowdonia & also experience a classic Victorian seaside resort.
E-mail: info@tanlanhotel.co.uk

Kerry & Peter Saunders   Tan Lan Hotel   Great Ormes Road   Llandudno LL30 2AR   Conwy
Tel: (01492) 860221 Fax 01492 870219 Open: FEB - NOV (Incl. Xmas & New Year) Map Ref No. 12

£17.50 to £18.00 | Y | N | Y

Firs Cottage

Nearest Road: A.470

A 17th-century Welsh cottage & comfortable family home, situated in the beautiful Conway Valley, with excellent views to the hills. Firs Cottage offers 3 very comfortable & attractively furnished bedrooms, as well as a beautiful garden in which to relax & plan visits to the many North Wales attractions, which are all within easy reach. Good food & a warm Welsh welcome will make for a memorable holiday at this charming home. The perfect spot for a relaxing break.

Jack & Mary Marrow   Firs Cottage   Maenan   Llanrwst LL26 0YR   Conwy
Tel: (01492) 660244   Open: ALL YEAR (Excl. Xmas)   Map Ref No. 13

Aberconwy House.   Betws-Y-Coed.

Column headers (rotated): rate £ from - to per person | children taken | evening meals | animals taken

---

£30.00 to £42.50

Y Y Y

(no smoking symbol)

VISA: M'CARD: AMEX:

Hafod Country Hotel

Nearest Road: A.470

Set in the lovely Conwy Valley, on the edge of Snowdonia, Yr Hafod (The Summer Dwelling) is a former 17th-century farmhouse, extensively furnished with antiques. The bedrooms each offer a highly individual sense of style. Warm hospitality at this award-winning hotel is complimented by outstanding food, while drinks can be enjoyed in the oak-panelled bar or in front of a log fire. Children over 11. Animals by arrangement.
E-mail: hafod@breathemail.net

Christopher & Rosina Nichols   Hafod Country Hotel   Trefriw LL27 0RQ   Conwy
Tel: (01492) 640029   Fax 01492 641351   Open: FEB - DEC (& early Jan.)   Map Ref No. 14

£29.00 to £34.00

Y Y N

(no smoking symbol)

Delfryn (The Old Rectory)

Nearest Road: A.5

Small country rectory dating from 1714, situated on the edge of Snowdonia in a beautiful, quiet, hilly setting. A private walled garden with views. Bedroom with balcony overlooking the pond. Meals are amongst some of the finest anywhere & are cooked to individual tastes & served with guests own wine. No corkage. Home-baked breads, biscuits & preserves. Homely atmosphere, log fires, small panelled dining room. Books, guides, classical music, grand piano. No T.V.s anywhere.

Mr & Mrs F. Hart Delfryn (The Old Rectory) Bettws Gwerfyl Goch Corwen LL21 9PU Denbighshire
Tel: (01490) 460387   Open: MAR - JAN   Map Ref No. 15

£24.00 to £26.00

Y Y Y

see PHOTO over p. 436

VISA: M'CARD:

Eyarth Station

Nearest Road: A.525

A warm & friendly reception awaits the visitor to Eyarth Station. A super, converted, former railway station located in the beautiful countryside of the Vale of Clwyd. 6 en-suite bedrooms. T.V. lounge, garden, sun patio & outdoor heated pool. Conveniently located for the many historic towns in the region including Conwy, Caernarfon & Ruthin & their castles, with medieval banquet 2 minutes drive away. Chester is also within driving distance. 1987 winner of Best Bed & Breakfast Award.
E-mail: eyarthstation@amserve.net

Jen & Bert Spencer   Eyarth Station   Llanfair D. C.   Ruthin LL15 2EE   Denbighshire
Tel: (01824) 703643   Fax 01824 707464   Open: ALL YEAR   Map Ref No. 17

£18.00 to £20.00

Y Y N

(no smoking symbol)

Llainwen Ucha

Nearest Road: A.525

A working farm set in 130 acres overlooking the very beautiful Vale of Clwyd. Offering 3 pleasantly decorated rooms with modern amenities, & accommodating up to 6 persons. All rooms are centrally heated. Good home cooking made with fresh local produce; vegetarian meals on request. Conveniently situated for visiting Chester, Llangollen, Snowdonia & the coast. Offa's Dyke & fishing nearby. Medieval banquets are held at Ruthin Castle throughout the year.
E-mail: bryn.parry@farming.co.uk

Elizabeth A. Parry   Llainwen Ucha   Pentre Celyn   Ruthin LL15 2HL   Denbighshire
Tel: (01978) 790253   Open: ALL YEAR   Map Ref No. 18

Eyarth Station. Llanfair D.C.

Golden Grove. Llanasa.

Column headers (rotated): rate £ from - to per person | children taken | evening meals | animals taken

Bach-y-Graig

Nearest Road: A.55, A.541

A super 16th-century farmhouse nestling at the foot of the Clwydian range, with undisturbed views of the surrounding countryside. Walk a 40-acre mediaeval woodland trail on the farm where the royal Black Prince once hunted, & enjoy the wealth of rare plants & flowers. All rooms have en-suite/private facilities, tea/coffee, radio/alarms & T.V.. A lounge with T.V., an inglenook with log fires & central heating. Central for Chester, Snowdonia & coastal resorts. Single supplement.
E-mail: anwenroberts@bachygraig.fsnet.co.uk

	rate £ from - to per person	children taken	evening meals	animals taken
	£24.00 to £24.00	Y	N	N

Anwen Roberts   Bach-y-Graig   Tremeirchion   St. Asaph LL17 0UH   Denbighshire
Tel/Fax: (01745) 730627   Fax 01745 730971   Open: ALL YEAR   Map Ref No. 19

Greenhill Farm

Nearest Road: A.55

A 16th-century working dairy farm, overlooking the Dee Estuary, which retains its old-world charm, with a beamed & panelled interior. Bedrooms are tastefully furnished, some having bathroom/shower en-suite. Relax & enjoy typical farmhouse food in the attractive dining room. (Dinner by prior arrangement.) Children's play area & utility/games room also available. A lovely home, within easy reach of both the coastal & mountain areas of North Wales.
E-mail: mary@greenhillfarm.fsnet.co.uk

	rate £ from - to per person	children taken	evening meals	animals taken
	£19.50 to £21.50	Y	Y	N

Mrs Mary Jones   Greenhill Farm   Bryn Celyn   Holywell CH8 7QF   Flintshire
Tel: (01352) 713270   Open: FEB - NOV   Map Ref No. 20

Golden Grove

Nearest Road: A.5151

Beautiful Elizabethan manor house set in 1,000 acres, close to Chester, Bodnant Gardens & Snowdonia, & en route to Holyhead. The Steele-Mortimer brothers & wives, having returned to the family home from Canada & Ireland, provide a warm welcome for their guests. The menu features home produce, including lamb & game, together with interesting wines & home baking (advance notice required.) The atmosphere is friendly & informal. Children over 12. Licensed.
E-mail: golden.grove@lineone.net

	rate £ from - to per person	children taken	evening meals	animals taken
	£37.00 to £37.00	Y	Y	Y

see PHOTO over p. 437

VISA: M'CARD:

N. & M. Steele-Mortimer   Golden Grove   Llanasa   Nr. Holywell CH8 9NA   Flintshire
Tel: (01745) 854452   Fax 01745 854547   Open: FEB - NOV   Map Ref No. 21

Pentre Cerrig Mawr

Nearest Road: A.494

Pheasants & badgers visit the gardens of this peaceful 17th-century country house. Convenient for Chester, Snowdonia, the coast, Holyhead & 50 mins' to Manchester or Liverpool. The principal rooms have beams & open fires. Bedrooms are en-suite with T.V., etc. & magical views across the valley. Country pubs, walks, riding, golf & theatre nearby. The atmosphere is friendly & welcoming. Home-baking & local organic produce. Animals by arrangement. Children over 8. Single supplement.
E-mail: pentre.cerrig@virgin.net

	rate £ from - to per person	children taken	evening meals	animals taken
	£37.00 to £37.00	Y	Y	Y

see PHOTO over p. 439

VISA: M'CARD:

Ted & Charmian Spencer   Pentre Cerrig Mawr   Maeshafn   Mold CH7 5LU   Flintshire
Tel: (01352) 810607   Fax 01352 810607   Open: ALL YEAR   Map Ref No. 22

Pentre Cerrig Mawr.   Maeshafn.

Wales
Glamorgan, Gwent & Gwynedd

The White House

| | £22.00 to £25.00 | Y | N | N |

Nearest Road: A.48

Experience the White House, a Georgian residence 5 mins walk to the historic town, local pubs & restaurants. 1 mile to the coast, the footpaths start 10 metres from the house. Accommodation is in 2 gracious bedrooms with en-suite or private bathrooms, easy chairs, colour T.V., tea/coffee-making facilities, refrigerator & hairdryer. Neville & Janet with a collection of teddy bears will be delighted to share their home & provide you with a scrumptious & varied breakfast.
E-mail: LLWHITEHOUSE@hotmail.com

Janet & Neville Farthing   The White House   Flanders Road   Llantwit Major CF61 1RL   Glamorgan
Tel: (01446) 794250   Fax 01446 794250   Open: ALL YEAR   Map Ref No. 23

Tregenna Hotel

| | £25.00 to £30.00 | Y | Y | Y |

Nearest Road: A.470, A.465

Family-run hotel with high level of comfort & class. 29 bedrooms with bathroom, 7 of which are designated for tourists & family use at special rates (50% reduction for children sharing). Telephone, tea/coffee service tray, colour T.V. in all rooms. Lunch, afternoon tea & dinner served 7 days a week. Brecon Beacons National Park 8 mins' drive. 45 mins' Cardiff/Wales Airport, 2 1/4 hours London Heathrow Airport. Animals by arrangement.
E-mail: reception@tregenna.co.uk

VISA: M'CARD: AMEX:

Michael Hurley   Tregenna Hotel   Park Terrace   Merthyr Tydfil CF47 8RF   Glamorgan
Tel: (01685) 723627   Fax 01685 721951   Open: ALL YEAR   Map Ref No. 24

The Glebe

| | £22.00 to £22.00 | Y | N | N |

Nearest Road: A.4042, M.4

The Glebe, overlooking this lovely part of rural Wales, is an ideal spot from which to explore this historic region with its numerous castles & abbeys & the book shops of Hay-on-Wye. Your friendly & helpful host is only too happy to help you plan if need be. Cardiff, capital of Wales, is 20 mins', London Heathrow Airport 2 1/2 hrs. The tastefully decorated bedrooms are centrally heated & have a hospitality tray. Breakfast menu. In the evening good pub fare is a pleasant country stroll away. Very convenient M.4 & M.5.

Mrs Beryl Watkins   The Glebe   Croes-Y-Ceiliog   Cwmbran   Newport NP44 2DE   Gwent
Tel: (01633) 450251/450242   Open: ALL YEAR   Map Ref No. 25

Abercelyn Country House

| | £18.00 to £28.00 | Y | Y | N |

Nearest Road: A.494

Set in landscaped gardens with its own mountain stream running alongside, this former rectory dates back to before 1721. Situated in the Snowdonia National Park, it is ideally located for walking or touring amongst the spectacular scenery. Bright & spacious en-suite bedrooms with views over Bala Lake, evenings relaxing before open log fires, & informal conversation over traditional breakfasts with hot home-baked bread, preserves & fresh coffee. Evening meals by prior arrangement.
E-mail: info@abercelyn.co.uk

see PHOTO over
p. 441

Mrs Lindsay Hind   Abercelyn Country House   Llanycil   Bala LL23 7YF   Gwynedd
Tel: (01678) 521109   Fax 01678 521109   Open: ALL YEAR (Excl. Xmas)   Map Ref No. 26

Abercelyn. Llanycil.

Wales
Gwynedd

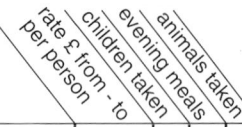

The White House

Nearest Road: A.487

The White House is a large detached house set in its own grounds, overlooking Foryd Bay, & with the Snowdonia mountains behind. Accommodation is in 4 tastefully decorated bedrooms, all with bath or shower, tea/coffee-making facilities & colour T.V.. Guests are welcome to use the residents' lounge, outdoor pool & gardens. Ideally situated for birdwatching, walking, windsurfing, golf & visiting the historic Welsh castles.
E-mail: RWBAYLES@SJMS.CO.UK

£20.00 to £22.00	Y	N	Y

R. W. Bayles   The White House   Llanfaglan   Caernarfon LL54 5RA   Gwynedd
Tel: (01286) 673003   Fax 01286 673003   Open: MAR - NOV   Map Ref No. 27

Ty'n Rhos Country Hotel

Nearest Road: A.487

Ty'n Rhos is a special place, set in a splendid location on the wide-open plain running between Snowdonia & the sea. Once a working farmhouse, it has now been transformed into a country house of great charm & comfort. Each individually designed bedroom is furnished to a high standard. 5 ground floor rooms have patio doors opening onto the garden. Award-winning Ty'n Rhos serves super meals. Quality allied to exceptional value are the keynotes at Ty'n Rhos. Children over 6.
E-mail: Enquiries@tynrhos.co.uk

£40.00 to £55.00	Y	Y	N

VISA: M'CARD: AMEX:

Nigel & Lynda Kettle Ty'n Rhos Country Hotel Seion Llanddeiniolen Caernarfon LL55 3AE Gwynedd
Tel: (01248) 670489   Fax 01248 670079   Open: ALL YEAR   Map Ref No. 28

Min-Y-Gaer Hotel

Nearest Road: A.497

A pleasant, licensed house in a quiet residential area, offering very good accommodation in 10 comfortable rooms, all of which have a bathroom en-suite. All rooms are non-smoking & have colour T.V. & tea/coffee-making facilities. The hotel enjoys commanding views of Criccieth Castle & the scenic Cardigan Bay coastline, & is only 2 mins' walk from the safe, sandy beach. Car parking on the premises. An ideal base for touring Snowdonia. Animals by arrangement.
E-mail: info@minygaerhotel.co.uk

£23.00 to £26.00	Y	N	Y

VISA: M'CARD: AMEX:

Mrs Rita Murray   Min-Y-Gaer Hotel   Porthmadog Road   Criccieth LL52 OHP   Gwynedd
Tel: (01766) 522151   Fax 01766 523540   Open: MAR - OCT   Map Ref No. 29

Gwrach Ynys Country Guest House

Nearest Road: A.496

A warm Welsh welcome awaits you at Gwrach Ynys, a 7 bedroom Edwardian country house set in 1 acre of garden, nestled between the sea & the mountains in beautiful Snowdonia National Park. En-suite bedrooms, individually decorated & furnished to a high standard. 2 comfortable guest lounges & a separate dining room. Evening meals are available by prior arrangement. Ideally located for exploring North Wales. Superb area for walkers, birdwatchers & golfers. Children over 3.
E-mail: bestbandb@gwrachynys.co.uk

£22.00 to £28.00	Y	Y	N

Deborah Williams   Gwrach Ynys Country Guest House   Talsarnall   Harlech LL47 6TS   Gwynedd
Tel: (01766) 780742   Fax 01766 781199   Open: MAR - OCT   Map Ref No. 32

The Wenallt. Gilwern.

	rate £ from - to per person	evening meals children taken	animals taken

Cefn Coch Country Guest House

Nearest Road: A.493

Cefn Coch is an old coaching inn on the edge of the Snowdonia National Park & is surrounded by over an acre of gardens & paddock. It has been tastefully renovated throughout & now provides quality accommodation. There are 2 attractively furnished bedrooms, each with an en-suite bathroom & tea/coffee-making facilities. Delicious evening meals are served. Guests can enjoy the extensive views of the local countryside. The beautiful Cardigan Bay coast is nearby. A delightful home.
E-mail: david@cefn-coch.co.uk

£23.00 to £25.00 N Y N

David Sylvester   Cefn Coch Country Guest House   Llanegryn   Tywyn LL36 9SD   Gwynedd
Tel: (01654) 712193   Fax 01654 712193   Open: FEB - OCT   Map Ref No. 33

The Wenallt

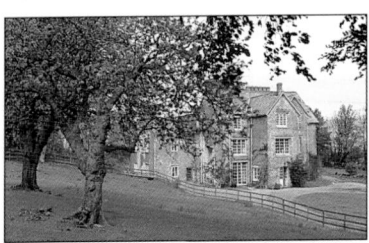

Nearest Road: A.465

A 16th-century Welsh longhouse set in 50 acres of farmland in the Brecon Beacons National Park & commanding magnificent views over the Usk Valley. Retaining all its old charm, with oak beams & inglenook fireplace, yet offering a high standard of accommodation, with en-suite bedrooms, good food & a warm welcome. The Wenallt is an ideal base from which to see glorious Wales & the surrounding areas & attractions. Licensed.
E-mail: thewenallt@talk21.com

£19.50 to £24.00 Y Y Y

see PHOTO over p. 443

B. L. Harris   The Wenallt   Abergavenny NP7 0HP   Monmouthshire
Tel: (01873) 830694   Fax 01873 830694   Open: ALL YEAR   Map Ref No. 36

Llanwenarth House

Nearest Road: A.465

A truly delightful 16th-century manor house, standing in its own beautiful grounds & surrounded by the tranquil scenic hills of the Brecon Beacons National Park. Elegantly furnished, tastefully decorated & with superb views, this house is a real pleasure to visit. Candlelit dinners, prepared by Amanda, a Cordon Bleu cook, are a delight. 5 en-suite bedrooms. Fishing, golf, climbing, walking & shooting nearby. No smoking in dining room or bedrooms. Single supplement. Children over 10.
E-mail: mandy@r-weatherill.fsnet.co.uk

£41.00 to £43.00 Y Y Y

see PHOTO over p. 445

Amanda Weatherill   Llanwenarth House   Govilon   Abergavenny NP7 9SF   Monmouthshire
Tel: (01873) 830289   Fax 01873 832199   Open: MAR - JAN   Map Ref No. 37

Great House

Nearest Road: A.48

Great House is a pretty 16th-century Grade II listed home on the banks of the River Usk, with clematis garden. Excellent stopover for those travelling to Wales & Ireland. Retaining much of its original character (including beams & inglenook fireplaces), it offers 3 bedrooms with T.V., etc. A drawing room with T.V. & woodburner. Within easy reach of superb golf course, fishing & forest trails. Caerleon is very near with its amphitheatre, museums & Roman Baths. Good pubs. Children over 10.
E-mail: price.greathouse@tesco.net

£25.00 to £28.00 Y N Y

Dinah Price   Great House   Isca Road   Old Village   Caerleon NP18 1QG   Monmouthshire
Tel: (01633) 420216   Open: ALL YEAR   Map Ref No. 38

Llanwenarth House. Govilon.

Wales
Monmouthshire & Pembrokeshire

Parva Farmhouse Hotel & Restaurant

Nearest Road: A.466

A delightful 17th-century stone farmhouse situated 50 yards from the River Wye. The quaint en-suite bedrooms, with their designer fabrics, are gorgeous, & some offer breathtaking views over the River Wye & woodland. The beamed lounge, with log fires, leather Chesterfields & 'Honesty Bar', is a tranquil haven in which to unwind. Mouthwatering dishes, served in the intimate, candlelit Inglenook Restaurant, reflect the owner's love of cooking. A super home, perfect for a relaxing break or for exploring beautiful Wales.

£30.00 to £38.00 — Y Y Y

see PHOTO over
p. 447

VISA: M'CARD: AMEX:

Dereck & Vickie Stubbs   Parva Farmhouse Hotel & Restaurant   Tintern NP16 6SQ   Monmouthshire
Tel: (01291) 689411   Fax 01291 689557   Open: ALL YEAR   Map Ref No. 41

The Old Vicarage

Nearest Road: A.487

Patricia & David welcome you to their elegant Edwardian home set in an elevated position with large lawned gardens & glorious views to the sea. Offering 3 comfortably furnished en-suite bedrooms with tea/coffee-making facilities. Situated in Britain's only coastal National Park, 1 mile from one of the most dramatic sections of the Pembrokeshire Coast Path at Ceibwr Bay, with the Preseli Hills & Teifi Valley nearby. Enjoy the timeless & leisurely tranquillity of north Pembrokeshire. Croeso!
E-mail: stay@old-vic.co.uk

£25.00 to £28.00 — N Y N

Patricia & David Phillips   The Old Vicarage   Moylegrove   Cardigan SA43 3BN   Pembrokeshire
Tel: (01239) 881231   Fax 0870 1362382   Open: MAR - OCT   Map Ref No. 42

Allenbrook

Nearest Road: A.40

Allenbrook is a charming country house set in its own grounds. It is adjacent to the beach & situated in the Pembrokeshire National Park on the coastal path. The house is very comfortable with spacious bedrooms fully-equipped with T.V. & tea/coffee-making facilities. All the bedrooms have en-suite or private bathrooms, & there is a large, comfortable guests' sitting room. A delightful home & an ideal spot for a relaxing short break or holiday.
E-mail: allenbrook@talk21.com

£25.00 to £25.00 — N N N

Mrs E. A. Webber   Allenbrook   Dale   Haverfordwest SA62 3RN   Pembrokeshire
Tel: (01646) 636254   Fax 01646 636954   Open: ALL YEAR   Map Ref No. 45

Knowles Farm

Nearest Road: A.4075

Relax, unwind & prepare to be pampered in this lovely south-facing family home overlooking the Milford Haven Estuary. Knowles Farm has access to farmland & ancient woodland & is within 15 mins' of the glorious Pembrokeshire coast. There are castles, ancient monuments & theme parks surrounding Knowles Farm, & lovely walks are on the doorstep. Riding, fishing, bird-watching & boating within minutes. After a day out, a special meal (with notice) in the lovely dining room.
E-mail: ginilp@lawrenny.org.uk

£23.00 to £25.00 — Y Y Y

Virginia Lort Phillips   Knowles Farm   Lawrenny SA68 0PX   Pembrokeshire
Tel: (01834) 891221   Fax 01834 891221   Open: EASTER - OCT   Map Ref No. 47

Parva Farmhouse and Restaurant. Tintern.

rate £ from - to per person / children taken / evening meals / animals taken

The Peacock Guest House

Nearest Road: A.4075, A.40

Set in its own grounds in the heart of the Pembrokeshire countryside. The Peacock offers attractive accommodation in 2 pretty bedrooms. 1 double en-suite & 1 twin with a private bathroom, each with T.V. & tea/coffee-making facilities. Excellent choice of breakfasts. A lovely place for exploring the glorious Welsh countryside & many attractions. Beaches 20 mins. Evening meals by arrangement. Licensed. Children over 12.
E-mail: Ros@peacockguesthouse.co.uk

| | £20.00 to £25.00 | Y | Y | N |

VISA: M'CARD:

Ros Mooney   The Peacock Guest House   Hoarstone   Martletwy Narberth SA67 8AZ Pembrokeshire
Tel: (01834) 891707   Fax 01834 891707   Open: MAR - OCT   Map Ref No. 46

The Old Vicarage

Nearest Road: A.4139

Situated in the coastal village of Manorbier with its beautiful beaches & castle, The Old Vicarage offers gracious accommodation with glimpses of Barafundle Bay. The en-suite bedrooms are furnished with antiques. Guests may enjoy the mature gardens or sit by a log fire in the drawing room. For the more energetic, the Pembrokeshire Coastal Path passes through the village. Beaches a 5-min. walk. Irish ferries from Pembroke (20 mins') & Fishguard (50 mins'). Children over 7.
E-mail: oldvic@manorbier-tenby.fsnet.co.uk

| | £25.00 to £30.00 | Y | N | N |

Mrs Jill McHugh   The Old Vicarage   Manorbier   Nr. Tenby SA70 7TN   Pembrokeshire
Tel: (01834) 871452   Fax 01834 871452   Open: ALL YEAR   Map Ref No. 49

Dolycoed

Nearest Road: A.40

Dolycoed, built at the turn of the century, retains many of its interesting original features. Standing in a sheltered position in Brecon Beacons National Park, it offers a warm, friendly, homely welcome to all. Accommodation is in 2 comfortable guest bedrooms, with radio & tea/coffee makers, & a guests' lounge with colour T.V.. There are many outdoor activities nearby including pony trekking, riding, fishing, watersports & walking. Dolycoed is ideal for a relaxing break.

| | £20.00 to £20.00 | Y | N | Y |

Mrs Mary Cole   Dolycoed   Talyllyn   Brecon LD3 7SY   Powys
Tel: (01874) 658666   Open: ALL YEAR   Map Ref No. 50

The Beacons

Nearest Road: A.40

Recently restored 17th/18th-century house retaining many of its original features. Well-appointed standard, en-suite & luxury period rooms. Enjoy a drink in the original meat cellar (complete with hooks) or relax in a comfortable armchair in front of the fire. The award-winning chef will spoil you with outstanding cuisine freshly cooked to your order. The Beacons is a delightful home & an excellent base for a relaxing holiday.
E-mail: beacons@brecon.co.uk

| | £18.00 to £29.50 | Y | Y | Y |

VISA: M'CARD:

Peter & Barbara Jackson   The Beacons   16 Bridge Street   Brecon LD3 8AH   Powys
Tel: (01874) 623339   Fax 01874 623339   Open: ALL YEAR   Map Ref No. 51

Glangrwyney Court. Crickhowell.

Wales
Powys

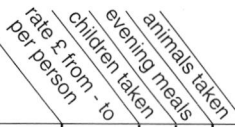
Shiwa Lodge

Nearest Road: A.40

Situated in Llangorse village, overlooking the lake & Brecon Beacons, Shiwa Lodge is well-placed for the activities in the National Park, visiting castles or browsing second-hand bookshops in Hay-on-Wye. The detached house has ample parking & pleasant gardens. Inside, the African style decorations brighten comfortable accommodation for the disabled & able-bodied. The peaceful surroundings offer those less active, a quiet world for relaxing, painting, reading or birdwatching.

E-mail: marie-gray@shiwa-lodge.fsnet.co.uk

| £20.00 to £25.00 | Y | N | N |

VISA: M'CARD:

| Mrs Marie Gray | Shiwa Lodge | Llangorse Village | Brecon LD34 7UG | Powys |
| Tel: (01874) 658631 | Fax 01874 658144 | Open: ALL YEAR | Map Ref No. 52 |

Ty-Isaf Farm

Nearest Road: A.470

Ty-Isaf Farm, situated in the attractive village of Erwood, offers charming accommodation in 2 attractive & comfortably furnished rooms with modern amenities & tea/coffee-making facilities. Plentiful English or Continental breakfasts are served. Special diets & packed lunches are provided by arrangement. Guests may choose to relax in the cosy lounge, with T.V. throughout the day. An ideal base for a relaxing break or for exploring this lovely part of Wales & its many attractions.

| £16.00 to £16.00 | Y | Y | Y |

| Nancy M. Jones | Ty-Isaf Farm | Erwood | Builth Wells LD2 3SZ | Powys |
| Tel: (01982) 560607 | Open: ALL YEAR | Map Ref No. 53 |

Glangrwyney Court

Nearest Road: A.40

Glangrwyney Court is a Georgian mansion set in 4 acres of established gardens & surrounded by parkland. All rooms are comfortably furnished with antiques & fine porcelain & paintings, & there is essentially a welcoming & homely atmosphere. There are 5 attractive & well-appointed bedrooms, each with a private or en-suite bathroom. During the winter, log fires burn in all the sitting rooms, & in the summer guests are able to relax with a drink in the gardens. Evening meals by arrangement.

E-mail: glangrwyne@aol.com

| £35.00 to £40.00 | Y | Y | Y |

see PHOTO over
p. 449

| Mrs C. Jackson | Glangrwyney Court | Glangrwyney | Crickhowell NP8 1ES | Powys |
| Tel: (01873) 811288 | Fax 01873 810317 | Open: ALL YEAR | Map Ref No. 54 |

The Bear

Nearest Road: A.438

The Bear is a 16th-century former coaching inn, in the centre of the famous book town. Attractive & comfortable bedrooms combine ancient beams & panelling with newly refurbished bathrooms. Ideal for book & antique browsers, Hay is also on Offa's Dyke footpath & the Wye Valley Walk; other outdoor activities are offered in this lovely area. Parking. Luggage transfers & packed lunches, if booked in advance. A choice of restaurants nearby.

E-mail: jon@thebear-hay-on-wye.co.uk

| £27.00 to £27.00 | Y | N | Y |

VISA: M'CARD:

| Sue Newall & Jon Field | The Bear | 2, Bear Street | Hay-on-Wye HR3 5AN | Powys |
| Tel: (01497) 821302 | Fax 01497 820506 | Open: ALL YEAR | Map Ref No. 55 |

York House. Cusop.

	rate £ from - to per person	children taken	evening meals	animals taken

York House

Nearest Road: A.438

Peter and Olwen Roberts welcome you to their traditional Victorian guest house quietly situated in beautiful gardens on the edge of Hay. Sunny mountain views are enjoyed by all the well-appointed en-suite rooms. Ideal for a relaxing holiday spent browsing in the world-famous bookshops, exploring the National Park and Kilvert country, or just enjoying the freshly prepared home cooking. Evening meals by arrangement. Private parking. Children over 8 years welcome.

E-mail: roberts@yorkhouse59.fsnet.co.uk

£26.00 to £28.00 — Y Y Y

see PHOTO over p. 451

VISA: M'CARD: AMEX:

Peter & Olwen Roberts	York House	Cusop	Hay-on-Wye HR3 5QX	Powys
Tel: (01497) 820705	Fax 01497 820705	Open: ALL YEAR	Map Ref No. 58	

Guidfa House

Nearest Road: A.483, A.44

Licensed Georgian guest house, situated in an ideal location for touring lakes, mountains, national parks & the coast. The bedrooms are all comfortable, non-smoking & spacious, most en-suite, all with colour T.V. & tea/coffee-making facilities. A ground-floor room is also available. Meals are prepared by Anne, who is Cordon-Bleu-trained. Dinner is a set menu, but special diets/requests can always be catered for with a little prior notice.

E-mail: guidfa@globalnet.co.uk

£26.50 to £29.00 — N Y N

VISA: M'CARD:

Anne & Tony Millan	Guidfa House	Crossgates	Llandrindod Wells LD1 6RF	Powys
Tel: (01597) 851241	Fax 01597 851875	Open: ALL YEAR	Map Ref No. 59	

Bron Heulog

Nearest Road: A.483

Bron heulog - means sunny bank in Welsh. This beautiful Victorian house was built in 1861, grandly situated in a 2-acre garden. The Victorians knew a thing or two about building, the walls are 2ft. thick! Fully restored, the house feratures a magnificent curved staircase & original fireplaces in every room. The Orchid, Sunflower & Bluebell rooms are all recently refurbished with Victorian style en-suite facilities & offer every comfort to guests.

E-mail: kraines@enta.net

£23.00 to £27.00 — Y N N

VISA: M'CARD:

Ken & Karon Raines	Bron Heulog	Waterfall Street	Llanrhaeadr Ym Mochnant SY10 0JX	Powys
Tel: (01691) 780521		Open: ALL YEAR	Map Ref No. 60	

Little Brompton Farm

Nearest Road: B.4385, A.489

Robert & Gaynor welcome you to this charming 17th-century farmhouse, situated on this working farm. The house has much original character, with beautiful old oak beams. Pretty en-suite bedrooms enhanced by quality antiques. T.V.. Offa's Dyke runs through the farm. Situated on the B.4385, 2 miles east of the beautiful Georgian town of Montgomery. Come & relax in peaceful, stress-free countryside. Animals by arrangement.

E-mail: gaynor.brompton@virgin.net

£22.00 to £22.00 — Y N Y

Gaynor Bright	Little Brompton Farm	Montgomery SY15 6HY	Powys
Tel: (01686) 668371	Fax 01686 668371	Open: ALL YEAR	Map Ref No. 61

rate £ from - to per person	children taken	evening meals taken	animals taken			

£26.00 to £26.00

Y Y N

Lower Trelydan

Nearest Road: A.490

Graham & Sue welcome you to their wonderful, award-winning black-&-white farmhouse, set on a working farm & listed for its history & beauty. Bedrooms are en-suite & tastefully furnished. An oak-beamed lounge, & a dining room where evening meals are served most nights. Home cooking a speciality. Licensed. Powis Castle, many beauty spots, leisure activities & walks are nearby. Capture the atmosphere of 4 centuries of history in this outstanding house. Disabled facilities.

E-mail: stay@lowertrelydan.com

VISA: M'CARD:

Mrs Sue Jones   Lower Trelydan   Guilsfield   Welshpool SY21 9PH   Powys
Tel: (01938) 553105   Fax 01938 553105   Open: ALL YEAR   Map Ref No. 63

£25.00 to £32.50

N N Y

Tides Reach

Nearest Road: A.4067

The warmest of welcomes awaits you at Tides Reach, where you will find a lovingly restored early Victorian town house elegantly furnished with antiques. There are 6 attractive bedrooms, each with private facilities. Well situated on the seafront in the delightful village of Mumbles (the gateway to Gower), only 4 miles from the city centre. An ideal base for business or pleasure & convenient as a stop on your way to Ireland.

E-mail: tidesreachmumbles@yahoo.com

Mrs Jan Maybery   Tides Reach   388 Mumbles Road   Mumbles   Swansea SA3 5TN   Swansea
Tel: (01792) 404877   Fax 01792 404775   Open: FEB - NOV   Map Ref No. 64

All the establishments mentioned in this guide
are members of
The Worldwide Bed & Breakfast Association

When booking your accommodation please mention
The Best Bed & Breakfast

Towns & Counties Index

Town	County	Country
Aberfoyle	Stirlingshire	Scotland
Abergavenny	Monmouthshire	Wales
Aboyne	Aberdeenshire	Scotland
Alnwick	Northumberland	England
Altrincham	Cheshire	England
Ambleside	Cumbria	England
Ampleforth	Yorkshire	England
Andover	Hampshire	England
Anstruther	Fifeshire	Scotland
Appin	Argyll	Scotland
Ardrishaig	Argyll	Scotland
Arundel	Sussex	England
Ashbourne	Derbyshire	England
Ashford	Kent	England
Auchtermuchty	Fifeshire	Scotland
Aylmerton	Norfolk	England
Ayr	Ayrshire	Scotland
Bala	Gwynedd	Wales
Ballantrae	Ayrshire	Scotland
Banbury	Oxfordshire	England
Barnstaple	Devon	England
Bath	Somerset	England
Bath	Wiltshire	England
Bedale	Yorkshire	England
Bedford	Bedfordshire	England
Berkhamsted	Hertfordshire	England
Betws-y-Coed	Conwy	Wales
Beverley	Yorkshire	England
Bideford	Devon	England
Bingley	Yorkshire	England
Bishop Auckland	Durham	England
Bishop's Stortford	Essex	England
Blidworth	Nottinghamshire	England
Bolney	Sussex	England
Bordon	Hampshire	England
Boscastle	Cornwall	England
Boston Spa	Yorkshire	England
Bourne	Lincolnshire	England
Bournemouth	Dorset	England
Bourton-on-the-Water	Gloucestershire	England
Bovey Tracey	Devon	England
Bowness-on-Windermere	Cumbria	England
Bradford-on-Avon	Wiltshire	England
Brampton	Cumbria	England
Brecon	Powys	Wales
Bridgwater	Somerset	England
Bridlington	Yorkshire	England
Bridport	Dorset	England
Brighton	Sussex	England
Bristol	Gloucestershire	England
Bristol	Somerset	England
Broadford	Isle of Skye	Scotland
Broadway	Worcestershire	England
Broadway	Gloucestershire	England
Builth Wells	Powys	Wales
Bungay	Suffolk	England
Burford	Oxfordshire	England
Burnley	Lancashire	England
Bury St. Edmunds	Suffolk	England
Buttermere	Cumbria	England
Buxton	Derbyshire	England
Caerleon	Monmouthshire	Wales
Caernarfon	Gwynedd	Wales
Callander	Perthshire	Scotland
Camberley	Surrey	England
Cambridge	Cambridgeshire	England
Canterbury	Kent	England
Cardigan	Pembrokeshire	Wales
Carlisle	Cumbria	England
Carmarthen	Carmarthenshire	Wales
Carnforth	Lancashire	England
Carrbridge	Inverness-shire	Scotland
Cartmell Fell	Cumbria	England
Castle Douglas	Dumfriesshire	Scotland
Chagford	Devon	England
Chard	Somerset	England
Cheltenham	Gloucestershire	England
Chester	Cheshire	England
Chichester	Sussex	England
Chippenham	Wiltshire	England
Chipping Campden	Gloucestershire	England
Cholsey	Oxfordshire	England
Christchurch	Hampshire	England
Cirencester	Gloucestershire	England
Clitheroe	Lancashire	England
Coalville	Leicestershire	England
Cockermouth	Cumbria	England
Cockermouth	Cumbria	England
Colchester	Essex	England
Corfe Castle	Dorset	England
Corsham	Wiltshire	England
Corwen	Denbighshire	Wales
Crackington Haven	Cornwall	England
Cranbrook	Kent	England
Cranleigh	Surrey	England
Craven Arms	Shropshire	England
Crediton	Devon	England
Crianlarich	Perthshire	Scotland
Criccieth	Gwynedd	Wales
Crickhowell	Powys	Wales
Danehill	Sussex	England
Dartmoor	Devon	England
Dartmouth	Devon	England
Dereham	Norfolk	England
Dorchester	Dorset	England
Dorking	Surrey	England
Doune	Perthshire	Scotland
Dover	Kent	England
Dumbarton	Dunbartonshire	Scotland
Dunoon	Argyll	Scotland
Duns	Berwickshire	Scotland
Dunster	Somerset	England
Durham	Durham	England
Duror	Argyll	Scotland
Duror in Appin	Argyll	Scotland
Easingwold	Yorkshire	England
Eastbourne	Sussex	England
Edinbane	Isle of Skye	Scotland
Edinburgh	Edinburgh	Scotland
Ely	Cambridgeshire	England

Towns & Counties Index

Town	County	Country
Emsworth	Hampshire	England
Evesham	Worcestershire	England
Exeter	Devon	England
Exmoor National Park	Somerset	England
Eyam	Derbyshire	England
Falmouth	Cornwall	England
Farnham	Hampshire	England
Faversham	Kent	England
Folkestone	Kent	England
Fordham	Cambridgeshire	England
Fordingbridge	Hampshire	England
Forres	Morayshire	Scotland
Fort William	Inverness-shire	Scotland
Gainsborough	Lincolnshire	England
Gatwick	Surrey	England
Girvan	Ayrshire	Scotland
Glasgow	Glasgow	Scotland
Glastonbury	Somerset	England
Goudhurst	Kent	England
Grange-over-Sands	Cumbria	England
Grantown-on-Spey	Morayshire	Scotland
Grasmere	Cumbria	England
Hadleigh	Suffolk	England
Harlech	Gwynedd	Wales
Harrogate	Yorkshire	England
Hartfield	Sussex	England
Haslemere	Surrey	England
Hastings	Sussex	England
Haverfordwest	Pembrokeshire	Wales
Haverhill	Suffolk	England
Hawkhurst	Kent	England
Hawkshead	Cumbria	England
Hay-on-Wye	Powys	Wales
Haywards Heath	Sussex	England
Heathfield	Sussex	England
Hebden Bridge	Yorkshire	England
Henfield	Sussex	England
Henley	Oxfordshire	England
Hereford	Herefordshire	England
Herstmonceux	Sussex	England
Hexham	Northumberland	England
Hillesden Hamlet	Buckinghamshire	England
Holbeach	Lincolnshire	England
Holsworthy	Devon	England
Holywell	Flintshire	Wales
Hope Valley	Derbyshire	England
Horsham	Sussex	England
Hungerford	Berkshire	England
Hunstanton	Norfolk	England
Hurstpierpoint	Sussex	England
Inverness	Inverness-shire	Scotland
Ipswich	Suffolk	England
Ironbridge	Shropshire	England
Isle of Anglesey	Anglesey	Wales
Isle of Islay	Argyll	Scotland
Isle of Mull	Argyll	Scotland
Isle of Wight	Hampshire	England
Jedburgh	Roxburghshire	Scotland
Kelso	Roxburghshire	Scotland
Kendal	Cumbria	England
Kentallen of Appin	Argyll	Scotland
Keswick	Cumbria	England
Kettering	Northamptonshire	England
Kilmarnock	Ayrshire	Scotland
King's Lynn	Norfolk	England
Kingsbridge	Devon	England
Kington	Herefordshire	England
Kirkbean by Dumfries	Dumfriesshire	Scotland
Kirkby Lonsdale	Cumbria	England
Knebworth	Hertfordshire	England
Knutsford	Cheshire	England
Launceston	Cornwall	England
Lawrenny	Pembrokeshire	Wales
Leamington Spa	Warwickshire	England
Leeds	Yorkshire	England
Leek	Staffordshire	England
Leigh	Gloucestershire	England
Leighton Buzzard	Bedfordshire	England
Leominster	Herefordshire	England
Lewes	Sussex	England
Leyburn	Yorkshire	England
Lincoln	Lincolnshire	England
Liskeard	Cornwall	England
Little Gransden	Cambridgeshire	England
Lizard	Cornwall	England
Llandrindod Wells	Powys	Wales
Llandudno	Conwy	Wales
Llanrhaeadr Ym Mochnant	Powys	Wales
Llanrwst	Conwy	Wales
Llantwit Major	Glamorgan	Wales
Loch Lomond	Stirlingshire	Scotland
Lochinver	Sutherland	Scotland
Lochwinnoch	Glasgow	Scotland
London	London	England
Long Stratton	Norfolk	England
Longhope	Gloucestershire	England
Looe	Cornwall	England
Ludlow	Shropshire	England
Lydney	Gloucestershire	England
Lyme Regis	Dorset	England
Lymington	Hampshire	England
Lynton	Devon	England
Maidenhead	Berkshire	England
Maidstone	Kent	England
Malmesbury	Wiltshire	England
Malton	Yorkshire	England
Malvern	Worcestershire	England
Mansfield	Nottinghamshire	England
Margate	Kent	England
Market Drayton	Shropshire	England
Marlborough	Wiltshire	England
Matlock	Derbyshire	England
Mayfield	Sussex	England
Melton Mowbray	Leicestershire	England
Merthyr Tydfil	Glamorgan	Wales
Midhurst	Sussex	England
Minchinhampton	Gloucestershire	England
Minehead	Somerset	England
Mitcheldean	Gloucestershire	England
Moffat	Dumfriesshire	Scotland

Towns & Counties Index

Town	County	Country
Mold	Flintshire	Wales
Montgomery	Powys	Wales
Morchard Bishop	Devon	England
Moreton-in-Marsh	Gloucestershire	England
Moretonhampstead	Devon	England
Morpeth	Northumberland	England
Narberth	Pembrokeshire	Wales
New Forest	Hampshire	England
Newbury	Berkshire	England
Newport	Gwent	Wales
Newquay	Cornwall	England
Newton Abbot	Devon	England
Northallerton	Yorkshire	England
Norwich	Norfolk	England
Nottingham	Nottinghamshire	England
Oakham	Rutland	England
Okehampton	Devon	England
Olney	Buckinghamshire	England
Oswestry	Shropshire	England
Oxford	Oxfordshire	England
Padstow	Cornwall	England
Penrith	Cumbria	England
Penzance	Cornwall	England
Perth	Perthshire	Scotland
Petersfield	Hampshire	England
Petersfield	Sussex	England
Pickering	Yorkshire	England
Pitlochry	Perthshire	Scotland
Plymouth	Devon	England
Polperro	Cornwall	England
Reading	Berkshire	England
Redhill	Surrey	England
Redruth	Cornwall	England
Retford	Nottinghamshire	England
Ripon	Yorkshire	England
Romsey	Hampshire	England
Ross-on-Wye	Herefordshire	England
Royston	Cambridgeshire	England
Rumbling Bridge	Kinross	Scotland
Ruthin	Denbighshire	Wales
Rye	Sussex	England
Saffron Walden	Essex	England
Salisbury	Wiltshire	England
Sandy	Bedfordshire	England
Scarborough	Yorkshire	England
Sedbergh	Cumbria	England
Sevenoaks	Kent	England
Shaftesbury	Dorset	England
Shaftesbury	Dorset	England
Sherborne	Dorset	England
Shipston-on-Stour	Warwickshire	England
Shipton-under-Wychwood	Oxfordshire	England
Shrewsbury	Shropshire	England
Sinnington	Yorkshire	England
Somerton	Somerset	England
South Brent	Devon	England
South Molton	Devon	England
Southampton	Hampshire	England
St. Andrews	Fifeshire	Scotland
St. Asaph	Denbighshire	Wales
St. Austell	Cornwall	England
St. Blazey	Cornwall	England
St. Briavels	Gloucestershire	England
St. Ives	Cornwall	England
Staffin	Isle of Skye	Scotland
Stirling	Clackmannanshire	Scotland
Stirling	Stirlingshire	Scotland
Stoke-on-Trent	Staffordshire	England
Stow-on-the-Wold	Gloucestershire	England
Stowmarket	Suffolk	England
Stragglethorpe	Lincolnshire	England
Stratford-upon-Avon	Warwickshire	England
Stroud	Gloucestershire	England
Sturminster Newton	Dorset	England
Swadlincote	Derbyshire	England
Swaffham	Norfolk	England
Swansea	Swansea	Wales
Tarporley	Cheshire	England
Taunton	Somerset	England
Tavistock	Devon	England
Teignmouth	Devon	England
Tenby	Pembrokeshire	Wales
Tenterden	Kent	England
Tetbury	Gloucestershire	England
Thetford	Norfolk	England
Tintagel	Cornwall	England
Tintern	Monmouthshire	Wales
Tiverton	Devon	England
Tonbridge	Kent	England
Torpoint	Cornwall	England
Torquay	Devon	England
Totnes	Devon	England
Trefriw	Conwy	Wales
Truro	Cornwall	England
Tunbridge Wells	Kent	England
Tywyn	Gwynedd	Wales
Uffington	Oxfordshire	England
Uttoxeter	Staffordshire	England
Wallingford	Oxfordshire	England
Wareham	Dorset	England
Warminster	Wiltshire	England
Warwick	Warwickshire	England
Wells	Somerset	England
Welshpool	Powys	Wales
Welwyn	Hertfordshire	England
Wheddon Cross	Somerset	England
Whitby	Yorkshire	England
Whitchurch	Shropshire	England
Wimborne	Dorset	England
Winchcombe	Gloucestershire	England
Winchelsea	Sussex	England
Winchester	Hampshire	England
Windermere	Cumbria	England
Witney	Oxfordshire	England
Woking	Surrey	England
Woodstock	Oxfordshire	England
Worthing	Sussex	England
Wrexham	Cheshire	England
Yelverton	Devon	England
York	Yorkshire	England

Recommendation 2002

Thank you for taking the trouble to supply this information .
We value your comments & will take appropriate action where necessary.
We regret that we are unable to reply to you individually.

Proprietors _____

House Name _____

Address _____

_____

Please give some general information about your stay, the house, rooms, food & hosts etc.

Date of stay _____

_____

_____

_____

_____

_____

_____

_____

Your Name _____

Address _____

_____

Reply to: W.W.B.B.A. P.O. Box 2070.
London. W12 8QW

Recommendation 2002

Thank you for taking the trouble to supply this information .
We value your comments & will take appropriate action where necessary.
We regret that we are unable to reply to you individually.

Proprietors _____

House Name _____

Address _____

_____

Please give some general information about your stay, the house, rooms, food & hosts etc.

Date of stay _____

_____

_____

_____

_____

_____

_____

_____

Your Name _____

Address _____

_____

Reply to: W.W.B.B.A. P.O. Box 2070.
London. W12 8QW

Complaint 2002

Thank you for taking the trouble to supply this information .
We value your comments & will take appropriate action where necessary.
We regret that we are unable to reply to you individually.

Proprietors _____

House Name _____

Address _____

_____

Please be specific about your complaint. State exactly what was wrong with your stay e.g. the room, food, house keeping etc.

Date of stay _____

_____

_____

_____

_____

_____

_____

_____

Your Name _____

Address _____

_____

Reply to:W.W.B.B.A. P.O. Box 2070,
London. W12 8QW

Recommendation 2002

Thank you for taking the trouble to supply this information .
We value your comments & will take appropriate action where necessary.
We regret that we are unable to reply to you individually.

Proprietors _____

House Name _____

Address _____

_____

Please give some general information about your stay, the house, rooms, food & hosts etc.

Date of stay _____

_____

_____

_____

_____

_____

_____

_____

Your Name _____

Address _____

_____

Reply to: W.W.B.B.A. P.O. Box 2070.
London. W12 8QW

460

Complaint 2002

Thank you for taking the trouble to supply this information .
We value your comments & will take appropriate action where necessary.
We regret that we are unable to reply to you individually.

Proprietors _____

House Name _____

Address _____

_____

**Please be specific about your complaint. State exactly what was
wrong with your stay e.g. the room, food, house keeping etc.**

Date of stay _____

_____

_____

_____

_____

_____

_____

_____

Your Name _____

Address _____

_____

**Reply to: W.W.B.B.A. P.O. Box 2070.
London. W12 8QW**

Complaint 2002

Thank you for taking the trouble to supply this information .
We value your comments & will take appropriate action where necessary.
We regret that we are unable to reply to you individually.

Proprietors _____

House Name _____

Address _____

_____

**Please be specific about your complaint. State exactly what was
wrong with your stay e.g. the room, food, house keeping etc.**

Date of stay _____

_____

_____

_____

_____

_____

_____

Your Name _____

Address _____

_____

**Reply to: W.W.B.B.A. P.O. Box 2070.
London. W12 8QW**

Recommendation 2002

Thank you for taking the trouble to supply this information .
We value your comments & will take appropriate action where necessary.
We regret that we are unable to reply to you individually.

Proprietors _____

House Name _____

Address _____

_____

Please give some general information about your stay, the house, rooms, food & hosts etc.

Date of stay _____

_____

_____

_____

_____

_____

_____

_____

Your Name _____

Address _____

_____

Reply to: W.W.B.B.A. P.O. Box 2070.
London. W12 8QW

Recommendation 2002

Thank you for taking the trouble to supply this information .
We value your comments & will take appropriate action where necessary.
We regret that we are unable to reply to you individually.

Proprietors _____

House Name _____

Address _____

_____

Please give some general information about your stay, the house, rooms, food & hosts etc.

Date of stay _____

_____

_____

_____

_____

_____

_____

_____

Your Name _____

Address _____

_____

Reply to: W.W.B.B.A. P.O. Box 2070.
London. W12 8QW